PROJECT MANAGEMENT

V. C. SONTAKKI

Himalaya Publishing House

MUMBAI • NEW DELHI • NAGPUR • BENGALURU • HYDERABAD • CHENNAI • PUNE • LUCKNOW • AHMEDABAD • ERNAKULAM • BHUBANESWAR • INDORE • KOLKATA • GUWAHATI

First Edition : 2006
Second Edition : 2009
Third Edition : 2012

Published by : Mrs. Meena Pandey
for **HIMALAYA PUBLISHING HOUSE PVT. LTD.,**
"Ramdoot", Dr. Bhalerao Marg, Girgaon, **Mumbai - 400 004.**
Phone: 2386 01 70/2386 38 63, Fax: 022-2387 71 78
Email: himpub@vsnl.com Website: www.himpub.com

Branch Offices:

New Delhi : "Pooja Apartments", 4-B, Murari Lal Street, Ansari Road, Darya Ganj, New Delhi - 110 002. Phone: 23270392, 23278631, Fax: 011-23256286

Nagpur : Kundanlal Chandak Industrial Estate, Ghat Road, Nagpur - 440 018. Phone: 011-2738731/3296733, Telefax : 0712-2721215

Bengaluru : No. 16/1 (Old 12/1), 1st Floor, Next to Hotel Highlands, Madhava Nagar, Race Course Road, Bengaluru - 560 001. Phone : 080-22281541/22385461, Telefax: 080-22286611

Hyderabad : No. 3-4-184, Lingampally, Besides Raghavendra Swamy Matham, Kachiguda, Hyderabad - 500 027. Phone: 040-27560041, 27550139, Mobile: 09848130433

Chennai : No. 85/50, Bazullah Road, T. Nagar, Chennai - 600 017. Phone: 044-28144004/28144005

Pune : First Floor, "Laksha" Apartment, No. 527, Mehunpura, Shaniwarpeth, (Near Prabhat Theatre), Pune - 411 030. Phone: 020-24496323/24496333

Lucknow : Jai Baha Bhavan, Church Road, Near Manas Complex and Dr, Awasthi Clinic, Aliganj, Lucknow - 226 024 Phone: 0522-2339329, 4068914, Mobile: 09305302158, 09415349385, 09389593752

Ahmedabad : 114, "SHAIL", 1st Floor, Opp. Madhu Sudan House, C.G. Road, Navrang Pura, Ahmedabad - 380 009. Phone: 079-26560126, Mobile: 09327324149, 09314679413

Ernakulam : 39/104 A, Lakshmi Apartment, Karikkamuri Cross Rd., Ernakulam, Cochin - 622011, Kerala. Phone: 0484-2378012, 2378016, Mobile: 09344199799

Bhubaneswar : 5 Station Square, Bhubaneswar - 751 001. Mobile: 9861046007, E-mail: orissa@himpub.com

Indore : Kesardeep Avenue Extension, 73, Narayan Bagh, Flat No. 302, IIIrd Floor, Near Humpty Dumpty School, Narayan Bagh, Indore (M.P.) - 452 007. Mobile: 09301386468

Kolkata : 108/4, Beliaghata Main Road, Near ID Hospital, Opp. SBI Bank, Kolkata - 700 010. Mobile: 09910440956

DTP by : **Sri Siddhi Softtek,** Bengaluru

Printed by : **Sri Manjunatha Printers, Bengaluru on behalf of - HPH**

With

Love and Affection

To

AARYN

PREFACE

More and more Indian Universities have fallen in love with the subject "PROJECT MANAGEMENT", Which is evident from the syllabi designed at graduate and post-graduate levels. Bangalore University has, of late, included this demanded subject at BBM course. I am, therefore, happy to present this title to those who are preparing for the said course at graduate level.

The entire subject matter is divided into THIRTEEN CHAPTERS arranged in a sequence of flow that percolates to the maximum. The last chapter is that deals with SKILL DEVELOPMENT component.

In preparing this book, I have freely drawn the materials from Indian and foreign authors who have provided a sea of information. Only relevant matter is taken up, pruned, tuned and tailored to the tastes of students keeping up to the boundaries of syllabus. I am thankful to those experts and academicians and practitioners who have mite in making project management a specialised subject.

I am also thankful to Shri. K.N. Pandey and Sons, Shri S.K. Srivastava and Dr. V.R. Naik who encouraged me to take up the work. I can not forget to thank those who have worked behind the certain to bring this book to light in a record time.

I hope that book serves the purpose for which its designed. I welcome constructive suggestions from the teachers and the taught to improve the quality and utility of this work. Every effort is made to give zero-defect book. However, with all the due care, some mistakes might have crept in. It is the teachers and the students who are to bring to the notice of author so that they can be corrected in the next print or edition.

V. C. SONTAKKI

Alpha Doller House,

7th Cross Road,

Kalyan Nagar,

Dharwad - Karnataka

580 007

SYLLABUS

Project Management

CHAPTER – 1: Introduction of Project Management : **15Hrs**

Understanding Project Management, Project Manager, Line Manager & Staff Manager, Inter Relationship& Interface, Defining Project Mangers, Functional Managers & Executive's role. Project Manager as a planning agent, Project Driven Vs Non Project Driven organization, Marketing in the Project Driven Organization, Position of the Project Manager, Programs and Projects, Vs Project Management, Project Life Cycles.

CHAPTER – 2: Project Planning : **10Hrs**

Identifying strategic project variables, Project planning, Statement of work, Project specifications, Milestone schedule, Work breakdown structure, Planning cycle, Management Control.

CHAPTER – 3: Feasibility of project : **10Hrs**

Technical feasibility, marketing feasibility, socio economic feasibility, Managerical feasibility and finacial feasibility.

CHAPTER – 4: Project Evaluation and Review techniques : **5Hrs**

Estimating activity time, Estimating total program time, PERT/CPM planning, Crash time

CHAPTER – 5: Project Management Fuctions : **10Hrs**

Controlling, Directing, Project authority, Team building, Leadership, communications, Project review meetings, Management policies and procedures.

CHAPTER – 6: Pricing Estimating & Cost Control : **10Hrs**

Types of estimates & Pricing Process, Labor distributions. Overhead rates, Material/Support costs, Pricing review, Budgeting for projects variance & earned value, Status reporting.

SKILL DEVELOPMENT :

- Prepare project life cycle chart.

BOOKS FOR REFERENCE :

1. Choudary S, Project Management
2. Joseph J Moder and Philips C.R., Project Management
3. Joy P.K., Total Project Management
4. Gopal Krishnan Rama, Text book of Project Management
5. Harold Kerzer, Project Management
6. Josh S, Project Management
7. Saprthe R.K., Project Management
8. Narendra Singh, Project Management and Control
9. Vasanth Desai, Project Management and Entrepreneurship
10. Bhavesh. M. Patel, Project Management

CONTENTS

Chapter 1

INTRODUCTION TO PROJECT MANAGEMENT

- WHAT IS A PROJECT?
- STANDARD DEFINITIONS
- BASIC CHARACTERISTICS OF A PROJECT
- PROJECT FAMILY TREE
- DISTINCTION BETWEEN 'TASK', 'PROGRAM', AND 'PROJECT'
- CASSIFICATION OF PROJECTS
- DISTINCTION BETWEEN BALANCING, MODERNISING, REPLACING, EXPANDING AND DIVERSIFYING PROJECTS
- PROJECT LIFE-CYCLE AND ITS PHASES
- PROJECT MANAGEMENT
- STANDARD DEFINITIONS
- STEPS IN PROJECT MANAGEMENT
- CREATION OF A PROJECT
- HISTORY OF PROJECT MANAGEMENT
- DAMING CYCLE FOR PROJECT MANAGEMENT
- EFFECTIVE PROJECT MANAGEMENT
- CHAPTER BASED QUESTIONS

BACKDROP

As we are approaching the practical subject PROJECT MANAGEMENT, we need a thorough under- standing of basics of such subject. Hence, this chapter focuses its attention on various basic concepts of project, project related concepts, project manager, his role, organisation for project management with emphasis on its unique features and other relevant concepts. That is, we are concentrating on PROJECT, PROJECT MANAGEMENT, to start with. The chapter with units Chapter Based Questions.

WHAT IS A PROJECT ?

Every one of us works on one task or the other which has a start up and deadline - from production employee to financial analyst, from banker to physican, from engineer to administrator, from armyman to zerox person. Irrespective of our occupation, vocation, discipline, position in an organization, everyone works on tasks that are unique, challenging and rewarding and involve people who do usually work to-gether.

A project is neither a physical objective nor an end result,but one which is to do with goings-on in between, which must be same whether one builds a high tech-process plant or merely hold and election, to deserve a common name and to be called as a project. We, very often hear of iron and steel projects, power projects, refinery projects, fertilizer projects, pesticides projects, water-supply projects where the word 'project' is common to all the plants. In each case, the 'project' is used for the plant but as soon as the plant is operational, the project is said to be completed. Take another case, that of project for methods improvement. The project is complete when methods improvement has been achieved. Anything that can be implicitly expressed can be a project which is not explicitly called as a project. The best examples are holding elections to Lok Sabha, Assembly, Municipal Corporation, Village Panchayat, even acquiring a degree, at lower level and higher level. Thus, a career, successful conclusion of social gathering, musical concert, club programmes all can be called as projects. One of the basic objectives of business units is to take birth, grow, expand, multiply and survive successfully. Successful survival demands good business ideas which are having high potentiality-passing the acid tests of cold facts of technical feasibility, economic viability, physical suitability, and above all, social acceptability. Once an idea concerned passes these tests, it turns into investment proposal and when investment is made after approval, it starts firing. Thus, a project is initiated to achieve a mission-whatever it may be. Hence, a project is completed as soon as mission is fulfilled Stated in other words. Project starts from scratch with a definite mission, generates activities involving both human and non-human resources all directed towards the fulfillment of the mission and comes to and end when the mission is fulfilled.

STANDARD DEFINITIONS

- **Project Management Institute of America (PMIA) :**
  "Project is a one shot, time-limited, goal-oriented, major undertaking, requiring commitment of varied skills and resources, a combination of human and non-human resources pooled together in a temporary organization to achieve a specific purpose."
- **Experts of ECAFE Report :**
  "The smallest unit of investment activity to be considered in the case of programming."
- **I.B.R.D. - WORLD BANK :**
  "An approval for capital investments to develop facilities to provide goods and services."
- **Mr. Little and Mr. Mirrlees :**
  "Project is any scheme or a part of scheme for investing resources which can be reasonably analysed and evaluated as independent unit. It may be any item of investment activity which can separately be evaluated."
- **Mr. Glitnger :**
  "The whole of complex of activities involved in using resources for benefits."
- **Dr. Albert O. Hirchman :**
  "The development-project connotes purposefuless, some minimum size, a specific location, the introduction of something qualitatively new and the expectation that a sequence of further development moves will be set in motion. Development projects are privileged particles of the development process."
- **E.L. Hanson :**
  "A non-routine, non-repetitive one-off undertaking normally with discrete time, financial and technical performance goals."

Thus, project connotes purposefulness, some minimum size, a specific location, the introduction of something qualitative, new and expectation that sequence of further development moves will be set in motion. It is a compilation to be made of the economic-advantages and the disadvantages attendant upon the allocation of country's resources to the production specific goods and services. It stands for objectives. It is a scheme, a design, a proposal of something intended or devised. It is an investment proposal carried out according to a plan in order to achieve a definite objective within a certain time and which will cease when the objective is achieved. Thus, project is a combination of inter-related activities to achieve a specific objective. That is, a project is any non-repetitive activity which can be modeled through analyzing the inputs, constraints, outputs and mechanisms which is abbreviated to the letters (ICOMs).

BASIC CHARACTERISTICS OF A PROJECT

1. **IT HAS PRE-DETERMINED OBJECTIVE/S :**

   Any product can not be without an objective or set of pre-determined objectives. Thus, a construction of a dam has the set of objectives. These may be : (a) Providing water for agricultural areas covering a state or states. (b) Generation of electricity. (c) Bringing green, white and blue revolutions. (d) Rehabililation of families whose belongings are likely to submerge in catchment area. These objectives differ from case to case. It is not same in the case of construction of a cold-storage, a hospital, school, college or an university, naturally objectives differ.

2. **IT HAS A DEFINITE LIFE-SPAN :**

   A project has dimension of time. A project can not go on and on for ever. It has its scheduling. As per the time table, it is to be completed, irrespective of its nature. Thus, a non-professional college student is to acquire the degree within three years-ten plus two plus three. On the other hand, professionals ten plus two plus four of five years depending on the nature of professional course. It is different thing that a student does not get the degree in three or five years, due to his inability or inefficiency or exigency. Thus, Konkan Railway was to be completed in five years in three states of Kerala, Karnataka and Maharastra and it was done. However, Zuari bridge on NH17 took almost double the time by Gammon India Limited. It was started as early as 1966 but completed and declared open only in 1982–the longest period. Sooner or later, the project, will have to come to an end.

3. **IT IS A SINGLE ENTITY :**

   A given project is a single entity which is entrusted to one responsibility center. That is, there will be one central authority which is totally responsible for its completion, or attainment of objectives. This central authority employs good many participants, who are specialists, in completing the project very successfully. These may be line and staff authorities where matrix type of organization works.

4. **IT IS A HALLMARK OF TEAM - WORK :**

   Any project warrants a team-work. Project is not one man job ; it is a joint activity and therefore, cogent and congruous teams are formed. These teams are constituted as part of total-team consisting of members drawn from different lines, skills, knowledge, expertise and leadership qualities are tested because, team building is not that easy and making it to work in unison, is another thing, without any conflict.

5. **IT HAS A LIFE-CYCLE :**

   Like any living creature, each project has its own life-cycle namely, start or launch, growth, maturity and decay. The periods of launch or introduction, growth, maturity and decay are not having same time period which differ from project to project, time to time and team of project management. This life-cycle is a matter of learning component where mistakes of one can be corrected in another.

6. **EACH PROJECT IS UNIQUE :**

Just as no two speicies are similar, or even a single specie, no member is identical in all respects, so also the projects. When we talk of a dam construction, one can not be identical to another as it is constructed under changing conditions though broadly they are called as dams. Even in case of the candidates who passed all their examinations from same school, high school, college, and university, they can not be branded as identical products as I.Q., differs and later on, performance capacity differs. Thus, a gold medalist might fail in ground realities while a rotton egg at early stage might be a Nobel Laurate–par exellence. Similarly, each project is unique. Take two steel plants of same capacity, same technology, constructed by same project unit, it is the location, infrastructure, their agencies and the people which make these unique one.

7. **CHANGE IS ANOTHER NAME FOR PROJECT :**

A Project faces changes in its life span–different stages of completion. Some of these changes may not have major impact on system while some changes are so sevre that their undercurrents are capable of changing the very nature of project. The basic aim or aims will have to be changed. In case of N.H.4. which is going to be four-line, one-way express-highway, it is not bound to be as originally planned because, we are dealing with mother earth or natural powers. Man is a slave of nature. Though he boasts of his containment or controlling of nature, he should not take it for granted. In India, projects have been drawn for the last 50 years to root out the problems of floods in West Bengal, Orissa and Bihar. In spite of government efforts, it has been an utter failure.

8. **PROJECT HAS A WIDE GAP BETWEEN DREAM AND A REALITY :**

Planning of a project is one thing and implementation is another. Things do not go as we calculate. It is easier to calculate book profits than the real profits or actual profits earned. There can not be a better example in India than that of utter failure of UTI-investments under UTI-64. The UTI went on taking savings of the people particularly middle-class–the back bone of India. People trusted it as an investment trust. However, now there is a panic among the members of UTI where investments are long-term. The Ex-finance Minister, Mr. Sinha and now Mr. P. Chidamberam have been pouring hundreds and crores of rupees through budgets. UTI is like pot which has good many holes at the bottom. The effort of government is like a crow which is trying to put pebbles to increase the level of water so that it can drink and make others to drink water. It is a dream. It has been a nightmare for honest humble savers who are known only when the project is implemented.

9. EACH PROJECT IS MADE TO ORDER :

Each project is made to order because, the requirements of each project are very much different. That is, the party to whom project is going to be handed over after completion, puts his own conditions in terms of time, cost and quality. These are the constraints under which the planners and implementers are to work. There can not be any deviation or dilution or any sort of compromise. It is so, that the contractee will demand heavy compensation. Customer needs are to be met at any rate and at any cost.

10. PROJECT IS A FINE CASE OF UNITY IN DIVERSITY :

A given project being unique, is a complex set of innumerable varieties. These variations are seen in terms of technology, materials, equipment, machinery, people, work-culture and ethics. What is important is that these variants are so intricately interrelated that they have to be pulled together to achieve the targets. If there is no unity of thought, purpose and action, it means that there is conflict which is opposite of coordination. Such conflicts speak of either incompletion or unwillingness to pull together.

11. A PROJECT IS A MARK OF HIGH LEVEL OF SUB-CONTRACTING :

By, nature, a project requires the services of specialized persons. Take a simple case of 5 storey - flat system. We have specialists who lay foundation, workers who raise the pillars and girders, centering and slab-work, constrution of walls, fixing doors and windows, plastering, polishing, concealed-wiring, pulling-wires, painting, sanitary blocks-fillings, carpentry work including lift-fixing, fire-fighting system, plumbing, drainage, septic tanks and so on. Here, depending on the complexity of work, nearly 75 to 80 per cent of work is done by sub-contractors.

12. A PROJECT IS A PACKAGE OF RISK AND UNCERTAINTY :

A Project is a business proposal. Another name for business is game where there are probabilities of high profits, no-profits - and losses. That is, there is greater amount of risk and uncertainty associated with projects. The degree of risk and uncertainty depends on how a project has been passed through the various life-cycle phases. A well defined project will have at-least degree of risk and uncertainty. It is worthwhile to note that risk and uncertainty are not the part and parcel of research and development projects. What is important is that there can not be a project free from the elements of risk and uncertainty.

PROJECT FAMILY TREE

A project stems from a plan which may be international, national-regional-state level, district level or even city level. A project is otherwise a programme or a work-package. Thus, a programme is a part of plan or plan itself. In a civilized society in which we live, we have number of programmes for the well-being of the society. It may be an education programme, a health programme, afforestation programme and so on. These programs lead to a project or projects–say hospital project, housing project, university project, bridge project, power-hydel or thermal-project and so on. These projects are culminated in work packages say, water-supply and distribution package, natural gas-supply and distribution package, power-supply contract, construction of foundations, erection of power generation plant, sewage water treatment plant, wind power line, construction of cooling towers. These tasks lead to activities. These may be preparation of drawings, designing of models, fabricating prototypes, laying down cables, laying down water-supply mains, excavation, preparation of specifications. This can be presented as in Fig. 1.01.

Thus, the smallest ramification of a plan is an 'activity'; pack of activities make a 'task'; tasks make a 'work-package'; work-packages make a 'project'; projects make a 'programme' and 'programmes' make a plan. This synergic difference is very important and one term is not same as another. Thus, a 'work-package' is not a project though it is identified for better management.

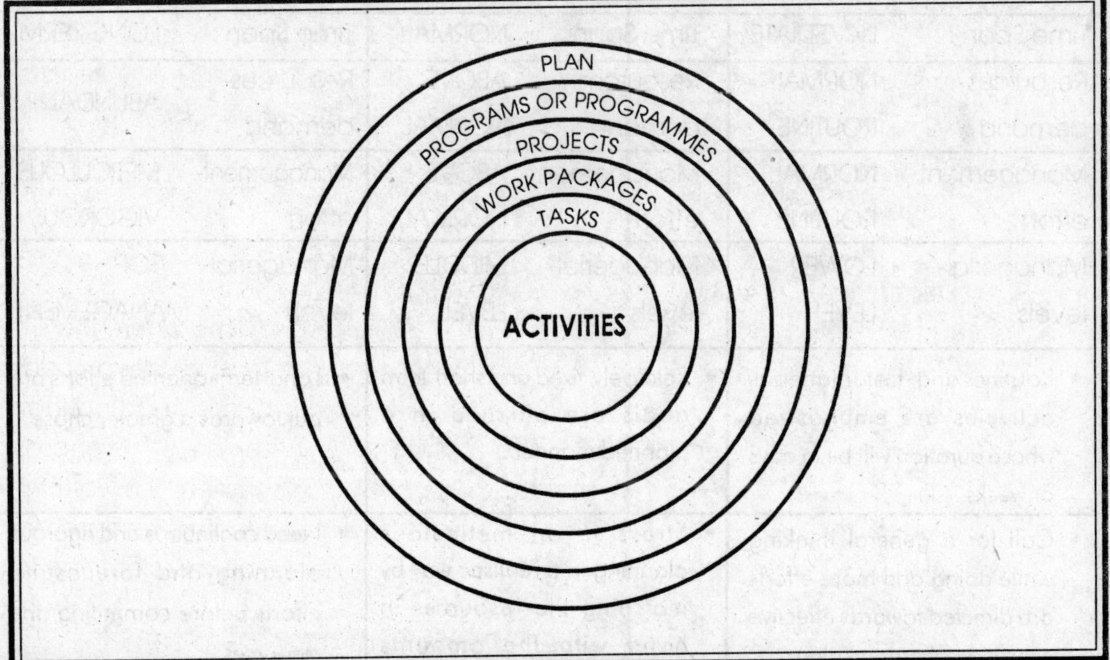

Fig. 1.01 Project Family Tree

DISTINCTION BETWEEN 'TASK PROGRAM' AND 'PROJECT'

Knowingly on unknowingly, people freely interchange the words task, program and project with one another. However, as the students of PROJECT MANAGEMENT, we cannot afford to do that because there is much difference between these terms.

As noted earlier, **task** is an immediate and spontaneous commitment to execute a set of duties by a single or a small group of people for immediate results. A project is fragmented into different **work packages** and each **work package** consists of certain tasks to be performed by the department concerned. A **project** is an assignment usually directed towards short-term results with limited resource base and fixed time frame. Projects are a limiting case of programmes where authority, responsibility, scope, budgets and the like get diluted as they move downwards in the hierarchy. A **program** is a comprehensive and long-term endeavour determining huge amount of resources for achieving the objectives. Generally, every program is divided into various programs or small programs according to time, scope, and complexity involved. The following chart makes clear the difference between Tasks, Projects and Programs.

TASKS		PROJECTS		PROGRAMMES	
Objectives :	CLEAR	Objectives :	CLEAR	Objectives :	VAGUE
Scope :	LOWER	Scope :	NORMAL	Scope :	HIGHER
Complexity :	LOWER	Complexity :	NORMAL	Complexity :	HIGHER
Time Span :	IMMEDIATE	Time Span :	NORMAL	Time Span :	LONG TERM
Resources-demand :	NORMAL ROUTINE	Resources-demand :	ABOVE NORMAL	Resources-demand	ABUNDANT
Management-effort :	NORMAL ROUTINE	Management-effort :	ABOVE NORMAL	Management-effort	METICULOUS VIGOROUS
Managerial-levels :	LOWER LEVEL	Managerial-levels :	MIDDLE LEVEL	Managerial-levels	TOP MANAGEMENT
• Routine and Instantaneous activities are emphasized whose duration will be in days or weeks.		• Relatively, fixed and short-term goals are pursued in a planned manner.		• Long-term oriented efforts are put towards a greater chose.	
• Call for a general thinking while doing and more efforts are directed towards effective execution of present plans.		• Stress is on meticulous planning in a realistic way by matching the resources in hand with the amounts needed.		• Need continuous and rigorous planning and forecasting efforts before commiting the resources.	

• The tasks are executed by foreman or team members single handedly or with a little help from peers at the lower level.	• Project Management or the project manager with his team members takes a leading role in planning and designing the project.	• Top level Management is involved in program setting and decision-making in an organization.
• Methods formulation, procedural setting and little experimenting, thorough processing, all help to execute the tasks efficiently and effectively.	• Growing, thinking, brain storming sessions, morphological analysis, financial appraisals, and the like shape the ideas of a project.	• Board meetings, Conferences, SWOT analysis and other pre-investment studies shape the decisions of a program.
• Simple time shedules, calendars, and daily diaries are used as the primary tools to check the progress of the tasks.	• PERT/CRM/GANTT Charts chaeles are the vial tools used for sheduling and monitoring the projects.	• Policies, objectives, guide lines, codes and the like are issued for the total program where strategic planning, experience of the senior management are the effective tools used.

CLASSIFICATION OF PROJECTS

What a project is made up of and its management for planning and execution will depend on how the projects are classified. The most significant variables that determine the exact nature of project category are its location, type, size, ownership, technology, scope, speed and time which, in turn, determine the efforts needed in implemcnting a given project. The following chart gives the full classification of projects.

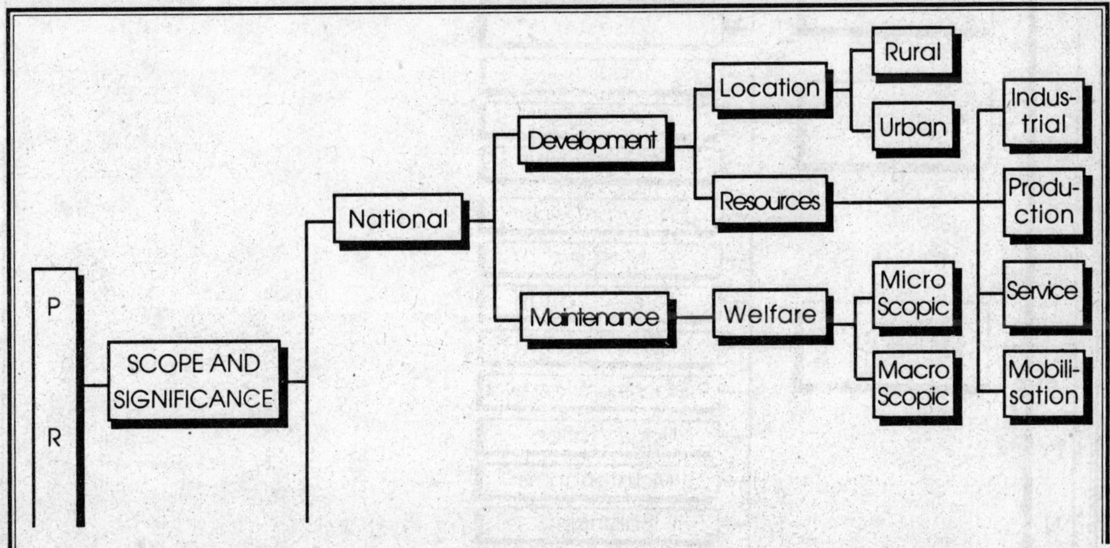

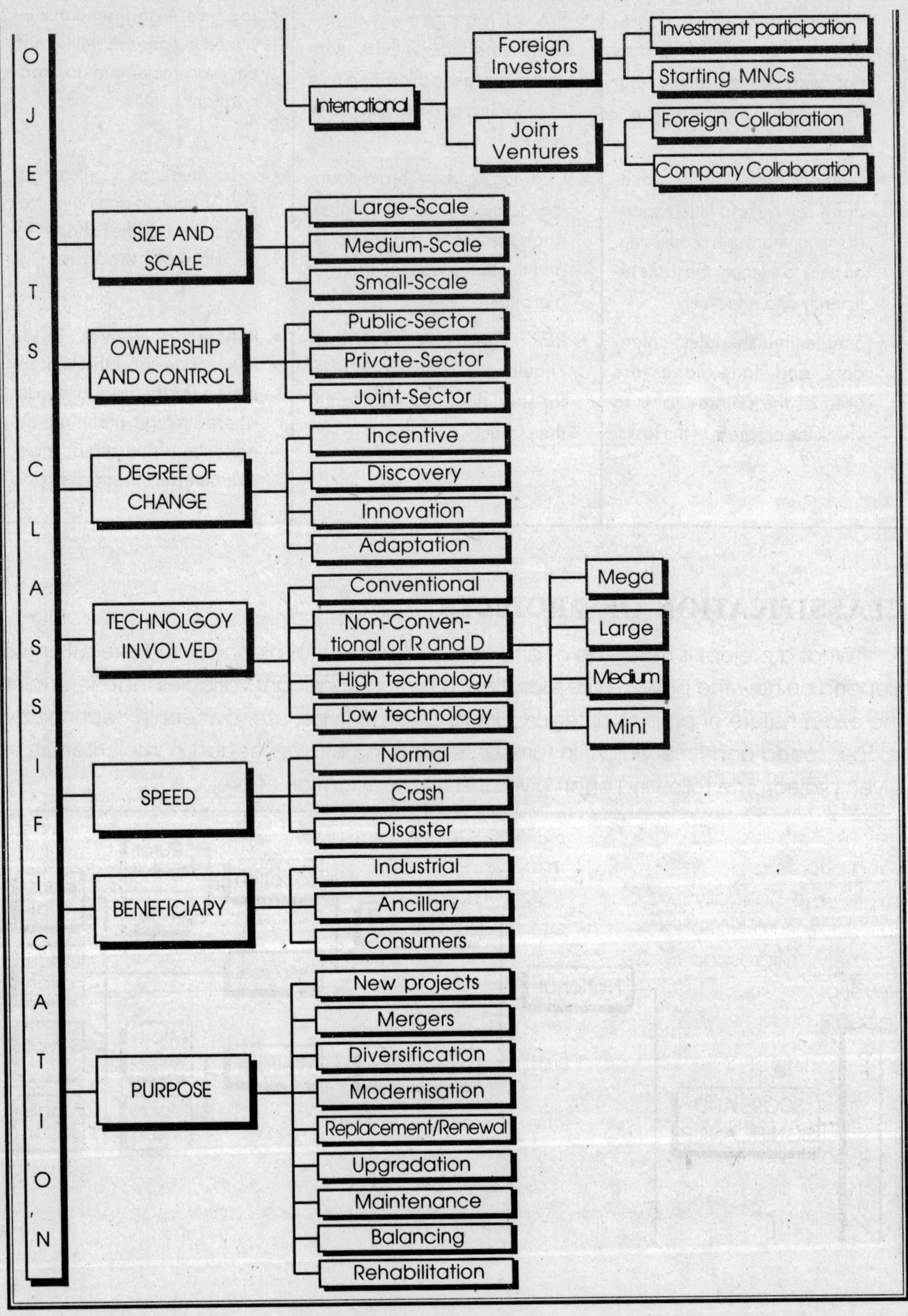
OBJECTS CLASSIFICATION
International
Foreign Investors
Joint Ventures
Investment participation
Starting MNCs
Foreign Collabration
Company Collaboration
SIZE AND SCALE
Large-Scale
Medium-Scale
Small-Scale
OWNERSHIP AND CONTROL
Public-Sector
Private-Sector
Joint-Sector
DEGREE OF CHANGE
Incentive
Discovery
Innovation
Adaptation
TECHNOLGOY INVOLVED
Conventional
Non-Conventional or R and D
High technology
Low technology
Mega
Large
Medium
Mini
SPEED
Normal
Crash
Disaster
BENEFICIARY
Industrial
Ancillary
Consumers
PURPOSE
New projects
Mergers
Diversification
Modernisation
Replacement/Renewal
Upgradation
Maintenance
Balancing
Rehabilitation

It pays to understand each base of classification that gives rise to further sub-classification. In the process, there is bound to be certain amount of over-lapping which cannot be avoided.

1. SCOPE AND SIGNIFICANCE OF A PROJECT

This is the first base that measures a project on the basis of scope and significance. Scope represents coverage or spanning speaking about the magnitude and the complexity of operations that are essential to complete the project in hand. The coverage speaks of its marketability. Accordingly, projects can be **National** and **International**. The point is how a project is to help in the development of a country or the countries and in what it brings about extension and maintenance of living standards of people in a given nation or nations. The national projects are those carried out in the national boundaries which can be 'Developmental' and 'Maintenance' type. Developmental projects are those which are newly develped to serve the national needs. Thus, super National Highway Plan - Connectivity programme in the finest example. On the other hand, maintenance projects are those, that take of maintaining the newly created and existing projects alredy working All hydle Power Projects are the examples of this kind. Futher, developmental projects can be 'Locational projects' and 'Resource projects' are futher branched into 'rural' and 'urban' projects taking geographical area as a base. In case of Resource projects, they are of four types namely, infrastructural, production, services, and mobilisation. These are self explained. Thus, infrastructural projects are to create infrastuctural facilities which are a must for industrial and non-industrial activities. Thus, projects providing roads, water supply, power-supply housing and the like are the examples of this kind. Production projects stand for connecting raw-materials into end products. These projects are dealing with erection of all kinds of plants to make consumer and non-consumer goods. There can be countless examples of these plants, factories or mills that produce goods for people and other industrial activities. Service projects are installing the service stations of all kinds, repairs, water-supply, communications, computer, goods and servises meant for general and private use. 'Modifications' projects are related with congregating the resources - which are basically related with finance, personnel research and development and so on. Turning to National maintenance, they are welfare projects which are of two types namely, 'microscopic' and 'macroscopic'. Microscopic projects are undertaken at unit level or individual level while Macroscopic at state or national level meant for common good.

Turning of 'International' projects where countries participate for the mutual benefits. There can be "foreign investment" projects and "joint ventures". That is, in case of "foreign investment projects', either the other country or countries contribute their finance or there is a possibility of starting MNC. In case of "Joint ventures" there can be collaborations between the nations - as to capital contribution and sharing of technology or technical known-how or both. Another possibility is that there can be collaborations between companies of the same nation lending to merger, amalgamations, or takeovers. Thus, we have foreign collaborations like Susuki and MUL, Honda, and Kinetic, ABB and Indian Railways. Again, we have case of coming to get their of Indian companies to better utilise their resourcing increase competitive advantage. HLL has taken over so many companies under its banner. So is the case with TATA and Other units.

2. SIZE AND SCOPE OF OPERATIONS

Taking the size and scope of business operations, these projects can be 'large', 'medium' and 'small' projects. The points of investment and time for compleling the projects are the bases classification. Small-projects are having an investment below 5 crores, medium between 5 crores to 100 crores and large-projects above 100 crores of investment. Taking time for completion, small-projects like 1 to 2 years, medium 2-5 years and large 5 - 10 years. Examples of small-scale are repairing a highway, remodelling a plant layout, construction of houses. Medium type of projects are contracts of a housing colony, flyover and construction of river bridges, dams, rehabilitation of people by construction of new township are examples of large projects.

3. OWNERSHIP AND CONTROL

Here, the basis of classifications is 'ownership'. Accordingly, these can be 'public-sector', 'private-sector', and 'joint-sector' projects. Public-sector projects are owned and controlled by governments either central or state or both. Thus, the projects of laying railway track, extracting mineral ores, generating nuclear power and like are the cases of public-sector. There cannot be better examples than Rourkela, Bhilai and Durgapur Steel plants in India. Private sector projects are widespread from snap faster to textile machinnery in engineering line, form hamburger to soiree in fast foods, from kids bicycle to sophiscated cars in luxury sector and the like. Privatisation policy has encouraged private projects to come up. All these industrialists have their projects managed through companies. Joint-sector is the joint ownereship by Central, State governements and private business people; HMT, SBI, Airlines, Insurance, and the like.

4. DEGREE OF CHANGE

The extent of 'change' that is involved in the base for classifying the projects. The most original changes can be invention and discovery. A pharmaceutical company might come out with new medicine which was not heard of earlier. Thus, pfizer of America given the 'Viagra' to improve sex life. Mr. Dahon, American manfactuaring company hs variety of folding bicycles for executives. When we talk of discovery, is searching something new which is already there given by the nature.When new routes are found out to far off places, it can be a case of discovery. When we talk of innovation the existing products are made more useful and valuable. Thus, the latest mobile is a telephone, camera, music - system and the like. The products which have multiple uses with the change of mode say, TV can be a sound gadget, computer, video-system, and so on. Finally, adaptation is changing the product to a certain extent to make it more acceptable. Thus, miniaturisation is the case of adaptation. The weight, design and the size of products are reduced to more acceptable products.

5. TECHNOLOGY INVOLVED IN A PROJECT

'Technology' plays a vital role in managing projects. In every field we see the impact of technology whether it is a product or source. These technological miracles are fast increasing, be it a camera, a pair of shoes, a soft-drink, or a food-item. The projects are sub classified into four categories - as conventional, non conventiaonal state of the art and low technology.

"Conventional technology" projects are those which use proven technology, thus making of cement, steel, chemicals, fertilizers, sugar, and the like. Even we can include cottage and village industrial units using the traditional technology in making textile items, sugar and so on. "Non-conventional technology" projects are those we come accross in case of small-scale sector. These units use contemporary mode technologing. Thus simple cranes, simple proceses of manufacturing.

"High-tech projects" are those which use high technology as used in oil refineries, nuclear power station, guided missiles. These involve huge investment. Based on the degree of high technology, these can be further classed into mega projects fairly large projects medium sized prjects and minimal projects. The basic of classification is investment and complexity.

"Low technology" projects are small in nature requiring lower invenstments. Thus, making of soaps, detergents, consmetics household items, handmade machinery and tools and the like.

6. SPEED

The 'speed' of completion is very important at times. These are the forms of expansion projects. These can be normally crash and disaster. "Normal expansion" projects are taken back completly in normal time durations. Thus, extension of state high-ways to national high- ways. As the phases of project are allowed to have the standard time for implementations. "Crash expansions" projects are those where time period is given due weightage. Therefore, sometimes the costs increase however quick expansion takes place. Thus, protecting the lives and property caused by floods, fire, landslides, earthquake, volcano, blockages in mining, post-blast operations and so on. Here, the project people work day in and day out to complete projects. These are costly but great time savers and reducing further losses of lives and property.

"Disaster expansion" projects are those which are taken up on priority basis. Thus, flood operations, collapse of bridge, bombardment of airport, they all call for emergency opertions. Here, cost is not a factor but time becomes more than money. The work goes on war-footing to restore the normally.

7. BENEFICIARY OF THE PROJECTS

The basis of such classifications is the parties that stand to 'gain'. Based on these, these can be industrial, auxillary and consumer projects. "Industrial projects" we mean where the industrial sector stands to benefit in the first instance. Later industries transfer the benefits to every member of society. Thus, the projects takes up exclusively for the birth and growth of any industry. Starting of road, construction provision of electricity, supply of water for processing and drinking purpose, starting of schools, colleges and other institutes of higher learning to make available skilled and semi-skilled people. On the other hand, "Consumer projects" are those that are started where the consumers are the main bene ficiaries. Thus, supply of eligible water, daily requirements of an average customer like household items, textile needs, services as banking, insurance , communication, transport and soon. The midway classification is projects where the intermediaries stand dialy gain. These are wholesale retailers, bankers, insurers, and the like by starting and running units in these lines.

8. PURPOSE OF THE PROJECT

Every project has a 'purpose' to serve. That is, the projects involve huge resources in terms of time, treasure and talent to attain a particular purpose or set of purposes. Based on the purposes served, these can be classed into certain categories as rehabilitation projects, balancing projects, maintenance projects, modernization projects, diversification projects, new projects, mergers and acquisitions. There is close alliance between the purpose and the degree of change involved. Hence, these can be possible overlapping.

"Rehabilitation projects" are those projects which are undertaken to rejuvenate or reconstitute the unit which is already crumbler. These are generally undertaken by the financially sound investing groups to revive sick units or worn-off projects. The chances of revival succses are very dim involving good deal of risk. The NTC programs has, taken up the task of rehabilitating the sick textile mills in the country. Banks have programs of finance such rehabilitation programme of projects. Though the success is far from reach, the efforts are made to rebuild on humanitarian grounds. Thus, a closure of a textile mill will mean throwing out hundreds and thousands of people rendering them jobless, shortage of production, miseries affecting those who dependent on these industrial activities. To safeguard the interest of all these, rehabilitations work is taken up as a welfare and social issue. At governmental level, the financial institutes like IRBs and SFCs come forward to help.

"Balancing projects" are those which are taken up to reach equilibrium in cases of imbalance. This is quite common in cases where the planned capacity is not balanced. Hence, balancing projects are undertaken to cope up with the changes in the "Supply side" of the economics of factors of production to increase the overll efficiency of plant and machinery by emphasizing the value addition, to the output through an equal proportion of input-mix. Hence, to reduce or eliminate the under-utilistion of the actual capacities and thereby enhance the effacing and effectiveness. Balancing between plant capacities is a continuous phase of many industries in their routine operations which are mainly driven on the market forces. In cases of blancing projects, even the decisions to make or buy play significant role. The overall idea is to make the unit to gain by keeping it is balance.

"Maintenance projects" are those which are undertaken to maintain the facilities created. The routined activity becomes special project when it calls for more than stipulated funds for regular maintenance. Maintenance projects involve the activities of overhauling the machinery, repairs and patching up activities at more than regular intervals. Put in other words, when the scope of normal maintenance task gets enlarged seeking additional support and coordination from other departments, then it becomes a maintenance project. These projects are financed through in house budgetary provisions without tapping outside sources. The basic aim of such projects is to see that the life-cycle of plant and machinery increases beyond the estimated future life.

"Modernization projects" are those where there is shift over to new tools and techniques and, hence machines from the existing ones. Modernisation is to keep pace with changing technological needs to be in the competitive advantaged position. The technologies change making the existing one as outdated and continuation of the same reflects higher cost, inferior quality production.

Modernisation helps in:

- Removing the stereotyped approach to production process.
- Encourages competitive spirit among the firms of the industry.

However modernisations is:

- Costly as it involves large investment.
- Longer transitory period dislocating facilities and resulting losses.
- Small firms cannot afford the luxusry of modernisation.

"Diversification projects" are those which are undertaken to improve the overall positions of a firm. The idea is to strengthen the competitive advantage. Diversification is to undertake such activities that support the existing activities resulting in increased sales, profits and putting investments in different baskets to play-safe. These diversification can be vertical or horizontal. Vertical diversification is to control up and down streams of the activities to be controlled and thereby gaining. Thus, a company manufacturing agro based products will now plan to own the farming and agricultural activities. This is what Godrej, Indian Tobacco Company, HLR are doing. Some companies may be only manufacturing, but now want to enter the marketing through their own units. Horizontal diversification is an attempt to make unrelated diversification. Thus, ITC has entered into salt, textiles, hotels, ready-garments, agro-products though it was basically a tobacco manafcturing company. Same is the case with Brooke Bond, Liption, Reliance group, Godrej and others.

Acquisition/merger projects are those where two existing companies merge with one another or one acquires the controlling share in another. Acquisition is the case where one company which is stronger acquires the assets of another which is comparatively weaker financially in marketing field or production area. The idea is to make the units combined to produce the synergy out of strength and weakness of one another. The idea may be to reach "Position No 1" in market or to come up as "market leader" than follower or challenger and so on. While in case of mergers, the aim is basically to get stronger together which works on two heads are better than one and four hands are better than two. Every day we come across good many cases of acquisitions and mergers.

New projects are those which have been undertaken to add capacity to the industrial -sector as an additional unit by using latest technological advancements. This adds to the industrial-sector capacity one side but makes a separate category itself as it is going, in for the latest technology and have lower cost and superior quality output. The idea is to reap the benefits of lowest cost and best possible quality output. It may be any line whether it is consumer durable or non-durable or purely it is industrial. Finally, the benefits are transferred to the members of society.

Distinction Between 'Balancing', 'Modernising', 'Replacing', 'Expanding' and 'Diversifying' Projects

The following chart gives the clear cut distinction with one another which helps to have much clear conceptualisation of projects.

Point of View	Balancing Projects	Modernising Projects	Expansion Projects	Replacing Projects	Diversifying Projects
◆ **Objective**	◆ To balance between the existing plant capacities and reach optimum efficiency	◆ To shift from the existing process to new process that brings new economies of scale	◆ Widening the scope of work in the similar line of operations	◆ Simply replace the old machine or a part of the process with new system to continue to function smoothly.	◆ Overall growth of enterprise from all angles. To capture new markets and explore new products.
◆ **Change factor**	◆ Little change is initiated due to change in the capacities of hither	◆ A good amount of change while shifting from one kind of	◆ There is a positive change leading to growth of business	◆ No much change as it reflects a simple replacement of old and	◆ A total change is involved which may be either way. Jump-

	to inbalanced processes.	operation to another. This may affect the employee knowledge too.	and will occur only if the management volunteer for such a change.	out dated mechanism with the new system unless the system is highly complicated and unfamiliar to the workers.	ing into and new from the existing one is a challenging feat where high risk is involved.
◆ **Conflicts in Organisation structure**	◆ There may be a little conflict between people working at different machines or processes which need to be balanced but mostly not a serious one to consider.	◆ Generally, a resistance to change to a new mecha nism or systems is exhibited from the working members. or shop-floor people but that can be manager by project manager by assuring them of sufficient training in the new system.	◆ Some confusion and choas may initially develop in functional department lending to misunderstandings and conflicts. Also some managers may be envied by others on being given the credit for expansion.	◆ Conflicts may arise between functional and the project manager as he has to seek their consent and help while replacing some systems with new ones. Again, this can be effectively medicated by top management.	◆ Conflicts and change are the hall- marks of diversification. The R&D team is always in forms of capturing new market or new products and the current product development teams strongly resist such risk ventures. This conflict may delay the decisions and many a time even the projects are abandoned if the pro-

					posal discussions are not handled delicately.
◆ — spirit	◆ This encourages little spirit among the organizational members of those departments where the process is operating below capacity.	◆ This reinvigorates the team effort on the new system as most of the members will be enthusiastic towards the new system.	◆ This demands competitive spirit on the part of all the members.	◆ This encourages competitive spirit and gives rise to increased output.	◆ To copeup with changing needs of the business as well as the society, one chooses to diversify the enterprise. Therefore, lack of competitive sprit on the part of may not help in diversifying the old business.
◆ **Costs involved**	◆ Little costs are involved in balancing which can be ploughed back from the depreciation mechanism or system and the remining can be arranged through internal sources such as deprecia-	◆ It is bit costly proposal yet can be easily manager by realizing fund out of disposal of old mechanism or system and the balance amount can be arranged though internal sources such as deprecia-	◆ This is a costly affair as it needs sufficient funds both from within the business and outside sources such as banks and financial institutions. However, this proposal is accepted only when the resurses are	◆ This will not be in generally costly as replacements are thoroughly investigated and only if such costs are not burden on the departments concerned, the project will be executed. Therefore, cost wise	◆ This calls for huge funds. This is a big gamble which an entrepreneur would be playing at his risk. though viability of the project logically explains and funds will be sought from financial institu-

	tion and other contingent funds.	tion and other contingent funds.	assure and the risk of funds insufficient is limited.	worry these is no worry at all.	tions, the public issues may also be opted as the main source of such funds.
◆ **Time Spent**	◆ This needs to be done within a short span of time as it is predetermined by the concerned authorities.	◆ This is also executed well within the time schedules prepared by the authorities and no or little delay is permitted.	◆ This is relatively a time consuming activity. It can not take place over night. Sufficient time is provided to researcheing to give their findings on such expansion projects.	◆ This needs to be executed on the dot. This does not consume much time as 'ready made systems are generally available and installation time is the only time that is needed. Any delay in installation impedes the production process and output.	◆ Planning is the fundamental principle is the diversification projects. Meticulous planning and time-scheduling are essential to enter into a new line of otherwise it would be very difficult to cope up with such a complexity.
◆ **Benefits derived**	◆ Immediate benefits are enjoyed in the form of increased output. Benefits are shared by the total department.	◆ Benefits arrive some what slowly because system costs need to be recovered initially and some lead time is also given to the members to	◆ Benefits with accrue only after commissioning the expended plant or when full scale production is in full swing. This is relatively long-	◆ Benefits will break even with cost of systems installation. Subsequently, some additional benefits may accrue both in the form of qual-	◆ Benefits in the form of profits, good products, and new markets and the like are matter of chance and the entrepreneur may have

		understand the system.	run oriented. The benefits will be shared by the total organisation.	ity output and profits.	to went for years to reap the true fruits of his efforts. The benefits are shared by all the stake - holders including management of the organization and customers.

PROJECT LIFE-CYCLE AND ITS PHASES

Every Project has a life-span encompassing at least five stages or phases. Each phase is different taking its own time and other inputs, just as human life is having life-cycle of birth, growth, peak-height,decay and death. Sometimes, human life comes to an end because death can occur at any time. However, there are definite stages which are logical. Similarly, project has five phases from start to end. These are:

1. Conception phase.
2. Definition phase.
3. Planning and organizing phase.
4. Implementation phase.
5. Project clean-up phase.

Though these are logical steps or phases, there is no need to follow this sequence. That is, all projects do not follow in reality this sequence and the span of each phase is not definite though estimates are made by experts. Let us know as to what are these phases, before we go the concept of project management.

This concept of project life-cycle can be nicely presented in the form of a diagram as given below.

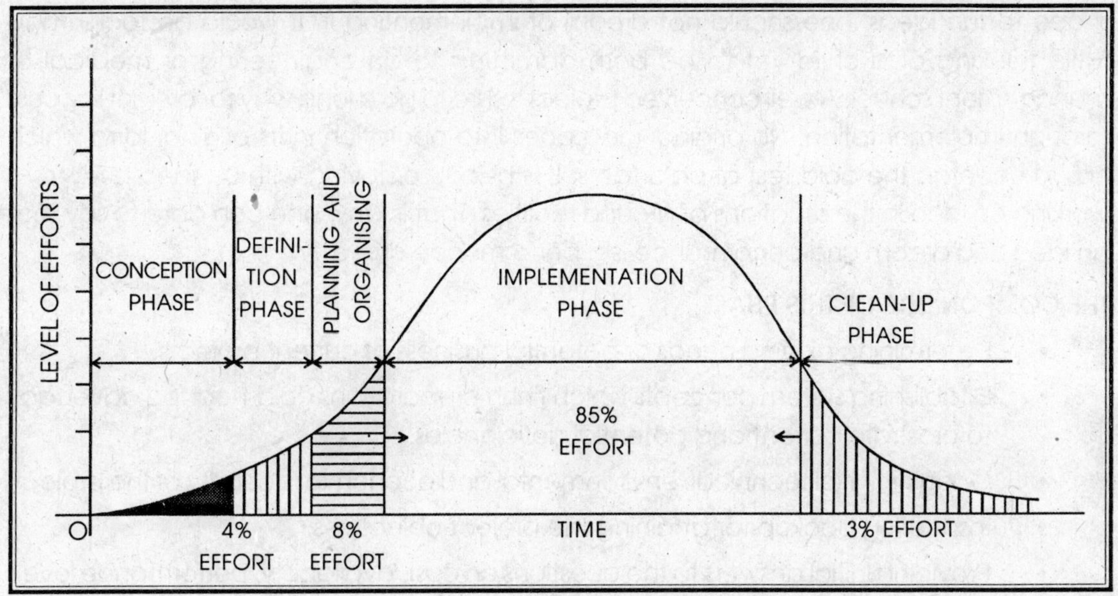

Fig. 1.02 Project Life Cycle Curve

1. CONCEPTION PHASE :

This is the first stage or phase where the project idea germinates. The idea comes to the mind when one seriously attempts to overcome certain problems. These problems may be non-utilisation of either the available funds, plant capacity, expertise or simply unfulfilled aspirations or desires. When one is after the problem, like an ant, he looks around to find the ways of overcoming them. It is also possible that an idea suddenly flashses in his mind and he starts surveying the environment; his well-wishers might provide him with idea or ideas. From whatever source he gets the ideas, these are to be written down in a systematic manner before they are compared to competing ideas.

Take case of any factory or plant which is operating at lower capacity than it has and is having high-power consumption resulting into higher cost of production per unit. This situation is not at all acceptable and, therefore, it pays to go in for new technology, replace some critical items selectively or scrap the plant altogether and go in for latest technology well within the resource constraints especially finance, keeping up of the man-power already working and raw-materials. Hence, these ideas need to be examined in the spot-light of one side objectives vis-à-vis the constraints. Finally, the business house has to work between these extremes– a compromise that gives the best results. This is, the fashion in which business ideas are usually conceived.

This exercise is, simple and logical and if done away with, the ideas that proceed might be blunders finally making a unit bankrupt. As it is the stage of giving birth and shape to the ideas, one should not dream of implementing it. It would be foolish and futile thinking of a child yet to be born admitting to an engineering or medical or management school. A well conceived project is sure to go a long way for brilliant success through implementation. No original idea goes into operation in its original form which has to undergo the acid test of cold facts. It is because, toying with an idea is far from working on idea in the situations of ground realities. That is why, one can dare to say that an idea or a dream and performance is a performance or reality.

THE COMPONENTS OF THIS PHASE

- Determining existing needs or potential business of current projects.
- Establishing system concepts which finish preparations cold-hearted advocacy to prostrate current and potential deficiencies.
- Gauging initial technical, environmental and economic feasibility of the project.
- Inspecting backup for attaining the project objectives.
- Providing initial answers to the questions on cost, availability, performance levels and their computability to other project programs.
- Identifying human and natural resources essential for effective management.
- Choosing initial designs that would satisfy the objectives.
- Determining initial project interfaces
- Designing an appropriate organisation structure for the project.

2. DEFINITION PHASE:

This definition stage of the project is to support the idea or ideas generated at conceptual stage by documentation or by defining it in concrete form. Facts relating to the idea are collected and presented. Take for example, the company is planning to produce aluminium for construction purposes. Then the idea has to ask several questions which are answerable in positive. These are relating to various imputs:

(a) **Quality and quantity of raw-material** namely, bauxite – especially the areas of deposits and how long they exist or last ?

(b) **Calculations as to the size or capacity of plant** – where it is to be installed working capacities are to be given. That is, how many aluminium ingots or how many kilograms of aluminium will be produced per day in one shift.

(c) **Location and the Site of Plant** – This has to be explained in terms of economy, environmental hazards, social implications and so on.

(d) **The technology to be Employed** – or the selection of process of conversion of raw-materials into end products - that is - bauxite into aluminium ingots. There should be optimum technology supported with reasons and there should be description of selected technology.

(e) **Layout of Project** – It is of considerable importance. What is the optimum location?, with reasons and drawings to be explained.

(f) **Plant and Machinery is yet another Aspect** – It describes the selection of a particular type of plant and machinery, the reasons for selection, detailed description of the selected equipment and machinery in terms of specifications and the cost availability.

(g) **Electrical and Instrumentation Works** – This is to do with the scheme of electrical installation from the factory power grid to the last points where the high and low-tension power is to flow. Schematic drawings will be of greater help.

(h) **Civil Engineering Works** – Selection of best possible civil works, reasons supporting and the description of selected civil works with cost estimates.

(i) **Plant Utilities** – These relate to fuel, power and water. The fuel may be wood, coal, oil, gas. What the factory needs – that is, plant needs how much? In case of each item, there should be detailed specification as to properties, quantities, source availability and the unit costs.

(j) **Manpower Needs and Organisation Design** – The type of organization – the structure giving clear picture of line and staff authorities – the pyramid of structure from top to bottom or organization chart, when various positions are identified, specify the professional, skilled, semi-skilled and unskilled employees – their selection – training, availability – and the cost estimates.

(k) **Financial Analysis** – This is to do with the total financial needs to start with bifurcated into fixed and working capital, sources of finance; details of production and distribution costs. It is to do with the financial viability of the project.

(l) **Schedule of Implementation** – This aspect of the second phase though last is of immense importance. This clears the ambiguities and uncertainties which are clothed with formation of a project idea at conceptual phase. It goes beyond that and estimates the amount and degree of risks. These are defined clearly. Based on all aspects – a cost-benefit analysis – the idea may be accepted or rejected. Before a project is accepted and go ahead with actual implementation, there should be second thought where the project idea accepted or not to be accepted, has to undergo many tests of not only its possibility but also its feasibility or viability.

THE COMPONENTS OF THIS PHASE :

- Dauntless identifications of the human and natural resources required.
- Fabrications of the final system performance requirements.

- Preparing the detailed plans required for the support of the project.
- Estimation of realistic cost, schedule and performance requirements.
- Spotting out those areas of the project where high risk and uncertainty exist, and delineation of plans for further analysis.
- Defining interface and interfacing of project activities.
- Ascertaining other necessary sub-system of the project
- Characterising the initial preparations of the documents required to support the project, namely, policies, procedures, job-description budget and funding papers, letters, memoranda and the like.

3. PLANNING AND ORGANISING PHASE :

Though this phase starts after definition phase, in practice, it starts with the idea generation or conception of project idea. This is the phase which is all-purvasive where it is bound to overlap again and again. This is to give green signal for go-ahead with implementation. Many firms prepare a document called" "Project Execution Plan". During this phase, the firms deal with the action steps to convert dream into a reality or a promise into performance. These vital aspects are:

1. Project infrastructure and supporting services.
2. Systems design and basic engineering package.
3. Organisation and the manpower.
4. Schedules and budgets.
5. Licensing and governmental clearances.
6. Finance – the oil of business lamp.
7. Systems and Procedures.
8. Identification of Project Manager.
9. Basis of design, general conditions regarding purchase and other contracts.
10. Site Preparation resources and materials.
11. Construction resources and material.
12. Work packaging.

Stated in other terms, this phase involves the preparation of project to take-off without any snags. This phase is more emphasing implementation and, hence, is part of implementation phase. It is because, it is not confining itself with merely paper work and thinking and good many doing activities. One knows that planning is process of making rational choice among the choices one has. It is a decision-making process. It says "Look before leap". If one jumps to implementation without planning, he is inviting the trouble.

There will be crises and crises only so much so that one has to burn his fingers. Plans, however sound, need effective implementation. Plans which are the designs of destiny are to be cleared in all respects before implementing them.

THE COMPONENTS OF THIS PHASE :

- Translation of perspicuous plans so concerned and defined over the course of antedating phases.
- Identification and management of the resources in order to facilitate the production processes such as inventory, supplies, labour, funds and so on.
- Affirmation of project production, specifications
- Manifestation of production, construction and installation.
- Final proceedings and dissemination of policy, consonant with targets.
- Retention of final testing to determine sufficiencies of hardware and continue to pursue.
- Ameliorations of technical, manuals and affiliated chronicle listing how the project is intended to operate.

4. IMPLEMENTATION PHASE :

This phase gives an idea about what company is doing because, the configuration on paper is seen that hectic activities are going on plant site. That is, project people are on work site for the first time, starting work as per the plan. Preparation of specifications for equipment and machinery, placing order for plant parts and machinery and other equipment lining up construction contractors, giving of construction drawings, civil construction and construction of equipment foundations, erection of plant machineries, electricals, piping, plumbing, instrumentation, testing, check-list, trial-run and commissioning of plant. Nearly, 80-85 per cent of total work is completed during this phase. Therefore, organization people are eager to start this phase. Since, it forms the bulk of the project work, people are eager to complete at their earliest. However, things go as per schedule already prepared to avoid risks and losses. As this phase, more or less, represents the whole project, every attempt is made to avoid delay to put the project on fast track. That is, overlap of sub-phases like engineering, procurement, construction and commissioning to a greater extent. This phase is not independent but parallel to the activities of the project cycle, taken earlier. The extent of fast-tracking is going to be slow if project designing and construction are done by different agencies. In case only one agency or party is doing all the work, fast tracking moves on at greater speed.

This phase is very crucial and complex and, therefore, needs greater co-ordination and control. The project conceiving, testing, and selection for implementation may take more time, but actual implementation goes on as per schedule. The following figure gives subphases of this implementation indicating the extant of fast tracking of this phase of project life.

Sub Phase No.	Sub-phase details	Number of months											
		1	2	3	4	5	6	7	8	9	10	11	12
1.	Detailed Engineering												
2.	Ordering	.	.	.	.	.	.	.	.	.	.	.	.
3.	Delivery												
	.	.	.	.	.	.	.	.	.	.	.	.	.
4.	Construction and Erection												
5.	Start-up												

Fig. 1.03 Sub-phases of Project Implementation for an engineering project.

THE COMPONENTS OF THIS PHASE :

- Actuate the project yield by the contemplated user or customer.
- Virtual linking of the projects product or service into existing oragnisational system.
- Evaluation of the technical social and economic sufficiencies of the project to meet actual operating conditions.
- Provision of the feed back to planners concerned with developing new projects.
- Evaluation of the adequacy of project supporting.

5. PROJECT CLEAN-UP PHASE :

This is a phase which is transition in which the hardware built with active involvement of different agencies is handed over physically to start production. For the project personnel, it involves clean-up task like drawings, documents, files, operation and maintenance manuals, catalogs are given to the clients or the owners of the project. To satisfy the client, the contractors and specialized experts are to undertake several test-runs. In case the client needs a change at this stage, that has to be met by the project experts and contractors. Finally, the project completion accounts are closed, materials reconciliation is carried out, outstanding payments are made, if any, and all the dues are collected during this phase. The most significant issue during this phase is that of planning the manpower – professional, skilled, semi-skilled and unskilled – involved in project work.

Once the project is completed, all employees can not be asked to go. Therefore, preparation for project cleaning is to start long time before the actual physical hand over. The first among the employees to move are the design engineers. Most of them move to new project sites and rest are retained at field for residual engineering. Then, the turn is that of other engineers. Their places are taken over by client- engineers for production and maintenance work. The new projects taken over will have new team. Each project being unique, same team can not work.

THE COMPONENTS OF THIS PHASE :

- Confirming that customer is satisfied with the work done and executing any small fluxes, harking to reply questions essential to achieve satisfaction
- Arranging relevant project files in proper form so that they can be reffered for future projects of similar type.
- Reviving equipment and facilities to earmark status for others to run through or decommission them.
- Ensuring that project accounts are maintained up-to-date, amply audited and closed out.
- Assisting project staff in being re-assigned.
- Discharging any outstanding dues on behalf of the project.
- Collecting dues of fees or payments from the clients and clearing the account.

PROJECT MANAGEMENT

WHAT IS IT ?

Project Management is an organized venture for managing projects. It involves specific application of modern tools and techniques in planning, financing, implementing, monitoring, controlling and coordinating unique activities or tasks to produce desirable outputs in consonance with predetermined objectives, within the constraints of time, cost, quantity and quality. Project management is basically involved in executing the projects. Project management is a discipline and philosophy. As a discipline, it is one of the richest sources of proven techniques for attainment of the goals allowing organisations to reduce the need for strict control and heavy rigidity. Project management is the application of knowledge, skills, tools and techniques to project activities in order to meet or exceed stake holders needs and expectations. In simple words, project managements encompasses the managerial tasks of planning, organising, directing, motivating, coordinating and controlling the activities involved in project a non-repetitive activity.

STANDARD DEFINITIONS

- **PROFESSOR HARVEY MAYLOR OF CANDIFF BUSINESS SCHOOL OF AMERICA :**

  Project management includes planning, organizing, directing and controlling activities in addition to motivating what are usually the most expensive resource on the project – the People. Planning involves deciding what has to be done, when and by whom? The resources then need be organized through activities such as procurement and recruitment. Directing their activities towards a co-herent objective is a major management role. The activities also need controlling to ensure that they fit within the limits set for them."

- **PRINCE :**

  Project in Controlled Environments – is a project management cell or structure within which plans can be formulated and actions controlled through the project life-cycle. Its major benefit is providing a degree of methodology standardization between projects. This allows managers to concentrate on details of their specific project, confident in a recognized and proven method.

  PRINCE defines project in terms of its products. **These are categorized as :**

  - Management – the planning, documentation and control actions of management;
  - Technical – the planning, documentation and review of technical aspects of project;
  - Quality – the planning, documentation and review of the quality control of the project system.

- **INSTITUTION OF CIVIL ENGINEERS :**

  Project management is expressed as "In order to carry out work efficiently, it is essential that a scheme of operations be first decided by those directly responsible for the execution. With such planning, the work can be broken down into series of operations and an orderly sequence or programme of execution evolved. Without a program, execution can only be haphazard and disorderly. The drawing up of a program at the beginning of the work does not mean, of course, that is drawn up once and for all and cannot be changed. The exact reverse is the case."

- **PROFESSOR HAROLD KERZNER :**

  "Project managements is the process of achieving project objectives through the traditionl organizational structure and over the specialities of the individuals concerned. Project management is applicable for any (unique, one time, one of a kind) undertaking concerned with a specify end objectives.

MR. OLSEN :

"Project management is the application of a collection of tools and techniques (such as CPM and matrix organisations) to direct the use of diverse resources towards the accomplishment of a unique, complex, one time task, within time, cost and quality, constraints. Each task requires a particular mix of these tools and technique structured to fit the task-environment and life -cycle (from conception to completion) of the task."

Thus, Project management is to do with project identification, formulation, appraisal, selection, implementation and management of projects. As **a process**, project management offers the organization a dynamic way to control change effectively in a structured manner. To achieve these desired results requires you to determine what needs to be done, by whom and when, before one attempts to start the work. In other words, project management is the management of a project. Therefore, project management involves planning, organizing, directing, co- ordinating, motivating and controlling. As **an approach**, project management is one that meets the pre-determined goals of a project or projects within the framework or limits set by the organisational span namely, materials, personnel, finance, time, results expected. Project management is that approach or modular work-approach which does the tasks of what is to be done, when is to be done? Where is to be done? How is to be done? And how best is to be done? within the limits of treasure, talent and time, of course, maintaining organizational integrity by use or intra and extra organizational resources. In essence, project management is about the management of a process of change and differs from normal requirements of the line manager's role. Project management has not remained taking the sequence of steps to complete project in time. It is more to do with scientific incorporation of the voice of the CUSTOMER, creating a disciplined way of prioritizing efforts and resolving trade-offs, working concurrently on all dimensions of the project teams and down-stream activities say in new product development integration with manufacturing, logistics and after-sale support – where 80 per cent of the costs are determined before they take over.

There are huge opportunities for eliminating waste of time and efforts in almost every project. In manufacturing, Toyota of Japan estimates that only 05 per cent of activities actually add value, 35 per cent are necessary but do not add value, whilst the remaining 60 per cent is a pure waste–Muda in Japanese! By reducing it to 50 per cent of it, the effort in designing a new car, they show that this 'Muda' can be reduced to a considerable extent by good project management.

STEPS IN PROJECT MANAGEMENT

Project management 'as a systems-approach' consists of five steps. These are :

1. **GROUPING OF WORK :** First, the total project is determined which will be the total job package. As project completion warrants highly specialized tasks and sub-tasks, closely related tasks are lumped into closely knit tasks so that specialists will undertake the work. This helps in two ways: work will have professional touch and simultaneous working will proceed as per the schedule drawn so that time is not wasted.

2. **ENTRUSTMENT OF JOB TO A SINGLE HEAD :** The entire project work is in charge of a person none other than a project manager. He is the whole and the sole having authorities and responsibilities and is accountable for his performance– over-under or normal. That is, it is he who manages the show as he thinks fit. That is, he plans, organises, directs, coordinates and controls the work which he gets through the efforts of others.

3. **INTERNAL AND EXTERNAL SUPPORT SERVICES :** Project management is not a joke. In performing his functions of management namely, planning, organizing, directing, co-ordinating, motivating and controlling, he needs internal support services and external support services. That is, he is enabled by the project organization through various departments or external agencies as suppliers, contractors and sub-contractors.

4. **BUILDING UP OF COMMITMENT :** Since the project work is to be completed well within the resource constraints, definite commitments are needed which can be achieved through negotiations, schedules, budgets and contracts. This needs good deal of give and take, coordination, communication and direction. It is so because, he is held responsible for his deeds and not his subordinates.

5. **CONTINUOUS MONITORING :** Project manager and his assistants are to see that each activity is going on as planned which is possible only when the planned activities are compared with actuals, deviations are determined, extent and nature of deviations are traced so that necessary corrective action can be taken, if need there be. This needs close-watch, detailed monitoring and strict-control so that promise is converted into performance and everything goes well as per prior calculations. If situations change, both external and internal, rescheduling is done and every attempt is made to achieve the goals without compromising in terms of cost, quality, quantity and time.

CREATION OF A PROJECT

To better utilize project management as an approach, there is need for creating a project. In systems-approach, project is viewed as a conversion or transformation of some form of input into an output. The following figure shows the inputs are some form of want or need which is satisfied through this process of conversion. The project will take place under a set of controls or constraints–those elements are generally from outside the project which either provide the basis for any assumptions or limit the project. The mechanisms are those resources that make the conversion process possible.

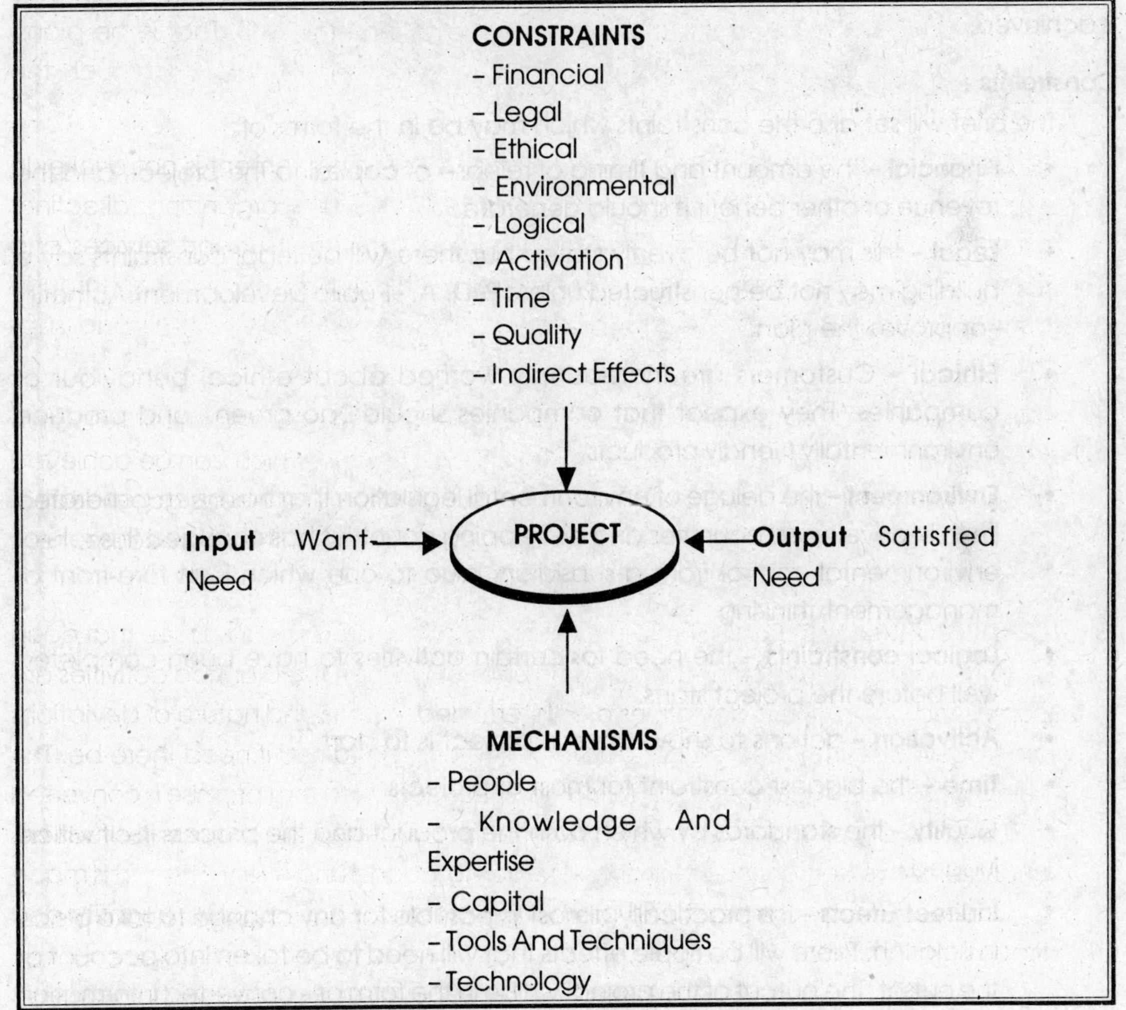

Fig. 1.04 Project as a Conversion Process

Inputs

For a project of even moderate intricacy, there will be some form of project brief - a document which provides a statement of want or need that is to be transformed by the project. There will be both statement of original needs and those which emerge during the course of project due to the customer's needs or perceptions that are changing which one can call as emergent needs. It is rather tempting to think of a project brief as an unequivocal statement from the customer. In actual practice, this is rarely the case and there will always be a degree of interpretation required from the project team. The brief needs to provide guidance as to what the nature of desire is–where there is a large creative element required of the project without putting unnecessary limits on the way it is achieved.

Constraints :

The brief will set also the constraints which may be in the forms of:

- **Financial** - the amount and timing of release of capital to the project, and the revenue or other benefit it should generate.
- **Legal** - this may not be overtly stated but there will be legal constraints say a building may not be constructed unless P. D. A. –Public Development Authority –approves the plan.
- **Ethical** - Customers are increasingly worried about ethical behaviour of companies. They expect that companies should "go green" and produce environmentally friendly products.
- **Environment** - the deluge of environmental legislation that has been generated both in developed countries and developing countries has changed the role of environmental control from a subsidiary issue to one which is at fore-front of management thinking.
- **Logical constraints** - the need for certain activities to have been completed well before the project starts.
- **Activation** - actions to show when a project is to start.
- **Time** - the biggest constraint for most of projects.
- **Quality** - the standards by which both the product and the process itself will be judged.
- **Indirect Effects** - it is practically almost impossible for any change to take place in isolation. There will be ripple effects that will need to be taken into account at the outset. The output of the project will be in the form of - converted information say a set of specifications for a new product - a tangible product - say a bunglow - changed people say, through a training project, the participants have gained new knowledge and so are part of the transformation process as well as being a product of it.

Output :

Output stands for "satisfied need". The expression "satisfied need" is very wide interpretation of the possible outputs of a project and includes say, a new bunglow from a construction project, processed information in the form of engineering drawings or a report and people with the necessary skills for a task because, the output of project involving special training. The output may be tangible or intangible.

Mechanisms :

The means of mechanisms by which the output is achieved are:

- **People –** those involved both directly and indirectly in the project.
- **Knowledge and expertise –** brought by the participants and outside recruited assistance say, consultants – to the project.
- **Capital –** the money that provides inputs or resources.
- **Tools and techniques –** the methods for organising the potential work with the available resources.
- **Technology –** the available physical assets that will be performing part of all of the conversion process.

HISTORY OF PROJECT MANAGEMENT

When human race started joint activities, of course, result oriented, people did engage in project management in a crude form. It is because, any activity or set of activities undertaken which are result-oriented and timebound, are projects. That is why, it was pointed out that every one is a project manager. These sets of activities were simple, then turned complex calling for the services of specialists. However, the study of subject where performance and methods are analysed, appears to have begun just prior to World War II in the chemical industry by **Morris** and **Hough** in 1937. It was in 1950s that further development took place towards establishing a methodology that was recognized today as project management.

During 1950s, the focus was on process and construction industries, the heavy engineering and defence sectors – particularly in America – began the development of the numerical techniques which today are seen as central to the subject. This part of the subject draws heavily on the work of Operations Research (OR) or management science, which is the mathematical treatment of complex situations such that understanding is achieved through numerical analysis and, hence, decision-making is enhanced.

This focus on mathematical reasoning has prevailed until very recently. The continued development of this idea or area has led to fragmentation of the subject, to the point where rather than just having project managers, there are specialists in particular areas of mathematics say, risk management. With the lapse of time, more recent approaches of the emerging area of technology management have brought in other management specializations such as human resource management. This element has expanded the scope of project management making it the management specialization today.

DAMING CYCLE FOR PROJECT MANAGEMENT

Managing change has been the watchword in this world of fierce competition. This is possible through the process of continuous improvement over what you have done. One of the champions of the change management **Dr. W. Edward Daming**, concentrated on change in quality than quantity. His original work was centred on the operational aspect of quality adopted with far greater vigour in Japan than his native America, but lately has been given more prominence in western management study. **Dr. Edward Daming** is famous for producing his 14 management points. The FIFTH of these is : "Improve constantly and forever every activity in the company, to improve quality and productivity and thus constantly and forever every activity in the company, to improve quality and productivity and thus constantly decrease costs". He stated this in 1986. The means by which his constant improvement is achieved is by the approch to projects can be configured as under:

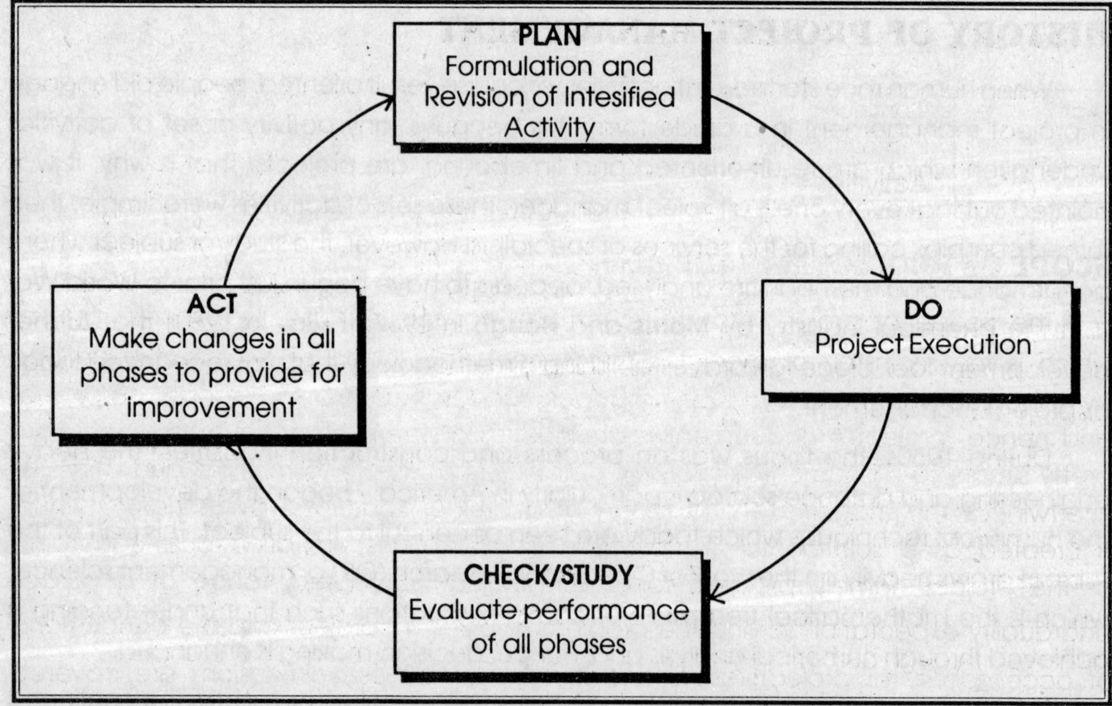

Fig. 1.05 Daming Cycle for Project Management

It is clear from the above figure that there are four steps for continuous improvement. The PLANNING STAGE involves the formulation and revision of statement of intended activity, whether formalized or otherwise. The DOING stage is the time when when the project is carried out which is the direct value-adding phase. The CHECK/STUDY stage involves a critical appraisal of both the project output as well as the process. The ACT stage is the phase when the project process is considered to see how the lessons learnt and gleaned from the review could be channeled back into the people involved in the process. The result is that all phases or stages of the process can be improved.

This **Daming cycle** for project management can be presented in the framework form with four dimensions namely, Activity- Phase- Key Issues and the Fundamental Question.

Activity	Phase	Key Issues	Fundamental Question
Plan	Project planning and Analysis	Goal Definition, Planning, Estimating, Resource-Analysis and Justification	How should a project be planned and the plans be evaluated ?
Do	Project Execution	Organisation, Control, Leadership and Decision-making	How should the day-to-day running of a project be undertaken ?
Check/ Study	Project Review	Assessment of results, feed-back of performance, change in the light of results	How can the 'management process' be continually improved ?
Act	Continuous Improvement Activities		

SCOPE OF PROJECT MANAGEMENT

The Scope of project management can not rule out the scope of a project which is the mainstay of project management. The scope of a project is defined by its objectives, constraints and budgets and schedules. The scope of project and hence, project management is obviously is quite wide, as projects range from pretty simple to monumental involving activities from simple to multiple and complex intertwined. The magnitude and range of a project is defined by its nature which is created as a solution to the problem, specifications, limitation and constraints of the project namely problem for which project is created, range of accuracy and quality expectation solving the problem involved in project and the benchmarks of acceptability of project results and its range. All these dimensions are covered up by project management. The scope and courage of any project lies in the abilities of project manager to handle unique problems by balancing through all the resource constraints. However, the external parties namely, stake-holders, promoters, financial institutions and the governments do play a dominant role either in reducing or enhancing the scope of a project. That is why, it is appropriate to say that scope is not the prerogative of either project manager or outside parties. It is rather the fine interplay of concerned parties which is a must to define the span and scope of project and project management. The following four dimensional cube helps us to understand the real scope.

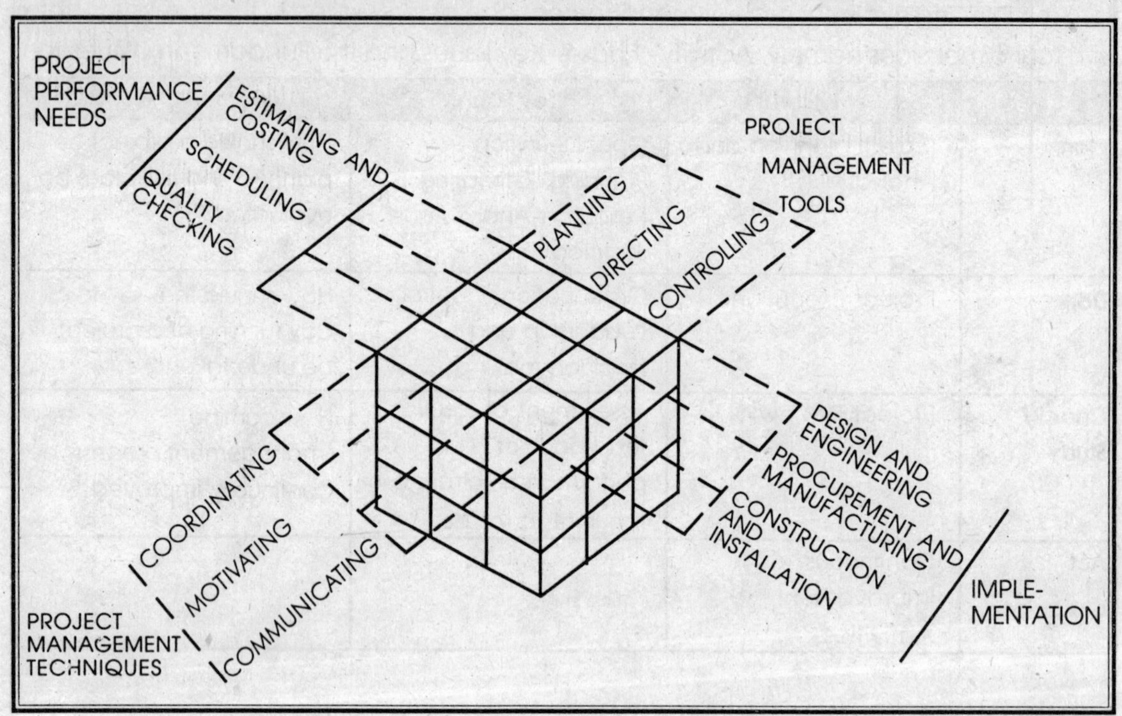

Fig. 1.06 Cube of Scope of Project Management

Before we conclude on project management scope : it will not be out of place if one looks at the flow chart which can be configured as under :

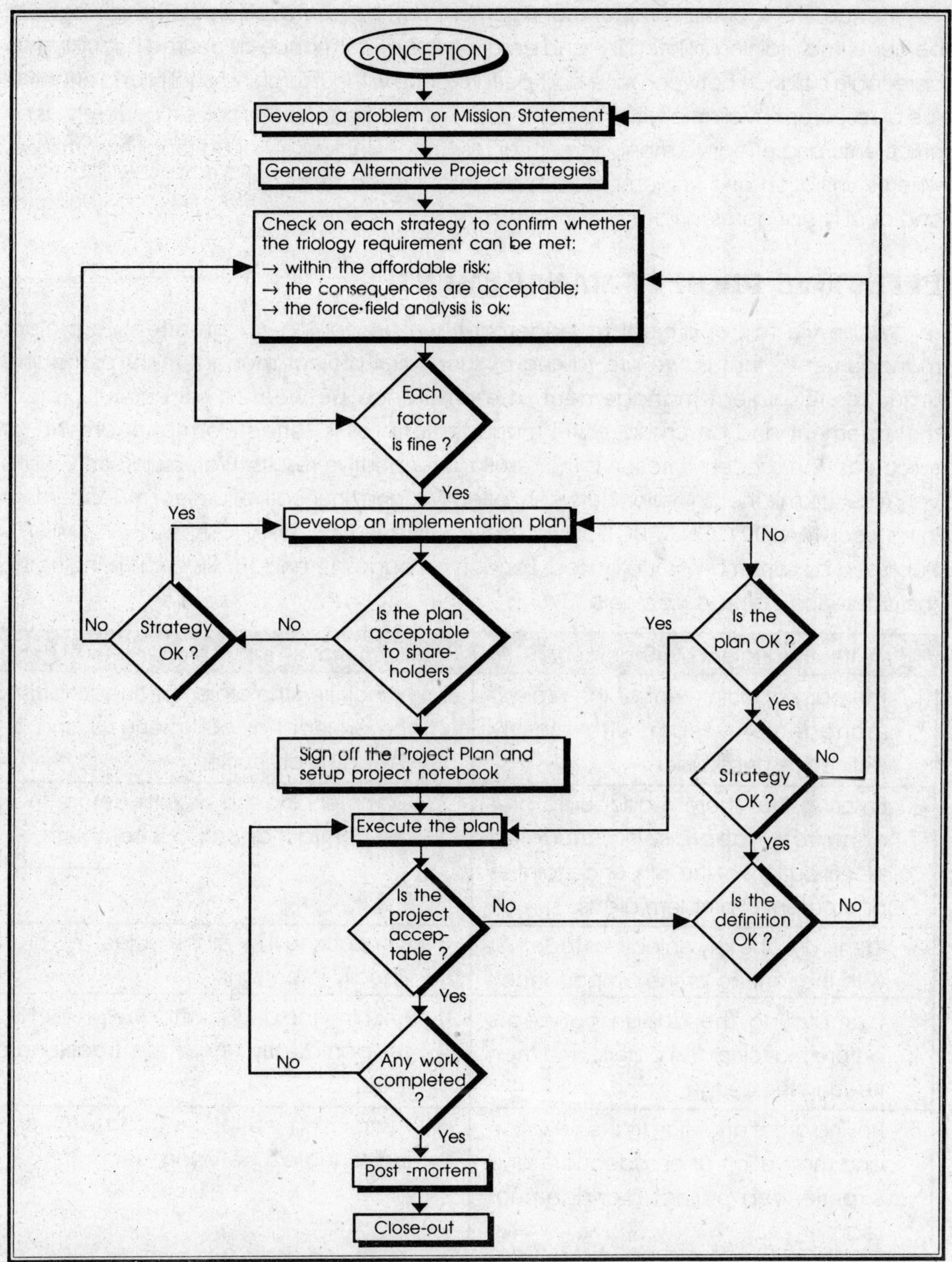

Fig. 1.07 Conceptual Flow chart of Project Management

Hence, the scope of project management can be portrayed by defining what is to be done, maintaining its integrity, and ensuring the performance as desired by striking an agreeable balance between time-cost-performance without furgoing quality and effective use of resources available with the organisation. Thus, it can be perceived perfectly as an efficeient and effective management of resources particularly of national importance, wherein initiation and implementation are inter-twined to the dimensions of time, cost and quality standards.

EFFECTIVE PROJECT MANAGEMENT

When we talk of project management, we are talking of "an effective project management". that is, we are talking of successful project management as against unsuccessful project management. The difference between a successful project management and an unsuccessful management lies is "effective management" of resources. The success criterion is the result rather positive results. Professor Keith F. Potts very nicely points the distinction between 'effective' and 'Ineffective' project management in his book MAJOR CONSTRUCTION WORKS: CONTRACTUAL FINANCIAL MANAGEMENT – Published by Longman group limited, London on pages 12 and 13. His chart bringing up the difference is reproduced here.

Effective Project Management	Ineffective Project Management
1. The early appointment of the project management team with clearly defined responsibilities.	1. Appointing the project manager after the project has commenced and is already in difficulties.
2. Ensuring that there is adequate pre-contract appraisal including identifications of the risks, uncertainties and potential problem areas.	2. Commencing the project before the pre-contract appraisal is complete.
3. Identifying the key objectives together with the ranking of their importance.	3. Considering that all the objectives are equally important.
4 Completing the design concepts before pla- cing the orders, and then freezing the design.	4. Finishing the design after the project is set particularly under the traditional route.
5. Poying great attention to the selection and motivation of an adequate and experienced project management team.	5. Appointing inexperienced staff with inadequate supervision.

6. Choosing the appropriate contract.	6. Using the same procurement strategy as is being done in production programs.
7. Selling up an effective communication network between the key participants before the commencement of the project.	7. Developing a computeriesd communication system all the year into the project that is not available to the participants.
8. Learning from past, approaching other clients with similar projects.	8. Assume that you have to reinvent the wheel on every project.
9. Strict control of design change proposals vested by a review board.	9. Issuing drawings without obtaining approval from the executive and without identifying the changes.
10. Ensuring that the time-cost model adequately reflects the financial consequences of alternative courses of action.	10. Considering the cost of alternatives merely on the basis of the bill of quantity rates.
11. Planning and replanning on daily basis if critical, otherwise on a weekly and monthly basis.	11. Planning the construction program at the site office wall and forgetting about it.
12. Visiting the site, if necessary, on daily basis, this motivates both senior staff and lhe operatives.	12. Staying remote and rarely visiting the site.
13. Driving the project forward, getting in there and making it happen.	13. Remaining desk bound with 9-5 mentality.
14. Being proactive, identifying contractors' problems early and offering solutions.	14. Considering that the contractor's difficulties are of no concerns to the project.
15. Communicating with the project management team on what needs to be done and how to do it.	15. Being a lower and keeping all your good ideas to yourself.
16. Thinking ahead and trying to control and influence the future.	16. Just letting it all happen without reacting to the events.
17. Constant attention to detail; urging people to complete their tasks.	17. Letting people get on with their tasks in their own sweet time.

CHAPTER BASED QUESTIONS

A. WRITE SHORT NOTES ON

1. Project
2. Project family - tree
3. Classification of projects
4. Project life - cycle
5. Stages of project life - cycle
6. Definition stage
7. Planning and organizing stage
8. Implementation stage
9. Project clean up stage
10. Project management
11. Steps in project management
12. Daming's cycle for project management

B. SHORT ANSWER QUESTIONS

1. What is a project ?
2. What is project family tree ?
3. What are the basics of project classification ?
4. What is project life-cycle ?
5. What is project management ?
6. What steps are involved in project management ?
7. What is creation of a project ?
8. What is Daming cycle for project management ?
9. What is the scope of project management ?
10. What is rehabitation project ?

C. ESSAY TYPE QUESTIONS

1. What is a Project ? What are its characteristics ?
2. What is a project family tree ? Distinguish between task, 'Program' and 'project'.
3. What is project ? How do you classify these projects ?
4. Distinguish clearly between BMERD projects (Balancing, modernizing, expansion, replacing and diversifications ?
5. What is project life-cycle ? What are its phase ?
6. What is project management ? What steps are involved in it ?
7. What is project management ? Explain its scope.
8. What is 'effective' and 'ineffective' project management ?
9. What is project management ? Explain Daming's cycle for project management.
10. What is Project management ? What is its importance? Trace its history.

* * * * * *

Chapter 2

PROJECT ORGANISATION AND PROJECT MANAGEMENT

- PROJECT ORGANISATION
- BASIC ELEMENTS OF ORGANISATION
- THE BASIC PRINCIPLES OF ORGANIZATION
- BASIC FEATURES
- ORGANISATION FOR PROJECT MANAGEMENT – A MODULAR APPROACH
- THE RELATIONSHIP BETWEEN PROJECT MANGEMENT AND LINE MANGEMENT
- DISTINCTION BETWEEN 'PRODUCT' AND 'PROJECT' STRUCTURES
- FUNCTIONAL TYPE OF ORGANISATION STRUCTURE
- THE BASIC CHARACTERISTICS
- SUITABILITY OF FUNCTIONAL TYPE STRUCTURE
- DISTINCTION BETWEEN 'PROJECT' AND 'FUNCTIONAL' ORGANIZATION AND MANAGEMENT
- THE PROJECT MANAGER
- BASIC EDUCATION FOR A PROJECT MANAGER
- ROLES AND RESPONSIBILITIES OF A PROJECT MANAGER
- AS A FUNCTIONAL MANAGER
- PROJECT MANAGEMENT AS A PROFESSION
- CHAPTER BASED QUESTIONS

BACKDROP

Studying Project Management without the 'Organisation' is meeting a person without body and without manager is meeting a person without head and heart. That is, project management is is rediculously incomplete without Organisation Structure and the manager to manage that organisation. Hence, this chapter is designed to know more and more about project organisation and project manager. The chapter ends with Chapter Based Questions.

PROJECT ORGANISATION

WHAT IS ORGANISATION?

The word ORGANISATION is used in two senses namely, as a STRUCTURE and as a PROCESS.

As a STRUCTURE, Organisation is the net-work of horizontal and vertical dimensions designed to attain certain common objectives. It is the mechanism or the frame-work of role whereby people functions and facilities are integrated to achieve common goals. Its is a group of people working towards the accomplishment of given goals. It is the structural frame-work of duties and responsibilities required of personnel in performing different functions within the company. It is essentially a blue-print for action resulting in a mechanism for carrying out functions to achieve the pre-set goals by the company management. It stands for an organism meaning a structure of body divided into so many parts which are held together by fabric of some relationship as one organic whole. In a stricter sense, the meaning of ORGANISATION remains narrower or static.

STANDARD DEFINITIONS

(1) **PROFESSOR RALF DAVIS:** defines it as "a group of people who are co-operating under the direction of leadership far the accomplishment of a common end."

(2) **MR. M. A. CAMEROON**: "It is the frame work of duties and responsibilities on which an undertaking works."

(3) **PROFESSOR HANEY L. H:** "Organisation is a harmonious **adjustment of specialized parts for accomplishment of some common purpose or purposes.**" In essence, it implies an internal arrangement of parts on scientific basis for effective and easy attainment of preset goals by the management.

As a PROCESS, Organisation is the crucial task of creating harmonious relationship between the parts of the enterprises. It is the function of identifying, grouping the work to be performed, defining, grouping the work to be performed, defining and delegating the people to work most effectively. It is the creative task of building and developing and maintaining the structure of **working relations in order to attained the common objective** or objectives.

(1) **PROFESSOR LOUIS A. ALLEN** : "Organisation is the process of identifying and grouping the work to be performed, defining and delegating responsibility and authority and establishing relationships for the purpose of enabling people to work most effectively together in accomplishing objectives".

(2) **PROFESSORS KOONTZ AND O DONNELL** : "Organisation is the grouping of activities necessary to attain enterprise objectives and the assignment of each grouping to a manager with authority ancestry to supervise it".

(3) **THEO HAIMANN** "Organisation is the process of defining and grouping the activities of the enterprise and establishing the authority relationships among them. In performing the organising function, the manager defines, **departmentalizes and assigns additives so that they can be most effectively executed.**"

This gives a broder sense and dynamic meaning. Thus, organization is designed to identify the total task to be performed, dividing and sharing so that the work can be performed with ease, economy and effectiveness.

The best thing its to combine the structural and functional contents of the word 'organization'. It is a mechanism of management by which a group of individuals will pool their efforts, energies, brains for the attainment of the objectives by defining and dividing the activities, responsibilities and authorities, It is an arrangement for the indoor administration of an enterprise. Organisation describes and prescribes the part to be played by each employee of the total task to be achieved effectively and efficiently. It is that organism which spells out the division of duties and responsibilities coupled with due authorities so that the group efforts result in final attainment of preset goals.

BASIC ELEMENTS OF ORGANISATION

The fundamental planks or elements of any acceptable organization are three. **PROFESSOR LUIS A ALLEN**, a renowned management luminary, identifies three basic planks of organization namely, division of labour, identification of source of authority and establishment of working relationships. It will not be out of place if we know these three primary planks of organisation.

- Division of labour
- Identification of source of authority
- Establishment of working relations

As a 'Structure' an organisation is featured by :

- It is the outcome of proposive or deliberate creation.
- It has a shape of a pyramid.
- It is more or less in prominent nature.

- Sacrifice of individual goals for the sucess of organisational goals.
- It is a design where it is a machine and the manager an engineer.
- Two dimensions off structural relations namely, vertical and horizontal.
- Structural relations can be charted.
- It is a means to a given end to be advised.

As a 'Process', it has the outstanding attributes namely

- Identification of total work.
- Dividing and grouping the work.
- Establishing the formal relations.
- Providing a measure to evaluate and control.
- Delegating authority and responsibility.
- Providing for working relation by accommodating industrial goals as a part of organizational goals.

THE BASIC PRINCIPLES OF ORGANIZATION

The Management thinkers of early days namely, **Henry Fayol, F.W. Taylor, U.L. Urwick** and their associates did develop some fundamental principles of organisations. These principles act as the guidelines for the creation and maintenance of sound, efficient and effective organization structure on one hand, smooth and frictionless functioning on the other. Though there are good many principles, the most important, hence commonly accepted, principles are outlined as under :

- The Principle of OBJECTIVE
- The Principle of CAPITALS/SPECIALISATION
- The principle of COORDINATION
- The Principle of AUTHORITY
- The Principle of RELATIONSHIP
- The Principle of DEFINITION
- The Principle of SPAN OF CONTROL
- The Principle of CHAIN OF COMMAND
- The Principle of UNITY OF COMMAND
- The Principle of UNITY OF DIRECTION
- The Principle of DISCIPLINE
- The Principle of BALANCE
- The Principle of CONTINUITY
- The Principle of SIMPLICITY

IMPORTANCE OF AN ORGANISATION

The **"isation"** Processes , of the latter half of the 20th century as opposed to **"isms"** of the first half, is having more sweeping sway on the organisations that have been working for years both in India and abroad. Liberalization, Privatisation and globalisation waves have changed the economic scenario. The organisations caught in this storm of change are both successful and failures. Taking the Indian case, Reliance, and HL are most successful ones as agaist Binnys, Scindia steamship and even Batas turning sick. The root cause of such result is the organizational base they have created, retained, pruned and adopted. A study of cross-action of successful Indian and foreign organisations reveals that it is the life-cycle of it and its attempt to adopt to internal and external forces. This highlights the significance of organization which makes or mars the very success of it. Its importance can be reduced to :

- It fosters administration.
- It boosts growth and diversification.
- It prepares spade-work for the use of latest technology.
- It creates conditions for creativity and initiative.
- It extracts best results from human capital.

PROJECT ORGANISATION STRUCTURE

'Survival' and 'Success' instincts have made the human race to go in search of new types of organization structure rather than carrying on with conventional structures we have come through. It does not mean that conventional organizational structures are useless because, even this day, they are playing important role. However, when better ways can be developed and used being more effective and productive, there is nothing wrong, old system or arrangement gives the way for new and improved system, to meet the challenges of change. One such modern organization structure is project structure.

WHAT IS IT?

A project is a task or an assignment where input and output relations are laid down well in advance. Project refers to any scheme of business to be undertaken in future. It might a project of construction of bridge, dam, administrative-building or a housing-colony on an establishment of a manufacfuring or marketing unit that provides facilities. Each has an objective to achieve, investment to make in human and money capital to make it payout in due course of time. In simpler terms, project is one which has purposes to achieve, provides satisfactions to the owner, satisfies the needs of stake-holders and users; it has time and pecuniary deadline and meets the needs of project team.

Projects are typically part of an organisaion larger than the project. The structure of the performing organization often constrains the availability of or terms under which resources become available to the project. Organisational structures can be characterized as spaning a spectrum from functional to projectised. The basic functional organization is a hierarchy with staff grouped by speciality, while in projectised organization staff is grouped by project and often collected. An ideal project organization involves an intelligent mix of these two structures at various levels, that is, forming a matrix organization. The wise management follows a "rewards system" in line with organizational structure failing which it counters the basic philosophy, leading to negative results. Thus, project structure consists of a number of horizontal organizational units to complete projects of longer duration. In a way, each project is vital and important to the organization for as soon as one is finished another ranks for completion. Therefore, a team of experts or specialists from different areas is designed for each project. Naturally, the size of the project team varies from project to project. What is more important is the activities of the project team are coordinated by project manager who has the authority to get advice and assistance from panel of experts both outside and inside the organization. The heart of project organization is to gather a selected and blended team of specialists or experts to work on and complete a particular project. It should be noted that the project staff is separate and independent of the function. The heart of project organization is to gather a selected and blended team of specialists or experts to work on and complete a particular project assigned. A project term is purely temporary set-up for once the project is completed, the team is disbanded and there will be reformulation of team suitable for working on another project. A typical project organization structure can be projected as under :

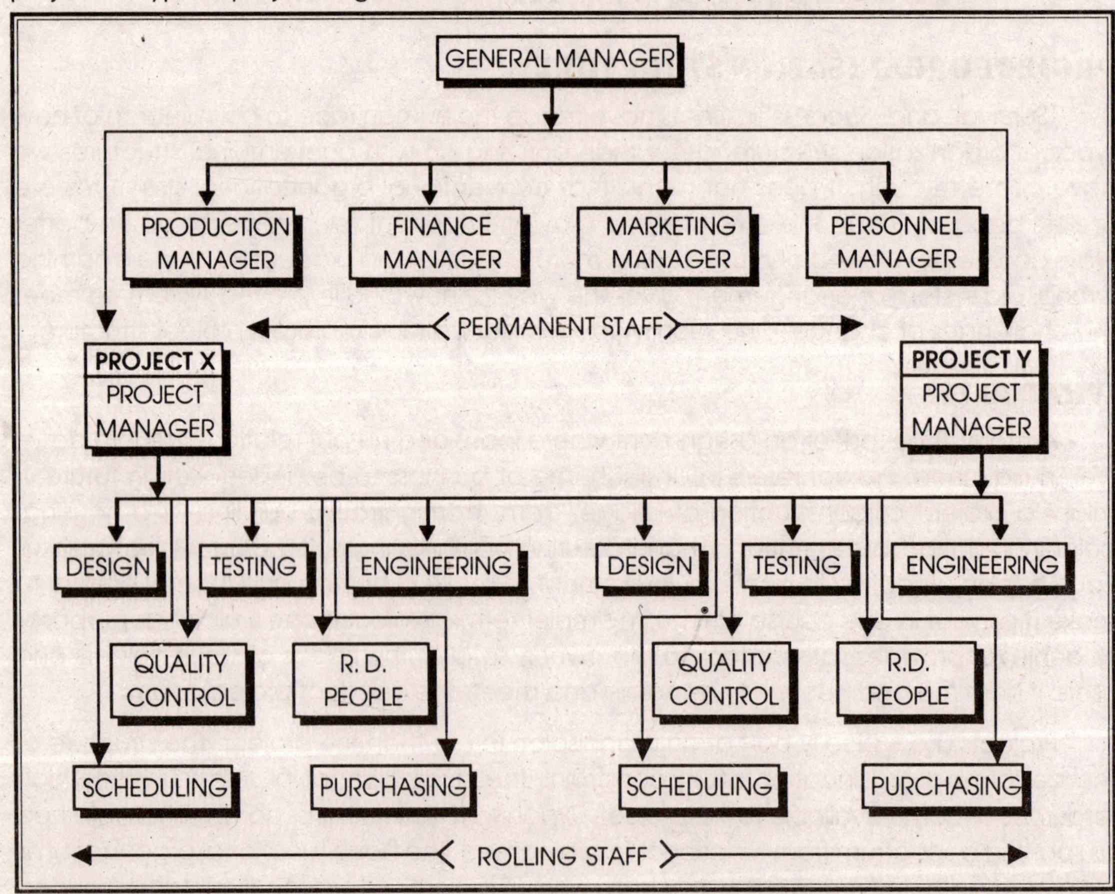

Fig. 2.01 Model of Project Organisation Structure

BASIC FEATURES

Project organization structure stands out as the traditional forms of structures have failed to meet the requirement's of pretty large multi-product managing variety of product and service tasks. The outstanding attributes of project structure are :

1. **PERMANENT AND ROLLING STAFF :**
The basic structure normally takes the functional form and the major departments namely, manufacturing, finance, marketing and personnel have a permanent staff concentrating on their major functions. These staff members are not hilted and tilted as they are the pillars of the basic structure. However, multi-product company has a number of assignments or projects which are important, some of which are taken simultaneously and separately. For each project to be completed, a team of experts or specialists is designed and allowed to work till project is incomplete. Once the project is complete, it is disbanded and made to join new team to take up another or other projects.

2. **UNDERTAKING OF UNIQUE PROJECTS :**
There is no meaning in designing a project organization structure if it has projects with nuclear or indefinite goals, that are infrequent and familiar to the present structure. It is more known for complex projects which have deep interdependence of tasks and which are crucial to the success of the organisation. The projects are challenging, thrilling and paying monetarily and non-monitarily to those who are involved in these projects. **George Terry** puts it rightly "it is a preferred means whenever a well-defined. Project must be dealt with, or the task is bigger than anything the organization is accustomed to". Exceptional line of aero-space, air-craft-manufacturing, ship-building, construction and professional areas like management-consultancy and so on.

3. **EMPHASIS ON HORIZONTAL RELATION :**
In project organization structures, the projects are subject to high standards of performance in terms of precision, specifications, units of tolerances. All these, needs due weightage to horizontal relations among specialists drawn from different lines as a team or task force. Project teams are so designed to facilitate the designing and development of product or new-products. Project management is so developed to deal with situations where production and marketing strategies do not fit into a purely functional type organization. The structure specifically speakes of horizontal relations than vertical as all specialists are at one plane.

4. **PRESENCE OF PROJECT MANAGER :**
One can not think of project organization structure without a head for project or projects undertake who is responsible for planning and implementation of the project assigned to him. The main components of project planning are establishing the desired

results – the objectives; determining the strategy is followed to achieve or exceed results; deriving a plan and scheduling showing when results are to be achieved; a budget to be established to back up achievement of results; projections of what will happen at certain specific points of time; organizational structure and policies for empowerment; establishing procedures for control and communication and setting standards of performance and methods of measurement of performance. On the other project implementation emphasizes on that the works is progressing according to the plan schedules; there has been no change of priorities for the individual; there are no problems being encountered; there are no problems anticipated; nothing has been forgotten in planning stage and project costs are running within the units of budget.

ORGANISATION FOR PROJECT MANAGEMENT – A MODULAR APPROACH

Any arrangement of project management is to achieve as to defining of what is to be done? Maintaining its integrity, and ensuring that it is done and performed as desired, within time and cost budgets for it, through a modular work approach, using organizational and extra organizational resources. The first task in project management is that of creating a project. This is possible even in a routine situation. Take the case of maintenance organization involved in routine maintenance, decides to go in for scheduled maintenance, a scope for using the project management approach is created. It, therefore, needs a project manager. The project manager, to handle the situation, takes certain steps to have modular approach to get certain benefits. These are :

1. **Projectise the Task :** Project manager projectises maintenance work as much as possible. That is, he creates number of projects may be daily, weekly, monthly, quarterly, terminally and annual maintenance of the entire plant.
2. **Set Targets :** Accordingly, cost and time targets for each of these projects are to be set as the guidelines or norms.
3. **Matrix with Maintenance Department :** Next thing he is expected is to matrix with maintenance department that provides for after maintenance still including labour and supervision. The maintenance department may be responsible for break down and running the maintenance work.
4. **Line up Vendors and Contractors :** These vendors and contractors are responsible for supply of materials and maintenance erection skills– who are to be identified and chosen.
5. **Matrix and Coordinate with Other Departments :** This also needs matrixing and coordinating with other departments that are responsible for preparation of drawings, specifications and procurement of material.

6. **Monitor and control :** He is expected to monitor and control these projects using schedules, budgets and contracts. The norms are fixed in terms of costs and time.

BENEFITS OF THIS MODULAR APPROACH :

The major benefits of such an approach that are apparent quite immediately are-reduced plant shut-down time and minimized maintenance costs. Such slashing down of valuable time and costs are possible because of the modular system that works giving much lee-way to the project manger :

(1) He will be totally concerned with completing the projectised maintenance work with the budget and schedule. He, unlike the maintenance manager, not concerned with the day to day maintenance-related problems. Further, as his performance is evaluated in terms of schedule and budget, he is impelled to stick to the terms of these.

(2) All maintenance work will be accommodated within the longest maintenance cycle time – better known as "critical path" – thus, reducing the total plant down time to the minimum.

(3) Each party will have a definite time and cost targets to work to. The work of these parties is subject to continuous monitoring and, therefore, the issues or the problems are reviewed and resolved even before they cause any damage. The parties, therefore, work in an environment conducive to meet the targets.

(4) The project manger concerned manages only what he has projectised. Hence, he is concerned with how to achieve the next target and not to look back. This approach makes Ihings work as people are geared themselves for the targets.

(5) As the project manager has the authority to take the things and make the decisions relating to his projects, decisions are made faster. This modular approach has full scope for lateral co-ordination that makes possible taking quicker decisions and prompt implementation.

THE RELATIONSHIP BETWEEN 'PROJECT' MANGEMENT AND 'LINE' MANGEMENT

In a conventional management hierarchy, lines or layers of authority and responsibility are clearly drawn. **"Line officers,"** strictly speaking the "doers" and functional or **"specialists"** are "thinkers". Long back, you had the opportunity of studying that management is the art of getting the work done from others. However, 'doing' and 'thinking' are part of it. What is more important is that one is incomplete without another.

The project manager has the line management role side by side functional management in that he is accountable for the projects that need functional management. The following is the typical organization structure for project management. The Fig. 2.02

indicates the project manager is being responsible for people drawn from each functional specialization in their activities in relation to the project. Examine thoroughly the project management structure given below.

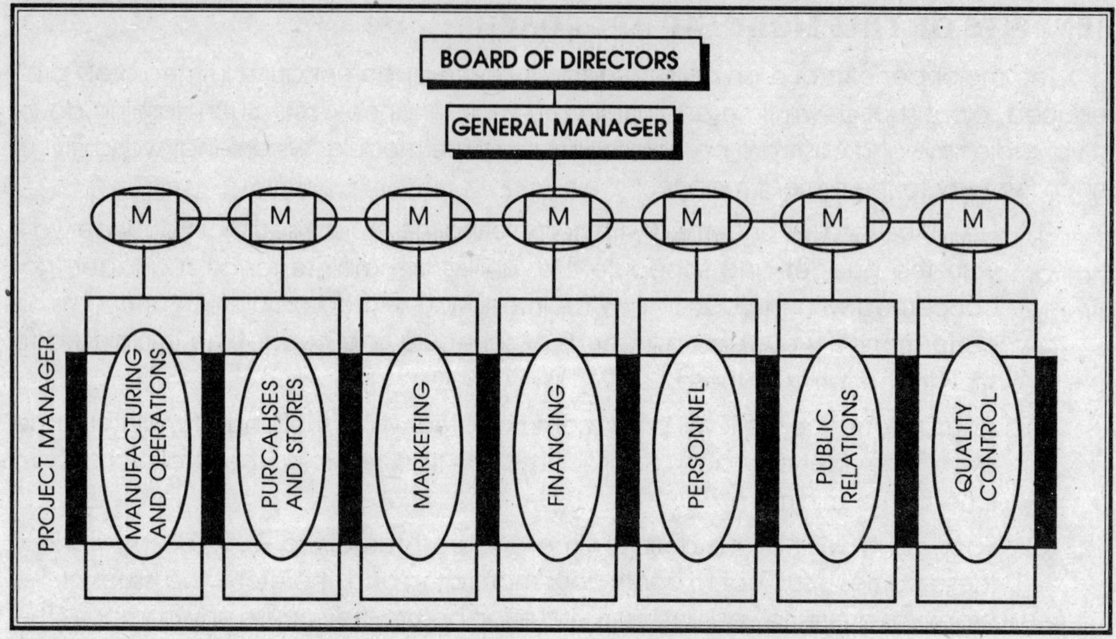

Fig. 2.02 'Project' Versus 'Line' Management

The project manager's role differs from that line manager in the nature of tasks being carried out. **The basic differences are :**

(1) A 'line manager' is responsible for managing the status-quo whereas, 'project manager' is responsible for not just managing the status-quo but for overseeing change.

(2) The 'line manager' authority is defined by the management structure whereas the project manager's lines of authority are not very clearly defined. They are fuzzy or fizzy.

(3) A 'line manager', has a set of consistent tasks, whereas, 'project manager' does not as his tasks are ever changing.

(4) 'Line manager's responsibility is limited to his own function or set of functions whereas, 'project manager's responsibility is cross- functional.

(5) 'Line manager' works on 'permanent' organizational structures unlike 'project manager' who works within the structures that last so long as a project is completed. That is, change over to new project implies change in structure.

(6) The 'line managers' tasks are described as more 'maintenance' while that of 'project manager' tasks are pre- dominantly innovative.

(7) 'Line manager's main task is optimization while the main task of 'project manager' is the resolving the conflict/s.

(8) 'Line manager's success is determined by the achievement of interim targets whereas, the 'project manager's success is determined by the achievement of stated end-goals.

(9) The 'line manager' has limited set of variables to work on, while in case of 'project manager' has variables made up of intrinsic uncertainties.

This split between the tasks can be considered as 'maintenance' or maintaining the status-quo and 'innovation' is changing. The fig. 2.03 makes it amply clear. It indicates the from line managers. The outcome of this is a change in the role of line-managers and a reduction in the difference in the roles of the "line" and "project" managers.

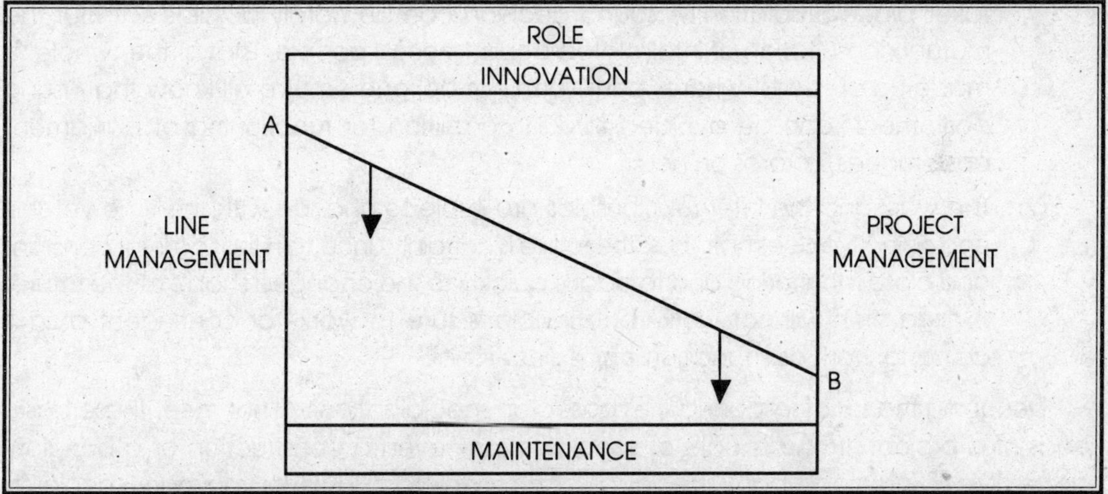

Fig. 2.03 Innovation/maintenance activities in Line and Project management

The major change in the project management practice has been its emergence as a management specialist in his own right – just as financial management, operations management, marketing management, personnel management and so on. In case of most of strategic projects, the function of project management involves variety of element comprising of :

- **Financial Management-** through the preparation of a financial case to meet the needs of project needs set out in the project brief or portfolio.
- **Personnel Management-** that calls for the identification of skills required, the selection of staff, their motivation and welfare too.
- **Operations Management-** where there are many parts of project that are repetitive in nature and can be treated as individual operations.

- **Purchasing and Logistics-** the identification of material and service needs, suppliers, their selection and management of logistics- location and transportation of materials.
- **Technical Specialisation-** say, new product development, engineering, programming quality management and so on.
- **Marketing Management-** that is projects generated for both internal and external customers warrant clear statement of needs drawn up and then to be sold to the customer.

All this leads us to the definite conclusion that the project management approach is neither fully functional nor fully line. **There are two important bases for this :**

(1) All work has interdependence and interrelationship with others. That is, nothing takes place is isolation. A sound decision can be hardly possible without the mutual consultation of interrelated departmental people. That is, the 'whole' is made up of 'parts' where 'parts' can not be ignored. We all know that 'hung parliament' can be avoided through coalition for functioning of parliament costs rupees 3 crores on hour.

(2) The work and the inter-relationships are liable to change with the time yet the end objective does not. Thus, The future is certainly uncertain that calls for constant and close monitoring and to adapt quickly to the changed shape of the future. A fixed plan will not work- but flexible is sure to work- or contingent plan is going to work as management is situational.

Designing the set of responsibilities based on specialization will not meet these basic needs of a project. If one speaks of specialization- even a construction of a bunglow can be divided into good many special tasks and specialists. However, too many specialists for each and every task of construction, the bunglow may not be constructed as too many cooks spoil the broth. Grouping and generalization of work as far as practicable is the dire need for the faster work- the project management, as opposed to extreme specialization and too much of division of labour because each finest idea- a novel way has its limits. Immediately following this is the need for trade-off-accepting lesser than the best, in one or more areas, for an overall benefit. By nature, all specialists may be against this, but no project can configure up in time and cost without this compromise- flexibility. Hence, a flexible and generalist approach than a rigid specialist approach is badly needed for project management.

What happens is that under the umbrella of functional specialization, the totality of the work is very often lost sight off. Wherever and whenever, functional specialization is dragged to an extreme which means some one is purely THINKING and some one is only TALKING. The real work is done by the third putting his heart and soul together and fourth one will do that follow-up. It means that only a PART OF HUMAN-BEING and not the WHOLE PERSON is involved in the planning and execution of a project. With such an arrangement also, no single individual except the chief executive can be held responsible for a work or a project from A to Z or start till finish. This situation adds fuel to the fire by creating problems of communication, coordination, commitment and control.

A work is smartly done if taken up as a WHOLE and assigned to ONE RESPONSIBILITY CENTRE. Any project is a work not a mere task of processing or conversion of INPUT into OUTPUT. Here, work is done when the objective for which the work was undertaken in the first instance is achieved. Anything done in between are only TIME and cost consuming MOTIONS. It means that any person has not done any work unless and until the said person is continuously busy with the planned schedule of motions till the final aim is achieved. This urge for achieving final aim is the greatest motivating force behind the project management approach.

In essence, project management demands a clear distinction between the PART and the WHOLE and MOTION and the WORK. Unless this is injected effectively in the minds of all the member of team or organization, rich and rare resources - time, talent and treasure - will be wasted in useless motions. That is, project management approach is a must for all of us irrespective of working on a multi-billion rupees like four way National Highway network or a simple cycle workshop. The heart of the problem is dedication, commitment on the part of each member of the project-team focusing the attainment of final aim in time and cost limits. Like functional management, project management will involve getting the work done through others and but with difference. That is, people from the environment which are more than the people within the organization-those people being external are not bound by the organization's ethics and discipline. That is, project management approach has to work within this environment or social setting. Majority of the people might find it unusual and may not like; one thing is sure, one has to get the work done without whose support project remains hung. What is needed is good deal of patience, lobster listening and grebbing negotiating capacity. The project management approach gets the work done through lateral and diagonal contacts where hierarchical protocol is almost non-existent, in practice. The result is quicker and clearer communication, quick and sound decisions. While free-wheel communication is working, sorting out the problems and decision making commensurate with responsibilities at lower level, the higher ups are always kept informed if the situation so forces.

This style of operation is the characteristic feature of project management approach irrespective of nature of the structure which may be purely projectised, matrix or functional. Therefore, the protocols of the organizational hierarchies, remuneration levels and designation are all unimportant as far as working relationships are concerned. It means that project management postulates that the human organization is created to manage a physical structure or a system which has a natural inter- relationships and interdependence and, therefore, the human-system must correspond to the physical system and respond to the demands of the physical system without creating any other artificial system based on class, creed, colour, or ideology. Ideally, the human organizational system should be a mirror image of the physical system. It, again, is not possible no matter how far we are liking to merinate with physical system. Again, like projectising the task, there is need for projectising the outlook- look to the future and bury the past. Past is past; what is important is what you are and what you will be? Therefore, project management wants orientation, commitment and achievement of target result.

EVALUATION

MERITS :

As a pull out from traditional form of organization, project organization brings home certain special merits. These are :

1. **LOGICAL APPROACH TO ANY CHALLENGE :**
   Project organization can provide logical and matching approach to any challenge in the form of a mega project with definite start and end and clearly defined outcome or performance. It cuts to size the manager's jobs to a significant and tolerable level, spans and spreads **decision-making** process by participation and facilitates lines of communication through lateral relations between the speciatists and in officials.

2. **ENCOURAGES INITIATIVE AND CREATIVITY :**
   Perhaps the greatest merit of project organization structure is that the success of the project organization is hinged on project success and, in turn, its success is depending on picking and choosing and frame a team requiring highly talented professionals known for acumen, greater degree of creativity. For a people of expertise, creativity, they need free-hand in dealing with the work assigned. Thus, work is a great motivator which is challenging nature. Therefore, project organization encourages individual initiative, crucial creativity and autonomy all that needed to accomplish the project.

3. **MATCHING TO MANY LINES OF ACTIVITIES :**
   Project organization has been found useful to accommodate wide variety of variations in situations and types of activities. The ever-increasing complexity of projects and intricacies involved and meticulous handling of each projects warrant people of knowledge, skill, expertise and acumen. Each project is unique and demands commanding flexible and adaptable approach. You name any project – say construction, space-craft, aero-plane and ship-building, management consultancy, advertising agencies, financial and cost accounting consultancy areas – all are accommodated with the fine blending of classical thinking and traditional approach along with teams and participative leading to better results.

4. **GUARANTEED SUCCESS :**
   Project organization structure creates an atmosphere where concentrated attention and integrated efforts are put in a complex project. Strict ground reality planning and stringent implementation procedures guarantee timely completion of projects

without having any damaging impact of organizational set up. It can be tailored to specific mission or project to consolidate diverse and varied actions towards the accomplishing pre-set goals in terms of time treasure and talent. The sponsor is happy as he gets work done in time. With quality and low costs; the employees get motivated that they have achieved the best results and the stake holders the owners because, they get decent return on resources employed.

5. **OPTIMAL UTILISATION OF RESOURCES :**
Project structure, by nature, gives more degree of flexibility in the utilization of scarce resources – material and human – as there is well planning allocation as per the forecasts, budgets which are put to acid test of cold facts based on cross-verification of experts drawn from different yet closely rated to project. While arriving at optimal allocation of resources internal and external environmental factors that have imping impact on resources and results are taken care of. There will be no intermixing of other projects.

DEMERITS :

All is not well with the project structure, though one boasts of the merits. One should take into account the demerits too, for each thing has both brighter and darker sides. These demerits are :

1. **FEAR OF LOSS OF JOBS :**
Nearly eighty percent of the staff is purely temporary whose fate has been clothed with the tenure and continuation of project. People working on a particular project have a fear of losing jobs as soon as the project is competed or to the bad luck the postponement or discontinuance of the work in progress. There is very strong feeling of insecurity and changing status of personnel's jobs generates worry about the career and degenerates and demoralizes as to work. There is no guarantee that soon after the completion of project, the personnel will be joining on new project. This feeling of job insecurity creates a problem of present.

2. **HEAVY BURDEN ON PROJECT MANAGER :**
Project manager has a tough time as he has to deal with professionals drawn from various fields. As they are experts and specialists, they very often differ in approach and interest. The structure is so designed that there is no clearly defined responsibility, clear lines and measurement parameters. Lack of a well structured and prescribed organizational process makes the jobs of a project manager **not only** frustrating but vulnerable. Further, lack of awareness of the details of project problems and personal prejudices, malice on the part of top-management it is likely that the morale and self confidence might be saped and sagged so much so that he feels like a stuff sandwiched between the line officers and specialists.

3. **DISPROPORTIONATE RESPONSIBILITY AND AUTHORITY :**
As a project incharge, he is held responsible for results of the project. The problems faced by the project manager are numerous and intricate as he has to discharge his duties and responsibilities without adequate authority. The conventional nature of project structure does not grant him the authority that is sufficient to get the work done. Therefore, he had to rely on his personal qualities and unofficial relations than officials. That is why, his major areas of headache are budgets, manpower and co-ordination and control. He is bound fail, in case the congenial atmosphere is not assured by top management. The problems of project management are really challenging and if he believes in traditional system of organization, he might not be able to work with a success.

4. **CONFLICTS AND CHAOS :**
Project is an adhoc arrangement with limited span of life. Uncertainties and fear are sure to create interdepartmental conflicts and Chaos. Personnel have the fear of being forgotten at the time of promotion due to separation from the mainstream. The decisions may not be sound though quick backed on scanty data caused by the pressure forth completion of project on hand in time and within the limits of budget. Excessive supervision and multiple might be the root cause of frustration and loss of confidence. The end results might be role conflicts, poor loyalty and under-utilisation of resources and project failures.

SUITABILITY OF PROJECT STRUCTURE :

Project organisation structure is most suitable in cases where :

1. The task or job involved is time bound and definable terms of specific goal or goals.
2. The task is unique, infrequent and unfamiliar to the organisation where it is made challenging, thrilling and paying.
3. The task is highly complex and multi-dimensional that calls for perspective thinking by people of specialisation calling for interdependence.
4. The task is that there is high degree of stake in the successful completion of the project. The stake is particularly in terms of time-where time is more than money.

DISTINCTION BETWEEN 'PRODUCT' AND 'PROJECT' STRUCTURES

Good many times, it so happens that both 'product' and 'project' structures appear, to be similar. Even when one studies in detail that he is bound to have confusion so much so that they are taken something synonymous or identical. However, a good deal of difference between the two. One can distinguish both 'product' and 'project' structures at least on Ten Counts. An an attempt is made to put in simple words, the difference between the two taking each basis. These differenting bases can be :

1. **ORGANISATION BASE :**
   Under "product structure" each product-line is organised as a separate division while, in case of 'project' structure each project is organised as a separate unit. Thus, product has a division while project as a unit. A product division can be done on the basis of process, customer geography and so on. This kind of treatment in case of project structure where functional can be basis and project can have staff.

2. **STAFF ARRANGEMENT :**
   In case of "product structure". each product division has functional staff of its own. Thus, a product-line having product A,B,C,D and E each has all the four functional staff namely, production, finance, marketing and personnel. Each becomes a self-contained block while in case of "project structure" two sets of staff are seen. There are, at the top common departments of manufacturing, finance, marketing and personnel. While in case of each project the specialists are drawn. That is, there is no duality of chain of command in case of "project structure" there is. Subordinates have one superior in case of "product structure" while in case of "project structure" there are two superiors.

3. **ACCOUNTABILITY :**
   On the basis of the responsibility for results one can have difference. In case of "product structure" he is totally responsible for the product division where he has sub-divisions interdepartments of production, finance, marketing and personnel. He is to plan is product in terms of quality, cost, quantity and time-dimensions set. Higher authorities will hold him responsible even if the fault lies with department or sectors or rank and file. In case of "project structure" the responsibility of completion of project or projects assigned to him in terms of time, cost, resources. He can hire and fire project staff drawn from different lines in getting the work done.

4. **OPERATIONAL AUTONOMY :**
   Autonomy stands for the freedom of handling the work or task. Operational autonomy stands for official autonomy in performing or getting performed the task. It stands for the freedom of decision-making, spending, empowering, rewarding and punishing the employees and mode of operation. In case of "product structure" the product manager has high degree of autonomy as he is self-contained block having every physical and service facility on the other hand in case of "project structure" the project manager has higher degree of operational autonomy as he has to handle two types of staff namely, functional and project. The first is permanent while second is temporary. The problems of planning, coordination, direction, controlling, communication all warrant, higher degree of free hand in working. Therefore, latter enjoys comparatively higher degree of autonomy than former.

5. **COORDINATION AND CONTROL :**

Coordination is opposite of conflict. It is to do with three things namely, timing, integrating, and balancing. One who has command over this co-ordination function, he will not have any problem of control. In case of "product sructure" this task is quite simple as he has only functional facilities brought at best level for each product division. Comparatively, the task in case of "project structure" is still more easy. It is simpler because, there is no interference and every person has full freedom in so far as his role is concerned. Work freedom acts as a great motivation and, hence workers will be "self-starters" than "shirkers".

6. **ANGLE OF ECONOMY :**

Economy stands the best use of available resources both, human and material. It means avoiding possible duplicacies, inefficiencies and wastes of all kinds. If, this criterion is applied, the "product structure" is quite expensive because, for each product division we are to have functional facilities in terms of personnel and physical facilities. There are good many chances of under-utilisation, inefficiencies and wastes as the business situations change and keep on changing. On the other hand, in case of "project structure", there is no duplicacy, and the available facilities are used economically and efficiently. The possible pockets of wastages are plugged; under-utilisation is located and cavities are filled. This happens in spite of duality of nature of staff as each looks from his point view of common success.

7. **DEGREE OF FLEXIBILITY :**

Flexibility is the ability to adjust to the changing circumstances. It is the elasticity or responsiveness as to how far a thing maches to a changed situation to make it more effective immune or capacity of manoeuvring. "product structure" is comparativly less flexible as the functions are duplicated for each product or product line a set up once done it becomes difficult to adjust to fast changing external and hence, internal forces. On the other hand, "project structure" made of two cades can be more flexible because the project staff is purely temporary and it can be moulded easily to the requirements of change though permanent staff need not be can be touched as it is fundamental. Thus, organisational stability is more guaranteed in case of "project structure" than in case of "product structure".

8. **JOB-SECURITY AND JOB-SATISFACTION :**

Job-security stands for the tenure of service and job-satisfaction is the mental gratification one derives from a job. In case of "product structure job-security is of high order as mostly it consists of permanent nature product-divisionwise. It might so happen that, though there is job-security, there might not be job-satisfaction as the whole time of work is done by the employees. On the other hand, speaking in terms of job-security, project structure can not guarantee as roughly 70 to 80 percent staff is temporary nature and are rendered redundant as soon as project is over. May be there might be re-employment. Thus, except in functional officers, the project officers face the problem of job insecurity while the degree of job-satisfaction is high because, they are exposed to variety of challenging activities.

9. **TIME-SPAN :**
Time-span relates to how long the entity is going to be continued. The concept of entity and going concern are of top importance for a success, reputation and comparison of performance. In this regard, "product structure" is more permanent and no specific time limits are laid down. Products are produced continuously might be the quantitative and qualitative change might be expected. Once a set up is made for a product division, it is permanent unless they withdraw the product from the market. However, in case of "project structure" it is permanent in the sense that it has a definite time span. Once the project is complete, the entire infrastructure is uprooted. That is, project has a definite time limit and hence, the organisation which is designed to meet the requirements of time bound project.

10. **UTILITY OF STRUCTURE :**
Utility of a structure can be spoken in terms of its suitability. "Product organisation structure" is more suited when a product is a profit centre, where it is essential to measure product division performance, new divisions can be opened with least disturbance in existing conditions, where is possible to grant greater degree of autonomy as a dose of motivation. While in case of "project structure" it is suitable where the task or project is time bound and has definite goals to achieve, the task is unique, challenging and infrequent; the task is highly complex calls for contribution of team of specialists and perspective thinking, is involved and where the task involves high degree of stake in terms of time, treasure, and talent, particularly time where time is money.

FUNCTIONAL TYPE OF ORGANISATION STRUCTURE

WHAT IT MEANS?

'Functional' or 'staff' type of organisation structure is one where the activities involved are grouped together according to certain functions like production, marketing, finance, personnel and so on and are put under the charge of different persons. All the persons in the organisation dealing with a particular function are put under the charge and care of a person controlling that particular function. The person incharge of a function is a specialist in his field and, therefore, contributes his best. Functional structure is most widely used in medium and large organisations manufacturing limited number of products. The term "functional" might have emerged from the idea that there are good many functions and activities that any organsation is to perform to attain its business goals. The growth and working is hunged on specialisation. Functional structure is designed by grouping the activities on the basis of functions required for the achievement of organisational goals. Such an attempt warrants that all the functions are to be classified into basic and secondary and supporting functions according to their nature and importance. Here, BASIC functions arc those which are a must for the very existence and survival of the unit. Thus, a manufacturing organisation must have production and marketing functions. Secondary functions are those which are the sub-divisions of the major or basic functions. When departments are created based on basic functions and departmental manager feels that his span of management or control is too wide to have effective management, he divides his department into sub-departments by dividing basic functions into sub-functions.

Thus, the marketing manager-incharge of marketing, can divide the marketing activities into say, marketing research, advertising, sales-promotion, personal selling, tele-selling and so on. In addition to sub-functions and basic functions, some supportive activities or functions are needed to fill in the gaps of basic and collateral functions. The best examples of this kind can be finance, accounting, legal, industrial relations, public-relations, credit, packaging, despatching and the like. The exact role of these supportive functions will depend on the requirements of departments and their arrangements. Thus, finance and personnel departed activities can be major in some organisation than supportive. There is no any hard and fast rule as what is fundamental, collateral and supportive.

Originally, this organisational structure was the brain-child of **MR. F.W. TAYLOR,** the champion of efficiency. He mainly applied it to production activities. His idea was that each should get his place as per his field of specialisation so that fullest advantage of division of labour can be taken. To day, however, it is very rarely applied in its original form. In functional structure, the authority relations might be in the form of line, staff and functional. In true sense, the concept of functional authority is very essential for functional structure.

THE BASIC CHARACTERISTICS

Functional structure enjoys certain specific characteristics which makes it very much different from pure line organisation on one hand, and line and staff on the other. These features are :

1. **SPECIALISATION BY FUNCTIONS :**
   The functionalisation of the organisation takes place in the first place. That is, the organisation is first divided into departments based on major functions such as production, marketing, finance and personnel. Then each departmental jobs are further divided into functions branching into matching specialisation. Specialisation is that state of art where a person does more and more of less and less.

2. **TALL STRUCTURE WITH LIMITED SPAN OF MANAGEMENT :**

As functional organisation structure is hinged on specialised activities, it is bound to be quite tall and a tapering pyramid like a cone where department is divided into major, minor and supporting functions where each person is to do a part of the total work which is already divided into certain parts. Though, tall, each department has its own autonomy so far as its internal functioning is concerned. As a result, the span of control will be quite limited that makes management of the departmental and, hence, organisational work quite easy, cosy and posy.

3. **SPECIALISTS HAVE AUTHORITY AND AUTONOMY :**

A specialist is not a line officer but a staff officer. Though line officers are known for getting the work done by virtue of their position and powers, they have to consult these specialists in the decision making process. As a result, the decisions are sound as they have professional or specialist touch. They enjoy powers and position by their specialised knowledge, skill and experience. They, therefore, enjoy autonomy in their functioning contributing their best. This idea and approach gives due weightage not only the major organisational goals but sub-goals at each layer of different departments. That is why **F. W. Taylor,** said "specialist a king in the domain of his area functioning."

4. **EXISTENCE OF LINE AND STAFF DIVISIONS :**

Though functional or staff structure is quite diametrical and that of line type, one can not simply imagine a hundred percent staff or a unit of purely specialists or functionalists. Though, there is highest degree of specialisation, the levels of management can not be eradicated. Thus, worker is to report his immediate boss say foreman, foreman to supervisor, supervisor to superintendent and superintendent to assistant production managers to production manager to the general manager and general manager who reports to the managing directors. Thus, in it is line cum staff arrangement.

5. **PROBLEM OF RESPONSIBILITY FIXATION :**

The responsibility and accountability for final performance can hardly be fixed for no one is responsible for product or service cost and profits or losses. Each department fully concentrates on a part of product but not in its entirety. In fact, only it is the top man who is pulling and pushing everything together. This also makes decision-making slow though sound decisions can be made. Therefore, functional structure is not responsive to the rapid changes that are common in the dynamic world of business.

The idea of functional organisation structure can be best understood through the following diagram.

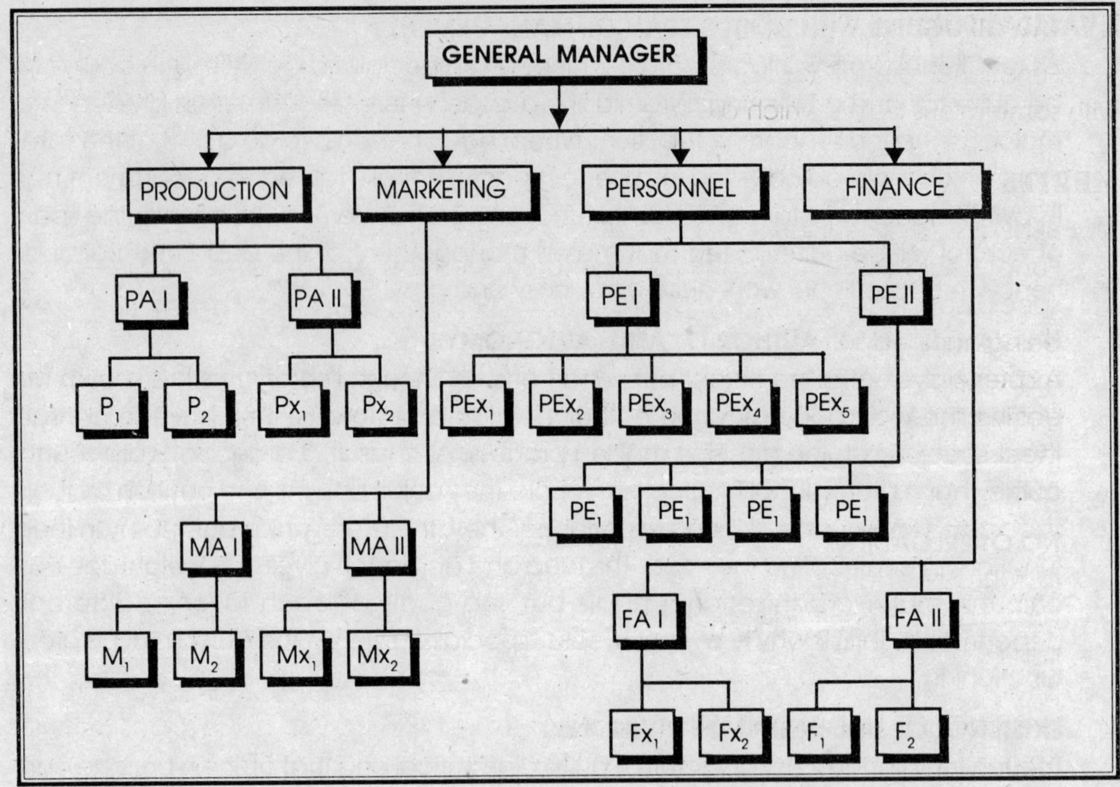

Fig. 2.04 Model of functional type of structure

Note:

PA I = Purchasing PA II Engineer
P_2 = Stores Section
Px_1 = Research and Development
MA I = Assistant Marketing Manager
M_2 = Industrial Goods
Mx_1 = Advertising and Sales Promotion Manager
PE I = Assistant Personnel Manager
PEx_2 = Employee Selection
PEx_4 = Employee Rating
PE_1 = Employee Relations
PE_3 = Employee Salary administration
Fx_1 = Accounts
F II = Assistant Financer
F_2 = Real Estate

P_1 = Quality Control and Inspection
PA II = Assistant Works Manager
Px_2 = Supervisor
M_1 = Consumer Goods
MA II = Assistant Marketing Manager
Mx_2 = Sales Manager-Personal Selling
PEX_1 = Public Relations
PEx_3 = Employee Training & Placement
PEx_5 = Assistant Personnel Manager
PE_2 = Employee Councelling
FI = Assistant Finance Manager
Fx_2 = Credit Dealings
F_1 = Budgeting

EVALUATION

Functional form of organisation structure is blessed with some plus points and baned with some minus points which are to be noted before one comes to its suitability.

MERITS :

1. **BENEFITS OF SPECIALISATION :**
   Functional form of organiation structure gives top priority for the concept of specialisation or division of labour in dividing the total work. Each piece of work is being handled with a touch of specialisation or division of labour. A specialist is the master player in his own area whose expertise, skill, acumen, dexterity can not be easily challenged. Such a person plans and implements the plans in his module of precise and perspectives, It brings excellence in performance. It reduces cost, improves quality and multiplies the output or performance level.

2. **NO OVERLOADING OF DUTIES :**
   In functional organisation, no officer or even the employees at lower level are overloaded with too many tasks. Functional army of workers are to carry out limited number of duties concerning their area of work or task. This reduces both physical and mental stresses and strains. The result is, he has the opportunity of contributing his best in total performance in so far as his responsibility is related. Result is strict discipline.

3. **WIDE SCOPE FOR EXPANSION AND GROWTH :**
   By its very nature, functional form of structure offers greatest vent or scope for wide range of spectrum of expansion and growth without dislocating the existing structure. It is because it is more, an extension of each department and its branches in lo further tentacles. It is like tree which starts from a seedling into a saple, a saple into a plant and a plant into a huge tree where a stem is divided into branches and branches into further tentacles. It looks like an arrangement of our daily usable vegetable namely cauli-flower.

4. **OPERATIONAL FLEXIBILITY :**
   Functional structure is known for its flexibility or easy adjustability. Any change in the organisation can be brought into play without dislocation or distortion and loss of operational efficiency. It is because each employee grows out of specialisation. Function as a whole can be cut by eliminating the positions at the lower levels without seriously affecting the total performance. Operational flexibility stands for introduction of changes to match to the changing needs that too without adversely influencing the level of efficiency.

5. **ECONOMY AND EFFICIENCY** :

The administrative set up is so systematically arranged that it encourages the idea of large-scale round about mass production where each 'm' of industry and commerce namely, materials, manpower, machinery, methods, money, marketing are in the hands of each specialist who turns out much out of these inputs. This brings in economy and efficiency finally resulting in productive use and higher profitability levels. There is no scope for misuse, waste, inefficiency, if taken in right spirit. Thus, functional organisation is designed to guarantee economy and efficiency.

6. **ATTRACTION OF TALENTED PERSONS** :

As functional organisational structure is woven on the woof and warf of extreme specialisation, it attracts the people with highly specialised personnel. These specialised people are class by themselves known for brains, education, tact, grit, wit, judgement, integrity, openness and special knowledge. These people are not only attracted but given an opportunity of developing leadership qualities by projecting outstanding skills. That is, the absence of an employee is not felt as others are ready to step into the shoes.

DEMERITS :

1. **DIFFICULTY IN LOCATING THE RESPONSIBILITY** :

The responsibility for ultimate performance can hardly be fixed in functional structure for no one is responsible for the product cost and profit or loss. It is because, each department contributes a section of a total product. Only the top man is made to pull on and up practically everything. This, in fact, overburdens the top officer with the problems of coordination and control. He finds it difficult to measure the exact contribution of each department.

2. **DELAYED DECISIONS** :

Functional structure sags and slows down the process of decision-making. The success of a company depends on sound and timely decisions. The first part is guaranteed that the decisions are soundest as each specialist is a brainy fellow and is able to contribute where the issue is put to acid test of cold facts as final decision is the outcome of multi-dimensional attack and refinement. However, the decisions are delayed as each specialist is to give his opinion. The complex and highly competitive world of business needs a minimum speed at which it is work else, it fails. It gives others to take advantage of the golden opportunity.

3. **BASE OF SPECIALISATION** :

Functional structure offers a good deal of leeway for conflict among staff on one hand and line and staff on the other. Differences of opinion and conflict of interests between the line and staff officers will defeat the very purpose of specialisation. Line officers blame the staff for their mistakes and staff for the mistakes of line officers.

Here, the authority that has upper hand and this leads to abuse of specialisation as their views might not be respected. This tug of war caused and fueled by conflicts are detrimental to the very existence and efficient working of an enterprise.

4. **ABSENCE OF RESPONSIVENESS :**
Functional structure bereft of responsiveness so essential for coping up with new and rapidly changing work commitments and requirements. Thus, if the organisation decides to add some new business line or activity, there is big question as to how to add this because it might mean a new functional structure as the new business can not be easily absorbed by the existing functional structure. This all happens because, staff-officers become ineffective as they do not have any authority to implement the plans of their own, nor do they command any influence as they can not force to accept their very best.

5. **IT IS EXPENSIVE :**
The functional pattern of organisation structure is quite expensive in terms of time, treasure and talent. It multiplies the number of specialists who are white elephants resulting in disproportionate rise in overhead expenses. Only very big and financially strong organisations can afford the luxury of such lavish spending and showmanship of specialisation.

6. **TOO MANY COOKS SPOIL THE BROTH :**
There is nothing wrong in having minute division of labour or specialisation. However, too far-stretched specialisation has its own limitations. When too many specialists come together, there is every danger of conflict of interests, thinking, and not pulling together as each specialist thinks that he is extra-ordinary in his own field and does like to overtake him. This creates a problem of high sense of discipline, decorum and coordination. A specialised organisation is as weak as it is strong. It is because, there full scope for the interplay of conflicts. Thus, too many doctors attending a patient might kill him than curing.

SUITABILITY OF FUNCTIONAL TYPE STRUCTURE

Functional structure make it most suitable under following situations based on its merits and demerits.

1. Where there is need and scope for too much of specialisation.
2. Where bringing clarity in organisation is a must. That is, where every one should understand his job clearly for its efficient clearance.
3. Where it promotes professional achievement that satisfies the specialist.
4. Where economy is brought about avoiding duplicity.
5. Where there is possibility of bringing into play effective coordination and control to assure quality and quick decisions.

DISTINCTION BETWEEN 'PROJECT' AND 'FUNCTIONAL' ORGANIZATION AND MANAGEMENT

The major differences— between the "project" and "functional" management can be drawn atleast seven grounds. These points of distinction are :

1. **LINE AND STAFF ORGANISATIONAL DICTOTOMY :**
   In case of 'Project' management, slag heap of the hierarchical model continues, but line functions are placed in a support position. A web of authority and responsibility relationship exists. While in case of 'functional' 'management, line functions have direct responsibility for accomplishing the objectives, the line commands and staff advises.

2. **SCALAR PRINCIPLE :**
   In case of 'Project' management, the elements of the vertical chain exists, but prime emphasis is placed on horizontal and diagonal work flow. Important business is conducted as the legitimacy of the task requires. As opposed to this, in case of 'functional' management, the chains of authority relationships is from the superior to sub-ordinate throughout the organization. Central, crucial and important business is conducted up and down the vertical hierarchy.

3. **SENIOR – SUBORDINATE RELATIONSHIP :**
   In case of 'Project' management, it is peer to peer manager to technical expert, associate to associate and the like relationships are used to conduct much of the salient. Contrary to this, in case of 'functional' management, this superior – subordinate is the most important relationship, if kept healthy, success follows. All important business is conducted through a pyramiding structure of superior and subordinates.

4. **ORGANISATIONAL OBJECTIVES :**
   In case of 'project' management, management of a project becomes a joint-venture of many relatively independent organisations. Thus, the objective becomes multilateral. As against this, in case of 'functional' management, organizational objectives are sought by the parent unit consisting of an army of sub organisations working within its environment the objective is unilateral.

5. **UNITY OF DIRECTION :**
   In case of 'Project' management, the project manager manages across functional and organizational lines to attain a common inter-organizational objective. As opposed this, incase of 'functional' management, the general manager acts as the one head for a group of activities having the same plan.

6. **PARITY OF AUTHORITY AND RESPONSIBILITY :**

In case of 'Project' management, considerable opportunity exists for the project managers responsibility to exceed his authority. Support people are often responsible to other managers (functional) for pay, performance reports, promotions and so on. While in case of 'functional' management, consistent with functional management, the integrity of the superior – subordinate relationship is maintained through functional authority and advisory staff 20 miles services.

7. **TIME SPAN :**

In 'Project' management, the project and hence the organisation is finite in duration. Contrary to this, in case of 'functional' management, the organisation tends to perpetuate itself to provide continuing facilitative support, hence it is infinite.

"PROJECT DRIVEN" VERSUS "NON-PROJECT DRIVEN" ORGANISATION

At macro level sturdy, there are two types of organisations namely 'project driven' and "non-project driven". The fundamental business of project driven organisations is the work done through projects where each project is a cost centre having is own income statement. The total profit of such a company is the sum total of the profits on all projects thinking that all projects are making profit. In a typical project driven organisation every thing hovers round the projects. The growth strategies of such organisations are clearly reflected in the type, size, location and nature of the projects chosen for bidding as well as the choices made as of how the resources refused are provided say, in house or out sourced to implement the projects as and when a contact is clinched. There cannot be better example than that of NASA.

The basic goals of every "project driven" organisation is to capitalize "on time" and "profitable delivery" projects of course maintaining highest levels of consumer satisfaction. Their goals are achieved when project managers, resource mangers, business mangers, consultants, executives team members, information technology processionals and accounting cadre work under one umbrella by dovetailing the tools to the goals to their specific roles and responsibilities the best practices for project driven, organisation are : * They have a well defined project management processes at projects, program and post folio levels. * The practices and procedures are standardizes, constantly monitored for continuous improvement. * The organisation structure is tailored to requirements of projectized organisation * Support projectized-organisation.

The firms of engineers, architects, constructor or contractor, software development forms who sell thus products and services on contract basis, telecommunications systems suppliers, consultancy and other professional services forms including these organisations which bid for work on a project by project basis.

As opposed to these, we have "non-project driven", organisation engaged his low technology manufacturing and service area. Here, profits or losses are measured on vertical or functional lines. That is, in case of such organisation projects exist merely of support the product lines or functional lines. The resources are assigned to those functional lines of activities that assure surplus instead of associating of projects. It is quite possible that non-project driven originations may also have a steadily stream of projects where all are usually designed of enhance the manufacturing operators. Some of the projects may be customer requested such as : * Introduction of statistical dimensioning concepts of improve process control * Bringing its process changes to improve the final product. * Introducers process change concept of future product dependability.

The following is the portrait of project driven, non-project driven and hybrid organisations:

PROJECT-DRIVEN (Project Management)	**NON-PROJECT DRIEN** (Product Management)	**HYBRID** (Program Management)
• Project Management has 'project' and 'line' responsibility	• Very limited projects	• Production driven but with mainly products
• Project Management is recognized profession	• Profitability form productions	• Stress on new product development
• Wide open multiple carrier paths	• products with longer life-cycle	• Short product life cycles
• Income from projects worked	• Limited carrier paths	• Marketing orientation
• Customer orientations	• Line and staff responsibility	• Need for faster development process

Experts give certain reasons as to why project management in a non-project driven organisation is not that easy. These reasons are : Heavy dependence up on subcontractors and outside agencies for projects management expertise. Projects are not only few but far between. Projects delayed because approval has to come form vertical chain of command. It is the reason as to why project work, lies too long with functional deportments. Neither the executives have enough time to manage the projects more they re ready to delegate authority to juniors. The projects can not be managed in a standardized way s each project has differing requirements and line span

MARKETING IN PROJECT DRIVEN ORGANISATIONS

Doing business in a turbulent water is not a joke. The organisation which wants to survive successfully, has to remains supple and variable matching to the ever increasing competitions by improving the product and survive values, designing and developing new market offerings that marinate perfectly with consumer specifications. Between the urgency of threats are consumer, opportunities, there s a strong temptations to react to one or the other. The managers or strategists are expected to understand the target customers and their expectations so that the firm can and value to the customer's expectations. Building a satisfied customer through instruction that works.

It goes without saying that ever increasing competitive forces have forced the marketers to go in for proven and innovative marketing strategies. For any project oriented business manager, clinching new contracts is an achievement. However, the practices of the project oriented firms are quite different form traditional product business calling for highly specialized and actually disciplined group or team efforts in each area of management namely, marketing, personal, finance and public, relations including technical competence in project fort folio. To succeed in project driven organisations, management experts have come out with a definite quantitative approach to marketing which is having the halt marks s notched below :

1. **OBJECTIVITY :**
   There is dire need for objectivity to the marketing as a science so that the marketing senses are put to acid rests of cold facts guaranteeing transparency and objectivity.

2. **BETTER UNDERSTANDING OF MARKETING IMPLICATIONS :**
   Marketing being dynamic needs a rigorous testing to understand the king of marketing namely, the customer. The idea is to keep lines satisfied by value addiction which is possible when marketers understand his bottom lines.

3. **DATA BASED ATTEMPT :**
   The role of marketing manger is not merely confined to just mange the slow. He has to collect, assimilate and disseminate detailed and maintains data regarding consumer as the hub of marketing wheel.

   This new approach has really helped to achieve greater success in moving form consumer satisfaction to consumer delight.

FEAURES OF PROJECT MARKETING

Definitely 'projects' are different from 'products'. Marketing of projects warrant an ardent ability of identify, follow and catch one of a kind business opportunities. Marketing of projects is featured by : * A systematic attempt * Customs design * Project life cycle * Technical capability * Risk and uncertainty * Maximising returns on marketing investment and * Consumer loyalty with employee retaining.

THE PROJECT MANAGER

A project is a work and work is to be got done and is not an individual effort end product. It is a joint and complex set of tasks which needs an able person called manager a successful manager. It is because, good project managers make things happen. And when they do, people notice. What is their secret to success? The bottom-line is that effective managers of project get the job done on time, within the budget, and according to desired quality standards. As facts stand today, in India, none of the present day generation project managers including the most successful, come from any of our white elephant Management Schools costing each 10-15 crores. These persons were given the jobs - where some succeeded and rest successfully failed. Those who succeeded were handful because quite few projects were completed in time, within the budgets, meeting quality standards. Good many seminars and workshops were conducted to identify and analyse as to why projects failed ? Unfortunately, these serious discussions left the role of project managers and their development. It may be because of two reasons : (1) None thought that success or failure of a given project depends on project manager. (2) None considers project managers as a special breed.

THE REQUIREMENTS OF A SUCCESSFUL PROJECT MANAGER

The role that a project manager is going to play is determined by at least four variables namely; (1) **the nature of the project-** the complexity, scale, position in hierarchy of projects; (2) **the nature of the organisation** that is being carried out in, for instance, sector, activities, organisational structure. (3) **the personality** of the project manager and (4) **the constraints** under which he is working. It is almost impossible to specify a generic list of characteristics for a successful project management. **The list of characteristics that is presented below by Mr. Harway Maylor, can be treated on the basis of scales on which** : (1) Initially, projects should be rated to determine the requirements of the person for the job and (2) individuals can be rated to determine their suitability for the job in hand. The characteristics of individuals may be classified as either attitudes or skills :

ATTITUDES :

Attitudes are those characteristics which are determined by the way a person thinks about a particular issue and which are reflected in the intent of that person. The attitudes which are desirable for a project manager are :

(1) **A desire not just to satisfy but to delight** customers and stake-holders alike.

(2) **Accepting of both challenges and responsibility.**

(3) **Being focussed on action,** rather than procrastination - getting the job done rather than avoiding critical or difficult issues.

(4) **A desire to make the best use of all resources** - minimising waste in all activities.

(5) **Does not lose sight of the light** at the end of the tunnel - is goal focussed.

(6) **Has personal integrity** - people find it very difficult to respect and take the authority of a person who has low integrity.

(7) **Is flexible about route** that must be taken to achieve the stated end-goals.

(8) **Has personal goals that are consistent** with those of the project organisation - the project team perceives that the project manager and the organisation are going the same way.

SKILLS :

The skills are those characteristics which a person has been trained in or has learnt and determines the tools available to that person regarding 'how' to handle a particular situation. The skills which are desirable for a project manager are :

(1) **Ability to determine the real needs** - or desires of the costomer. This is done through "getting close" to the customer via visits and both formal and informal discussions and asking the relevant questions.

(2) **Analytical skills** - to turn the data into information and break the project into comprehensible component parts.

(3) **Technical skills** - the project manager need not be a technical specialist, but must atleast be capable of comprehending the work that is being carried out, and "speaking the language" of the people involved.

(4) **Team skills** - are those abilities of the individuals to motivate and enthuse the team because many battles have been won against poor odds.

(5) **Ability to delegate effectively** - not trying to do everything personally.

(6) **Ability to manage own time** - one can not expect to manage other people unless he shows that he can manage.

(7) **The balancing of stake-holder perceptions** of project progress - otherwise known as being able to "sell ideas".

(8) **Negotiating Skills** - resolve potential conflict situations so that all parties can said to have 'won'.

(9) **Problem solving** - or facilitating problem solving skills - finding the alternative choices and select the most apt under given situation.

(10) **Question all assumptions made by stake-holder** - at all stages of activities and if one can keep his head cool all about him losing theirs.

All the above are internal factors of the person. Their role and the way that is managed by the organisation are just as important. This consideration will centre around four factors namely, Responsibility - the scope of the control of the project manager as they perceive it, **Authority** - the organisation's view as to the scope of control of the project management **Accountability** - the set of outcomes that are determined to be under the control of the project manager and **Credibility** - the organisation must stand behind the project manager and back the decisions that are made. Not doing so, removes the individual's credibility and, hampers, authority.

BASIC EDUCATION FOR A PROJECT MANAGER

It is quite obvious that a project manager should have a degree in engineering and advanced education in project management and training in effective project management or both. In the light of this, almost all Universities thinking of formal education in project management are planning for post-graduate programs after a basic engineering education. This is so because, a basic degree in engineering comes from acceptance of the fact that an engineer's main business is design, operation and maintenance of systems, though the emphasis is mainly on hardware systems. The hardware-systems form the core in any project and the concern for effective performance of the hardware is so overriding that almost all recruitment ads for project managers look for an engineer having a basic degree in hardware system of the project. Whether this is necessary is subject to debate. However, education planners have agreed to put hardware system that forms the heart of any project. It is the usual experience, in practice that the engineers by virtue of their technical education are incapable of compromising with quality or quality standards. It is quite usual that they overdo it but when it comes to time and cost, the same concern rarely exists. They think of glittering designs not commensurate with cost. So far as time is concerned Indian project managers feel that it is cheap and easily available. Indian project managers or engineers have to learn that time is not only money but more than money. That is, a basic education in engineering does not commit a person to time and cost as opposed to quality. However, commitment is the essence of professionalism for there can not be a profession without a high sense of commitment.

True and practical education is supposed to change the very attitude, knowledge, skill and behaviour. The mental frame is couched for commitment. Therefore, any education programme shall not be merely a short-term training programme. It is not to undermine short-term programs; they are good indeed for imparting the skills in preparing networks, development of performance budgets, design of systems, performance evaluation, project reviews and so on. However, they are not preparing the trainees to correct uncertainties without any complaint, continuous management of projects and managing project through installation of self-controlling systems.

In this regard, one should appreciate the universities abroad that they have realised this lacuna and have started post-graduate programmes in project management. Better late than never, India too has gone ahead with such programmes. The Project Management Association, New Delhi, is the first organisation to introduce part-time post graduate courses in project management spreading over a period of one year. Universities too have followed suit to give a kick-start by introducing post graduate courses ranging from one year to two years. Hence, one can hope for qualified project managers to change the very face of project management professionalism.

ROLES AND RESPONSIBILITIES OF A PROJECT MANAGER

These project managers can be either permanent employee of a company or they may be consultants. In view this 'employed' and "self-employed", the roles and responsibilities are sure to differ. However, we take the roles and responsibilities of a project manager as 'employed' only.

ROLES AND RESPONSIBILITIES OF AN EMPLOYED PROJECT MANAGER :

As employed on permanent basis, he has at least a dozen set of his roles and responsibilities. These are :

1. **Defining and Maintaining the Integrity of a Project** : An effective project manager defines clearly the project so that it is easy and clear for both higher ups and lower downs to understand and size up. What is more important is that he has to maintain the integrity of a given project as it is his brain child. That is, he has full confidence and faith in his project.

2. **Development of Project Execution Plan** : It is well known that a project manager, like any other manager, has to "plan the work and work the plan." That is, planning is something and implement it is some thing. For proper implementation, he has to plan - giving step by step - sequential execution of a project which is routing and scheduling, dispatching and follow up action all rolled into one.

3. **Designing Organisation for Execution of the Plan** : Defining a project and developing project execution plans are not done in thin air. The planning and execution need a definite structure or a system. An organisation is a structure of relationships that work to attain the goals. It is he who is to design appropriate organisation that arranges for the inputs to reach output target.

4. **Setting Targets and Development of Procedures** : In a way, planning phase itself is to do with setting the targets or norms in the light of goals to be achieved, though it is a part of control system. He has to develop viable and effective systems and set of procedures for attainment of project objectives and targets.

5. **Negotiation for Commitments** : A significant part of management's time is taken by meetings and since project work is about getting results, anything a project manager can do is to 'reduce' talking and 'increase' doing. As a project leader, he has to hold different kinds of meetings such as regular informal one-to-one sessions with team member, regular project team meetings; negotiation meeting with functional managers and project review meeting with key stake-holders. These negotiation meetings are of two kinds namely, (1) with external stake-holders-suppliers, consultants and the like and (2) with other functional managers. The first type of meetings usually involve some form of contract that is subject to legal status. This

requires specialist knowledge that one can aquire or seek from consultant. He has to use his power of negotiation to achieve win-win result where everyone is happy. Negotiation skills are different that need preparation, bargaining and concluding so that there is commitment.

6. **Direction Coordination and Control of Project Activities** : Project manager is totally responsible for all the functions of management from planning to control of which direction, coordination and control have a special weightage. These functions insist upon team work or joint work as project is not a one man show. The subordinates need direction, their working in terms of time, efforts and interests are to be balanced which is delicate task of coordination. The last phase is control-continuous monitoring to see whether everything is going as planned so that differences can be traced, reasons can be found out, and corrective action can be taken, if any.

7. **Contract Management** : Contract management is managing contracts which are of two types namely, "business contracts" and **"internal contracts"**. Project manager has appropriate authority by virtues of project charter and organisational arrangement. This authority allows him to use in-house resources. However, all projects can not be executed with only in-house resources. He has to depend on external resources or organisations where he has no direct authority, This entails some arrangement which we call as contract and authority so acquired as contractual authority. In case this authority is acquired in-house through a contract, the process is known as 'internal' contracting and all other contracts for the acquisition of authority can be termed as business contracts. Contract management is very complex in case of business contracts, which is an art and science too. A business contract management warrants a step by step success - starting with 'enquiry' and ending with 'contract' juxtaposed in between -the 'offer', 'acceptance' and 'agreement'. Each is a crucial phase.

8. **Non-human Resource Management Including Fiscal Matters** : Project manager's job is not only to manage the human- content which is really significant. However, non-human resources on which the human resources are to work are also important namely, materials, parts, project scaffoldings, models, technology and, hence, machinery and equipment. All these are only a dream, in case he does not know how to manage finance, the crux of every project whether it is of a few lakhs or crores of rupees.

9. **Projectising and Problem Solving** : Projectising is to take whole task or the project and dividing into viable and manageable parts in a congruous manner so that totality is not forgotten in the name of division of the whole into parts. This means building of commitment in completing the entire project in time within cost limits and quality standards. It is creating a framework of norms and performing in those outer limits. All project work is laced with problems. It is an intrinsic characteristic of

the process of change that problems will surface from time to time. One can expect them and one should regard then as an opportunity with a challenge. Unfortunately, one can not see the whole problem - only the "tip of the ice-berg." This needs understanding the whole problem by going deep to its very root. Problem solving involves ihe tasks of diving below the surface - Asking why is it occurring ? to establish cause and effect relations - state the problem - action planning and implementing the solution.

10. **Man Management** : It is already said that even a project manager is provided with superior quality inputs-materials, money, machines and tools, the project goals can not be achieved because of the manpower - the prime mover in all activities. A good project manager builds a team-and' sub-teams, allocates duties dnd responsibilities, directs them, coordinates them, motivates them and controls their performance. A good project manager knows how to manage team as a diplomate with working relations for best results.

11. **Satisfying Customers, Government and the Public** : The sole objective of any business activity is to earn decent rate of return for our investments in terms of time, talent and treasure by satisfying or even delighting the customer-the king, government-the custodian and public - the volatile group - which is supporting or opposing any business activity. This is more applicable to project management than to any other line as there is stake of the firm, government and the society.

12. **Attainment of Project Objectives, Cash Surplus and Improved Productivity** : It is our experience that projects whether private or for public have not met-all-namely, objectives, cash surplus and higher productivity. In fact, if a project is planned scientifically and executed effectively, well within the limits of time, cost and qualty, there are no problems at all. However, if our wishes were horses every body would have been able to ride on. External forces do allow us to attain the targets. A project manager who follows contingent approach is wise because management is situational. Again, profitability, liquidity and productivity are conflicting. If you want to increase one, the other has to be compromised. Inspite of those, the project manager attains target, generates more funds and the productivity is improved. That is, the resources-both human and physical-are used both economically and efficiently that lead to optimum use thereby increasing the productivity. For better understanding, one should know the role of a **"Project manager"** and role of **"functional manager"** in a project organization.

AS A PROJECT MANAGER

1. **HE IS THE PROJECT HEAD :**
   Project manager is in charge of a project or projects assigned to him. He is the whole and sole of the project. Hence, he frames and lays down the basic policies and

strategies to achieve the project objectives. In other words, in the light of defined goals, he designs policies and strategies that lead to easy and effective attainment of preset goals. Policies set boundaries for overall activity within the organisation; these are the guidelines for decisions. A policy helps in predicting actions and decisions of others - broad, general and comprehensive. An example of policy might be to promote the person from within. On the contrary, strategy provides direction for the deployment of resources to meet the cnvironnientat opportunities and threats. It is an imperative plan concerned with the external environment. Example of strategy might be that the competitors are cutting the price which can be counter acted by aggressive advertising.

2. **HE DETERMINES THE DIMENSIONS OF TIME, TREASURE AND TALENT :**
To implement the project a dream a promise, he determines meticulously the time required to complete the project, the resources - with material and human with specifications of a project. He draws a budget in terms of time deadline, draws personnel of all kind from functional and project needs and arranges for the money that sets rolling and gliding the budget which has been sold to the top management and he has "go ahead" signal and support from the top management. It is more and organising function of the essential of the project. Organising is the meticulous and detailed task of understanding the total project, breaking it into viable tasks and to assign these tasks to tasks forces or the team to convert promise into performance, a dream into reality.

3. **HE CO-ORDINATES THE PROJECT ACTIVITIES :**
Mere planning and organising has no meaning unless there are the attempts to integrate, time and balance the project activities, he integrates the project people interest, time the project activities and sub-activities and balance the subgroup interests and individual expectations. As an integrator he draws a schedule of various operations and communicates to the functional groups. He is accountable for motivating the personnel working under his guidance supervision and control without the use of lien authority.

4. **HE SETS OR CONTROLS MECHANISM :**
Management of project and project activities implies controlling of business variables. In fact, control of costs of each cost centre by his executive behaviour. In project management timely completion of projects is of top-importance because costs vary in the time and level of activity. In other words, controlling of project is a three step process (a) measuring the progress towards an objective, (b) evaluating what remains to be done, and (c) deriving action plan to achieve the results The control system is the methodology one employs through clearly defined procedure to ensure that the project on track of progress. The whole purpose of the system is to allow effectively -

collection of information about what is really happening, compare this with what you have planned to happen, analyse the variances exposed, derive actions you can reasonably take and implement action plans to keep the project on track.

AS A FUNCTIONAL MANAGER

1. **USE OF LINE AUTHORITY :**
   Functional manager search major functions has his subordinates and he is to use line authority over subordinates in order to ensure uniformity of his functional area for all the projects. Thus, the success of project depends on the extent and nature of assistance and cooperation of each department such as production, finance, marketing and personnel. He is to see that no project suffers at the cost of another by extending his services in required amount, quality and time. It is because, each project is important and the tells up on the reputation of the concern.

2. **ACTS AS A DISCIPLINARIAN :**
   Line-authority granted to the functional manager gives a real sense of discipline and decorum in his functional area. That is, he concentrates fully on his departmental activities and sub-activities and uses his power to see that there is pre-play discipline and resultant good effects. That is, efficiency and, economy of operations is guaranteed. In project structure there is duality of authority and therefore, he is to be extra careful for, the failure of project reflects on his share of responsibility. He is not the ultimate authority and he is accountable to the higher authorities namely, general manager. Therefore, he is a tough gue who insists in high degrees of discipline.

3. **ALLOCATIONS OF PERSONNEL, RESOURCES AND SERVICES :**
   At the request of each project manager incharge, he extends personnel, resources and services for the performance of each project. Each project undertaken is important and is going to be a success in case project manager he gets resources, personnel and services adequately, timely and priority basis without discrimination of any kind. The personnel he is allocated is expected to perform his duties to the fullest satisfaction of project manager else, he is going to complain. That is why, functional manager is extra cautious in depending personnel from his department with resources and services package. Subordinates of his are to obey the orders both the project-managers and his.

4. **PERFORMANCE EVALUATION :**
   Functional manager as he allocates the personnel, resources and service facilities to complete each project, he has every right to call for feed back, as to how each personnel, resource and service facilities extend are used, In fact, he is to keep track of performance of each personnel in so for as his contribution is concerned in each project as an individual and as the member of project team. It is because, the

personnel are paid for their work and accountable for their performance - whether just, over and under performance. In case of deficiencies and inefficiencies they can be taken to task.

PROJECT MANAGEMENT AS A PROFESSION

There is no doubt that project management is both a science and an art. Now the question is whether it is a profession. By applying the tests of any profession, project management is a profession. A **profession** to be called so should fulfil certain conditions. These are :

(1) It should form substantial body of knowledge.

(2) It should have an association of its own at national or international.

(3) Compulsory acquisition of knowledge-a formal period of learning both theory and practice.

(4) Application of knowledge and skills so acquired to solve business problems under he situations of ground realities

(5) Service above greed.

That a professional charges a reasonable remuneration as he or she is serving the society than making it a source of earning based on greed and graft. In fact, today, it is a beginning in India and in the days to come, it is going to be certainly a big profession like any other profession. Project managers have a bright future to build the nation by contributing in an innovative way to faster economic development of the nation. It is the case of self growth through the growth of an economy

CHAPTER BASED QUESTIONS

A. WRITE SHORT NOTES ON

1. Project management
2. Project manager
3. Functional role of a manager
4. Line role of a manager
5. Project management as a profession
6. Organisation
7. Principles of organisation
8. Functional organisation
9. Project organisation
10. Skills of a project manager
11. History of project management
12. Modular approach

B. SHORT ANSWER QUESTIONS

1. What is Project Management ?
2. What is the role of project manager ?

3. Is Project management a profession ?
4. Wnat skills he should have as a manager ?
5. What attitudes he should have as a manager ?
6. Trace the history of project management ?
7. What is modular approach to project management ?
8. Explain Role of project manager as line officer.
9. Discuss Role of project manager as a functional officer.
10. What is the importance of an organisation ?

C. ESSAY TYPE QUESTIONS

1. What is organisation? What are its elements and principles ?
2. What is project organisation structure? Explain its features, merits and demerits.
3. What is project organisation? Explain its merits and demerits and state specifically where it is suitable.
4. What is modular approach to project management? What are its benefits ?
5. How do you distinguish between '**product**' and '**project'** organisation ?
6. Discuss the role of project manager as '**line-officer**' and '**staff**' officer.
7. Who is a project manager? What factors make him successful ?
8. Distinguish clearly between **'successful'** and **'unsuccessful'** project management.
9. What is the position of a project manager in the organization ? What are his educational qualifications ?
10. Discuss the roles and responsibilities of an employed project manager.

* * * * * *

Chapter 3

PROJECT PLANNING PART-1

- ❖ WHAT IS PROJECT PLANNING ?
- ❖ SCOPE OF PROJECT PLANNING
- ❖ OBJECTIVES OF PROJECT PLANNING
- ❖ CHAPTER BASED QUESTIONS

BACKDROP

As we have noted earlier, a project is a special work plan which is to be completed within certain time to fulfil certain preset objectives by the efficient use of resources at the command of an undertaking. The basic principles of management are applicable to any project as is the case with any other work plan or activity. Hence, the fundamental functions of management namely, planning, organising , directing, coordinating, motivating and controlling are basically the same for managing project. However, as it is a special set of tasks, there are some unique features and problems in managing the projects. Hence, any scientific project management can be basically divided into two parts namely "Project formulation" and "Project implementation". "Project formulation" involves basically all kinds of planning-calling for detailed project report, technical appraisal, financial appraisal, economic appraisal, social benefit appraisal and clearance and sanctioning of the project. The "Project implementation" part calls for organizing and controlling functions. Organising takes care of specifying and scheduling work, initiating the project, clarifying the authority and the responsibility relationship and obtaining the resources. The control system, directing and controlling and finally terminating the project. Here, in this chapter, we are concerned with project planning in detail, of course, some of the aspects need further detailed treatment which will be taken up in the separately broken parts as chapters. This chapter ends with Chapter Based Questions.

WHAT IS PROJECT PLANNING?

Project planning is like a thread that makes a garland covering different flowers or beads - from the very stage of conception to commissioning and handing over the work to the clients on the other. Project planning means and includes all the essential activities involved in completing the project such as breakdown structure, statement of work and accurate time estimates and schedules that help further in anticipating the possible snags in a project to be overcome successfully. In project planning, a 'plan' is the starting point that provides the means to satisfy the needs of a project sponsor and helps in making the way clear to reach the desired destination. It becomes the start of the project managers input to ensure that the potential problems are identified well in time and can be easily assessed on the basis of which further estimating and resource allocation may be done without hesitation. Generally, most of the project decisions are taken during the preliminary planning phase unless preliminary planning is done carefully, decisions based on semi-baked ideas the plans may go fut. Hence, planners are to be committed to the satisfactory performance taking project planning right from its stage of initiation to finish. That is, there is no scope for any kind of slackness or complacence. In the process, it clears up estimation and allocation of resources—time and material— which are vital for performance of all project or project activities. This, project planning is to do units drawing a plan, setting the premises, establish largest, levels of details, and time scale of plans. It is equally important to give thought to establish a strategic framework, before starting on the plan in detail.

SCOPE OF PROJECT PLANNING

The scope of project planning signifies what exactly is covered under this caption of project planning. This is the study of components or aspects of project planning and following are the different aspects that come under the umbrella of project planning.

1. **PROJECT OBJECTIVES :**

   Every project has certain objectives. The objectives specify as to what is to be done and how, and by what time. The objectives of a project should be specific and challenging but achievable. Thus, a multipurpose community development project in case of irrigation, can have specific objectives: 1. To irrigate the dry land in the catchment area of 100 kilometers. 2. To generate and supply electricity for industrial and domestic purpose at reasonable cost. 3. To rehabilitate the households affected by the implementation of the project. 4. To create infrastructural facilities that encourage industrial and commercial achievements. 5. To supply drinking water to the households in the catchment area of 100 kilometers.

2. **FORECASTING AND ESTIMATION OF RESOURCES :**

   To work on a given project, we need resources in terms of treasure, time, and talent. The requirement of resources of a project are forecasted and estimated well in advance and suitable arrangement is made to meet the same. The requirement of manpower, materials and machines are worked out time-wise projective and activity wise. This is essential so that arrangement for their procurement and allocation for use may be scientifically planned. This exercise provides a basis for forecasting the requirement of funds in total.

3. **PROJECT ORGANISATION :**

   A project, if it is to see the light of the day, has its own organization. As already noted, organization specifies the management statements, delegation of authority, authority and responsibility relationship, line of control and so on. There are alternative organization structures namely, functional, project, product, matrix and so on. The most viable structures are project structure and matrix structure having been designed to accommodate project type of activities. This is a part of planning because, each project organisation is unique having its own problems and focuses.

4. **RESOURCE PLANNING :**

   Resource planning is planning of resources–manpower, finance, machines, materials and so on. Financial planning deals with the quantum and cost of finance so that funds sre available at any time without any blockade. The material planning is to procure material at least cost, in time and in adequate quantities. The manpower planning is to procure develop and maintain skilled, semi skilled and unskilled work-force.

5. **LAYING DOWN OF POLICIES, PROCEDURES AND STANDARDS :**

A policy provides general guidelines for decision-making and individual actions. Procedure is a detailed method of carrying out a policy. A standard specifies a level of individual or group performance, defined as adequate and acceptable. A project being a unique activity, warrants not only laying down the policy but also procedure and standards so that the work may move or glide along the chased course.

6. **PROJECT WORK PLANNING :**

Project work planning comprises planning the activities to be carried out at different stages; there sequence and specific requirements such as by what time to start and by what time to finish and the like. Each project involves certain activities to be carried out at different stages. The sequence of those activities has to be planned with the help of Network charts, Gantt charts and Bar Charts and the like. The ramifications of this are; work schedule, work break, down structures, work package, sequenced planning. Let us touch these:

A "work schedule" is prepared to integrate individual or group activities into network and show when a particular activity is to be started and completed. A "Work-break down structure" is natural decomposition of the project and its results. It is done through level by level break-down of project work such as from system to sub-systems, from sub-system to tasks and from task to sub-tasks and from sub-task to work package. For the creation of the entire project and its decomposition into systems, sub-systems, tasks and sub-tasks and work-packages is required.

A "Work Package" is the smallest element appearing at the lowest level. This specifies the work to be done to achieve an intermediate objective. Break down of a project into work-packages is done so that specific responsibility for a work package may be assigned to a particular person and resources for its completion, may be allocated.

"Sequenced planning" is mainly concerned with setting forth the chronological order of the work-packages or activities. It is done starting with the terminal task of the project and working backwards, to determine which particular tasks must be completed before succeeding tasks can be take up.

7. **PROJECT TIME PLANNING :**

Time is an important element in a project as every project is expected to be completed within a given time. This is applicable not only to a project as a whole but also to its various activities. In this process, first the time requirement of each individual activity is estimated, and then various activities are scheduled in a logical manner, and then the overall, time requirement for the project is estimated. The components of this time-planning are: sequence planning, master-programme schedule and project activities.

"Sequence planning" is mainly concerned with setting forth the chronological order of work packages or activities. It is done starting with the terminal task of the project and working back-wards, to determine which particular task must be completed before succeeding tasks can be taken up.

"Master programme Schedule" is a document giving the dates of major events and control points for management. For preparing a master program schedule, detailed specifications regarding time, resource and cost of activities are prepared, inter-relationships between activities are identified, sequence of activities is decided, responsibility for each task or activities is fixed.

"Project activities" are those which are to be finished to complete a project. Every project consists of good many activities. Thus, major activities forming the part of any manufacturing project may include: Finalisation of technical parameters. Selection of technology. Preparation of a layout plan. Indification of infrastructural requirements. Preparation of detailed project report. Preparation of specifications of buildings, plant equipment, auxiliaries, service and so on. Tendering and placement of orders. Civil work includes procurement of supplies, creation of plant and equipment. Recruitment and training of manpower. Project comissioning.

8. **MONITORING AND CONTROL MECHANISM :**
   Every Project is subject to monitoring and controlling so that project work may go on frictionlessly without external intervention. The major aspects of monitoring and control are time, cost, quality and performance or results.

9. **PROJECT BUDGETING :**
   Project has a budget. Project budgeting is based on estimates of costs of goods and services required to be acquired and payments to be made to attain project objectives on the one hand, and expected performance and results, on the other. Through budgeting, the plan is given a more concrete shape. It is particularly useful for both planning and monitoring of performance to keep the things in check.

OBJECTIVES OF PROJECT PLANNING

Planning is the first step in management of any activity or set of activities and, hence, a project. The objectives of sound project planning are:

1. **ANALYSING :**
   Planning or project planning aims at visualizing as to how a job will be done? In what order? and with what resources? by dividing into convenient manageable parts or activities. Each activity is to be readily identifiable as a definite piece of work, ideally relating to the project management structure and fully under the control of a specific individual.

2. **ANTICIPATING :**

This is another point that speaks of its objective. That is, project planning focuses its attention on the potential problems with the intention of reading the risk, associated and to find the ways and means to overcome them. Risks and uncertainties are quite common. However, the extent of risk and uncertainty differs from case to case.

3. **SCHEDULING :**

Perhaps very important aim is to not only allocate the resources but to guarantee the best use of resources with assured positive results. This scheduling does the wonderful work of identifying the best resource-mix for a given project.

4. **COORDINATING AND CONTROLLING :**

What is more important is uninterrupted work on a given project. Project completion calls for participation of all the parties and their cooperation and support is a must. This is done through planning that leads to coordination and control of all business variables.

5. **PROVISION OF INFORMATION :**

The aim of project planning is to provide relevant information to help in planning better, so that future planning may be much improved and stronger. These objectives of project planning will not accrue automatically. What is needed is whole -hearted support from the top-management to swear by planning and hence, control. Another basic requirement is provision of adequate and timely resources to the project management team. Before we take up the mainstays of project planning, it is advisble to have a glance at the following model of project planning.

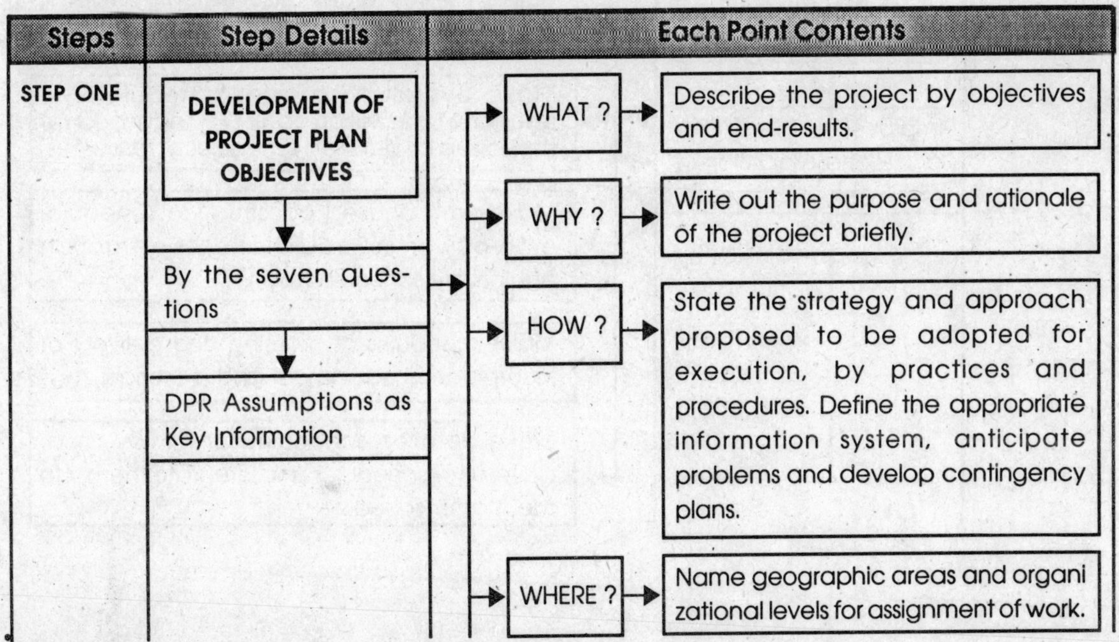

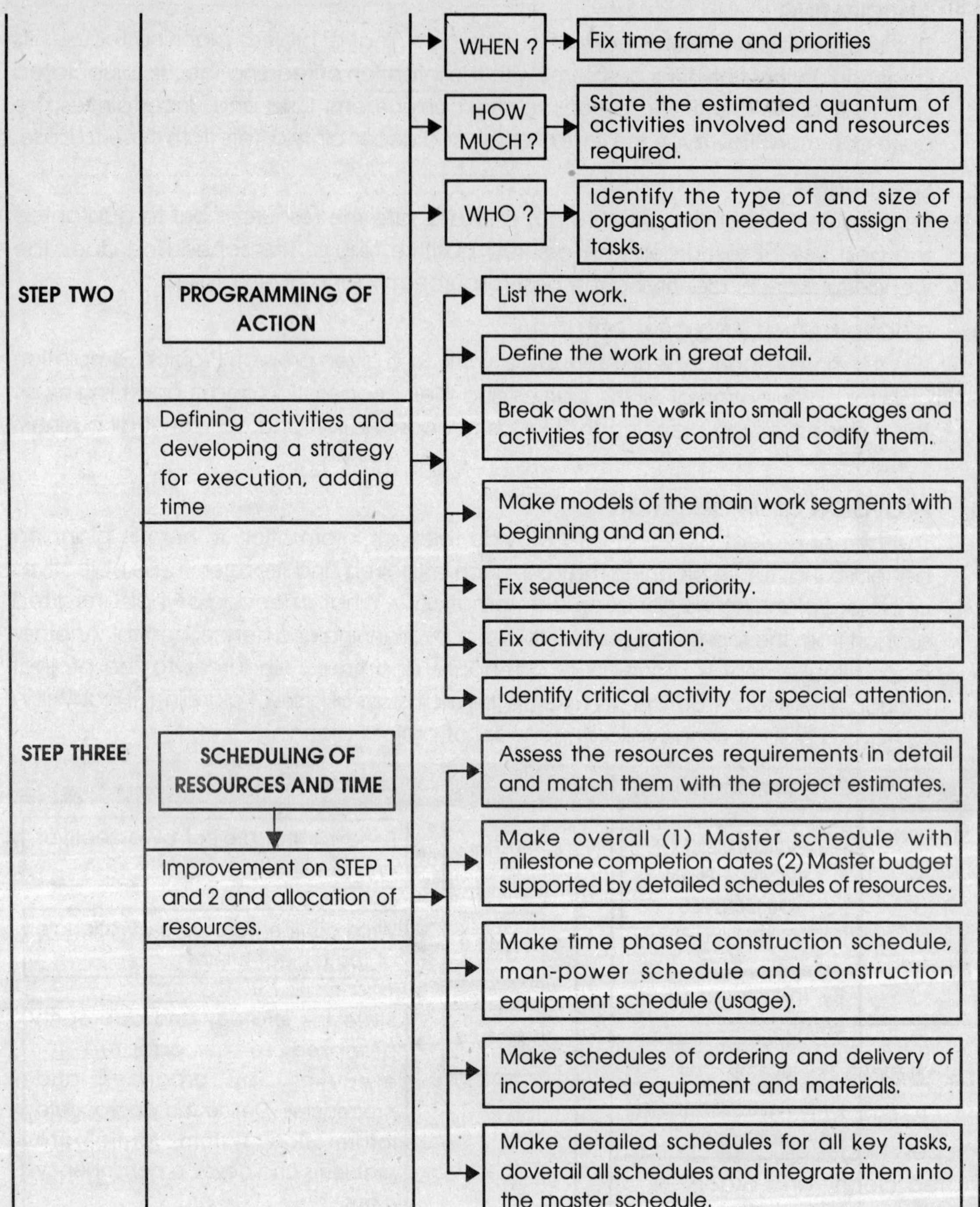
WHEN ?
Fix time frame and priorities
HOW MUCH ?
State the estimated quantum of activities involved and resources required.
WHO ?
Identify the type of and size of organisation needed to assign the tasks.
STEP TWO
PROGRAMMING OF ACTION
Defining activities and developing a strategy for execution, adding time
List the work.
Define the work in great detail.
Break down the work into small packages and activities for easy control and codify them.
Make models of the main work segments with beginning and an end.
Fix sequence and priority.
Fix activity duration.
Identify critical activity for special attention.
STEP THREE
SCHEDULING OF RESOURCES AND TIME
Improvement on STEP 1 and 2 and allocation of resources.
Assess the resources requirements in detail and match them with the project estimates.
Make overall (1) Master schedule with milestone completion dates (2) Master budget supported by detailed schedules of resources.
Make time phased construction schedule, man-power schedule and construction equipment schedule (usage).
Make schedules of ordering and delivery of incorporated equipment and materials.
Make detailed schedules for all key tasks, dovetail all schedules and integrate them into the master schedule.

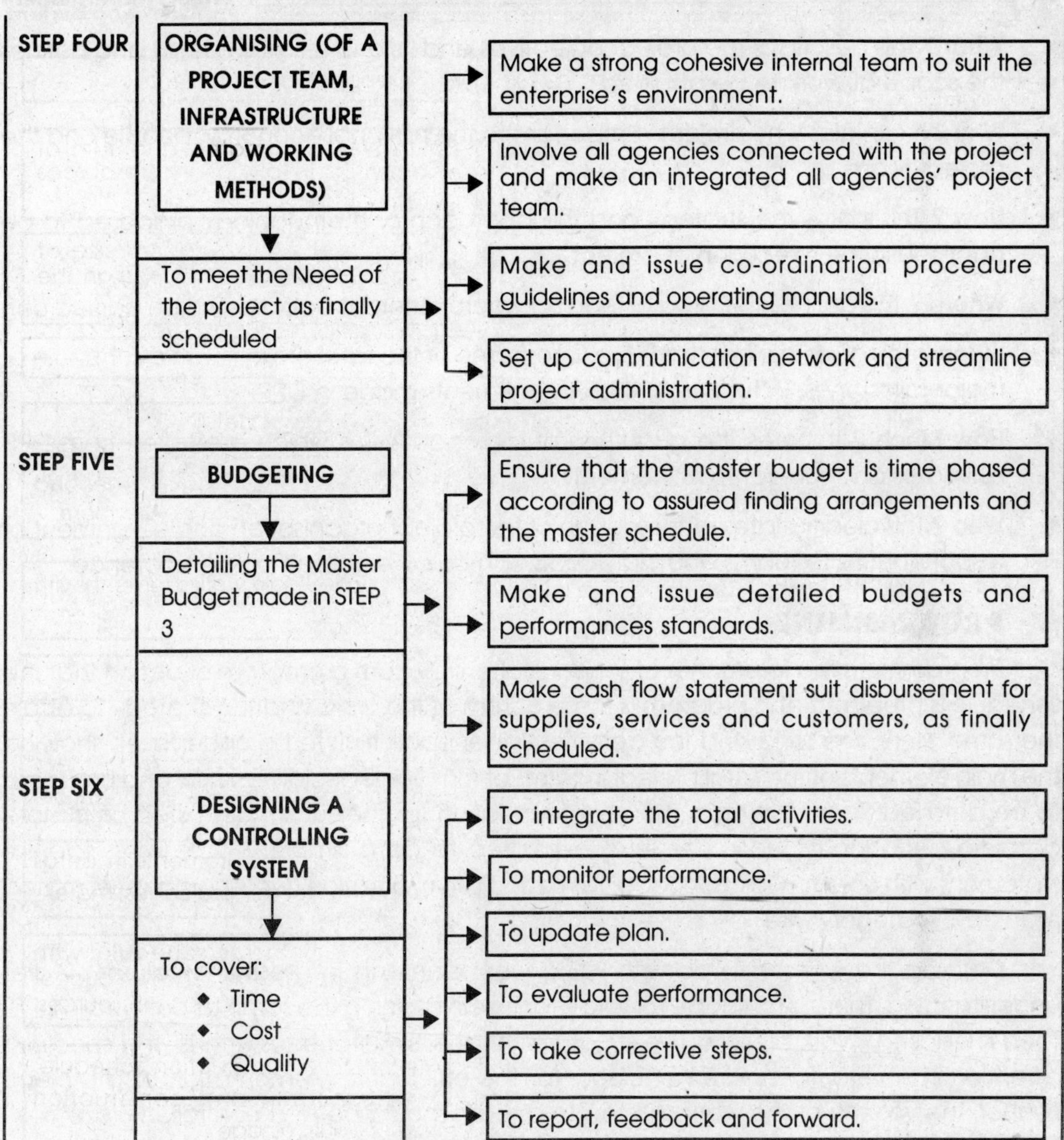

1. DEVELOPMENT OF PROJECT PLAN OBJECTIVES

Before drawing up a detailed plan, it is customary to define the scope of its Plans success hinges on clear understanding of the plan objectives. Therefore, they are to be stated clearly and orderly and to see that they are achievable, measurable, easily comprehensive and consistent with the resources levels fixed in detailed Project Report (DPR) estimates. Planning aims to achieve the project completion by the best use of time and resources. The 'W's are going to answer this objectives part.

- **What ?** This describes the project objectives and its end results in detail and defines the scope of work to be attained.
- **Why ?** It explains why project is important to the national economy, people and the project team.
- **How ?** This states the strategy and the approach or methodology proposed to be adopted in the execution of project.
- **Where ?** This defines the area or leading where different activities will be carried out.
- **When ?** This gives in clear terms the time-frame of the total project with a schedule of major milestones, in tune with the commitments made in DPR.
- **How Much ?** It states the quantities of major activities which are taken from DPR estimates and subject to refinement.
- **Who ?** This clearly states of the design of the project organisation and assignment of responsibilities to teams and individuals with due weightage on competence.

2. PROGRAMMING

Programme is the forerunner of schedule. It is only from a program of action that the schedule is prepared. This program is the program of the tasks and the strategy to attain the same. Here, the tasks and the activities under each task to be undertaken showing the main elements of the total project in terms of functions, disciplines, skills and crafts are to be detailed. These lists form the very foundation for the subsequent step of a more detailed definition of work. The list is expected to be a simple, phase wise, tabular statement with columns for task code, task description/duration (working day)/estimated man days (category wise).

Defining the work, is to do with listing work elements in greater detail for clearer understanding. There is no scope for uncertainties in defining the same as outlined in DPR. Then it leads to 'Work break down structure'. That is, simultaneous efforts and specialist attention in several forms are necessary for the efficient implementation of a project. Further, the volume of the work allotted to a team should be of a controllable size only. This is the reason why, work breakdown structure (WBS) is made. WBS is a function of programming. It is highly specialized task of breaking down the total project work into manageable self-task contained and independently excecutable work packages and down the line activities, areawise or functionwise or craftwise or process stagewise. WBS is prepared by studying the design and engineering characteristics and requirements of the project, and breaking down the project into smaller units or elements, In different levels as: Level 1: Total project. Level 2: Major segments of the project. Level 3: Tasks of every segment. Level 4: Activities in every task. Level 5: Elements in every task or activity.

Next aspect of programming is codification. Codification of tasks and related project accounts facilitates effective management and control. It is an usual practice in all large projects to use structured codes for identification, reference, accounting, integration and computerisation of drawings and technical documents, WBS contents, costs, purchase orders, budget commitments equipment and materials schedules, off-site and infrastructure facilities, man- power and other inputs, contracts, bills, progress reports, performance evaluation, income, and expenditure, assets and liabilities and the like. The numbering structure should be logical, related and level related. Coding can be done either numerically or alphabetically or alph-numerically. The actual structure of codification depends on the type, size and accounting needs of the project and the enterprise. The coding system and numbers must be made known to every one connected with the project.

The next aspect of programming is modeling the work. That is, graphic models of the main segments and important elements of the work is a must. These models are helpful in understanding the variables to one who is to handle and translating the plan into reality. The modes are expected to indicate the various angles of the type and magnitude of the work to be putin, and the technical, functional and logical relationship of the various activities, involved in the work. Addition of time duration to every model with a beginning and an end is done here. As calender dating may be impossible at this stage, the same is fixed in terms of project months or project days, starting from the zero date.

The next step in preparing is fixation of sequence priority. A project is an integrated whole unit into which hundreds of tasks and thousands of work elements are integrated. Therefore, work programming is to be done with the interrelationship of work in mind. Interfacing of the models will establish this interrelationship. It is possible to carry out many work elements independently upto their assembly stage, but in a project with few hundred thousand identifiable work elements, one can not afford to leave half of them executed out of sequence and wait for mass finishing, assembly, connections and testing towards the end of the project. This is sure to cause good deal of confusion, wastage, lockup of money and in most cases remobilization and even some rework. Further, in a large project, different work packages may have different phased out commissioning dates for technical and financial reasons, necessitating a correspondingly phased out completion of work. Furthermore, for economic or technical reasons, some segments may have to be accomplished or priority over others. For these reasons, a definite sequence and priority have to be given due weightage while programming.

The next requirement of programming is fixation of Activity Duration. Every activity shall be allotted a realistically estimated time duration so that the sum total of all such durations minus the net overlapping would be equal to the project duration. There is a theory for time estimation under PERT; in actual practice the time-duration is fixed on the basis of previous on the job experience of the planners and line managers. The planner, is well qualified and highly experienced. It is usual fix a shorter than permitted duration, keeping a few days up-one's sleeve as a 'buffer time' for any possible slippage. This provision is contingency time. Scheduled completion time plus contingency time is the target time.

Identification of critical activities is the last in the programming phase of project planning. If one looks at the total project model, placing individual segments' models end-to end or drawing a time-phased master bar chart, plotting all the important segments with the indication of their interrelationships, one finds that some items have fairly long-floats or slack time between starting and finishing as their finishing does not hold up other activities; but at the some time, some other items are so critical that the preceding items' tie in and succeeding items' start are dependent on their finishing. These latter items have to be separately identified and listed for special management attention towards their completion, in the interest of timely completion of the project. These are generally referred as "Red List" items.

3. SCHEDULING

Scheduling is the substantial improvement on programming. This improvement is activated in some manner as a tailor improves his marking and shaping to give the final shape to a suit while taking a trial of the hand stitched model. Scheduling is principally the exercise of laying down and integrating time, resources, and the main-work elements of engineering, procurement and constructions in the most efficient manner to achieve the project execution. Resources availability and their economic levels of distribution, time duration for individual activities and for the total project, and the estimated costs are interrelated through the scheduling exercise. This interrelationship is established through: Forward and backward scheduling. Resource assessment and matching. Master scheduling and master budgeting. Construction schedule. Manpower schedule. Construction equipment usage schedule. Ordering and delivery schedule for incorporated equipment and materials. Schedule of maintenance spare-parts. Critical activities, red list or desk top control chart. Other supporting schedules. Integrating of schedules by using the standard principles and techniques of scheduling.

4. PROJECT ORGANISATION

A good project organization in which all individuals concerned constantly interact for achieving project objectives is vital for the success of any project. A project-team takes over the project responsibility from the study team as soon as the statutory clearances are got and funding arrangements are made. In the scheduling stage, what is generally done is to check and redesign the organization which was defined at the commencement of the project when the study team was disbanded. In this stage, the organization is given a more formal character and strengthened with clearly defined responsibilities with commensurate authority.

After defining the work and making WBS, one is abel to determine the exact size of the project team, and the form of organization necessary to manage the project successfully. The size of the organization depends on work load, the specialization involved and the complexity of the project. The distribution of work, between the owner and the contractors will also have an impact on project organization size.

Form of organization depends on four factors:

1. Whether the project enterprise is starting its business life with the setting up of the project on hand.
2. Whether the project is undertaken by an ongoing production unit, as on additional facility or renovation or modernisation.
3. The geographical locations of the HO, the project site and the principal project office.
4. The management philosophy of the project enterprise.

As we have already discussed earlier, there are three different forms of project organisation namely, functional, project and matrix. Each is having its own set of merits and demerits and suitability list. Please refer the concerned chapter for details. Here, organizational part is to do with: Integration of project terms. Management through consulting agencies. Appointment of a competent project manager. Appointment of good planning manager. Strengthening the project team. Making efficient commercials arrangements. Making a responsibility matrix. Teaching the officers the decision making process. Setting up the project offices and infrastructural facilities. Initiation of the project. Introducing project log books. Provision for conflict management and organizational effectiveness all go a long way in successful organisations.

5. PROJECT BUDGET AND FUND FLOW STATEMENT

During pre-feasibility studies and feasibility studies, budgets and fund-flow statements were made. It is the time now to recheck, revise them wherever necessary and time phased to suit the schedule. Master budget and master fund-flow statements are to support the master schedule and the detailed sectionl budgets and fund-flow statements should support the time-phased work, break-down structure and detailed schedules. While the budget is prepared on financial commitment basis, fund-flow is made on receipt and payments basis like a cash-flow statement. There is generally a time gap between commitment and disbursement. The concerned authorities must ensure that WBS, OBS schedule and budget breakdown structure are perfectly integrated. Further, one must ensure that the funding agency or financial institution agrees with the budget and fund-flow statement, and gives an assurance of fund-flow before the plan is released for final implementation.

6. THE CONTROL SYSTEM

Control follows planning. If is so because "no planning no control". The objective of control system is to control the schedules of time and cost, achieve required quality and reduce the risks associated with the projects. This can be possible through: Integration of the total activities. Fixation of performance standards. Monitoring of performance. Plan up-dating. Performance evaluation. Corrective and preventive actions. Having an effective reporting system.

CHAPTER BASED QUESTIONS

A. WRITE SHORT NOTES ON

1. Project planning
2. Scope of project planning
3. Objectives of project planning
4. Programming
5. Scheduling
6. Scheduling of resources
7. Project organization
8. Budgeting
9. Control system
10. Controlling in time
11. Controlling Cost
12. Controlling quality
13. Work Break down Structure
14. Modeling the work

B. SHORT ANSWER QUESTIONS

1. What is project planning ?
2. What are project plan objectives ?
3. What is programming ?
4. What is work modelling ?
5. What are critical activities ?
6. What is scheduling ?
7. What is master schedule ?
8. What is Master Budget ?
9. What are principles of scheduling ?
10. What is project organization ?

C. ESSAY TYPE QUESTIONS

1. What is project planning ? What are its objectives ?
2. What is project planning ? What is its scope ?
3. What is programming ? Explain steps involved in it.
4. What is scheduling ? What are the different dimensions of it ?
5. What is project organisation ? What type of organisation you recommend and why ?
6. What is project organising ? What steps are involved us it ?
7. What is controlling system ? What it is made up of in project organisation ?
8. What is budgeting and cash flow ? What is expected of these in project management ?
9. What is breakdown structure ? What is its use ?
10. How project plan objectives are developed ? What purposes they serve ?

* * * * * *

Chapter 4

PROJECT PLANNING PART-2

- WHAT ARE BUSINESS OPPORTUNITIES?
- STEPS IN GENERATING AND SCREENING PROJECT IDEAS
- TURNING IDEAS INTO BUSINESS OPPORTUNITIES
- INITIAL EVALUATION PROCESS
- SWOT ANALYSIS
- APPENDIX - 1 WHAT IS ENTREPRENEURSHIP?
- WHO IS ENTREPRENEUR?
- STANDARD DEFINITIONS
- WHAT IS ENTREPRENEURSHIP?
- STANDARD DEFINITIONS
- WHAT IS INTRAPRENEURSHIP?
- NATURE AND CHARACTERISTICS OF ENTREPRENEURSHIP CHARACTERISTICS
- FUNCTIONS OF AN ENTREPRENEUR
- RISKS AND REWARDS OF SELF-DEVELOPMENT
- RISKS INVOLVED
- REWARDS THAT FOLLOW
- CHAPTER BASED QUESTIONS

BACKDROP

Foundation for founding the successful business venture is the prudent search of promising project ideas. It is very easy to say "get into the right business at right time for sure success"; it is not that easy to get into right business at right time because really promising and good business opportunities are more elusive. Identifying such elusive opportunities warrants fertile imagination. Close sensitivity to environmental changes and realistic and pragmatic clearcut assessment of what the firm can do. This task is not easy because, it is partly 'structured' and partly 'unstructured' and partly hinges on 'convergent thinking' and partly 'divergent thinking; it calls for partly 'objective' analysis of quantifiable variables and partly 'subjective' analysis of qualitative variables. These variables are partly subject to control and partly not; that these are of two types controllable and uncontrollable. What is more important is that identification is the result of triggering process rather than mere analytical exercise. The idea of identification sounds very simple but it renders much difficult to design and develop procedures or methods or techniques of it as there is no one standard way of or theory to guide this task. These difficulties get more complicated in the hierarchy of decision making. In the light of this background, an attempt is made to throw light on the different dimensions of project idea generation and screening. Therefore, let us try to understand as what are business opportunities and a definite logical framework for generating and screening the project ideas and other relevant aspects. The Chapter ends with the Chapter Based Questions.

WHAT ARE BUSINESS OPPORTUNITIES ?

An opportunity is the potential idea on which one can make his fortune, name and fame. Basically, opportunities are ideas which have something to give a fair chance of exploitation by which the individual or a group of individuals on one hand and the society on the other stands to benefit. Therefore, business opportunities are basically ideas which can be converted into most profitable opportunity for the benefit of one and all in the society where one has an important role to play in exploiting it directly or indirectly. Any person who is worth calling entrepreneur, has good many ideas, and therefore, opportunities of which he selects and also works on it. That is why, a good entrepreneur has an exhaustive list of ideas which have business potentials. These ideas are like rough diamonds which are to be washed, selected, shaped, polished to make them to shine and shine for ever.

STEPS IN GENERATING AND SCREENING PROJECT IDEAS

The process of generating and screening business or project ideas can be one which shall consist of at least eight logical steps. These are :

(1) Generation of ideas

(2) Monitoring the environment

(3) Corporate appraisal

(4) Scouting for project ideas

(5) Preliminary screening

(6) Project rating index

(7) Sources of positive net present value

(8) Essential qualities of a successful entrepreneur. Let us go into the details of these so that one can have grip over the basics of idea generation and screening — the process of separating chaff from grains.

1. GENERATING PROJECT IDEAS :

Generating ideas does not mean necessarily invention of entirely a new idea. The existing idea may be modified or adapted which is called as innovation rather than invention. Generating ideas has two basic aspects namely, (A) Check the sources of ideas (B) Creativity.

A. CHECK THE SOURCES OF IDEAS :

The basic ideas which are hidden that hold fortunes for any person of curiosity and creativity can be taken from any one of the following possible sources. This can be called as well scouting for ideas.

1. **Better Understanding of Economy and Economies :** Economy is a system that speaks of economic dynamics. When we talk of Indian or American or Japanese economy, we know that it stands for an arrangement, wherein different aspects of economies are involved namely, production, consumption, exchange and distribution of wealth. Economy is an arrangement which stands for-how the resources both human and material are used in making valuable useful goods and services and thereby bringing its growth and benefits along with the possible dangers. Thus, India is a vast country rich in resources both material and human - warranting for their effective or optimal use. That is why, almost all developed nations are ready to enter India or Indian borderless world where both foreigners and Indians will be benefilted. A decision to go in for a business needs a thorough study of costs and benefits which is otherwise called as Economics. Knowledge of economics is the ABC of doing any business - big or small - that has a profit potentiality.

2. **Changing Needs of Society :** Change is essential part of life. It is a spice of life which cannot be avoided but to be accepted. Things are changing in every aspect of-life because the life-style concept - the value system has been undergoing a sweeping change. In the past, taking loan was a sin; today, it is status symbol. Our likes and dislikes, tastes, preferences are changing. The changing life-styles have created many business opportunities. Thus, the concept of 'beauty' has attracted the attention of many specialists who together manufacture "beauty queens" as "Miss India", "Miss World", "Miss Universe".

Today's beauty contests are not confined only to vital statistics body but extented to sharpening of mind; Today, it is a combination of beauty and brain. Therefore, contests all over the world though reach various stages, finally only one "Miss World" is selected as winners up. Makers of Miss "India", "World" or "Universe" are specialists who combine all the essential qualities for victory. Thus, there are specialists who care for communication as to how to walk, how to talk, how to smile, how to laugh, how to express their feelings; some care for grooming; some care for attire or dress design and what not? In information technology, Indians have upper hand and preferred to others by advanced nations because of high performance and low cost.

3. **Emerging Trends in the Society :** This is a fast changing world where concepts and ideas in every walk of life change. The present trend is "Life is short-lived and one must enjoy it at any cost." That is why, more and more people are travelling far and wide, spending their leisure time which is precious because, they want "break" in their lives which are very hectic, mechanical and full of tensions. They want to work hard and take total rest at week-ends, month-ends or year- ends. On the other hand, people who are very much time-conscious are going in for fast-foods than routine type of foods and food habits. Thus, they prefer a tooth-paste to have daily one brushing; some people donot have time to bathe for whom bathing tablets are available. People want today a cigarette without smoke, a car without air pollution, a medicine without side-effects, a pair of shoes that needs no polish, dresses and clothing that hardly need ironing and so on. People are not stagnant, but keep on moving from rural to urban areas, cities to metro-polies and from metro-polies to mega-polies where the life and life-style has different meaning, speed, earning and spending. Thus, changing trends give good many ideas.

4. **Extensive Travelling and Wide Reading :** Both these activities give good exposure. A widely travelled person has enriched knowledge about cultures, heritages and plus and minus points of people, places and situation he faces. He knows the finest shades of meaning and synergic expression. It is nicely joked that there is something like American-way of laughing. That is, when a joke is cut in the group, all are expected to laugh as if they have totally understood the joke, else people call them or him or her as fools or duds; a person who has not understood the joke, tries to recollect it and get it and then he laughs for second time. We have a similar thing in case of India, as 'Indian mentality' which is dubbed as 'crab- mentality'. It means pulling the legs of those who are trying to get excellence in their tasks, achievements. Similarly, wide range of reading makes a person, well-informed citizen and more knowledgeable though he has not widely travelled. Today, information technology means have made the world

very small and one is getting closer. On TV, we can be in America, Australia, Paris, London, and practically any where. In the past, cricket matches we attended personally; instead now we have that cricket stadium on screen in our drawing or TV room at finger tips, a remote control panel button. Thus, today, world is more informed through travelling, reading, viewing and listening. For a keen observer, any thing can be a good source of ideas on which he can make or mar his fortune. Even an ad you read or see everyday keeps you updated in every walk of life.

5. **Analyse the Performance of Existing Industries :** A thorough study of existing industries in terms of their profitability and capacity utilisation is of much help. The analysis of profitability and break even level of various industries indicates promising investment opportunities, that too which are risk free. An examination of capacity utilisation of different industries provides information about the potential for further investment. This kind of study is rendered more useful if it is done on regional basis especially for products that involve heavy transportation costs.

6. **Examine the Inputs and Outputs of Various Industries** : An analysis of the inputs needed for various industries bring to light good project ideas. Such opportunities exist when (a) materials, purchased parts or supplies are presently being procured from different and distant sources that involve time lag and transportation costs and (b) good number of firms make internal component parts which can be supplied at a lower cost by a single producer who enjoys economies of scale. Similarly, a study of the outputs of the existing industries reveal opportunities for adding value through further processing of main outputs - by products as well as waste products. It is because a producer's waste can be wealth for another.

7. **Review Imports and Exports** : An analysis of import statistics over a period of say five to eight years is of much help in understanding the trend of imports of various goods and the potential for possible import substitution. Home made products which are presently imported are advantageous for at least three reasons namely, (a) it improves the balance of payments situation (b) it generates employment opportunities (c) it provides market for supporting industries and services. Similarly, an indepth examination of export statistics is of much use in learning about the export possibilities of different products.

8. **Explore the Possibility of Reviving Sick-Units** : Industrial sickness is one of the essential features of underdeveloped and developing nations. It does not mean that, it is absent in case of advanced nations. In a country like India there are large number of sick units which are either closed or on the verge of closure.

These sick units can be brought back to normal health by sound management, injecting additional dose of money as working capitals providing complementary inputs. Taking over of sick units is not a bad idea where one is giving a fresh lease of life, making profits without waiting for longer gestation period and resources are saved from being wasted.

9. **Identifying Unfulfilled Psychological Needs** : In case of products which are well-established having multi brand groups such as bathing soaps, detergents, cosmetics, tooth-pastes the question is one of manufacturing but whether the product or a brand is able to fulfil all the psychological needs of consumers. The spectrum analysis is useful in this direction which takes into account the significant factors influencing brand choice which are identified - positioning of existing brands on the continuum in respect of the factors so identified and finding out the gaps that exist in relation to consumer psychological needs that are identified.

10. **Visit Trade Fairs and Exhibitions** : Both national and international trade fairs provide an excellent opportunity of knowing about new products and developments. These present exposure to the latest arrivals and modified versions of products where one can think of further improving upon these.

11. **Heed to Suggestions of Financial Institutions and Developmental Agencies** : Each nation and each state of a nation is interested in promoting development of industrial ctivities. Hence, the state financial institutions, development corporations and other developmental bodies undertake studies, feasibility reports and offer suggestions to potential entrepreneurs. These provide readymade opportunities to those who are interested.

12. **Investigation of Local Materials and Resources** : Project ideas can stem from investigation of availability of local sources and skills. Thus, local materials and skills which are dormant are activated. Research institutions such as NCAER (National Council of Applied Economic Research) and other such bodies publish surveys of various regions showing the potential of industrial development. These surveys assess the resources both human and material, infrastructural facilities, marketing possibilities for different products. Even private research units do undertake market surveys and give the details of different products at local, national and international level.

13. **Study of Plan Outlays and Governmental Guidelines** : Government of every nation plays a significant role in economic development as the custodian of a nation. Indian five year plans and sectoral outlays that are proposed act as very useful indicators of investment opportunities. Indirectly, they point out potential demands for goods and services required by different sectors. The Department

of Industrial Development of Government of India is a good and reliable source of information. Annual publication gives a detailed information about structure and location, production performance, licenced and installed capacity, exports, and the future scope of different industries.

B. CREATIVITY :

For a person who is creative, each and every problem is an opportunity. One of the essentials of an entrepreneur is creativity or presence of critical bent of mind. He is to be creative and innovative. Creativity is that quality or trait that gives not only an edge for recognising needs, generating business ideas, manufacturing and marketing but also it helps in solving the problems effectively. A problem has alternative solutions and the best of them is to be chosen. A person who faces a problem and finds a novel solution is able to quickly convert the problem into an opportunity that has solutions, will not only survive but excel all others in the race. A creative mind set speaks of his ability to solve the problem easily, quickly and logically. Experts have given certain rules for creativity namely :

(1) Creativity accepts every problem as an opportunity

(2) Problems are not exercises for giving up

(3) Every problem has more than one solution

(4) One has to think side ways or laterally

(5) Creativity is a gift where one gets more and more ideas in an internal environment.

Most of us tend to limit our thought process into traditional and standard ways of doing the things which often become obstacles to creativity and our mind set is rendered to be happy with routine experience and peer pressure. If one is to be creative, one has to come out of this region and start thinking side ways or laterally. There can be many examples but more often quoted is a puzzle of NINE DOTS. Where one is to connect all the nine dots by straight line without lifting the pen or pencil. Fig. 4.01 makes it amply clear.

Among the maximum possible solutions, only three are given. It is the question not of only solutions but selecting the best in that it is viable from all angles. Accordingly, among three alternatives, alternative ONE is the best.

The concept of creativity is based on the idea "The very best can be improved", though there are variety of methods of creative thinking, we will touch only two most widely used namely, brain-storming and attribute listing.

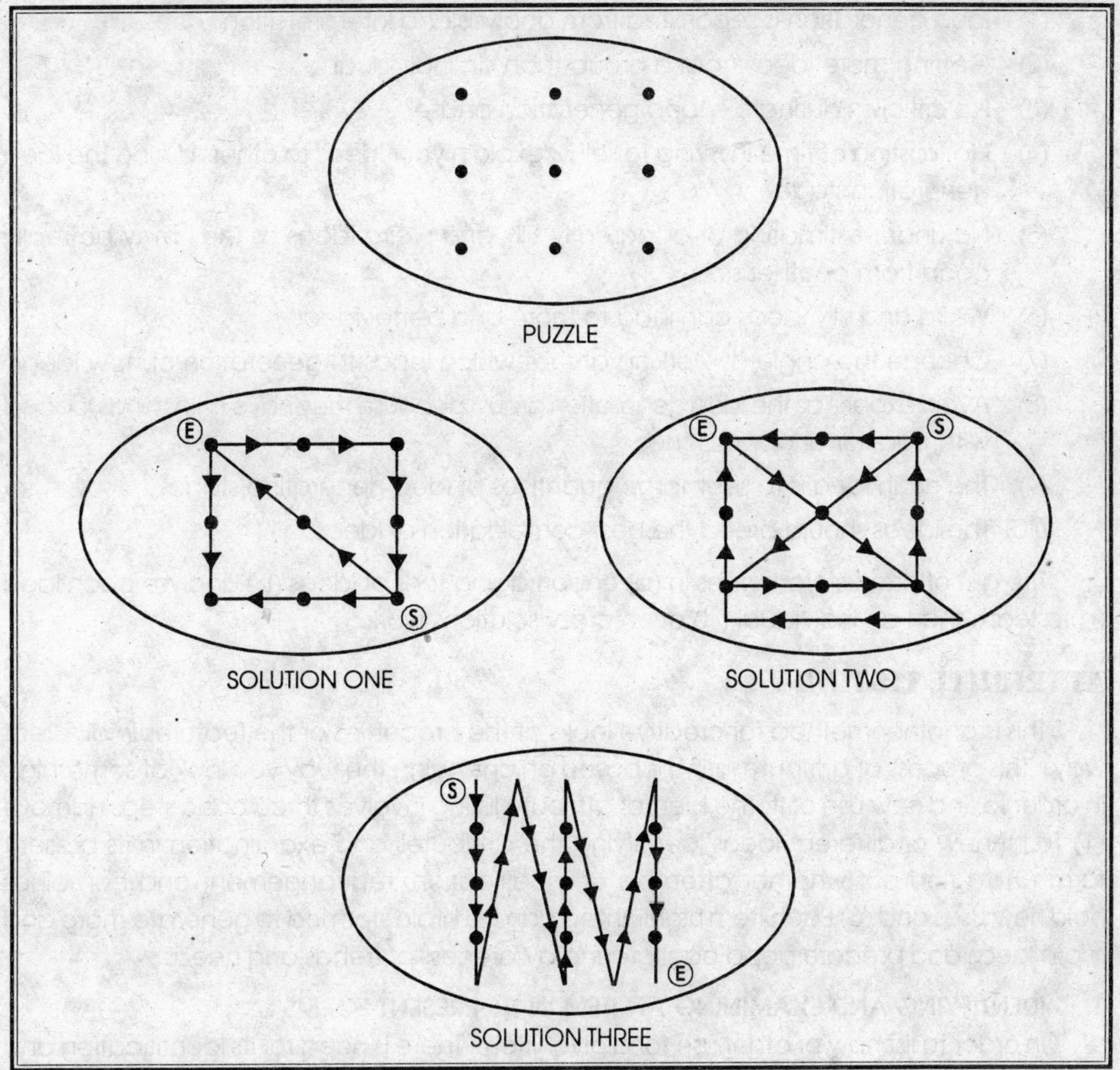

Fig. 4.01 NINE - DOT PUZZLE

BRAIN-STORMING :

Brain-storming is a process of detaching analysis of ideas from the actual development of ideas. Conventional way of thinking takes time to think through an idea and takes additional good deal of time to justify and sell the ideas to others. However, some times, non-conventional thinking gives birth to more ideas ensuring the best possible solution.

PRINCIPLES OF BRAIN-STORMING :

There are variety of ways to approach brain-storming of which what is common is that the rationale or principle behind remains the same. The principles are :

(1) Idea generation is separated from analysis and interpretation

(2) Getting more ideas from a group than an individual

(3) No criticism during the idea generation phase

(4) No wasting of time in trying to sell or explain your ideas to others during the idea generation stage

(5) No under-estimating of apparently silly and weird ideas as they may be really good from another side

(6) Weird and silly ideas can lead to more and better ideas

(7) Change the angle of working at that which leads to generation of new ideas

(8) Avoid experts as the idea generation group because they have rigid minds loaded with traditional approaches

(9) The main idea is to seek large quantities of idea generating stage

(10) The ideas should breed the best combination of ideas.

The gist of brain-storming lies in (a) encouraging tons of ideas (b) analyse each idea (c) a team than an individual (d) even crazy solutions work.

ATTRIBUTE LISTING :

This is another method for creative looks at the properties or the features in different ways. This process of attribute listing is based on changing the way you look at something in order to find new use of it. The idea of attribute listing involves three basic steps namely, (1) To list new or different ideas identifying the attributes and examination in its present form (2) To find out whether attempts of modification, rearrangement and combines hold new uses and (3) Each item highlighted can be brain stormed to generate more and more ideas and prepare good background awareness of trends and needs.

1. IDENTIFYING AND EXAMINING AN ITEM IN ITS PRESENT FORMS :

In order to list new or other use for a given item, there is need for its identification and thorough examination. Let us take a simple case of wornout tyre which is a waste if not recycled or put to other possible uses. The basic questions about attributes of an item can be: Does its SHAPE suggest other uses? As tyre is round it can be a good swing. Does its WEIGHT suggest other uses? As the tyre has the weight, it can hold down cloth or tarpantins. Does its COLOUR suggest other uses? The tyre being black in colour, it can be used as a carbon black for charcoal. Does its TEXTURE suggest other uses? Tyre is both strong and clastic and works as a good shock absorber in case of boat bumper or a protective barrier. Does its DIMENSION suggest other uses? Being round in shape as a ring, it can be made to work, as a flower pot in public gardens or houses or bunglows. Does its PROPERTIES suggest other uses? Tyre being inflamable, it can be a strong source of fire under hard conditions.

2. **FINDING OUT THE USES IN MODIFIED, REARRANGED OR COMBINED FORM :**
What you can do if you REVERSE it ? Being round, it can be used as a wheel socket. What can you do if you COMBINE with something else ? It can be a marine float with bamboo shoots or raft or styrofoam. What can you do if you MULTIPLY it ? In case it is cut into four, six or eight equal parts, they can be hanging vases. What can you do if you SHRINK it ? Being elastic, it can be moulded into an ash-tray or a flower design. What can you do if you ENLARGE it? Being expandable, it can be a medium of grand size. What can you do, if you REARRANGE it ? Can be cut into soles for shoes or can be mixed with asphalt as an addictive. What can you do if you CHANGE the material in it? It can be a bouquet centre piece in a bunglow hall.

3. **BRAIN-STORMING OF HIGHLIGHTED ITEMS :**
Being the third step of attribute listing, each highlighted item can be further brainstormed with a view to generate more and more ideas by referring it to a group ready for brain-storming session. It is equally possible, as it helps in having a good background awareness of both trends and needs.

C. NEED RECOGNITION :

Any human need is an opportunity, provided it is matching, met as conditioned by consumer specifications. It is impossible to produce a product as to each individual need or needs because, each individual is unique and has a different patterns of his expectations. Though, it is possible, it is not feasible to meet individual requirements in strict sense of the term. Hence, we are more concerned with those needs that are more general giving us a marketable surplus. Here, marketability is preferred to technical specifications. Many a times a producer makes even technically feasible products but have failed to market them. At times, even the best products can not be marketed successfully.

In recognising the human needs, **Abraham Maslows theory** of need hierarchy is widely accepted who classifies human needs into five categories as BASIC, SAFETY, SOCIAL, EGO and SELF-FULFILMENT needs. Speaking practically, basic needs may be-food-stall, tents shelter related products; safety needs may be locking systems, insurance, fire-extinguishers, shoes, guns; social needs may be say all kinds of deodorants and perfumes, watches, ties, occupational attires, two-wheelers, four wheelers and so on; ego needs may be say a watch made of solid gold studded diamonds, luxury sports bikes and cars, shoes, dress-materials; self- fulment needs may be one which are not fulfilled by others. It may be an artist stocks costly books as master pieces; a computer personnel having latest computer, a teacher par excellence using latest books and journals and interest facility for having latest knowledge.

D. TREND RECOGNITION :

One is able to anticipate needs and develop a clear vision of the future that holds of successful products, services and directions to follow and get an edge in competitive forces by developing an awareness of future trends. Certainly, trends occur because the world faces changing events say war, climatic change, shifts in economies, change in economic position, may be from public to private sector and vice versa, demographic changes, technological changes, socio-psychological changes, ecological changes, psychological graphics say, a trend in favour of sounder and fitter health, more liesure time to reduce daily tension and pressures of mechanical and successful life. These trends on illustrative basis can be : trend towards rural develop nerit, trend towards greater health fitness; trend towards extensive use of computers; trend towards market for unmarried persons; trend towards two income families; trend towards increased productivity; trend towards open economies.

E. FAD RECOGNITION :

Just as needs are to be recognised, fads are also to be identified. A fad is a short-lived business opportunity for which people get widely excited for a while. It is very common in such goods as clothing, sports games, shoes, where passion for fashions and styles is very strong but for a shorter period. For an entrepreneur who knows the art of encashing on such fads, the world of fad for products and services is a gold-mining treasure. Good planning and implementation of fads can yield rich dividends. Such business lines for fads do not last for more than three to five years. Therefore, initial profit margins should be one of the highest with the lowest investment. It is equally possible that some fads continue and enlarge the span over five years giving long lasting business and this longevity is supported by changed value system. Thus, demand for sport bicycles, surf-boats, jeans, water-beds, water slides, adventure sports items, go on increasing. Here, full advantage can be taken as elongated fad stage cycle.

TURNING IDEAS INTO BUSINESS OPPORTUNITIES

By this time, it is already considered the areas of different sources of ideas-recognising needs recognising trends - identifying varied travel background - recognising fads. In addition, it brought to the surface the methods of expanding the possible ideas through basic methods namely brain storming and attribute listing. With these, a basket of ideas can be prepared or a pot-pourri-a collection of nice variety of flowers from which one can select the best. The basket is quite exhaustive. However, for the want of spatial constraints, these are just listed as sources of generating ideas as said and compiled by experts. These can be : Borrow or copy the idea of others on which we can improve as Japanese do it. Interview good many people on a particular idea where you might get solution for your problem. Look for better way of doing the things. Turn a science fiction into a fact-turn fantasy into a reality. Convert an event into opportunity. A problem is an opportunity seeking the solution. Waste is an opportunity as marry rose four rags to riches. Analyse the weakness of existing business to do better. Convert your hobby or sport into a business venture. Thus, a hobby of palm reading leads of world class palmist of highest accuracy. Combine the ideas; often new ideas can come out of combining the existing ideas and new business opportunities. Create a novelty, small pleasure or cheap thrill so that children can be your customers for tomorrow's products. Create different uses of common products. Create different products of same kind made up of different inputs or medium. Buy an idea available for sale from researchers and research units which can be commercialised. Check-out foreign suppliers. The officials like consulates and embassies and chambers of commerce that have the lists of firms what they have for exchange for your product or service. Think of import replacement or import substitution. Study and analyse plans and policies of your State, District or Taluka as a part of local government development prorammes. Review Trade Magazines that list business opportunities. Review patents and copyrights that might have escaped your attention. Create an opportunity say coaching classes with attached soft-drinks parlours or cyber cafes. Relook on what has failed as second look gives a flicker. Add value that local materials can be converted into end products with local technology. Break the bulk. Buy in bulk and pack in small convenient sizes to make them more useful and economical. Design new partitions. Package a similar product to better the needs of target size packets. Specialise in larger market. Let your market be part of total market. Undertake after market repairs and salvage that attracts customers. Attempt to be an export agent for a local product who knows your product might click in an international market. Add service to an existing product or service idea to have consumer loyalty. Be small but smart because small is not only beautiful but equally effective.

Any ideas, however, promising can not be called as business idea unless it has business potentiality. Two questions are to be answered to see any idea can be converted into business opportunities. These two big questions are :

(1) Does it have potential to be profitable? These potentials refer 'marketing' 'production' and 'financial'. Speaking about marketing potentiality, can the product or products or services or services be successful in market place? Turning to production potentiality, can one produce the required volume and quality at decent margins? Coming to financial potentiality — can financial goals be satisfied? It speaks cf satisfactory R.O.I, or target rate of return or profitability.

(2) Does it satisfy your individual or personal constraints? That is, does it fit well within the frame-work of firm's resource constraints.

INITIAL EVALUATION PROCESS

The starting question is, is it worth the effort? The initial investigation or evaluation process can be smartly lumped into two stages namely *(i)* Basic evaluation and (ii) Personal constraints.

Basic Evaluation : Basic evaluation is nothing more than 'cost benefit' analysis in a rough way. It is a common sense approach. This evaluation gives whether the opportunity has something to move ahead or forget. For this, one should take a practical case of manufacturing and selling say a plastic gun or toy-gun. Take an annual feast or jatra or local famous festival fast approaching and **Mr. Jerry** has sufficient time to produce and sell toy-guns which will be very attractive, cheaper having large-sale potential. It may be a Ganesh Festival or a Military Feast. The points here to consider are :

(1) A reasonable market price of Rs. 25 each

(2) Cost of production of each unit Rs. 16.

(3) Selling Expense of Rs. 2.00 each.

(4) Persons attending festival or fair or feast for say three days; about 75,000 persons where 50 percent are the children - the prospective customers and 50 per cent of the children are expected to buy toy-guns. The results can be presented in the form of a simple Income Statement as under :

Units Demanded : 50 per cent of 50 per cent of 75,000 persons that is 18,750 toy-guns thinking each child buys one toy gun.

Sales Revenue.	18750 X Rs. 25.00 =	Rs. 4,68,150/-
Less cost of Production	18750 X 16.00 = Rs. 3,00,000/-	
Selling Exp.	18750 X 2.00 = `Rs. 37,500/-	3,37,500/-
Gross Margin :		Rs. 1,31,250/-
Less provision for contingencies		
@ 20% on	Gross Margin	Rs. 26,250
	Net Margin	Rs. 1,05,000

Profitability Indicators

1. Percentage Rate of Return on Sales :

$$\frac{\text{Net margin}}{\text{Sales}} \times 100 = \frac{\text{Rs.}1{,}05{,}00\ 0}{\text{Rs.}4{,}68{,}75\ 0} \times 100 = 22.40\%$$

2. Rate of Return on Capital Investment (ROI) :

$$\text{ROI} = \frac{\text{Net margin}}{\text{Total Investment}} \times 100$$

$$= \frac{1{,}05{,}000}{3{,}37{,}500} \times 100 = 31.111\%$$

Here, investment is taken as investment made in all production and selling expenses. These indicators or investigations reveal a signal of "Go Ahead" — as it pays to produce and market toy guns with better financial potentialities.

Personal Constraints : One is bound to be fascinated by the amount of profit potential than personal constraints. What is more important is though, it is profitable, one should see whether the proposal fits within one's own personal constraints. One should not be carried away by possible profit alone. These personal constraints may be good many. On illustrative bases, these can be :

(1) Whether we have real interest and exploitation of the opportunity?

(2) Whether we are able to contribute whole or part of our valuable time?

(3) Whether we are happy with the rates of return on sales and investment as calculated?

(4) Is it worth the efforts put in?

  (a) Is it legally allowed?

  (b) Is it within our social status?

  (c) Is it going to improve our image?

(5) Do we have people of our choice, to make a viable team? Whether opportunity has top priority in our lists?

(6) Will it provide thrill, fun, a sense of high achievement?

(7) Is it matching to our life-style?

(8) Do we have market and marketing knowledge and ability?

(9) Do we have enough finance from the time we start production, till production is converted into sales and back to hard cash?

Taking these two derivations, **Mr. Jerry,** comes to the following conclusions regarding production and sale of toy-gun in festival or feast season of three days :

(1) It can be a good part-time task

(2) It is thrilling and fun filled

(3) Return per unit sold is enough

(4) It is legal

(5) It has market potential

(6) It is within the levels of skills of production and sales management.

(7) It fits within the financial resources that are easily available at reasonable cost.

Even if we have the confidence of reaching the conclusions, the conclusions should be put to acid test of cold facts because, what is possible on paper is not possible and feasible in reality. Hence, three more steps are to be tested to see whether the proposal passes the acid test and still gives in the green signal to go ahead. These are market research — Action and Basic Cycle. Let us know what these mean as applied to the opportunity of producing and selling the toy-guns at the annual festival or feast.

Market Research : Instead of jumping to conclusion and making final decision, it pays to further testing the validity of the opportunity. The answer is market research where one can not take tilings for granted. Marketing research is the technique which helps one how far, one's reach is to near reality as there is always vast gap between the cup and lips. Market research is gathering of information systematically, recording, analysing, interpreting and then take up the decision.

Action : Then the plan of production and sales are to be implemented step by step both in terms of all dimensions of legality, economies, efficiency through managerial skills. This covers a host of actions as to where-when-how much-to produce and how to arrange for finance, and personnel for production and marketing?

Basic Cycle : What is said above is fundamentally a cycle for planning and implementing the business plan so couched. It needs constant vigilance. Calculations, Coordination, motivation, monitoring of each activity involved in making toy- guns and the sale of the stock. Calculations are done from time to time, in terms of profitability, inputs and outputs, financial implications and other personal constraints as the show needs continuous adjustment.

This preliminary look gives a kick-start which may warrant change, in the light of situations so that revision, modification, improvement are needed. What is needed is, systematic approach for better results.

SWOT ANALYSIS

Unfortunately most of the business firms follow a very casual and hotch potch approach to generate project ideas. SWOT analysis represents a conscious, deliberate and systematic effort by an organisation to identify opportunities that can be fruitfully exploited. SWOT is an acronym for strengths, weaknesses, opportunities and threats. It means analysis and assessment of comparative strengths and weaknesses of a business firm in relation of competitions on one hand and the environmental opportunities and threats which a firm may be exposed to face. As such SWOT analysis is a systematic study of identified action of all those aspects and strategies that best suit the individual firm's position in a given situation. It is logical and rational thinking that a proper strategy improves organisation's business strengths and opportunities at the same time reduces its weaknesses and threats.

WHAT ARE STRENGTHS ?

A strength is a power and excellence with resources, skills and advantages in relation to competition and requirement of the community a firm serves or plans to serve the same. A strength is a distinct or clear cut technical superiority with best technical know how, financial resources and the skills of the people who make the organisation's goodwill and image in the markets for products and services, labour and finance, firm's access to best distribution network. The discipline, morale, attitude and the culture of the employees with a sense of belongingness all count. Thus, it refers to the competitive advantage which a firm can exert in markets for finance, labour, products and services.

WHAT ARE WEAKNESSES ?

Weakness is the incapacity, deficiency in resources including limitations, such as technical, financial, manpower, skills, brand image, distribution pattern. In other words, it refers to all sorts of constraints or obstacles which deter or check movement or progress in a certain direction and may also inhibit an organisation in gaining a distinct competitive advantage.

Firm's strengths and weaknesses are a matter of interpretation and how the resources can be best utilised to achieve the best results as compared to other, similar computing organisations. These are purely internal forces and factors required to be studied and assessed from time to time since more and more competitive organisations with state of the art of technology and services are entering in the market and competitive forces are heated up making them more intensified.

WHAT ARE OPPORTUNITIES ?

An opportunity is an external factor or force in the business environment that changes because of external forces such as governmental policy, industrial policy, monetary policies, political situation at local, state, national and international level, formation of the trade blocks, trade barriers including changes in social, legal and cultural environment in the business world. That is, opportunities are created out of changes on which a wise, creative units harp. Any opportunity Is a major favourable advantage to a firm, provided the same can be availed strategically. Proper analysis of environment and identification of a new market, new improved consumer group with better product substitute or suppliers relationship could represent opportunities for a concern. Thus, changes in EXIM policy may bring in opportunities to some export houses, an amendment of MRTP Act, FERA (FEMA). Excise, Sales tax, Customs duties, Corporate taxes might bring opportunities. Policies of W.T.O. as members may avail opportunities under the policies of globalisation, privatisation and liberalisation.

WHAT ARE THREATS ?

A threat or environmental threat is a challenge posed by an unavoidable trend or a development that leads to the erosion of the company's position in absence of purposeful action. Threat is always an unfavourable environment for a firm, say slow market growth, entrance of resourceful multinationals or transnationals, increased bargaining power of buyers or suppliers because of large number of options, quick rate of obsolescence due to the hyper technological change adverse situations because of change in government policies, rules and regulations. All these put the organisations in a helpless and forlorn position putting in disadvantageous or handicapped situation posing a serious threat to the smooth running of an organisation.

In a nutshell, SWOT analysis is very significant weapon in today's world of faster changes in every walk of life and very important for strategic decisions. Such analysis and evaluation can be undertaken effectively through a brain-storming session in the full participation of key persons of all the related departments, preferably the departmental heads. SWOT analysis is undertaken in different ways in a strategic choice decision. The most common way provides a logical framework guiding systematic discussion as the environmental force and counter force, and thus making a choice of strategy as is necessary, fit and proper to the unique business situation that prevails in case of each individual concern.

Let us lake the same case of **Mr. Jerry** of manufacturing and marketing of toy-guns in an annual festival or feast The situation of **Mr. Jerry** will be facing a square of strengths and weakness on one sfde and opportunities and threats on the other as presented below :

STRENGTHS		WEAKNESSES	
1.	Good understanding of market situation	1.	Poor communication skills
2	Putting of hardwork	2.	Loosing temper quickly
3	Strong tendency to complete the task	3.	No latest technology in makmg toy guns
4.	Really willing to take moderate risks	4.	No guarantee of team work
OPPORTUNITIES		**THREATS**	
1.	Pretty large children as coustomers than other competitors	1.	Market survey reveals presence of competitors
2.	Toy guns are a novelty at first time	2.	Possible sudden rains or troubles at the festival time
3.	Ready and dependable suppliers of inputs get in time	3.	Government licence is difficult to get
4.	Toy guns are quite new and people want is to know and are curious	4.	Getting Government licence in time a problem

Thus, SWOT analysis helps him take up the same business idea or go in for another as per his decision.

2. MONITORING THE ENVIRONMENT

Fundamentally, a promising investment business idea enables the entrepreneur or the firm to exploit the opportunities covert in the environment by drawing on his or its competitive strengths. Business Environment takes the following shape

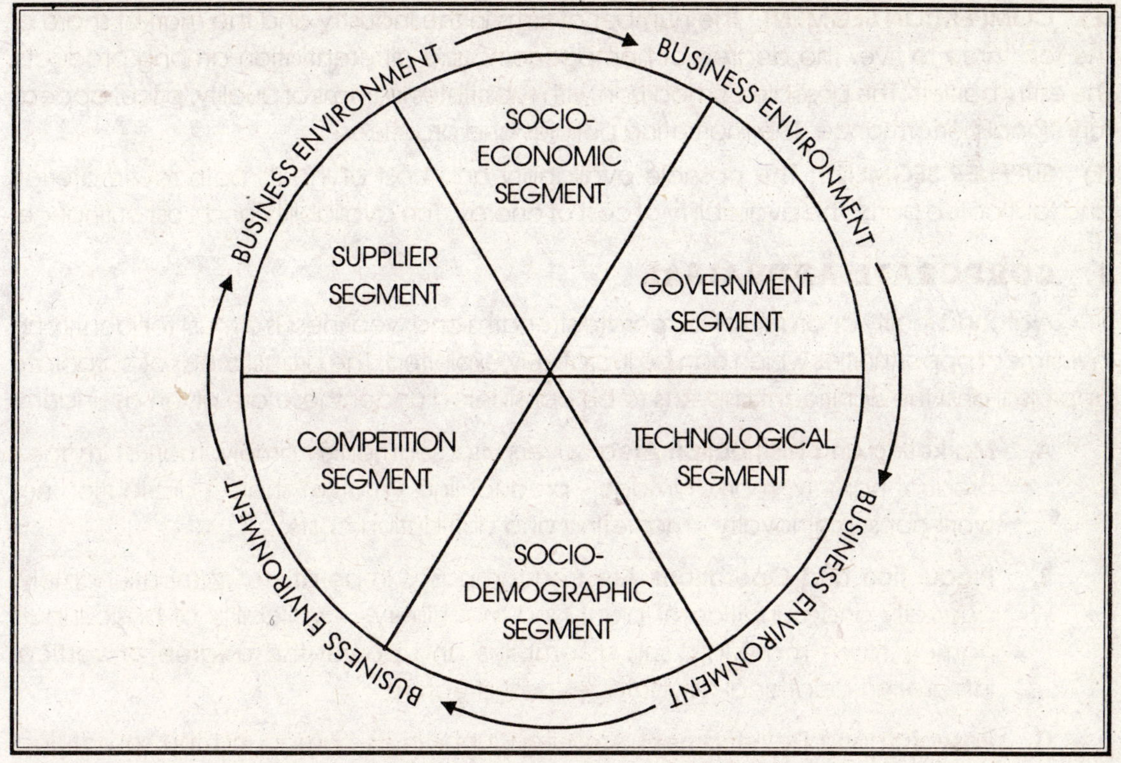

Fig. 4.02

Therefore, the firm must-meticulously and systematically monitor the environment and assess its competitive abilities. To monitor the environment, the business environment can be divided into at least six broad and meaningful segments. These sectors and their dimensions to be monitored are :

(A) ECONOMIC SEGMENT : The State of the economy. The overall rate of growth. The sectoral growth rates - primary, secondary and tertiary. The cyclical fluctuations. The rate of inflation. The linkage with the world economy. The trade surplus or deficit. The balance of payment situation.

(B) GOVERNMENT SEGMENT : The Industrial Policy. The Government Programmes and Project. The Tax Design. The Subsidies, Incentives and Concessions. The Import and Export Policies. The Financing Norms. The Lending Conditions of Financial Institutions and Commercial Bank.

(C) TECHNOLOGICAL SEGMENT : The State of Present and Emerging New Technologies. The Possible access to the Technical Know-how, foreign as well as indigenous. The Degree of receptiveness on the part of industry. The possible transfer of technology

(D) SOCIO-DEMOGRAPHIC SEGMENT : The population trends. The Age shifts in population. The income distribution. The educational profile. The state of employment of women. The attitude towards consumption and investment.

(E) COMPETITION SEGMENT : The number of firms in the industry and the market share of the top three to five. The degree of homogeneity and differentiation among products. The entry barriers. The possible comparison with substitutes in terms of quality, price, appeal, functional performance. The marketing policies and practices.

(F) SUPPLIER SEGMENT : The possible availability and cost of inputs both raw-materials and fabricated parts. The availability of cost of energy. The availability and cost of finance.

3. CORPORATE APPRAISAL

A ground reality appraisal of corporate strengths and weakness is a must for identifying investment opportunities which can be lucratively exploited. The broad areas of corporate appraisal and the significant aspects to be considered under these are given as under :

A. **Marketing and Distribution Area** covers vital segments namely, market image - product namely, market image - product line - market share - distribution net work-consumer loyalty - marketing and distribution costs.

B. **Production and Operations Area** encompases imperative segments namely, capacity and condition of plant and machinery - availability of basic inputs namely raw - materials, sub-assemblies and power-the degree of vertical integration-locational advantages-cost structure.

C. **Research and Development Area** impounds in its compound the sensational segments namely, research capabilities of the firm-track record of new product developments - laboratories and testing facilities and coordination between the research and operations.

D. **Corporate Resources and Personnel Area** surrounds the delicate yet impinging segments such as corporate image, doubt about with governmental and regulatory bodies - dynamism of top management - competence and commitment of employees - and the state of prevailing industrial relations.

E. **Finance and Accounting Area** is to do with the segments namely, financial leverage and borrowing capacity - cost of capital - tax position - relations with shareholders and creditors - accounting and control system and cash flows and liquidity.

4. SCOUTING FOR PROJECT IDEAS

Ironically, good project ideas are quite elusive though they are the touching stones to success. This fact makes the project planners to tap a variety of sources to identify them. The experts have given certain suggestions in this regard. These are :

1. **Analysis of the Performance of Existing Industries :** A careful study of the existing industries is useful especially of their profitability and the capacity utilisation. The analysis of profitability and break even level of various industries brings in focus

promising investment opportunities. That is those opportunities which are comparatively more profitable and risk-free. A clear scanning of capacity utilisation of various industries reveals information about the potential for additional investment. Such detailed study is rendered more useful if it is done regionwise especially in case of products which have heavy transportation and haulage costs.

2. **Fish-eye View the Inputs of Various Industries :** A closeup analysis of the inputs needed for various industries may help in fishing out project ideas. Opportunities do exist when (a) materials, supplies and bought parts are presently being procured from distant sources adding to time lag and transport costs (b) several firms produce internally some parts or components which can be supplied at lower cost by a single manufacturer who enjoys economies of scale or cost advantage. On the same lines, a study of the outputs of the existing industries might bring to surface the opportunities for adding value through further treating or processing of main outputs, by products and even waste products for a trash of one is a rich treasure for another.

3. **Review of Imports and Exports :** An indepth analysis of statistics of imports over a period of five to ten years is of great help in understanding the trend of imports of various items of goods and the potential for import substitution. Home made goods which are presently imported have certain merits for several reasons : (a) it helps to improve the balance of payment situation (b) it generates gainful employment opportunities (c) it provides market for supporting industries and services. Similarly, export statistics are useful in learning about the export possibilities of various products.

4. **Study Plan Outlays and Government Guidelines :** The government of the nation as the custodian and a mentor plays a significant role in the planned economy. Five year plans give priorities sector wise and, therefore, targets - that indicate the potential demand for goods and services of different sectors of the economy broken over year-wise Government of India publishes good many publications on various sectors. To give an example, "guidelines to Industries" published by Department of Industrial Development is a rich source of information for a period of one year. The information covers various dimensions like structure and location - production performance, capacity both licenced and installed - exports and future scope of various industries. Again one can not overlook projections over a period of short, medium and long term.

5. **Take Account of Suggestions of Financial Institutions and Developmental Agencies :** Both at national level and state level, financial institutions and development agencies provide ready specialised studies, feasibility reports, and package of suggestions to the entrepreneurs in making. These being authentic, are reliable source of identifying really promising projects.

6. **Probe Local Materials and Resources :** Quite likely that a search for project ideas may, start with a deep probing of local resources and skills. Different ways of adding value to locally available materials may be examined. The skills of local artisans those have been passed on from one generation to another may suggest the products that can be profitably produced and marketed. The national bodies like NCAER - publish detailed surveys of different regions of India of potential industrial development. These surveys highlight the clear assessment of resources - both human and material - infrastructural facilities including outlets and markets for variety of products.

7. **Examine Economic and Social Trends :** A careful and close study of economic and social trends is of great assistance in projecting demand for all types and kinds of goods and services. Changing economic conditions and social situations bring in new trends, life styles, caused by change in value system, economic uplift, philisophies, outlook all bring demand for new goods and services. Today's cult is "consume first and pay later". "Life is short lived-enjoy it-beg, borrow or steal". "Work less earn more." Ambitions, tenacity to excel others in social and, therefore, economic status have changed the traditional style of living and goods and services. For a keen and creative observer, these trends are golden opportunities.

8. **Keen Watch of New Technologies :** Technologies are fast changing in every walk of life make the present products and services outdated. The latest technology has an edge over the older ones in terms of quality improvement, quantitative increase and cost reduction. Though India spends less than one percent of GDP on research, Indian brain is not lagging behind. India has large network of research laboratories and stations under the shade of national bodies such as CSIR — Council of Scientific and Industrial Research. We do have private bodies engaged in fundamental and applied research. New ideas, new products, processes and techniques for existing products developed by research laborations may be investigated for commercialisation. Even individuals have fine ideas which can be exploited.

9. **Get Clues from Consumption Abroad :** All countries are not equal in all fields. There is gap between under-developed, developing and developed nations. Since, production has to be in tune with consumption patterns, one can learn from the consumption patterns of other countries. There is nothing wrong in copying others if it is beneficial. The concepts of fast foods, amusement parks, pre-fabricated houses, digital gadgets, gel pens, smokeless cigarettes, automobiles running on gas, water, urine, mosquito repellents, harmless pesticides, fertilizers, tubeless tyres, collasible kitchen wares, and so on metal frames of doors and windows, rondent destroyers and so on. Indians have made dosa-idli-samber an international food item as pizza, hot dogs, hamburgers have been invading less developed countries.

10. **Explore the Possibility of Reviving Sick Units :** Industrial sickness is quite common in indisciplined nations. Good deal of investment is blocked and employees are thrownout and consumers are deprived of the fruits of an ongoing healthy industrial unit. Industrial sickness is mainly caused by lack of discipline in the field of finance, and heterogeniety in other inputs and efficiency. There has been misuse of resources. The degree of industrial sickness that the units suffer from varies-as bad, worse and worst like a person who is injured by burns graded is first, second, thirds and fourth degrees. Instead of leaving these sick units turning bad to worse or worst, they can be brought back to normal health instead of starting altogether new units; it is because only marginal efforts and inputs are needed as it is a case of cutting the dead wood.

11. **Spot Unfulfilled Psychological Needs :** A product might meet the physical need of a customer, but may not be really happy psychologically. We have good many brands of toiletories and cosmetics which meet physical needs. Consumers are buying these because there are no alternatives. Hair dyeing is a common thing now, but is a very tedious job. Attempts are made to present hair dyes in liquid form, powder form, cream form may be oil based, shampoo based : yet consumers are not satisfied. Hair dying should be hassle free-needing no special efforts. Mosquito menace has been the major issue before society. In this regard, repellent creams came, coils, pads, vaporisers came but yet not total satisfaction. Researchers are at constant work to give an effective repellent and a fool proof rodent or rat trap. They are yet to give. The psychological needs can be met by conducting spectrum analysis.

12. **Attend Trade Fairs and Exhibitions :** National and international trade fairs and exhibitions are the fora giving ample opportunities to know about new products, processes, ideas and developments. These themes can be attempted or improved upon.

13. **Encourage Creativity in Generating New Product Ideas :** Creative thinking is the lateral thinking that gives birth to new ways of doing the things. It makes a person to think in terms of modifying, rearranging, reversing, magnifying, minifying, reducing, substituting, adapting, combining and so on.

14. **Blessing in Disguise Factors :** It is strange but true. Many a times, accidents, disabilities, chance factors pave the way for new product ideas. Today, plastic sachets, plastic bottles, boxes have thrown glass industry to the corner. Recently, plastic carry bags which are non-bio-degradnable are used in hot mix used in metalling the roads. The result is that life of road is enhanced and layer gets stronger almost three times. This has solved the problem of environmental pollution hazards. Again, a person who is physically handicapped is able to develop his own device because he knows what is his problem in all its girth. Even doctors

and designers might fail. Some times nuisance may lead to new product development. Examples of this kind are walkman-cassettee player, nappies and huggies and so on. A social worker from Gujarat has succeeded in producing better milk than natural milk from peanuts.

5. PRELIMINARY SCREENING

The earlier stages have made available large number of good project ideas. All good ideas can not be accepted for implementation because of these good, classed as very good and very-very good ones. That is, these can be good, better and the best. These concepts of what is 'good', 'better', and 'best' are comperative subjective in nature. In case these are quantified, subjectivity is called giving no scope for personal bias. The very idea of screening the ideas is to eliminate the ideas which are not promising or paying one. The preliminary screening of ideas taken into account how far the idea in question fulfils the following criteria - a set of points. These aspects hover round :

1. **Compatibility with the Promoter :** The project idea must first favour the interest, personality and the resources of the promoter or the entrepreneur. As rightly put by **Mr. A.Murphy,** a real opportunity has three features namely, (a) It fits the personality of the entrepreneur. That is, it squares with his abilities, training and proclivity or inclination (b) It is accessible to him (c) It offers him the prospect of rapid growth and high return on capital invested.

2. **Consistency with the Governmental Priorities** : The project idea to be feasible should fit in the frame work of governmental priorities. It is consistent provided it gets 'yes' answer to the following questions : (a) Is the project consistent with national goals and priorities ? (b) Is it environment friendly ? (c) Is it easier to get foreign exchange requirements for the project ? (d) Is it hurdle free to get licence for the project ?

3. **The Availability of Inputs** : Any project can not be worked out of thin air. It needs resources and inputs, both basic and subsidiary. Certain questions and the answers to them-prove it. These are : (a) Are the capital requirements of the project within the manageable limits ? (b) Is it possible to get the required technical know-how easily ? (c) Are the required raw materials available in plenty at reasonable prices ? If they are to be imported - is it difficult and costly ? (d) Is power supply for the project obtainable at reasonable rates from external sources ? Does it pay to generate internally ? These questions have specific relevance because countries like India have shortages at one end and plenty at another caused by lethargy and unaid under exploitation.

4. **Market Adequacy :** Market adequacy stands for presently existing market and potential growth in the future at decent rate of return. Market adequacy can be judged in terms of the following factors, (a) Total present domestic market (b)

Competitors and their market share (c) Export markets (d) Quality price profile of the product in comparison with competitive products (e) System of sales and distribution (f) projected increase in consumption - with dimensions of quantity, quality, value (g) Barriers to the entry of new firms (h) Socio-economic and demographic trends - favourable to increased consumption (ii) Patent protection. In India, demand for goods is ever on the increase because of low per capita consumption and increasing per capita income, except in situations of recessionary phase of business cycle. In that respect Indian entrepreneurs are better placed as demand follows supply.

5. **Cost Reasonability** : The cost structure of the proposed project must allow realisation of a acceptable or decent rate of profit with the competitive prices prevailing. Reasonability of costs applies to the following aspects namely (a) Cost of material inputs (b) Labour costs (c) Factory overheads (d) Administrative Overheads (e) Selling and distribution overheads and (f) the economies of scale (g) service, costs - that play important role in retaining and generating new satisfied customers.

6. **Acceptability of Risk Level :** Another name for business is risk - or game of risk. Greater the risk more rewarding will be a line of activity. Therefore, the desirability of a project is critically dependent on the risk featuring it. In the assessment of risk which is a very difficult task, the following factors are to be given due consideration. These are : (a) Vulnerability to business cycles (b) Technological changes (c) Competition from substitutes (d) Competition from imports (e) Governmental control over price and distribution. Though operational controls are imposed by government of India from time to time in the areas of production, distribution, price, exports and imports, the present approach controls reveal three features namely, (1) Partial control than total (2) better responsiveness to inflationary forces and (3) Liberalisation - that is - it is not control conscious as in the past.

6. PROJECT RATING INDEX

Preliminary screening can be done through **Project Rating Index**. That is, this process can be reduced to an Index that rates a project based on the score. The steps involved in determining rating index are : (1) Identification of factors relevant for project rating (2) Assigning of weights to these factors. The weightage is one that reflects relative significance. (3) Rating the project proposal on various factors using a suitable rating scale. Generally, it is five-point scale or a seven-point scale. (4) Multiply each factor with the weightage to get factor score and (5) Adding all the factor scores to get overall project rating index.

Following is the construct of Project Rating Index. It considers 8 factors, factor weights using five point scale.

Factors	Factor Weight	Rating					Factor Score
		Very Good	Good	Average	Poor	Very Poor	
		5	4	3	2	1	
1	2	3	4	5	6	7	8
1. Input Availability	3.00			✓			9.00
2. Technical know-how	1.00		✓				4.00
3. Cost Reasonability	0.50		✓				2.00
4. Market Adequacy	1.50	✓					7.50
5. Complementary relationship with other products	0.50		✓				2.00
6. Stability	0.75		✓				3.00
7. Dependence on firm's strengths	1.75	✓					8.75
8. Consistency with governmental priorities	1.00			✓			3.00
	10.00			Rating Index			39.25

Note : As per evaluation standards of firm, a score 35.00 and above are **"acceptable."**

7. SOURCES OF POSITIVE NET PRESENT VALUE

Many people think that there is no dearth of NPV projects that was positive and can be identified easily. However, the truth is that there are not abundant NPV positive projects. Things appear so because of imperfections in real market - product and factor markets - lead to entry barriers which cause positive NPVs. Therefore, there is an urgent need of understanding of entrybarriers which will clear the way for identifying positive NPV projects. These entry barriers are :

1. **Economies of Scale :** Economies of scale stand for the decline in the cost per unit produced and sold with increase in the scale or size of production or distribution. Whenever substantial economies of scale are present, the existing firms are likely to be larger in size. It means the more pronouncing economies of scale will mean more or greater cost advantage to the existing firms. To take advantage of the economies of scales, the new entrants require pretty hefty investment in plant and machinery, research and development and market development. This hefty investment needs act as entry barrier. Thus, greater the capital requirement, the higher and stronger the barrier to entry. This is particularly true in industries like oil refineries, mining, iron and steel, aluminium and so on.

2. **Product Differentiation :** A firm can create an entry barrier by diffentiating successfully its products from those of rivals. The bases of differentiation may be one or more of the following. (a) Effective advertising and superb marketing (b)

Extending extra ordinary services (c) providing with innovative product features (d) high quality and dependability.

3. **Cost Advantage :** A firm can be assured of better earnings if it enjoys cost advantage as against its rivals. Cost advantage stems from one or more of the following : (a) accumulated experience and comparative edge on the learning curve. (b) monopolistic access to low cost materials (c) a favourable location (d) more effective cost control and cost reduction.

4. **Marketing Reach :** A firm that has penetrating marketing reach has definitely a competitive advantage over others. There are good many examples of international and national repute. Take the case of H.L.L. number ONE consumer company which has both breadth and depth of distribution and work as compared to its competitors. By 2001 end, it had 6,50,000 outlets spread over 1,27,000 villages, served by 7,500 stockists and 2,800 vans. More than 8,000 sales persons supported the selling effort of 550 territory sales personnel. That is why, it has been a market leader in FMCG sector. Take another example of Amul-Cooperative of Gujarat where daily 20,00,000 men and women, bring milk from 20,000 villages worth 5 crores leading to operation white revolution making it possible sale of milk products - butter, cheese, chocolates, cookies, covering entire nation. This has been a success in cooperative sector which has led people of T.Nadu to go ahead on same lines. Pizza huts - outlets are fast appearing in competition to McDonalds.

5. **Technological Edge :** Technological superiority encourages a firm to enjoy excellent returns. Internationally, IBM and Xerox earned superior returns over longer periods of time due to technological edge had over their rivals. Microsoft - the international giant in electronics rules the world. Sony corporation in sound gadgets. At national level Laxmi Machine Works, Dr. Reddys Laboratory, Venkteswar Hatcheries hence, excelled their competitors because of technological superiority.

6. **Government Policy :** A government policy which protects a firm from invasion by its competitors enables it to earn superior returns. The government policies that create entry barriers may be absolute or partial. These can be : (a) restrictive licensing (b) import restrictions (c) high tariffs (d) environmental controls (e) special tax concessions and rebates.

   For many years majority of industrial firms were granted protection under the umbrella of encouraging home industrial units instead of exposing them to competition. Of late, the process of globalisation, liberalisation and privatisation has exposed these local players to foreign or international players thus making them to come down from seventh heaven to ground realities of hell.

8. ON BEING AN ENTREPRENEUR

Who is an entrepreneur ? What are his traits that lead to success ? PLEASE REFER, THE APPENDIX GIVEN. As a matter of passing reference it suffices to say that a successful entrepreneur is one who has the qualities or traits of : (1) Willingness to make sacrifices (2) Strong leadership qualities (3) Impeccable decisiveness (4) Self-confidence in the project as it is his brain child (5) Strong marketing orientation - as production is one thing and marketing is another (6) Strong ego coupled with will power.

APPENDIX - 1

WHAT IS ENTREPRENEURSHIP?

For every person who has a head and heart, there are three options before him or her to keep him or her busy and contribute to his or her development and economic development of his or her country at large. The three alternatives are **Wage-Employment-Self-Employment** and the **Employer.** With the fast growing population, in spite of jobs created, the people are running after jobs. There is growing competition and, therefore, it is very difficult to tap the first two options namely, getting employed and self-employed. The best option is the last namely, accepting the challenge of becoming an 'employer' than being an 'employee'. Before we know about the last option, let us know little about the first two options.

1. **Getting Employed :** Getting employed is the most common practice. Under this option, a person works for a wage or salary under an employer may be an individual or a firm. The activities can be manufacturing, trading or other related services. Under this system, there is definite relationship between the employer and the employee. The employer expects his employee to be devoted, regular, punctual and efficient in his line of activity. For his services, the employee gets his monthly wage or salary and other benefits; the employee is to work under the guidance and control of owner or employer. Though he has a freedom of taking decisions, he is responsible for implementing the decisions. Such wage-employment option has certain merits such as jobs security, chances of moving up by promotion to higher posts. However, his employment is of routine type, repetition and he finds it boring. Hardly, he has chance to use his innovative skills and abilities, liberty of action and sense of achievement. Therefore, he may not have job-satisfaction. Again, vast majority of people are in the race and it is very difficult to get the gainful jobs, matching jobs particularly in countries like India where people are running after jobs both educated and uneducated, skilled, semi-skilled and unskilled.

2. **Self-employment :** The Second option for any individual is that of self-employment. Self-employment is to create employment for oneself. A self- employed person makes use of his educational background, own money and undertakes any line

of activity, may be manufacturing, trading or service sector. As a self-employed person, he can be a manufacturer, producer, trader, or rendering services in different capacities. A pan-shop, a tea-shop, highway-dabhas, poultry-products, fruit-vending, barbers' saloon, cobbler's rapair shop, tailor's centre, a loundry, greengrocer, electric and electronic machanic's unit, milk-bar, fast-food centre, florists point, garages and what not? There are countless opportunities for self-employment. Most of the uneducated and educated youths are attracted to this line. Again, professionally and technically qualified persons do not like to work under somebody. They like full freedom and, therefore, they start their own service centres. Take the case of journalists, doctors, engineers, teachers, chartered accountants, cost accountants and management consultants. Self-employment gives scope for full exploitation of ones own personal skills and abilities. He is master of his own. Whatever he earns is his own - which motivates him to the fullest extent. It is quite possible that these self-employed persons might succeed in employing others a assistants but is not a necessity. This is a mid-way or golden path that many gifted and qualified persons who choose and succeed.

3. **Entrepreneur-the Employer** : The term 'entrepreneur' **'intrepreneur'** and **'entrepreneurship'** have attracted the attention of all in the context of economic growth in a rapidly changing socio-economic and socio-cultural climates, particularly in industry both in developed and developing countries 'Entrepreneur' and 'entrepreneurship' are economic terms.

WHO IS ENTREPRENEUR?

The term 'entrepreneur' is French word which is associated with the entrepreneurial functions. That French word is a verb namely, 'entreprendre' which means to 'undertake'. An entrepreneur is a person who brings us overall change through innovation for the maximum social good. He is a person handling ventures spun-off from a large business such as a company created as a subsidiary to produce the products of a new invention. On the other hand, 'intrepreneur' is a person who is able to innovate and make lasting changes for the betterment of the business organisation.

STANDARD DEFINITIONS

- **Mr. Richard Cantillon** defines the term 'entrepreneur' :

  "a person who purchases factors/services at certain price with a view to selling the product at certain prices in the future."

- **Professor and economist Mr. Schumpeter :**

  "any person who is innovative for profit earned by an entrepreneur is a reward for innovativeness."

- **Dr. Peter Drucker :**

  "Innovation is the scientific tool of entrepreneurs the means by which they exploit changes as an opportunity for a different business or a different service."

It is capable of being presented as a discipline, capable of being learnt and practised. Entrepreneurs smell and search purposefully for the sources of innovation, the changes and their symptoms that indicate opportunities for successful innovation and they need to know and to apply the principle of successful innovation.

Thus, an entrepreneur is a person who is responsible for setting up a business or an entreprise. He is one who has the innovative skill for innovation and who looks for high achievements. He is an agent of change and works for the good of people. He puts up a new greenfield projects that create wealth, generate employment opportunities and bring the growth and prosperity in other sectors.

WHAT IS ENTREPRENEURSHIP?

In broad sense, the word entrepreneurship is the "process of starting and running one's" own business. It has the roots in French language which stands for the word to "undertake." Today, however, it is known by other words as "adventurism", "risk-taking", "thrill-seeking" "innovating" and the like.

STANDARD DEFINITIONS

- **Professor B. Higgins :**

  "Entrepreneurship" is *"the function of seeking investment and production opportunities, organising an enterprise to undertake a new product, process of raising capital, having labour, arranging the supply of raw materials, finding site, introducing a new technique and commodities, discovering new sources of raw materials and selecting top managers for day-to-day operations of the enterprise."*

- **John Kao and Howard Stevenson :**

  "Entrepreneurship is the attempt to create value through recognition of business opportunities, the management of risk-taking appropriate to the opportunity, and through the communication and management skills to mobilise human, financial and natural resources necessary to bring a project to function."

- **William Diamond :**

  "Entrepreneurship is equivalent of enterprise which involves the willingness to assume risk in undertaking an economic activity particularly a new one. It may involve an innovation but not necessarily so. It always involves risk-taking and decision-making, although neither risk nor decision-making may be of great significance."

- **Professor A.H. Cole of Cambridge :**

  "Entrepreneurship is the purposeful activity of an individual or a group of associated individuals, undertaken to initiate, maintain or aggrandise profit by production or distribution of economic goods and services".

In a nutshell, entrepreneurship is the creative and innovative response of the environment and an ability to recognise, initiate and exploit economic opportunity.

At this stage, it is worth emphasising that the words 'entrepreneur'and 'entrepreneurship' are inseparable and they represent the same as 'Scholar' and 'Scholarship' 'teacher' and 'teachership', 'salesman' and 'salesmanship' 'fellow' and 'fellowship'. The latter part speaks of function of the former. For our discussion, we do not have any difference in the words 'entrepreneur' and 'entrepreneurship' and are used in the same sense. However, there is lot of misunderstanding of the word 'entrepreneur'. Some people call these entrepreneurs as 'greedy' 'power-hungry' and are 'born'. These are not correct. They are not necessarily 'greedy', 'power-hungry' and are 'born' because, the main concept of entrepreneur is 'innovation' and 'risk-bearing'.

WHAT IS INTRAPRENEURSHIP?

Intrapreneurer is entrepreneur of special attribute. The word 'intrapreneur' was coined in America, during 1970s where the senior executives left the big corporations in which they were working. They left the job because, the top management of these corporations were not encouraging the innovative ideas of these executives. These enterprising executives after leaving the jobs, started their own enterprises. Because of their innovative approach, they succeeded much more effectively than those corporation which they worked. Infact, these intrapreneurs were threat to the very survival and success of those big corporations. As a result, those corporations were forced to think on the lines as to how retain these employees of innovative approach. They wanted to stop the flight of these brilliant people. In 1976 **Mr. Norman Macras** wrote in London Economist that successful big corporations should become **"Confederations of Entrepreneurs".** The idea was promising and the opportunities awaiting entrepreneurs inside large corporations could be tremendous provided it could be made workable. **Mr. Gifford Pinchot III** an eminent American expert wrote his famous book **Intrepreneuring** in 1985 and used the term 'intrapreneurs' to describe the persons who resigned from their well-paid executive positions to the positions to launch their own ventures.

Infact, **Mr. Gifford Pinchot III** suggested that well-established companies should learn to make use of the entrepreneurial talent within to avoid the possible stagnation and decay or decline. It is these intrapreneurs who would introduce new production, service and processes which enable the company to grow and succeed in a changing environment. What was, therefore, needed was a system and an organisation culture within a large organisation that allows the executives to operate like entrepreneurs. These persons driven not by monetary gains but a deep desire of personal achievement. Hence, the companies should provide such extra-ordinary executives with adequate financial resources and the autonomy essential for development and application of their rich fund of knowledge or the ideas that they have for sale. **Mr. Gifford Pinchot III** suggests the creation of a system which provides the identified executives a status within the corporation similar to that of an entrepreneur in the society. These **"intra-corporate entrepreneurs"** are "intrapreneurs".

The idea of "intrapreneurship" calls that the managers inside the company should be encouraged to be entrepreneurs within the firm rather than moving out. For an entrepreneur to survive in an organisation, he or she needs to be sponsored and given adequate freedom to implement his or her ideas failing which the entrepreneurial "spark plug" will not ignite at all. The entrepreneur who starts his own business generally does so because, he has his high aspiration to run his or her own brain child and does not like to have somebody coming in a way. In other words, he or she wants to a "free-bird" to enjoy the freedom and achieve the goals of "esteem" or self- actualisation - the greatest achievement where others do not want to reach this zenith point of dizzy heights.

Good many corporations in America started practising the intrepreneur concept as suggested by **Mr. Gifford Pinchot-III.** Even well before Pinchot's suggestion, International Business Machines (IBM) the corporate giant adopted the concept of Independent Business Units (IBUs). Each unit was promoted and run by an executive intrapreneur as if he was an independent entrepreneur. More than a dozen of such units are now working in this company. The best known of these units is the one manufacturing and marketing personal computers with a sales turnover of more than 5 billion dollars. Similarly, General Motors (GM) launched Satwin Corporation as an entrepreneurial subsidiary. This programe is aimed at promoting new ways of making, selling and servicing and is headed by the executives of the parent company. Other corporations of America are American Corporations — that is, Dupont, AT and T, Texas Instruments, Data general are also providing intrapreneurs in this own way. American Telephone and Telegraph Company (AT and T) has set up the Epicentre for entrepreneurial venture. Commenting on this trend,

Jack Welsch, Chairman of the General Electrical Company of U.S.A. observes

"One Key to alluring entrepreneurial managers to flourish to give them a sense of ownership of their entrepreneurial managers as if they were small autonomous business, create an environment that exalts risktaking. We have got take the puritive aspects out of the management process in order to get enough bubbing up of idea. Such bubbing up is the only way for us to win."

What these large bureaucratic companies have is a strong and healthy risktaking culture where risk taking managers are assured of security and rewards. As entrepreneurial culture requires constant generation of new ideas, it needs managers to listen and respond to new ideas and willing to risk the future, a system that rewards managers who have generated and experimented with good ideas.

NATURE AND CHARACTERISTICS OF ENTREPRENEURSHIP

An entrepreneur, by his nature, possesses special qualities or traits, aptitudes, competencies and skills. The studies, conducted all over the world, reveal that an entrepreneurship has a definite nature which is clear by the characteristics. These are outlined as under :

1. **He is Achievement Oriented :** Any person worth calling as an entrepreneur is highly achievement-oriented. He is ambitious and initiates action to achieve the goals within the best parameters of performance. He sets his standards of excellence. He knows his weaknesses and strengths. As soon as he achieves one goal, he goes to another much higher goal.

2. **He is the Symbol of Imagination and Superior Talents :** Entrepreneur has imagination. He is a rich source of creative imagination. To achieve the set goals, he uses his imagination matched with intuition. He follows unconventional methods and techniques to reach the goals. He welcomes new ideas as keen observer. He demonstrates superior talent to identify and exploit the opportunities. In fact, he takes a fair chance to convert the threats and obstacles into favourable situations and opportunities.

3. **He is Optimistic, Flexible and Mobile :** Entrepreneur is always optimistic and positive. His failures do not discourage and dampen him. He takes these as bases of improving upon. He is always flexible in his approach; as a open minded person, he adjusts to any circumstances but at any rate he wants to achieve. He is a mobile person in terms of ideas, attitude and actions. He is a pace-setter or trend-setter.

4. He **is not the** 'Boss' **but the 'Manager' :** Whatever an entrepreneur does, he does as a manager but not as a boss. That is, he seeks advice from others in planning and implementation, if need there be. Feedback is the backbone of his way of managing. He learns from his own experience. He prefers outstanding performance to rich rewards as he knows rewards are the pay-off for the performance. Data feed-back and action course are matching.

5. **He has Interpersonal Skills :** Owning and managing an enterprise is not a joke. When he manages, he plans, organises, directs, coordinates, motivates, and controls his resources particularly manpower. Today, management is management people and not material, money, machines, markets. In planning and implementing, he believes in participative type of management. He is to get the work done through others by understanding the people who are his colleagues and juniors. He is a problem-solver and he is not discouraged by a problem. Any problem, he welcomes, studies its dimensions and gives solutions in a smiling way as he has the knack of playing with problems.

6. **He is a Risk-taker :** Business is full of inherent risks. He takes moderate risks, well calculated, unlike the gamblers who take a blind chance or believe in luck. He never takes high risks. Moderate risks taken with courage, increase the chances to win the game of business, surely. He does not believe in **'luck'** or divine happenings in his favour as he is known for tremendous self-confidence and not overconfidence. He attributes the success or failure to himself alone. It is because, finally he is the decision-maker though he might consult others. He has the values of freedom and ownership, he plans soundly and acts smartly.

7. **He is Industrious :** Entrepreneur is preoccupied with number of business activitives. Hardwork adds shine to the gold of intelligence or his mental capacity. There is no substitute for hardwork. The work of entrepreneur is such that he is the focal point. He acts as the hub of entire business enterprise occupying the centre of the total nerve system. Industry and honesty coupled with integrity pay rich dividend. It is but natural that he has both physical and mental strength. He is the buffer or the shock-absorber of the shocks of business.

FUNCTIONS OF AN ENTREPRENEUR

An entrepreneur is holding the key position in the society and has a social responsibility. As a successful entrepreneur, he is supposed to perform at least nine functions as explained by the experts in the field of entrepreneurship development. These nine fine functions are :

1. **Function of Innovation :** Entrepreneurship is highly creative activitiy. He is basically an innovator who is always trying to bring in something new. It may be a new idea, new product, new service, a new method, a new source of raw-material, new manufacturing method, new way of financing, new way of marketing or a fine combination of these which has not been tried and exploited earlier. By nature, an entrepreneur foresees the potentially profitable opportunity and tries to exploit it. Innovation encompasses the major activity of problem solving. Entrepreneur is not merely an innovator but is one who assumes the risks. He is a keen observer and waiting for the opportunity to pounce upon it. He is working under the conditions of uncertainty and risks where decision-making is a tough job.

2. **Function of High Achievement :** He is **achievement-oriented** or **result-oriented**. Achievement-orientated is the motive or tendency to strike for success in situations involving an evaluation of one's performance in relation to some standard or excellence. Those people who run after high achievement are more likely to succeed as entrepreneurs. Entrepreneur's interest in profits is not an achievement. People with high achievement standards are not influenced by monetary rewards as compared to the people with low achievement. The achievement motive is, by assumption, a relatively stable and enduring feature of an entrepreneur; those

persons who have high level performance do not believe in luck or divine forces. Those are ready to take well calculated risks, they are engaged in continuous struggle to achieve more and more. This kind of behaviour of struggle for success is called as **A Type Behaviour** by psychologists.

3. **Function of Organisation Building :** Entrepreneur has the special skill to build an ideal and suitable organisation. The ability to build an organisation is highly critical skill that is needed for an industrial development. This skill speaks of an ability to 'multiply oneself' by effective delegation of duties. In that sense, the entrepreneur is not only innovative but an **'Organisation builder'** or an architect who harnesses the new ideas to build the relations and structure that works for the longest time. Really, creating a new organisation is innovation, as it marks the renewal skill which facilitates the economic and effective use of resources of all kinds. The absence of this skill, the innovations fail to stimulate economic development.

4. **Function of Group Solidarity :** The entrepreneur acts as a model for his juniors or successors. Experts are of the opinion that entrepreneurial characteristics are found in clusters which may qualify themselves as entrepreneurial groups. Entrepreneurial activities are generated by a particular and peculiar family background, experience as a member of a certain group and as a reflection of general values. This is proved by **Mr. Young's** theory of change. Accordingly, a group becomes reaction when there is a coincidence of three conditions namely, when a group experiences low status recognition, when desired of access to important social networks and when the group has better institutional resources than other groups in the society at the same level. We also see in the family of entrepreneurs or for that matter in families of other sections of the society, the earlier generation achievement is attempted to cross and achieve higher targets. That family, social-groups, reference-groups and general values shape up the probable entrepreneurs or entrepreneurs-in making.

5. **Function of Leadership Skills :** Leadership abilities and skills in directing the enterprise are important factors in manager at effectiveness. Lead is to guide, direct, supervise, integrate and energise the efforts of others towards a common goal. It also means to excel or to outstand. A leader is one who influences the behaviour of others in any organised activity. Leadership is the relationship in which one person, the leader influences others to work together willingly on related tasks to attain that one which the leader desires. Entrepreneur, as a leader, should lead the team and he should possess the competence which can be interpersonal and administrative. Interpersonal competence deals with the ability to relate, treat people in considerate and effective way. On the other hand, administrative competence is the ability to achieve organisational goals within the frame-work set.

6. **Function of Linking the Missing Gaps** : One of the challenging tasks of new or innovative entrepreneurship is to fill in the gap or make up the possible deficiencies or lacunae which exist. There may be gaps of all kinds-knowledge about production, marketing, financing and personnel. A true entrepreneur is one who identifies all these gaps and fills ; function of inputs to get expected output in terms of lowest cost, highest quality, and adeqaute quantity. An able entrepreneur is measured in terms of inputs, completing capacity and providing the positive motivational binding. These missing links act as blockades in goal attainment and smooth sailing.

7. **Function of Status Withdrawal** : Change is certain in this uncertain world of business. Entrepreneur is a creative personality who solves the problems in an innovative way. The reaction that is projected by entrepreneur to sudden change or withdrawal of a given status or stand is very significant. It is because, if he is not able to adopt and adapt to the changes, he is not an entrepreneur of class. He is involved by the sudden changes of any kind. He should withstand the storm like a rock. These changes may be within the family bonds, within the close groups, within the industry or within the environment. Status withdrawal means change in the existing setup under which he is working.

8. **Function of Socio-economic and Political Structure** : Experts in the field of entrepreneurial argue that marginality is not going to generate entrepreneurship where additional factors are at constant work. That is, the entrepreneurs are not evenly distributed in the entire population. It is because, minorities in terms of religion, ethnicity, migration, displaced elites, fair sex, all have provided most of the entrepreneurial talent. However, all the minorities are not significant sources of entrepreneurship. The supply of entrepreneurship depends on three structures found in common namely, limitation structure, demand structure, opportunity structure and the actual incidence of entrepreneurs is due to inadequate or incorrect perceptions of various structures. One thing is sure that entrepreneurship depends on specific combination of circumstances which are difficult to create and much easier to destory.

9. **Function of Religious Belief** : Experts like **Max Weber** analysed religion and its impact on enterprising culture. He says that the spirit of capitalism is a set of attitudes towards the acquisition of money and the activities involved in it. **Mr. Max Weber** has also distinguished between the **"spirit of capitalism"** and "spirit of adventure". The spirit of capitalism is subject of strict discipline which is incompatible with giving freedom to impulse. This spirit of capitalism can be generated only when mental attitude in the society is favourable to capitalism. According to **Max Weber,** it is the "Protestantethics" that provides this mental attitude while Hinduism lacks such an attitude. Theory of **Max Weber** suited the

colonial rulers who wanted to encourage European entrepreneurship in India. However, the researchers criticised his theory as Indian situation for that matter other colonies have unique situations and spirits. Indian Hinduism is so strong that it is a single system, Indians have value system based on **'Hindutva'** and these values were not totally vanished by external forces because, like other religions, Hinduism is not against the spirits of capitalism and adventure.

RISKS AND REWARDS OF SELF-DEVELOPMENT

'Self-development' or 'self-employment development' is to create employment for one self. Self-employed person owns and manages his own line of activity or business. It may be trading, manufacturing or both concerned with product or service. Such self-employed is the supreme judge of his business affairs where he provides his own capital out of savings, loans from friends and relatives or institutions and takes sound decisions and implements at his own risk and hence, he is to enjoy the fruits, be it sweet or bitter. Self-employed person has the full freedom. The word entrepreneurship is very often used as a broad definition for the proces of starting and running one's own business. The term 'entrepreneur' is increasingly being reserved for the type of persons who is highly determined, confident, creative, market oriented, capable of smelling the opportunity and a great visionary to translate dream into a reality. Though these are called as reckless-risk- takers, they do take well calculated risks as there is relation between risk and reward. An entrepreneur is one who has thrill in starting a business and building it. Such persons are unique and valuable assets of an economy.

That is why, entrepreneurship development is emphasized in India and in other such countries. Government of India has undertaken specially designed **EDPs- (Entrepreneurial Development Programmes)** because of their importance in meeting the socio-economic needs. These, are :

(1) To bring about increase in national income.

(2) To make possible, balanced regional development.

(3) To decentralise economic power.

(4) To reinvest the profits which is called as take financing or ploughing back of profits.

(5) To solve unemployment and under-employment problems.

(6) To harvest the vigour of youth.

(7) To give woman a special and deserving place.

As a part of programme of self-employment and entrepreneurial development, special attention is given to small enterprises. Small enterprises are more suitable for self-employment and entrepreneurial development because of certain specific reasons. These supporting reasons are :

(1) They are labour intensive.

(2) They contribute towards exports to the tune of 40 per cent.

(3) They have higher per cent output of capital invested and per unit of energy used. That is, both capital and energy are best exploited.

(4) Ploughing back ot profits to gear up national production.

(5) They are highly flexible and innovative than large firms.

(6) They reduce economic and regional disparities and foster social stability and dispersal of economic power.

(7) They enter local markets in solving problems of new and under employment.

(8) They are environment friendly.

(9) They help us harnessing the youth vigour.

(10) They support large and medium units.

Today, small enterprises or small business is a big business which acts as a driving force for national growth because, they create more jobs, unemployed and under-employed are self-employed, allow creativity and flexibility, make persons to develop an ability to identify and exploit the business opportunity, provide full scope for nationalism, local ownership and control rather than by multinationals, possibility of greater economical and political stability as self-ownership is key of productivity, matching to local environment and culture exploiting local inputs, they are on frontiers of new and innovative technologies, migration is reduced, improve life-style of socially abandoned persons, it is possible to preserve the cultural values and personal profit, triggers creativity and initiative to develop new ventures and opportunities.

Thus, a country can create entrepreneurs and self-employed through the process of education. Country should plan for developing the persons who come forward to accept free thinking, willing to take risks, capable of identifying and developing gainful opportunities particularly within the borders of their skills or discipline. Only such persons will accept change and change for the better.

Let us, now take stock of pros and cons on risks and rewards associated with small enterprises or business or self-employment efforts :

RISKS INVOLVED

1. **One man show :** Self-employment attempt is unique where you have to sail your ship of business venture all alone. No body is there equal to you. You are the supreme judge pertaining to all business events good or bad.

2. **All decisions are yours :** As an entrepreneur a self-employment and self-employment attempt, all the decisions in various aspects of business are to be taken by you and you are responsible for the results. You have to accept both profits and losses single handy.

3. **Danger of losing confidence :** Generally, a person who behaves in self-employment and self-development has tremendous self- confidence. However, at times the business circumstances, particularly external, are beyond your control. The deadly developments might dampen your spirit of adventurism and you may lose self-confidence, a sure sign of withdrawal.

4. **Hard work is a must :** Unlike an employed person, self-employed has no fixed hours of work say 8 hours with standard breaks for lunch, tea and rest. The word business means 'business' which takes his long hours of time. There are cases where these self-employed people have worked in the range of 12 hours to 16 hours a day with limited number of holidays. As alone, you cannot run away from business and business house.

5. **Impact on family and social life :** Though you are all alone in your business, you have a family life and being a member of community or society, you have social life. Family members expect you not only to support them with decent earnings, they want your company, contribution, love and affection. Even society expects you to respect. Your schedule is so tight that it may not be possible for you to meet family and social needs in full.

6. **There may not be work satisfaction :** First of all, there is no work security. You are not secured. Any happening in your life - illness, death, disability, incapacity make your work unsecured. Always you feel unsecured. Added to that, you may not be happy with the work or business that you are doing as compared to others or you might feel that this is not your line where you are a misfit or a line that you have chosen and working and might have satisfaction though it is paying in monetary terms.

7. **You have to be very flexible :** As a self-employed person doing/working in a particular line of business, you are expected to be highly flexible and not rigid that dilutes and compromises your set of principles, ideology, thinking and acting. You are a tight-rope dancer where balancing at any rate and cost is a must. A person who is not adjustable to the changing tunes and currents will sink and die. As a wiseman, he is to move along with the current to be successful in business life. This needs a great deal of sacrifice which you may not like.

8. **Danger of depression :** Business is a game and you are player. However, active and hard working you are, always you are not a winner. Along with success one should accept defeat or loss. It is common in venturing. However, the extent of loss might be so great that you get depressed and not left with any potential to continue further. Again, the working capacity goes on diminishing with the passage of time, as you are getting old. What is shocking is your family has to face the shock and be prepared to accept poor life-style which is very difficult.

9. **You may not become master :** Though you have ventured a line of activity with the fond hope of becoming a master in the field, always it is not possible. Success depends upon both internal and external factors; you may not reach goal of achieving something unique because, you have your own strengths and weaknesses. In case the personality strengths and weakness are not matching to your line of business strengths and the weaknesses, such case of misfit, mismatch, you may not to be a master in field leading to so many psychological and physical problems and effects.

REWARDS THAT FOLLOW

Self-development through self-employment has its plus points also. Another name for business is risk-bearing and handling. Where risks are there, rewards follow. There is balance between risks and rewards, In other words, greater the risk more will be the reward; both monetary and psychological. The rewards associated with self-employment are :

1. **You are the master :** As a self-employed person, he is independent. He is not depending on anybody or anybody's mercy. He is not to salute anybody as is the case with employed person who has his boss or higher authority. Here, he is the boss, owner, manager and aboved all employer too. This is the greatest satisfaction that he is not controlled by others. He is king of his own kingdom of business. He reigns supreme. As a owner, he can control his activities and expects his business to move it in a direction and at a pace he likes.

2. **You are the decision-maker :** As a owner, manager he is to take each and every decision on his own without interference of anybody. This gives him the golden opportunity to develop self- confidence. What he thinks is right. As an entrepreneur, he is exposed to variety of situations and he develops a critical bent of mind to take sound and timely decisions. He has the opportunity of making use of his creative ideas, methods to get the best results. He has fair chance of experimentation.

3. **All profits are yours :** Whenever a person wishes to enter any line, he has a positive attitude of winning. By creative thinking and hard work, he strives hard to make his business unit to yield a profit. The risk-reward formula makes him to put up his best because whatever he earns as a surplus, he is the only person to enjoy. Nobody is there at any level to share it. This prompts him to be alert, keen observer and diplomat to exploit the situation. Monetary gain is the geatest motivating factor.

4. **Job satisfaction :** Most of the self-employed persons have chosen this line not only for monetary rewards but to get a kind of satisfaction or sense of achievement. Job-satisfaction is a kind of relation that exists, between the person and the job where he has the satisfaction as he becomes one with the job or assignment. It gives an opportunity as a challenge, and thrill adventurism. His position is like a motor-cyclist or race-car driver where surrounding risks are there along with thrill and monetary

rewards. Recently we see adventure games, popularly called as 'X' games where thrillable achievements are the motivating factors.

5. **Community status :** Self-employment opportunities if exploited properly are sure to give not only job satisfaction but good and attractive monetary rewards. He makes his life and fortune that bring his name, fame, popularity and above all a social standing or status. For a real entrepreneur, monetary gains are not that important. What he is interested is that he is occupied by the society as an achiever-a pace setter an uncommon personality altogether different from others. He stands out in his community or society as a model to whom others copy. This success makes others to follow his line.

6. **Quality of life :** Self-employment gives full scope for self- development of overall personality. He is always experimenting, as he is creative and not very happy over what he has already achieved. It is beacuse, the best he has achieved can be improved upon. He is at constant hard-work to do it in a better and easy way, commercial way, effective way that gives him scope for facing variety of situations that make him to gain experience in multiple job functions. All his achievement in each field leads to a good living and life. He turns prosperous and others also.

7. **Involvement of family :** As a strict self-employed person, he cannot do full justice to his family life. The reason is simple that he is married to his business venture so much so that his wife, children, relatives and family members hate him as he cannot involve in family expectations or aspirations other than money. As an achiever, his goal is to achieve. However, he can avoid that and add spice to his personal and business life by encouraging his family members say wife, son, brother to assist him so that his business and family relations and commitments are fulfilled.

8. **You are the agent of economic development :** The greatest reward perhaps, is the role that he plays namely, the agent of economic development. By starting small venture developing at and developing himself, he uses the resources of society as inputs and responsible for bringing out products and services useful to the society. He earns, makes others to earn, ploughs back his profits and utilises the savings of others and forms capital which is to bring further economic development. Thus, he acts as catalytic agent of economic prosperity and progress for self and others.

9. **Not a burden to the state :** In a sense, nobody is a burden to the state to which he belongs or a country to that effect. What is happening in all under-developed countries is that jobs are few though governments are committed to create more and more jobs. Really, more jobs are created through rational process of planning. However, the persons qualified and unqualified are more in supply than jobs created. Most of the educated youth are taking degrees and diplomas and they take these degrees and diplomas as the passport to job entry. Every one is joining the rat-race where a few people succeed. If these youths go in for self-employment schemes, and

self-development opportunities, they are reducing the pressure on economy, their families and community and so on. It is in this sense, that an entrepreneur is not a burden as he is trying to be self-made and independent hankering to prove his ability.

CHAPTER BASED QUESTIONS

A. WRITE SHORT NOTES ON

1. Entrepreneur
2. Project Rating Index
3. Positive Net Present Value
4. Preliminary Screening
5. Corporate Appraisal
6. Scouting for Project Ideas
7. Monitoring of Environment
8. Creativity
9. Sources of business ideas
10. Brain storming
11. Extensive travelling and reading
12. Fad recognition
13. Trend recognition
14. Personal constraints
15. SWOT analysis.

B. SHORT ANSWER QUESTIONS

1. What are business opportunities?
2. What is generation of ideas?
3. What is screening of business ideas?
4. What is monitoring of environment?
5. What is corporate appraisal?
6. What is scouting for project ideas?
7. What is project rating index?
8. What is positive net present value?
9. What is SWOT analysis?
10. What is brain-storming?

C. ESSAY TYPE QUESTIONS

1. What is a business opportunity? How is business opportunity converted into a project idea?
2. What do you mean by generating and screening of business ideas? What steps are involved in it?
3. What do you mean by monitoring of environment? What does it cover in its fold?

4. What is corporate appraisal? What aspects of corporation or company are taken into account?
5. What is scouting for project ideas? What suggestions have been made by experts in this regard?
6. What is project rating index? How is it constructed? What does it indicate?
7. What is net present value? What are sources of positive net present values?
8. Who is an entrepreneur? What are his qualities and traits?
9. What do you mean by need recognition-Fad recognition-Trend recognition?
10. "The ideas that flash are like rough diamonds which are converted into diamonds that shine by idea generating and screening process". Explain.

******

Chapter 5

PROJECT FEASIBILITY STUDIES - PART-1

- WHAT IS A FEASIBILITY STUDY?
- SCOPE OR SPAN OF TECHNICAL FEASIBILITY
- POINTS PERTAINING TO MANUFACTURING TECHNOLOGY
- THE NEED FOR CONSIDERING ALTERNATIVES
- CAPTER BASED QUESTIONS

BACKDROP

Once we complete the market and demand analysis, there is need for further suitability of the project as to whether it is feasible or viable in other dimensions so that the project idea is put to acid test of cold facts before it is accepted for formulation and implementation. It is because, wrongly assessed project proposals might appear quite good at early stage and may be, tempted to waste scarcely available resources of the society. Any hurry in doing so is repenting at leisure. Therefore, there is need for feasibility studies which are Technical feasibility, Financial feasibility, Economic feasibility and Managerial feasibility. In addition, certain analyses are to be conducted. In this chapter an attempt is made to study in detail two feasibility studies namely, technical and financial. Rest of the studies will be discussed in ensuring chapters at relevant point discussion. The Chapter ends with Chapter Based Questions

WHAT IS A FEASIBILITY STUDY?

"Feasibility study" is the process of investigating a problem and developing a solution in depth to determine it's economic viability and worth of development. Project feasibility is a test where prima-facie viability of the investment is evaluated.

This evaluation is based on secondary but comprehensive data. There are several possible perspectives about feasibility stage as to what it entails. When does it take place and which parties are involved ? The initial investigations by users is really an "preliminary feasibility" study. If the users decide to pursue further the idea, they solicit alternatives for solutions from one or more contractors. Each competing contractor performs his own internal feasibility study to assess the merit of the solicitation and evaluate its capability for submitting a winning proposal and getting or snatching a profitable contract with the user. The purpose of the user's solicitation which is called as Request For Proposal-RFB or Invitation to Bid-IB-might be to find a contractor to perform the feasibility study, in which case the feasibility study stage begins only after a contractor in selected. Alternatively, the process that a contractor follows in responding to the RFP may itself be considered a feasibility study.

The specifics or specifications of the feasibility study stage include the user requesting proposals for solutions, contractors doing feasibility studies and preparing proposals, the user evaluating the proposal, and joint user-contractor negotiations for a project contract. This process of acquiring outside services through solicitation and evaluating proposals and establishing a contractual agreement is a part of process known as "procurement management", which includes monitoring of project work for conformance to the contract and closing out the contract later. Because feasibility study is usually a time consuming exercise that requires expertise, the user typically chooses to bring in a contractor. Sometimes, the contractor is brought in as early as the initial investigation. The user notifies one or more contractors - internal or external -by sending them a document called "Request For Proposal" -RFP -a request for quotation or invitation to bid. The dual purpose of RFP is to outline the users idea - problem or a need - and solicit suggestions -proposals. For solutions -with an intent of awarding a contract for the best one. RFP are sent to companies on the users bidders list. The user describes his problems, objectives and any requirements in the RFP. Contractors choosing to respond send proposals, and the user assesses and awards a contract to one of them to perform the work. The RFP must be clear, concise and complete if the user expects the proposals equally clear, concise and complete. Finally, the ability of contractors to develop good solutions, perfectly matching to fit the users needs will depend, in part, on their understanding of user's requirements. Similarly, the ability of the user to select between contractors will depend on the information the contractors provide.

Each competing contractor must determine if it is capable of preparing winning proposal and they should win it so as to perform the proposed work. The amount a contractor spends in preparing the proposals and the proposition of contract it wins significantly affect its company overhead because expenses for lost proposals must be charged to overheads. It is only in rare cases that winning contracts are reimbursed for their proposal expenses. The feasibility of winning and concluding a project depends on numerous factors such as -whether competitors have got a head start: whether the contractor has sufficient money, facilities and resources to invest in the project; whether performance on the project is likely to be good for or damaging to the reputation of contractors.

Some times, contractors respond to RFP knowing that they can not possibly win the project, doing just to maintain a relationship with the solicitor, remain on user's list or keep the field competitive. Sometimes, users sound RFP with no intent of ever signing with a contractor; they do it simply to gather ideas. Sometimes, proposals are submitted to potential users without RFP. When a project group believes that it has a system or solution to satisfy a need or solve a problem, the project manager works with his marketing department to identify perspective customers and then notifies them with an unsolicited proposal. Other times, the project manager identifies follow-up work related to a current project and submits an unsolicited proposal to the current customer.

DISTINCTION BETWEEN "PRE-FEASIBILITY STUDIES" AND "FEASIBILITY STUDIES"

One need not be carried away by the strong and wrong feeling that 'feasibility studies' are "feasibility studies" whether they are 'pre' – or 'Post'. There is vast difference between the "pre feasibility studies" and 'feasibility studies'. The distinction can be on at least seven grounds. These are outlined as under:

1. **MEANING :**
   "Pre-feasibility" studies are the studies undertaken by the business house prior to feasibility studies. These can be called as 'mini' or 'trial' feasibility studies. That is, it is the starting step in project planning. As opposed to these, "feasibility studies" are the

most complex types of tests which a project is to survive in the final analysis. It may so happen, that a project manager thinks the projects, on cursory approach, are good. However, how good they are based on the strongest and stringent tests of cold facts where a project is to withstand. Then only it is passed for further planning and implementation.

2. **OBJECTIVE INVOLVED :**

In case of "pre-feasibility" studies, the basic objective is to determine whether or not the project idea needs further investigation. As against this, in case of "feasibility studies" the aim is to determine the true, profitability of the project and decide to go ahead or not.

3. **THE SCOPE IT SPANS :**

Speaking from the scope or coverage, a "Pre feasibility" study reveals an overview of the projects proposal through pre-feasibility reports which may have to be silver tongued when ever called for. As opposed to this, the "feasibility documents" cover maximum of the project proposal to facilitate the decision-making of going ahead or not. It is the feasibility report of the project that acts as the base for cut-off point.

4. **THE TYPE OF RESEARCH INVOLVED :**

In case of "Pre-feasibility" studies a fine combination of the secondary and primary research methods is used. Mostly, secondary type of information is obtained and surveys are conducted through informal sources to get the information. Contrary to this, is case of "feasibility studies" all types of research methods are employed. Basically, primary research having formal and informal net works are flushed to obtain the full information an the project.

5. **THE TIME SPAN INVOLVED :**

In case of "Pre-feasibility" studies, as it is a trial attempt, relatively shorter duration efforts are put in. These efforts can range between three months to six months depend upon the type and size of the project. Contrary to this, in case of "feasibility studies" as collection of adequate, authentic, update information is the basic input and aim, it is a time consuming affair. The general span of time is twelve months to twenty four months depending on the nature of the proposed project.

6. **COSTS INVOLVED :**

In case of "Pre-feasibility" studies the cost involved in conducting pre-feasibility studies are one of the minimum. To be exact, the costs range between 0.25 per cent and 1.50 per cent of the total project cost. Contrary to this, the cost incurred in case of "feasibility studies" are really high as they project the true and full scope of the project studies. They generally range from 1.50 per cent to 3.00 per cent in case of small and medium projects and 0.25 to 1.50 per cent of the project costs of large projects. Note, eventhough the per cent cost is less in case of large projects, the amount incurred is essentially larger.

7. **THE ACCURACY OF THE INFORMATION :**

In fact, the accuracy of the information plays significant role in taking vital decisions in case of projects. However, in case of "pre-feasibility" studies, the degree of accuracy is comparatively lower which is to the tune of 60 to 70 per cent. As opposed to this, in case of "feasibility studies" much weightage is given to this point of accuracy. It is because accurate results are outcome of accurate information collected and analyzed. Hence, accuracy rate ranges between 85 per cent to 95 per cent or even more.

A. TECHNICAL FEASIBILITY

Technical feasibility or analysis encompasses the technical areas of project, namely, material inputs and utilities, manufacturing process or technology, product mix, plant capacity, location and site, machines and equipment, structures and civil-works, project charts and layouts, work schedule. Indepth analysis of these aspects paves the way for knowing where each project stands for, each has an alternative to select the better one or the best one. Thus, technical feasibility assesses the technical viability for coming to a conclusion as to whether it fulfils the expected norms. Each of these are considered in detail.

SCOPE OR SPAN OF TECHNICAL FEASIBILITY

As mentioned in the starting paragraph, technical analysis covers atleast nine points:

1. MATERIAL INPUTS AND UTILITIES

Technical analysis in this regard covers defining of the materials and utilities needed, specifying their properties in exact detail and setting up their supply programme. It should be noted that there is very close relationship between the study of materials and utilities and other dimensions of project formulation especially those concerned with location, technology and equipments. Material inputs and utilities are classified by experts into four broad categories as: (i) Raw-materials. (ii) Processed industrial materials and components. (iii) Auxiliary materials and factory supplied. (iv) Utilities.

(i) **Raw-materials :** Raw-materials which are semi-processed or processed can be further grouped into

(a) Agricultural products.

(b) Mineral products.

(c) Livestock and forest products.

(d) Marine products.

In analysing AGRICULTURAL PRODUCTS the priorities of parameters are quality, quantity, dependability of supply and potentiality. The answers to these questions must be sought. What is the present marketable surplus ? What is the present area under cultivation ? What is the yield per hectare? What is the likely increase in the area of cultivation ? What is the likely increase in yield per hectare ? In case of MINERAL PRODUCTS, the detailed information is to be collected as to. What are the maximum exploitable deposits ? What are their properties ? What is the exact location, spread, size and depth of deposits ? Extent of viability of open-cast and underground mining ? There is need for indepth verifiable information regarding the composition of ore, level of impurities, need for benefits and physical chemical and other properties. In case of LIVESTOCK and FOREST PRODUCTS, secondary sources of data on them do not provide a dependable basis for estimation. Therefore, a specific survey, in general, is to be obtained with emphasis on quantum and quality of these products. In case of MARINE PRODUCTS, scientific assessment of the potential availability of marine products and cost of gathering is difficult and costly. Extensive preliminary marine operations are a must for the feasibility study.

(ii) **Processed Industrial Materials and Components :** Processed industrial materials and components refer to base metals, semi-processed materials, manufactured parts, components and subassemblies. These form an important complex of inputs for wide variety of industries. To get authentic and sufficient information, answers of the following questions must be sought. What are their properties - physical -mechanical- chemical and electrical ? What amount or quantum the project needs ? What are the domestic sources ? What are foreign sources subject to limits laid down by Authorities ? Extent of dependability on supplies and suppliers ? What has been the price trend in the past ? What will be the future trend ?

(iii) **Auxiliary Materials and Factory Supplies :** Any manufacturing unit or project needs variety of auxiliary materials and factory supplies like chemicals, additives, packaging materials, paints, varnishes, oils, grease, cleaning materials, consumable stores in addition the first two categories of materials. Here, also the questions relating to quality, quantity, cost, dependability of supply are considered.

(iv) **Utilities :** Utilities stand for power, water, steam, fuel, gas which play a constructive role in converting raw-materials into end products. Correct assessment of these in terms of location, technology, plant capacity and the like is a must. These utilities turn critical, at times, and become limiting factor in achieving highest level of efficiency or lowest level of cost. Therefore, there is need for detailed input output analysis. That is to produce say 100 units or 1,000 units, what would be the quantum of input - its cost or availability ? What hurdles play significant role in this regard ? What measures help in augmenting the adequate, regular and economical supply ?

2. MANUFACTURING PROCESS/TECHNOLOGY

The methodology used in converting materials into final products in known as a technology. For manufacturing a product, alternative technologies are there. To manufacture steel either Open Hearth process or Bossemer process can be used that represents a technology. In making cement the possible processes are Wet or Dry. In making paper using bagasse as the input, the manufacturing company can use one of the three processes namely, Soda process, Simoin Cusi process or Kraft process. These technologies are always changing from good to better and from better to best. Even, what is today the best can be suppossed in case better than the best is made available. Research and development efforts make possible the best because, even the very best can be improved upon over a period of time.

POINTS PERTAINING TO MANUFACTURING TECHNOLOGY

Feasibility study, especially technical, is to focus its attention on the significant aspects of choice of technology, acquisition of technology and the appropriateness of the technology.

I. CHOICE OF TECHNOLOGY

The choice of technology or technical knowhow is influenced by good many variables of which the most important one are :

A. **Plant capacity :** There is close relationship between the plant capacity and manufacturing technology. In order to meet a given plant capacity requirement only a specific production technology may be viable.

B. **Major inputs :** Basic inputs play significant role in choosing a manufacturing technology. For instance, in manufacturing of cement the quality of lime stone decides whether the manufacturing unit should go in for 'Wet' or 'Dry' processing. In case of country like India, a technology based on indigenous inputs may be preferable to that of imported inputs because there is every uncertainty and risk of imports.

C. **Investment outlay and Production cost :** The impact of alternative technologies on investment expenditure and production cost should be carefully assessed over a period of time. It is because production cost and the technology are closely related in that the cost and quality is based on the technology and that is based on its cost.

D. **Proof of success :** The technology adopted must well be proven by its success for use by other units. That is, a latest technology may not be always the best. One which is tried, tested, and trusted by successful units in the line is more acceptable.

E. **The Product-mix :** Product-mix stands for the main products, co-products and by-products that are resulting by use of a particular technology. In other words, the technology must be judged in terms of the total product-mix generated by it including saleable by-products. It speaks of flexibility in product pattern and compliance with indigeneous requirements.

F. **Latest advancement :** The technology adopted is one which is the latest or one which is adaptable for updating easily with least cost and tune. It is because, no technology lasts longer as it becomes obsolete in near future. The losses arising out of obsolescence can be avoided or reduced in case the firm goes in for more enduring technology.

G. **Ease of absorption :** Technology, however, latest and effective, has no meaning unless it is easier to be absorbed by the company. Very often it so happens that high-level technology may be not easily percolating to the absorbing firm due to some reason or reasons. Genuine Products of India finalised the German technology being very effective and proven but failed because Indian firm did not have the calibre of operating on due to lack of trained employees.

II. ACQUIRING TECHNOLOGY

In case the technology is available openly, then the detailed information can be obtained even at the feasibility study stage. If the know-how is available with the owner, then this step-that is-evaluation of process, can altogether be eliminated. What would still be required is development of a comprehensive technology package which alone can define the technical configuration of the project and its battery limit conditions. If the know-how is not available with the owner, it has to be acquired from outside sources. The acquisition of technology from some other enterprise may be possible through (a) technology licensing (b) outright purchase (c) joint venture.

A. **Technology Licensing :** This is the most popular way out of acquiring technology. Under this arrangement, the technology licence gives the licencee the right to use the patented technology and get the concerned know how on a mutually agreed basis. The suppliers of technology generally provide a technology package which may consist of some components which are not essential. Therefore, it becomes essential to break the package into component parts such as technology, proper engineering services, supply of intermediate products, supply of equipment by the licensor, use of a trade name, among other things. Every effort should be made to acquire only the essential and matching components of the technology package. The contract for technology licensing should be carefully studied with all the care with regard to: 1. Definition of technology to be acquired. 2. Cost of technology licensing. 3. Guarantees provided by the licensor. 4. Duration of the technology licensing. 5. Purchase of intermediate products, components and other related inputs.

B. **Outright Purchase of Technology :** This method is in vogue in certain kinds of industries. This alternative is most appropriate when: 1. There is no possibility of significant improvement in technology in the foreseeable future. 2. There is hardly any need for technological support from the seller of the technology.

C. **Joint-Venture Arrangement :** This is also very popular method under which the supplier of the technology may participate technically as well as financially in the project. Financial participation is normally in the form of equity holding. Experts are of the opinion that financial participation is likely to strengthen the motivation of technology supplier to transfer improvements without hesitation.

III. APPROPRIATENESS OF TECHNOLOGY

The phrase "appropriate technology" stands for those methods of production or process of production which are most fitting to the local, economic, social, cultural and environmental conditions. The proponents of appropriate technology feel that the said technology should stand the test of criteria fulfillment. Evaluation is to be done in terms of the following questions. These pertinent questions are: 1. Whether the technology uses the local raw-materials ? 2. Whether the technology employs the services of local labour force ? 3. Whether the goods and services produced cater to the basic needs ? 4. Whether the technology protects and maintains the ecological balance ? 5. Whether the technology is in harmony with the social and cultural values of the area ?

3. PRODUCT-MIX :

Product-mix is one of the major components of marketing mix is so designed as to meet the requirements of target market or segment or segments of the entire market for the company's products and services. All other mixes namely price, place and promotion mix go in consonance in a congruous way in requirements of a product-mix. It goes without saying the product-mix is guided by market forces or requirements. In the production of most of the items, variations in size, quality, design are aimed at satisfying the broad range of consumers. For instance, a ready garment manufacturer of trousers and shirts will have a wide range of items of size and quality to suit individual differences in consumers both physical and mental. Wide range of sizes, patterns and quality play significant role in enabling to garment-maker to earn good profit through higher profitability. What is true of clothes is true of toiletories especially soaps. Thus, each company comes out with three colours, three sizes, fragrance variance, variation in inputs, packaging and promotion package. These varieties meet the requirements of poor, middle and rich class. The idea is to arrive at total maximum profit.

Hence, while planning the production facilities, good deal of flexibility accommodating the changing needs of product-mix is a must. Greater the flexibility in production facilities, greater are the chances of the firm to enrich its power to survive, grow and diversify in different situations. The degree of flexibility chosen is based on a universal and careful analysis of the additional investment requirements for enjoying varying degrees of flexibility.

4. PLANT CAPACITY

Plant capacity or production capacity signifies the volume or number of units that a plant can produce during a given period, may be per day, per month or per year. Thus, Toyota of Japan manufactures 20,000 automobiles per day out of which 700 land on American soil alone. According to experts "Plant capacity is defined in two ways namely, "feasible normal capacity" and "nominal maximum capacity". The feasible normal capacity stands for the capacity attainable under normal working conditions. This is established on the basis of installed capacity, technical conditions of the plant, normal stoppages, down-time for maintenance and tool changes, holidays and shift patterns. On the other hand, nominal maximum capacity is the capacity which is technically attainable and this normally corresponds to the installed capacity guaranteed by the supplier of the plant. Here, it is taken as the first concept for capacity analysis.

A. **Factors that govern the plant Capacity decision :** In case of industrial projects, especially in case of process type of industries, there is a certain minimum economic size determined by the technological factor. In case of cement manufacturing a minimum size is of 300 tons per day so as to use the "rotary kiln" method or technology, failing which the plant will have to utilise the "vertical shaft" method which is better suited for lesser quantities of production. In assembly line say calculator and computers, CAM technology is suited when the turn out is in thousands of units per day while MAM technology is acceptable for less than these number of units.

B. **Input constraints :** In case of developing countries input constraints are quite common as these are not sur plus economies but economies of shortages. There may be great potentials but not readily available. Thus, power supply may not be available to the extent needed; basic raw-materials may be in short supply, foreign exchange reserves may be insufficient to buy these inputs. These limiting factors deserve special attention that come in the way of normal attainment or target results.

C. **Cost of investment :** The relationship between capacity and investment cost is a very significant factor of consideration when the serious input constraints are not easily procurable. Generally, the investment cost per unit of capacity declines as the plant capacity increases. This relationship is expressed in the form of an equation as under:

$$C_1 = C_2 \left(\frac{Q_1}{Q_2} \right)^a$$

where C_1 = Derived cost for Q_1 units of capacity

C_2 = Known cost for Q_2 units of capacity

a = a factor reflecting capacity-cost, relationship and this is in the range of 0.2 and 0.9.

To illustrate, say D.K. Company's known investment cost for 10,000 units of capacity for the manufacture of a machine in textiles is Rs. 20,00,000. What will be the cost for 50,000 units of capacity, if the capacity-cost factor is 0.4.?

The derived investment cost for 50,000 units of capacity will be :

$$C_1 = \text{Rs. } 20{,}00{,}000 \times \left(\frac{50{,}000}{10{,}000}\right)^{0.6}$$

$$= \text{Rs. } 20{,}00{,}000 \times (5)^{06}$$

$$= \text{Rs. } 20{,}00{,}000 \times (3)$$

$$= \text{Rs. } 60{,}00{,}000$$

D. **Market conditions :** The expected plant capacity is influenced by the anticipated market for the product or service. It means that a plant of higher capacity is welcome, if the market for the product is likely to be very strong and enduring. Intelligence lies in starting with a plant with lower or small capacity when the market for product or service is uncertain and fluctuating. Even in case of first situation, it is better to start small with least initial capacity to cope up with the initial demand level and the capacity can be added with the sustained rise in the demand caused by growth of market.

E. **Internal resources of the unit :** The most significant internal resources are management and finance. These two have deep impact on firm's capacity decision. It means that the scale of operation is dictated by these two powerful resources. That is, one cannot go beyond these means that set limit on scale of operation.

F. **The Government Policy :** Government policy has great bearing on capacity level a firm is to operate. For a long time, in the past, Government of India's policy was to distribute the additional capacity to create in certain lines of industrial activities among the firm's irrespective of economics of scale. In recent years the things have changed where the concept of "minimum capacity" is followed. This has been true particularly with the exposure of economy to the competitive forces where privatisation, liberalisation, disinvestment and merger policies have been common for successful survival.

5. PLANT LOCATION AND SITE

After assessment of demand, size and input requirements, the next consideration is that of plant location and site. Plant location is a major and quite irrevocable managerial decision. Plant location means and includes three things namely, selection of a requisite region, credible community and suitable site.

Selection of a REGION is a broad decision. The planners take those factors that determine the most general area where the plant is to be located. That is, it demands collection of information of more general nature. Such information is now made available by the most authentic sources such as: 1. National Council of Applied Economic Research. 2. Ministry of Industrial Development. 3. Indian Federation of Chambers of Commerce. 4. Department of industry of each State. 5. Geological survey conducted by Geological Society of India. 6. Meterological and Topographic Society of India.

While selecting a particular region the following factors are given priority: 1. Abundant and quality availability of raw-materials. 2. Proximity to fuel and power. 3. Means of transport. 4. Market place. 5. Meterological conditions and topography.

Selection of a PARTICULAR COMMUNITY is the next step. That is once the entrepreneurs have selected the region of their choice, they are expected to go in for second round selection process and that is selection of a particular community or locality. The selection of a community or locality calls for rigorous factors like: 1. Quality and quantity of labour-force. 2. Existence of supplementary and complementary industrial units. 3. Banking and credit facilities. 4. Local taxes, rents, rates and insurance charges. 5. Water-supply in terms of adequacy, quantity and quality. 6. Momentum of an early start. 7. Personal factors. 8. Historical factors. 9. Political stability -peace and tranquility. 10. Extent of state assistance.

The final round selection is selection of space or SITE where industrial plant is going to be located. The important factors that decide the choice of suitable site are: 1. The price of the land. 2. The type of the choice. 3. Ease of waste disposal. 4. Potentiality of future expansion. 5. Existence of commercial services and amenities. 6. The health conditions prevailing at site and surrounding area. 7. Statutory restrictions. 8. Panorama and beauty of site. 9. People's attitude. 10. Existence of religious and social institutions.

Taking all these factors, the most advantageous location is that at which the cost of gathering material and fabricating it plus the cost of distributing the finished product to the consumer is the least.

6. MACHINERIES AND EQUIPMENT

It is the technology that determines the exact requirement of machineries and plant capacity. It is also influenced by the type of project. For a process industrial plants, say petro-chemical unit or pharmaceutical unit, the machineries and equipment required should be such that the various stages of manufacture are matched well. The choice of machines and equipment for other units of manufacturing is much wider as machines can perform the same functions with varying degrees of accuracy. For example, the configuration of machines required for manufacturing of refrigeration, aircoolers may be of various forms. To determine the kinds of machines and equipments required in case of manufacturing industrial plants, the following procedure is generally followed:(a) Estimate the likely levels of production over given period of time. (b) Define various machines and operations. (c) Calculate machine hours required for each type of operation. (d) Select machineries and equipment required for each function.

The equipments required for the project may be classified into seven categories such as: 1. Plant process equipment. 2. Mechanical equipment. 3. Electrical equipment. 4 . Instruments. 5. Controls. 6. Internal transportation system. 7. Others.

What is more important is that, there is need for taking into accounts of spare parts and tools required. This aspect is divided into two parts namely,

(a) Spare-parts and tools to be purchased with the original equipment.

(b) Spare parts and tools required for operational wear and tear.

Possible Constraints while Selecting Machines and Equipment :

The following considerations warrant due weightage while selecting machineries and equipment. These are: 1. Shortfall of electricity - the available supply is less than what is needed to start-with. 2. Hurdles in moving equipment or divided plant to remote places. 3. Lack of cooperation on the part of employees when they are meant to advanced technological or numerical control of machines. 4. Import restrictions in importing certain types of machines and equipment.

Procurement of Plant and Machinery :

The procurement of plant and machinery and equipment takes two forms. One, different manufacturers of industrial machines and equipment may be approached to select the best: Instead, turn-key contract can be entered into for entire plant and machinery and equipment with a single supplier. While selecting a supplier or suppliers, the factors that matter the most are: (a) Desirability. (b) Level of technological sophistication. (c) Standing or reputation of suppliers. (d) The expected delivery schedules. (e) The terms of payment. (f) The required performance guarantees which may be mechanical, input and output guarantees.

There is nothing wrong in hiring the services of external technical expertise in case the in-house technicians are lacking the desired level of technical expertise and acumen. The outside agencies or consultants not only select the right kind of package of machineries, equipment and tools but also undertake the responsible job of supervising the installation of the same or erection of plant.

7. STRUCTURES AND CIVIL WORKS

For an industrial project, structures and civil works can be divided into three broad categories, namely, I. Site preparation and development. II. Buildings and structures. III. Outdoor works.

I. **Site Preparation and Development :** Actual work of site preparation and development calls for at least six types of coherent yet vital set of activities. These are: (a) Grading and levelling of site. (b) Demolition and removal of the existing unwanted structures.

(c) Relocation of existing pipe-lines, cables, roads, power-lines. (d) Reclamation of swamps and draining and removal of stagnant water. (e) Connections for the utilities from the site to the public net-work, electric power - both high-tension and low-tension, water for drinking and various industrial purposes, communications - telephone, telex, roadways, railways. (f) Other activities of site preparation and development.

II. **Buildings and Structures :** Building and structures are of five types namely, (i) Factory or process buildings. (ii) Ancillary buildings required for stores, warehouses, laboratories, utility supply centres, maintenance services and others. (iii) Administrative buildings. (iv) Staff- welfare buildings, cafeteria, medical centre, gymkhana facilities, recreation buildings. (v) Residential buildings.

III. **Outdoor Works :** The outdoor works cover (a) Supply and distribution of utilities such as water, electricity, steam, gas, communication and the like. (b) Handling and treatment of emission, wastages and effluents. (c) Transportation and traffic arrangements such as roads, rail-tracks, paths, parking areas, sheds, garages, traffic signals and so on. (d) Outdoor lighting. (e) Landscaping. (f) Enclosures and supervision that include boundary wall, fencing barriers, gates, doors, security posts, sewerage openings and the like.

8. PROJECT CHARTS AND LAYOUTS

Project charts and layouts are prepared once data are collected on major dimensions of the project namely, market size, plant capacity, production technology, machines and equipment, buildings and civil works. Conditions obtaining at plant site and supply of inputs to project. These charts and layouts clearly define the scope of the project and provide the basis for detailed project engineering and estimation of investment and production costs. The major charts and layouts are :

A. **General Functional Layout :** This layout potrays the general relationship between equipment, buildings and civil works. The primary consideration is to facilitate smooth and economical movement of raw materials, work in progress and end products, and preparing this general layout. It means that the layout should attempt to get easy flowing work in one direction without hurdles. Accordingly stores, workshops, canteen, rest-rooms and other serve stations must be situated functionally with towering position of main factory buildings.

B. **Transport Layouts :** This shows the means and the distances of transport outside the production line.

C. **Utility Consumption Layout :** This layout plan shows major consumption points of utilities such as power, gas, water, compessed-air and their required quantities and qualities. These layouts make available the basis for developing specifications for utility supply installations.

D. **Communication Layout :** This layout clarifies the things as how various points of the project will be connected with telephone, telex and Intercom and inter-connecting channels.

E. **Organisation Layout :** This layout plan shows or depicts the organisational set-up of the project along-side the information on personnel required for various departments and their inter- relations even reaching grass-root level of each work position.

F. **Plant Layout :** Plant layout is related with the physical layout of the factory. These layout of production facilities can be of two types namely, 'process' and 'product'. Even fixed layout can be another possibility. The important considerations in preparing the plant layout that deserve due weightage are: 1. Consistency with production technology. 2. Smooth flow of goods from one work station to another or one stage to another. 3. Effective use of space. 4. Scope of expansion. 5. Minimisation of costs. 6. Safety of the work force.

G. **Material Flow Diagram :** This diagram depicts the flow of materials, utilities, intermediate products, final products, by-products and emissions. A quantity flow-diagram showing the quantities of flow can be prepared along with the material flow diagram.

H. **Production Line Diagrams :** These diagrams show how the flow of the production is likely to progress alongwith the key information for the main equipment.

9. WORK SCHEDULE

Work schedule is the plan of the work relating to installation and initial operation. The work schedule serves at least three purposes. These are: 1. To anticipate the problems that are likely to crop up during the installation stage and suggest the possible and feasible ways of over-coming them. 2. To establish the phasing of investments looking to the availability of funds. 3. To develop a plan of operation.

It is generally found that the required inputs such as raw- materials and man-power are not available in adequate quantity when the plant is ready for commissioning or the plant is not ready when the raw-materials arrive. It goes without saying that in the first case the plant remains idle while in second case the material is likely to deteriorate or create problems of storage or both. In order to avoid the possible lossess arising out of idle-plant capacity or idle capacity and the determination of stocks of material, work schedule should be drawn in detail with care, clarity and ground realities. This helps in making use of available inputs by adjusting plant capacity utilisation or at least commissioning to start with.

THE NEED FOR CONSIDERING ALTERNATIVES

Ultimately, if original idea stands the tests and rigorous investigation, it is given green signal as it is accepted as the viable project at least in technical terms. However, the idea given is to be converted into a concrete proposal, which is a must. Atempt should be made to find alteratives of transforming ideas into concrete project. These alternatives are likely to differ in one or more of the given aspects, namely, nature of project, production process, product quality, scale of operation and scheduling and location.

I. **Nature of Project :** Each project has its own plan of manufacturing. A plan may be to manufacture all processing and producing components itself and assemble into final products. Alternatively, project may think of manufacturing basic parts and buy from the outside reputed concerns and assemble them into final products. Much depends on unique individual situation. Basically, it is a question of make or buy all products and assemble, or make all products and assemble or a combination of the two-whichever is viable from the point of view of project.

II. **Production Process :** In processing a compound or mix of inputs, there are alternative processes. The availability and characteristics of raw-materials, the cost-structure and the nature of market served are the key factors that are to be considered while deciding about the manufacturing process.

III. **Product Quality :** Except in case of precision products such as thermometer, lactometer, watches, calculators and so on, the choice with respect to quality standards is fairly large. This is especially true in case of consumer products both durable and non-durable. The quality decisions as to the standard range depends on the features of the market, the elasticity of demand, consumer preferences, and the nature and extent of competition.

IV. **Scale of Operating and Scheduling :** In good many cases, several scales of operation are not only possible but feasible both technically and financially. The choice of particular scale or level of activity depends on the financial resources at the command of the unit, the nature and extent of competition, the nature of demand and the economies of scale. Scheduling or time phasing refers to the installation of capacity whether done in one shot or phase-wise. The capital cost of capacity installation is usually lower when it is done at one shot. However, the cost of idle capacity will be very high if installed capacity is not fully utilised. In fact, the trade-offs between these costs determine the optimum pattern of time phasing. The commanding factor is the nature of effective demand.

V. **Location :** It is established fact that location and size are closely inter-related. It is quite possible that demand could be met by (a) a single plant for the entire market (b) one large plant for bulk of the market with a few. Smaller plants for the remaining market (c) Several plants of similar size spread over the market areas. Again, the choice depends on trade-offs between the economies of the scale in manufacturing vis-a-vis the economies in distribution.

Last but not the least, while evaluating the various alternatives, the interlinkages among the fundamental facets of the projects like product or service, demand, plant capacity, production technology, location, investment outlay, financial resources, production costs, selling price and profitability must be taken into account. The intertwined linkages of various facets can be much more clear from the Fig. 5.1.(Page 21).

B. FINANCIAL FEASIBILITY

Demand and price estimates are derived from market feasibility study. Project costs and operating costs are derived from technical feasibility study. The estimates need to be supplemented with (a) tax implications depending upon the prevailing tax laws and (b) financial costs emanating from the financing alternative are considered for the project. That provides enough information for the calculation of the financial bottom-line of the project. The financial feasibility involves the detailed financial analysis. To judge a project from the financial angle, there is need for information about the following project dimensions namely, cost of project, means of financing, estimates of sales and production, working capital requirement and its financing, estimates of working results, break event point, projected cash flow statements and projected balance sheets. An attempt is made the manner in which the above information is gathered, prepared, summarised and presented for sound financial evaluation. Before one goes deep into these financial estimates and projects, it pays to know how they are interrelated.

1. COST OF PROJECT

Cost of project signifies the total expenditure associated with a project wherein long-term funds are needed. Basically, it is capital expenditure. In other words, it is the dead investment or sunk investment made in land and site development, buildings and civil works, plant and machinery, technical know-how and engineering fees, expenses on foreign technicians and training of technicans abroad, miscellaneous fixed assets, preliminary and capital issue expenses, preoperative expenses, provision for contingencies, margin money for working capital, initial cash, losses and so on. A brief description of each item is of much use to have better understanding.

A. LAND AND SITE DEVELOPMENT :

This cost comprises of: (i) Basic cost of land including conveyance charges. (ii) Premium payable on base-hold and conveyance charges. (iii) Cost of levelling and developing. (iv) Cost of laying approach roads and internal roads. (v) Cost of gates. (vi) Cost of tubewells. (vii) Cost of fencing.

Cost of land varies from area to area. It is highest in urban areas, lower in semi-urban areas and lowest in rural areas. Again, the cost of site development varies widely depending on the location and the topography of the land.

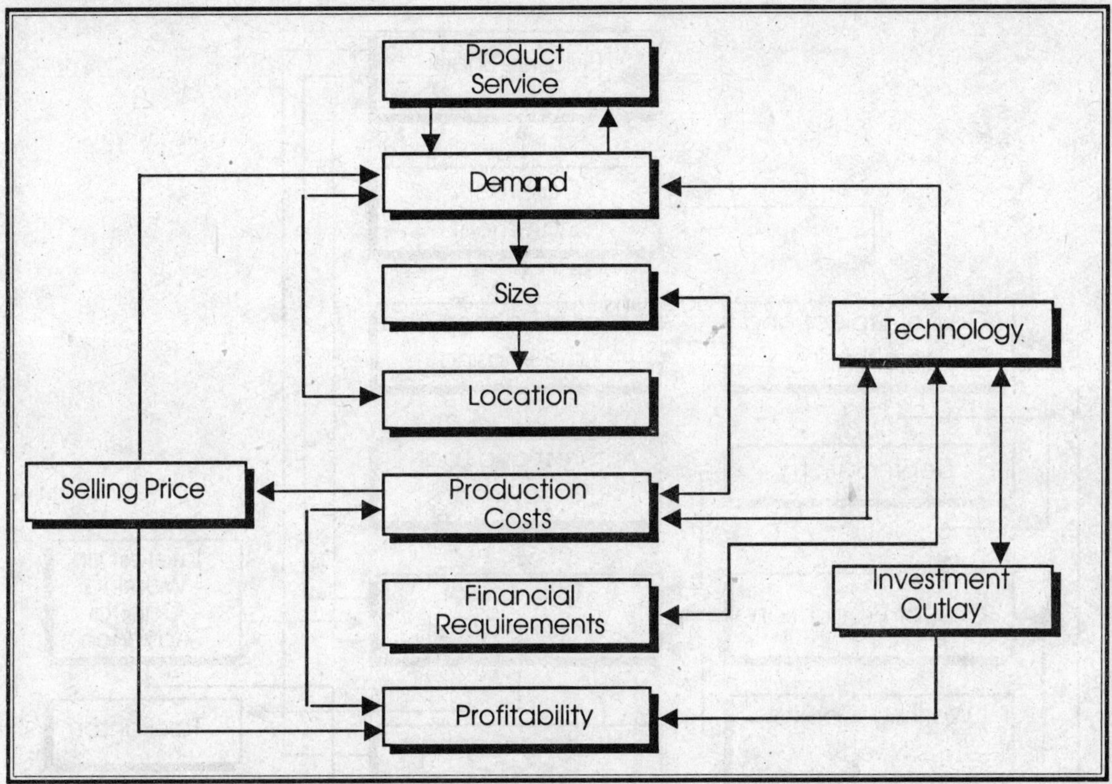

Fig. 5.01 Key Project Facets and their Inter-linkages

B. BUILDINGS AND CIVIL WORKS :

The cost in these include: (i) Buildings for the main plant and installations including equipments. (ii) Buildings for auxiliary services such as steam-supply, work- shops, laboratories, water supply, gas-supply, electricity-supply. (iii) Godowns, warehouses, sheds, and other open yard facilities. (iv) Buildings promoting services such as canteen, guest houses, time office, excise house, rest rooms, recreation hall and so on. (v) Residential quarters for employees. (vi) Special structures like silos, tanks, wells, chests, basins, cisterns, hoopers, bins and other structure for installing plant and equipments. (vii) Garages. (viii) Sewers, drainage, pits and the like. (ix) Other civil engineering works covered under earlier heads.

It is the kind of structures as needed by processing requirements of manufacturing that decide the cost. Once the kinds of structures required are specified, cost estimates are based on plinth areas and rates of various types of structures. To a certain extent these costs differ from location to location.

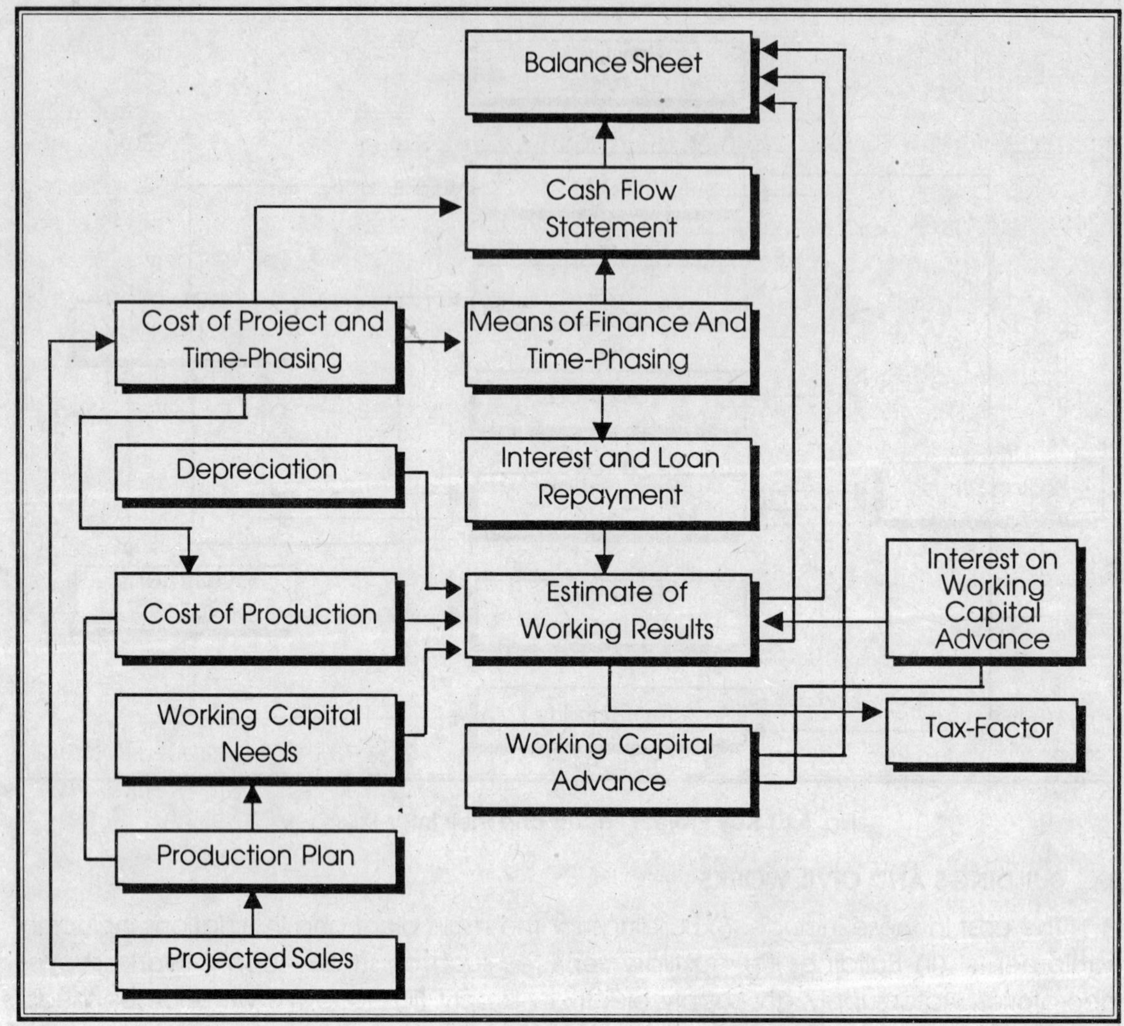

Fig. 5.02 Diagram depicting Financial Projections

C. PLANT AND MACHINERY :

The cost of plant and machinery covers the items:

(i) Cost of imported machinery - a sum total of FOB value, shipping, freight, insurance cost, import duty, clearing, loading unloading and other transportation charges to the site.

(ii) Cost of indigeneous machinery-the sum-total of expenses namely, FOR, sales tax, octroi, and other taxes, railway or roadways freight and other transport costs to the site.

(iii) Costs of stores and spares.

(iv) Erection charges - foundation and installation charges. The cost of plant and machinery is based on latest available quotation duly adjusted for escalation.

The provision for the escalation charges is equal to the latest annual rate of inflation applicable to plant and machinery multiplied by the length of delivery period.

D. TECHNICAL KNOW-HOW AND ENGINEERING CHARGES :

Making a project and see that it works, is not a child's play. There is need for utilising the services of technical consultants or collaborators from home or abroad or both. Their expertise in technical matters in preparing project report, choice of technology, selection of plant and machinery, detailed engineering all-go in no waste. These payments are of two types. The amount payable for having technical know-how and engineering services in setting up the project is the part of project cost. On the other hand, the royalty payable each year- a certain percentage of sales - is an operating expenditure charged to the cost of preparing projected profitability statements.

E. EXPENSES ON FOREIGN TECHNICIANS AND TRAINING OF IN-HOUSE TECHNICANS ABROAD:

The expenses of foreign technicians for their services in setting up and supervising the trial-runs-include their to and fro travel, boarding and lodging and salaries and allowances as agreed. Again, training of in-house technicians abroad calls large expenditure in their travel, stay abroad and other training related expenses.

F. MISCELLANEOUS FIXED ASSETS :

Miscellaneous fixed assets are those which are subsidiary to the main manufacturing fixed assets. This comprises of the items like furniture, official machinery, equipment, appliances, tools, vehicles, railway siding, diesel generating sets, transformers, boilers, piping systems, lab equipment, workshop equipment, effluent treatment plants, fire-fighting equipment and the like. The other expenses include the expenses incurred for procurement or use of patents, licenses, trade-marks, copyrights and so on and compulsory minimum deposits to be made with utility service rendering units.

G. PRELIMINARY AND CAPITAL ISSUE EXPENSES :

Preliminary expenses cover wide range of expenses incurred by promoters identifying the project, conducting the market survey, preparing the feasibility report, drafting of memorandum and articles of association and incorporating the company as an artificial person. On the other hand, capital issue expenses are capital raising expenses. These comprise of capital issue expenses namely, underwriting commission, brokerage, fees to managers and registrars, printing and postage expenses, advertising and publicity expenses, listing fees and stamp duty.

H. PRE-OPERATIVE EXPENSES :

Pre-operative expenses are those that are incurred from incorporation till the commencement of commercial production. These are: establishment expenses; rent rates and taxes; travelling expenses; interest and commitment charges on borrowings; insurance charges; mortgage expenses; interest on deferred payments; start-up expenses and other miscellaneous expenses. Preoperative expenses are directly linked to the project implementation schedule. Implementing the project as per the schedule is almost impossible and delays are caused which push up theses expenses. As it is a common phenomenon, the financial institutions allow delay - ranging between 20 and 25 per cent in the project implementation acts schedule and accordingly grant a cushion in the estimate for pre-operative expenses. Of these pre-operative expenses capitalised by apportioning them to fixed assets particularly those incurred between the initial stage and setting up of plant and machinery; the expenses till commercial production from the stage of setting up machinery and plant are treated as deferred revenue expenditure.

I. PROVISION FOR CONTINGENCIES :

There is need for providing for contingencies because there is slip between the cup and lips. That is, unforeseen expenses and excessive price like can not be neglected. These are already incorporated in cost estimates. The procedure for calculating provision for contingencies, as suggested by experts is made up two steps: (a) Divide the project cost items into two categories namely, "firm" and "non-firm" cost items. "Firm" cost items are those which have already been acquired or for which definite arrangements have been made. (b)Set the provision for contingencies in the range of 5 and 10 per cent of the estimated cost of non-firm cost items. Instead, make, 10 per cent for all items, if the implementation period is up to one year, including the margin money for working capital. Beyond one year, provisions for an additional 5 percent is to be made.

J. MARGIN MONEY FOR WORKING CAPITAL :

Major share of working capital needs are provided by commercial banks and trade creditors. A certain portion of working capital requirement, however, has to come from long-term sources of finance. This is called as "margin money for working capital". This margin money is, some times, utilised for meeting over-runs in capital costs. Eventually, this leads to a working capital problem or worse crisis, when the project is commissioned. To fight this, the financial institutions stipulate that a portion of the loan amount, to be blocked initially, equal to the margin money for working capital, so that it can be released as and when the project is completed.

K. INITIAL CASH LOSSES :

It is common to see that majority of the projects incur cash losses in the initial years. Though, it is a fact, the promoters do not disclose these initial cash losses because they want the project to appear quite attractive both to the investing class and financial institutions. Such kind of window-dressing affects the liquidity position of the project and damage the operations. Therefore, there is nothing wrong in accepting the fact and making provision for the estimated initial cash losses either directly or indirectly.

2. MEANS OF FINANCE

Each project cost is expressed in terms of monetary units say rupees, dollars, pounds and so on. The question is now the promotors to finance the projected cost of project. The normal means of finance open to the needy entrepreneurs are: Share Capital, term loans, debentures, deferred credit, incentive sources and other sources. Let us touch each in brief and see how the promoters plan the means of finance.

A. Share Capital :

Share capital is the amount contributed by the owners of the company. These shares are share-capital of the company are of two types, namely, preferential and equity. Equity share capital is a risk-capital or venture capital and equity shareholders are the residual claimants in the returns and refund of capital in the event the company is closed. Therefore, they are not guaranteed a fixed rate of return. However, equity shareholders have the power which is in the form of voting right-one share one vote. That empowers them to participate in deciding the destiny of the company and those depending on the artificial person. On the other hand, preferential shareholders have preference as to the fixed return and refund of capital, but have no voting rights.

B. Term - Loans :

Term-loans are those that are provided by the financial institutions as well as commercial banks. These funds are secured and returnable over longer period of time ranging between 5 to 15 years or even more. These are rupee term loans and foreign currency term loans. These are used for the investment of these finds in long-term or fixed assets which might be bought in national and international currencies. This forms the major source in financing schemes of expansion, modernisation, and renovation of existing set up.

C. Debenture Capital :

Debenture capital represents borrowed capital unlike share capital which is ownership. Being a loan, debenture holders get fixed rate of investment whether company makes profits or not. These are of different types. However, most common are convertible and non-convertible. Convertible debentures are those that can be converted into shares wholly or partly after stipulated period. Non-convertible debentures are pure long-term loans. Mostly they are secured having fixed or floating charge on the assets of the company. They do not have rights of voting.

D. Deferred Credit :

In industrial market, the suppliers of plant and machinery and equipment, grant deferred payment facility though it is an outright purchase. Instead of making one payment, cash down is made and total balance it is spread into part payments. It should not be considered as installment purchase.

E. Incentive Sources :

Government plays significant role in industrialisation process. As a part of package of incentives to the industries, government-through its agencies-grants certain initial capital, or loan to encourage starting of new units to achieve geographically well spread areas. Seed capital invested is a certain percentage of total capital needs of an industrial unit. If is give at nominal low rate. Again, capital subsidy is another form which is given to attract entrepreneurs to locate their units in a particular area. Even tax deferment or exception of tax holidays are declared for the same purpose.

F. Other Sources :

The other sources of long-term and medium-term loans are unsecured loans, public deposits, leasing and hire-purchase finance. The unsecured loans are provided by promoters to make clear that they have stake in project. It is the difference between total equity capital and the minimum amount provided by promoters as directed by financial institutions. Lease and hire-purchase finance is borrowing from the individuals and institutions who grant term-loans.

PLANNING OF MEANS OF FINANCE

It is quite evident from the above discussion that we are having different means of financing the project. The question is what shall be the structure or make up of total capital. What will be the exact structure or financial plan, is determined by two sets of factors namely, norms set by Regulatory Bodies and Financial Institutions and the key business considerations.

Coming to the norms set by Regulatory Bodies and the Financial Institutions, the financial plan should conform to the government or regulatory bodies or financial institution that lend the finance. The purpose of regulation is to have financial discipline so that the resources of society are not wasted and the parties contributing the same should not be cheated. The guidelines and conditions of financial institutions are those based on financial experts or veterans who know what is what?

Turning to key business considerations, any financing decision has to respect the dimensions of cost, risk, control and flexibility. Speaking of cost of capital, borrowed capital is cheaper as it is a fixed rate and exempt from corporate tax unlike share capital where earnings are subject to tax. Coming to risks, risks stand for loss-monetary and non-monetary. Again, these risks are classed into two categories as 'business' and 'financial'. Business risks are those that arise in the form of variability of earnings before interest and taxes caused by fluctuations in demand and variations in prices and costs. On the other hand, financial risks are those that arise mainly from financial leverage. This concept of leverage is the proportion in which we are mixing equity capital and debt capital and preference capital. Though debt capital is cheaper in cost, it is supported by a minimum of earnings. The mix should be low risked-both financial and business from the angle of equity shareholders. These risks - both business and financial- are quite opposite in impact. Coming back to control, the principle says with minimum of ownership funds maximum control should be exercised over total funds and business affairs. Business an ongoing activity - leads to growth and expansion of the firm where it should be easy to raise funds easily, quickly and at least cost. The parameters of flexibility measure the adjustability to the changing business situations.

3. ESTIMATES OF SALES AND PRODUCTION

Profitability of projects assessment starts with the forecast of sales or sales revenues that will pave the way for estimates of production - for, you must produce what you can sell well. Therefore, while estimating the sales revenues, the undermentioned points deserve due attention.

1. Don't assume high capacity utilisation in the first year of operation. The firm may not have any technical snags and the technology involved in simple, one should think of high level capacity working. It is because resource contracts may be key factors such as material shortage, limited power, entering successfully into market and so on. Taking a time phase of five years to reach high level capacity, in the first year one can think of 45 per cent to 55 per cent, second year 55 per cent to 75 per cent, 75 per cent to 90 per cent fourth year and fifth year may think of 90 per cent and above but certainly not alone 100 per cent. This use of installed capacity differs from case to case due to ground reality situations.
2. It is assumed that whatever is produced is sold. This avoids adjustments for inventories especially finished goods.
3. The selling price selected should be one which is realisable by the units net of excise duty. However, there is room for adding dealer's margin or commission as a part of selling expenses.
4. The selling price used is one which is presently prevailing. Here, it is assumed that changes in selling price will be matched by proportionate changes in the cost of production - an assumption though commonly accepted is not very much convincing. In case, a portion of production is saleable at controlled price, take the controlled price for that portion.

It is important to note that sales and production are closely inter-related. It is because of this, that both may be estimated at a time. The format of estimates of production and sales can be presented in the format followed by **All India Financial Institutions of India.** However, for the sake of more clarity, it is slightly modified. This format gives estimate for five years as against four years originally followed by **A.I.F.I.I.** For the benefit of readers this modified format is given as under:

Estimates of Production and Sales

The details are to be furnished separately for each product and until the plant reaches maximum capacity utilisation.

Particulars	Product I				
	1st Year	2nd Year	3rd Year	4th Year	5th Year
1. Installed capacity (Quantity per day per annum)					
2. Number of Workings Days					
3. Number of Shifts					
4. Estimated Production per day (Quantity)					
5. Estimated Annual Production (Quantity)					
6. Estimated Output as Percentage of Plant Capacity					
7. Sales (Quantity) (after adjusting stocks)					
Product					
I					
II					
III					
IV					

4. COST OF PRODUCTION

Working out the cost of production is based on the estimated production. The major ingredients of cost of production are Material cost, Labour Cost, Utilities cost and Factory overhead Cost. A touch of each points throws much light on cost of production as to what it is ?

A. Materials :

Material cost is a major component of cost of production. The material cost encompasses the cost of raw-materials, chemicals, component and consumable stores required for production. Material cost is the function of the quantities in which these materials are required and prices defrayed on them. The undermentioned points are worth pondering while arriving at material cost. (A) The requirements of different material inputs per unit of output are to be established on the ground of one or more of the following: (i) theoretical norms of consumption (ii) experience of the industry (iii) performance guarantees and (iv) specification of machinery suppliers. (B) The total requirements of different material inputs per unit of output with expected output during the year. (C) The material prices of inputs are defined in CIF terms (Cost, insurance and freight). (D) The present costs of different material inputs is considered. Put in other words, the factor of inflation is ignored. As we know already, the factor of inflation is ignored in estimating the sales revenue also. (E) In case the seasonal fluctuations in prices are normal or regular, the same must be counted while estimating material input cost.

B. Labour :

Labour cost is the labour content of the cost. In other words, it is the cost of all manpower employed in the factory. Labour cost is the function of the number of employees and the rates of remuneration. The manpower re quirement rests on the number of operations or helpers needed for operating various machines and manning various services. The general norms prevailing in the industry are used to calculate the number of supervisory and administrative staff. Estimation of employee renumeration rates are the prevailing rates in the industry and industrial area should be recovered with. The remuneration is the complex of basic salary, dearness allowance, house rent allowance, conveyance allowance, medical reimbersement, leave travel concession, provident fund contribution, gratuity contribution, bonus payments, among others. Due weightage should be given to vocations, overtime-work, night time work, work on holidays and so on. The labour cost estimates must provide, for annual investment say 3.5 per cent to 7 per cent. During initial and earlier years, lower labour costs may be taken when the capacity utilisation is much lower.

True labour costs will be one which are calculated during the year in which maximum capacity is utilised.

C. Cost of Utilities :

Utilities basically cover power, water and fuel. The requirements of these utilities are determined on the basis of norms specified by collaborators, consultants on one hand and consumption standards in the industry on the other, whichever is higher. The cost of power includes only the cost bought out power estimated based on power-tariff structure of the State Electricity Boards. The cost of captive power is reflected in the cost of fuel. The cost payable to local authorities and charges payable to other firms for water or steam or both may be shown separately. In case total water requirements are met out of own ground water facilities, water charges need not be shown separately. The cost of fuel, furnace oil, coal, fire wood, bagasse and the like - is somewhat difficult to estimate very accurately.

D. Factory Overheads :

Factory overheads or on-costs refer to depreciation, repairs and maintenance, rents and taxes, insurance on factory assets, consumables, motive-power and lighting (which are considered under power costs) and factory related expenses. Repairs and maintenance expenses are lower in initial stages and go on increasing. Rent, taxes, insurance and rates are one which are prevailing. As a precautionary measure, some provision should be made in addition to the total of overall factory overheads.

5. WORKING CAPITAL NEEDS AND FINANCING OF IT

Working capital has two acceptable concepts namely, current assets only and current assets minus current liabilities. In other words, the former is 'gross' and later is 'net' concept.

In estimating the working capital needs and planning for its financing, the following points deserve special relevance. These are:

(a) Contents of Working Capital : Working capital is the investment made for a period of one year including raw-materials and components - both indigeneous and foreign, work in progress or work in process, stock of finished goods, debtors, bills payables, and operating expenses.

(b) Sources of Working Capital : The possible sources of working capital are - working capital advances provided by commercial banks, trade credit, arrivals and provisions and long term sources of financing.

(c) Limits on Working Capital Advances by Commercial Banks : These limits are two: (1) The aggregate permissible bank finance is specified as per the norms prescribed by Tondon Committee- appointed by R.B.I. (2) Provision of margin money to be provided by the firm against each current asset.

(d) Suggestions of Tondon Committee : This committee suggested three methods for determining the maximum permissible amount a bank can finance for working capital. Of these methods, the maximum permissible bank finance is computed according to the second one, is as follows:

"Current assets as per the Norms laid down by Tondon Committee (0.75) - Non bank current liabilities like trade credit and provisions." It means that at least 25 per cent of the current assets must be supported by long-term sources of finance.

(e) Margin Variation for Each Current Asset : Though there is no hard and fast rule or formula for determining the margin amount, it ranges within which margin requirements for various current assets are given as below:

Raw-materials	–	10 to 25 per cent;
Working process	–	20 to 40 per cent;
Finished goods	–	30 to 50 per cent;
Debtors	–	30 to 50 per cent;

To estimate the working capital needs, the amount of bank finance available, and the margin for working capital to be provided from long term services, FORM IX-B of the Application Form is used by the **All India Financial Institutions**. Instead of four years, one can take five years - as modification. The form is large enough to cover all the details for only one year, and therefore, four or five forms are to be filled to cover consecutive period of four or five years.

6. ESTIMATES OF WORKING RESULTS

This estimates of working results is nothing but profitability projections. Once the firm comes out with estimates of sales revenues and cost of production, the next sequential step is to prepare profitability projection or estimates of working results. The estimates of working results may be prepared along the lines as laid down below :

(a) Cost of Production	- - - -	
(b) Total Administrative Expenses	- - - -	
(c) Total Sales Expenses	- - - -	
(d) Royalty and Technical know-how payable	- - - -	
(e) Total Cost of Production (a + b + c + d)		- - - -
(f) Expected Sales		- - - -
(g) Gross Profit before Interest		- - - -
(h) Total Financial Expenses	- - - -	
(i) Depreciation	- - - -	
(j) Operating Profit (g-h-i)		- - - -
(k) Other Income		- - - -
(l) Preliminary Expenses written off		- - - -
(m) Profit/Loss before Tax (j - k - l)		- - - -
(n) Provision for Taxation		- - - -
(o) Profit after Tax (m -n)		- - - -
Less Dividend on		
- Preferential Capital	- - - -	
- Equity Capital	- - - -	- - - -
(p) Retained Profit		- - - -
(q) Net Cash Accrual (p +i + l)		- - - -

Before going to the FORM XII of the Application Form used by All India Financial Institutions working for presenting estimates of working results, let us know what "a...q" points mean that will be the part of XII FORM.

A. COST OF PRODUCTION :

This is the sum total of the cost of materials, labour, utilities and factory overheads. (This expression cost of products has different meaning in Cost accounting - where it is referred to as Production Cost.)

B. TOTAL ADMINISTRATIVE EXPENSES :

These comprise of: (a) administrative salaries (b) remuneration to directors (c) professional fees (d) lighting, postage, telegrams, telephones and office supplies (e) insurance and taxes on office property and (f) miscellaneous items.

C. TOTAL SALES EXPENSES :

These comprise of: (a) Commission payable to dealers (b) packing and forwarding charges (c) Salary of sales staff with an annual increase of say 5 per cent (d) Sales-promotion and advertising expenses and (e) Other miscellaneous expenses.

It is the nature of industry and the kind of the competitive conditions prevailing that determine selling expenses. Therefore, the experience of similar units in the industry may be the guideline, generally, these expenses vary in the range of 5 per unit to 10 per unit of sales value.

D. ROYALTY AND KNOW-HOW PAYABLE :

It is payable annually and the rate varies between 1 and 5 per cent of sales. Again, such royalty payment is for limited number of years say 5 to 10 years as they are likely to revise.

E. TOTAL COST OF PRODUCTION :

It is the sum total of cost of products (production cost to be specific), total administrative expenses, total sales expenses and royalty and know-how payable. Again, "Cost of production" in strict sense, stands for production cost and administrative expenses.

F. EXPECTED SALES :

The expected sales figures are drawn from the estimates of sales and production prepared earlier in the financial analysis and projection exercise.

G. GROSS PROFIT BEFORE INTEREST :

This is nothing but the difference between expected sales value and cost of production (production cost).

H. TOTAL FINANCE EXPENSES :

Financial expenses cover interest on term-loans, bank borrowings, commitment charges on term-loans, commission for bank guarantees. Of all these, the first two are main. In estimating interest on term-loans, two things should be cared for: (a) present rate charged by financial institutions (b) the interest amount goes on decreasing as per the repayment schedule. On the other hand, interest or bank borrowings may be estimated as under: (a) Determine the total requirement of working capital (b) Find out the quantity of bank borrowing that would be available against the total working capital requirement, and (c) Calculate the interest charges on the prevailing rates of interest.

I. DEPRECIATION :

It forms an important item especially in case of capital intensive projects. To arrive at depreciation charge the points given below are most relevant. (a) Contingency margin and pre-operative expenses provided in estimating the cost of project should be added to fixed assets proportionately to determine the value of fixed assets for arriving at the depreciation charge. (b) Preliminary expenses in excess of 2.50 per cent of the project cost (excluding working capital margin) should be added to fixed assets proportionately to ascertain the value of fixed assets for determining the depreciation charges, (c) The Income Tax Act specifies that written down value method (WDV) of depreciation should be used for tax purposes. It specifies, further, the specific rate of depreciation applicable to different kinds of assets, (d) However, Company Law for the purpose of financial reporting allows both W.D.V. method or SL (Straight Line) method. From 1988 onwords, the depreciation rates under the Companies Act have been delinked from those under Income Tax Act. The key depreciation rates under the Companies Act are as under:

Details	In Percentage Terms					
	SHIFT					
	Single Shift		Double Shift		Triple Shift	
	WDV	SL	WDV	SL	WDV	SL
1. Buildings (other than factory)	5.00	1.63	-	-	-	-
2. Factory Buildings	10.00	3.34	-	-	-	-
3. Plant and Machinery (General Rate)	15.00	5.15	22.50	8.09	30.00	11.31

J. OPERATING PROFIT :

It is as clear as crystal which equal to (g – h - i)

K. OTHER INCOME :

This signifies an income arising from transactions not part of the normal operations of the firm. The examples are profit on sale of asset, scrap value realised. It is also true that non-operating loss may be there caused by loss on sale of asset excessive waste.

L. PRELIMINARY EXPENSES WRITTEN OFF :

Under the rules, preliminary expenses upto 2.5 per cent of the cost of project or capital employed, whichever is higher, can be written off or amortised in ten equal annual instalments.

M. PROFIT/LOSS BEFORE TAX :

This is equal to (j-k–l)

N. PROVISION FOR TAXATION :

Arriving at tax burden is, perhaps, one of the most difficult tasks. Stated in simple terms, there is need for arriving at taxable income as per the provisions of the Income Tax Act. Then apply appropriate rules of tax to calculate tax burden.

O. PROFIT AFTER TAX :

Profit after tax is equal to (m – n)

P. RETAINED PROFIT :

It is also called as retained earnings or ploughing back of earnings. It is equal to the difference between PAT – Dividend payable to preference and equity paid-up capital.

Q. NET CASH ACCRUAL :

The net cash accrual from operations is equal to (Retained profit + depreciation + preliminary expenses written off + Other non-cash charges.)

7. BREAK EVEN POINT

The estimates of working results or profitability are found on the postulations that project would operate at given levels of capacity utilisation in the future. The purpose behind this is to not only know projected profit but to know the level up to which losses are incurred in capacity utilisation. Break event point is a point where total revenue is equal to total cost. That is, BEP is no profit no loss point.

Calculation of break event point of units or sales, there is need for classifying the total cost into variable and fixed costs. Put in simple words, period costs are fixed and product costs are variable. Using costing terminology, variable costs include direct material, direct labour, direct expenses and variable overheads - factory, administrative and selling and distribution - all inclusive. Therefore, fixed expenses are those other than variable. The formulae for calculation of Break Even Point of Units and Sales can be;

$$\text{BEP Sales} = \frac{\text{Total Fixed Cost}}{\frac{S-V}{S}}$$

where, S = Sales price per unit

V = Variable Cost Per unit

$$\text{BEP Units} = \frac{\text{Total Fixed Costs}}{\frac{S-V}{S}} \times \frac{1}{5}$$

$$= \frac{\text{Total Fixed Costs}}{C}$$

where S = Unit Selling Price

V = Unit Variable Cost

C = Unit Contribution (S-V)

Break Even Point for A New Project

In case of a new project, the capacity utilisation level goes on increasing over a period of say 3 to 5 years. That is why, the fixed costs are planned in such way as to step up as capacity utilisation level goes up. It does not mean that there will be zero fixed costs if no production is there unlike in case of variable costs. Generally, the fixed costs incurred during 3rd or 4th year to start with as capacity utilisation reaches rated capacity utilisation.

8. PROJECTED CASH-FLOW STATEMENTS

A Cash-Flow Statement shows the movement of cash into and out of the firm at any time and its effect on the cash balance with the firm. This state is also called as "How come - how gone cash" statement. A cash-flow statement is nothing more than a cashflow budget. The format for preparing cash-flow statement can be that of sources and application of funds in a vertical form or it can be in horizontal form with opening and closing balance of cash - both cash and cash at bank.

The usual practice of preparing cash-flow statement is on half yearly basis and annual basis for the operating period for managerial purposes for consecutive ten years. Source experts are of the opinion that it is much more meaningful if prepared on quarterly basis for the construction period and half yearly basis for the first two to three years for managerial purpose. The latter alternative is of greater help in financial planning, project evaluation and control of funds.

A typical format for cash-flow statement can be one as which is given under:

A. SOURCES OF FUNDS

1. Share capital paid up ....
2. Profit before tax for the year ....
3. Depreciation provision for the year ....
4. Development Rebate Reserve ....
5. Increase in Secured medium and long-term borrowings for the project ....
6. Other term loans ....
7. Increase in unsecured loans and deposits ....
8. Increase in bank borrowings for working capital ....
9. Increase in liabilities for deferred payment to machinery supplier-including interest ....
10. Sale of fixed assets ....
11. Sale of investments ....
12. Other income: a ....

    b ....

    c ....

    Total Rs. (A) ....

B. APPLICATION OF FUNDS

1. Capital expenditure for the project ....
2. Other normal capital expenditure ....
3. Increase in working capital (Current assets other than cash- current liabilities other than short term bank borrowings) ....
4. Decrease in secured medium and long-term borrowings
   - All India Institutions
   - State Finance Corporations
   - Banks ....
5. Decrease in Unsecured Loans and deposits ....
6. Decrease in bank borrowings for working capital ....
7. Decrease in liabilities for deferred payments to machinery suppliers including interest ....
8. Increase in investments in other companies ....
9. Interest on Term Loan ....
10. Interest on bank borrowings for working capital ....
11. Taxation paid ....
12. Dividend paid equity and preference ....
13. Other expenditure ....

Total Rs. (B) ....

Operating balance of cash in hand and Bank ....

Net Surplus/Defict (A-B) ....

Closing balance of Cash and Bank ....

9. PROJECTED BALANCE SHEETS

Balance sheet is a sheet of balances of assets and liabilities reflecting the financial position of the company as on a particular date. The format of Balance Sheet is to as per the Part I of Schedule VI attached to the Indian Companies Act, 1956. The assets and liabilities appear in a well arranged sequence which is to be adhered to. Following is the skeleton of a Balance Sheet giving captions of each head of asset and liability.

BALANCE SHEET OF....

As on....

Liabilities	Amount Rs.	Assets	Amount Rs.
1. Share Capital	....	1. Fixed Assets	....
2. Reserves and Surplus	....	2. Investments	....
3. Secured Loans	....	3. Current Assets	....
4. Unsecured Loans	....	4. Miscellaneous Exp.	....
5. Current Liabilities and Provisions	....	5. Profit and Loss A/c (Loss)	....
Total Rs.	....	Total Rs.	....

Readers are aware of the items of each head of liability and asset. In case, they are not, they are advised to go through the concerned chapter in any Financial Accounting Book. Actual preparation of projected Balance Sheet calls for the information regarding:

(1) Balance Sheet of the year end.

(2) The projected income statement to be used for projected year.

(3) The sources of external financing proposed to be used in projection year.

(4) The proposed repayment of debt - long - medium and short-term - during the year of projection.

(5) The outlays and disposal of the fixed assets during the year of projection.

(6) The changes in the level of current assets during the year of projection.

(7) Changes in other assets and certain outlays like pre-operative and preliminary expenses that are capitalised - during the year of projection.

(8) The cash balance at the end of projection year.

MULTI-YEAR PROJECTIONS

Having marshalled the fundamentals of projection, it should not be difficult to have multi-year projections based on the given information both pre-operative and operative periods. For sake of simplicity, we will take construction (preoperative) period and first two years of operative period.

ILLUSTRATION

Sun Rise Corporation Limited was set up in the year 2000 and started in 2002 being its first year and 2003 the second year. The company produces metal component parts used in automobile industry. The given information is:

1. **Proposed Outlays and Financing of Sun Rise Corporation Ltd.**

Details	Construction Period 2000-2001	1st Year 2001-2002	2nd Year 2002-2003
	Rs.	Rs.	Rs.
OUTLAYS			
Preliminary and Preoperative Expenses	4,00,00,000	–	–
Fixed Assets	40,00,00,000	40,00,00,000	20,00,00,000
Current Assets	–	40,00,00,000	20,00,00,000
Term Loans	30,00,00,000	30,00,00,000	15,00,00,000
Short term Bank - Borrowings	–	24,00,00,000	12,00,00,000

II. **Projected Revenues and Costs of SUN RISE Corporation Ltd. for 2002 and 2003.**

Details	Year 2002		Year 2003	
Sales	Rs.	60,00,00,000	Rs.	1,20,00,00,000
Cost of Sales (excluding interest and depreciation)	Rs.	60,00,00,000	Rs.	80,00,00,000
Interest burden	Rs.	9,60,00,000	Rs.	12,80,00,000
Depreciation	Rs.	4,00,00,000	Rs.	5,60,00,000

Additional Information

1. **Assumptions Made :**

   1. The tax rate for the company is 60 per cent.
   2. No deductions or reliefs are available.
   3. Preliminary and pre-operative expenses will be written off during the first two years of operation, and
   4. No dividend will be paid in the first two years of operation.

Required :

(1) Prepare Projected Profit and Loss Statements

(2) Projected Cash Flows - Statements and

(3) Projected Balance Sheets.

SOLUTION:

I. PROJECTED PROFIT AND LOSS STATEMENTS OF SUN RISE CORPORATION LTD.

Details		1st Year Operation 2001-2002		2nd year Operation 2002-2003
Sales	Rs.	60,00,00,000	Rs.	1,20,00,00,000
Cost of Sales (excluding interest and depreciation)	Rs.	60,00,00,000	Rs.	40,00,00,000
Interest	Rs.	9,60,00,000	Rs.	12,80,00,000
Depreciation	Rs.	4,00,00,000	Rs.	5,60,00,000
Losses Absorbed		–	Rs.	13,60,00,000
Profit Before Tax	Rs.	13,60,00,000	Rs.	8,00,00,000
Tax		–	Rs.	4,80,00,000
Profit After Tax	Rs.	13,60,00,00,000	Rs.	3,20,00,000

Note: Figures in bracket indicate negative figures.

II. PROJECTED CASH FLOW STATEMENTS OF SUN RISE CORPORATION LIMITED
For the Years 2002 and 2003

Details	Construction Period 2000-2001	Operative 2001-2002	Period 2002-2003
SOURCES OF FUNDS			
1. Issue of Shares	Rs. 20,00,00,000	Rs. 30,00,00,000	-
2. Profit Before Tax and interest added back*	-	(Rs.21,00,00,000)	Rs. 34,40,00,000
3. Depreciation provision for the year	-	Rs. 4,00,00,000	Rs. 5,60,00,000
4. Increase in secured medium and long-term borrowings for the ProjectRs. 30,00,00,000		Rs. 30,00,00,000	Rs. 15,00,00,000
5. Increase in Working Capital through Bank borrowings	-	Rs. 24,00,00,000	Rs. 12,00,00,000
TOTAL (A)	Rs. 50,00,00,000	Rs. 84,00,00,000	Rs. 67,00,00,000

APPLICATION OF FUNDS :

1.	Capital Expenditure for the Project	Rs. 40,00,000	Rs. 40,00,00,000	Rs. 20,00,00,000
2.	Increase in Working Capital	–	Rs. 40,00,00,000	Rs. 20,00,00,000
3.	Interest	–	Rs. 9,60,00,000	Rs. 12,80,00,000
4.	Other Expenditure (Preliminary and Preoperative)	Rs. 2,00,00,000	–	–
5.	Taxes	–	–	Rs. 4,80,00,000
	TOTAL B	Rs. 44,00,00,000	Rs. 89,60,00,000	Rs. 57,60,00,000
	Opening Balance of Cash and Bank	–	Rs. 6,00,00,000	Rs. 40,00,000
	Net Surplus/Deficit (A-B)	Rs. 6,00,00,00,000	Rs. 5,60,00,000	Rs. 9,40,00,000
	Closing Balance of Cash and Bank	Rs. 6,00,00,000	Rs. 40,00,000	Rs. 9,80,00,000

Note : *This item does not take into account losses absorbed.

III. PROJECTED BALANCE SHEETS OF SUN RISE CORPORATION LIMITED DURING CONSTRUCTION AND TWO OPERATIVE YEARS

At the end of 2001, 2002 and 2003

Liabilities	End of Construction period	End of 1st year operation	End of 2nd year operation	Assets	End of Construction period	End of 1st year operation	End of 2nd year operation
	2001	2002	2003		2001	2002	2003
Share Capital	Rs.20.00	Rs. 50.00	Rs. 50.00	Fixed Assets	Rs. 40.00	Rs.76.00	Rs. 90.40
Reserves and Surplus	–	–	Rs. 00.16	Current Assets Cash	Rs. 06.00	Rs. 0.40	Rs. 09.80
				Others	–	Rs. 40.00	Rs. 60.00
Secured Loans Term Loan	Rs. 30.00	Rs. 60.00	Rs. 75.00	Miscellaneous Expenses			
Short term Bank Borrowings	–	Rs. 24.00	Rs. 36.00	Preliminary and Pre-operative Expenses	Rs. 4.00	Rs. 04.00	Rs. 04.00
				Profit and Loss A/c	–	Rs. 13.60	–
Total Rs.	50.00	134.00	164.20	Total Rs.	50.00	134.00	164.20

Note : All figures in crores of rupees.

CAPTER BASED QUESTIONS

A. WRITE SHORT NOTES ON

1. Feasibility study
2. Technical feasibility study
3. Financial feasibility study
4. Technical feasibility consideration
5. Financial feasibility considerations
6. Plant location and site
7. Machineries and equipments
8. Structures and civil works
9. Project charts and layouts
10. Cost of project
11. Estimates of working results
12. Projected cash flows - statements
13. Projected Balance sheets
14. Break even point
15. Means of finance.

B. SHORT ANSWER QUESTIONS

1. What is a feasibility study ?
2. What is technical feasibility ?
3. What is financial feasibility ?
4. What is cost of project ?
5. What are the means of finance ?
6. Estimates of sales and production - What do they mean ?
7. What are estimates of working results ?
8. What is no profit no loss point ? .
9. What are projected cash flow statements ?
10. What are projected balance sheets ?

C. ESSAY TYPE QUESTIONS

1. What is a feasibility study ? What are suggestions for defining User's needs ?
2. What are users needs in project feasibility studies? What are the hurdles that come in the way of getting correct information ?
3. What is a technical feasibility study ? What is its scope ?
4. What are inputs ? How are they classified for technical feasibility study ?
5. What is manufacturing technology ? What points should cover this vital aspect ?
6. What is product mix ? What is its make up? How does it come into picture as a part of technical feasibility ?
7. What is plant capacity ? What factors do govern plant capacity decision ?
8. What is plant location and site? What factors do govern the selection of a region, community and a site ?
9. What is the scope of financial feasibility ?
10. What are projected cash flow statements ? How is estimation of cash-flows made ?

* * * * * *

Chapter 6

PROJECT FEASIBILITY STUDIES PART-2

- A. SOCIAL COST BENEFIT ANALYSIS
- SHADOW PRICING OF SPECIFIC RESOURCES
- ENVIRONMENTAL APPRAISAL OF PROJECTS
- TYPES AND DIMENSIONS OF A PROJECT
- MAJOR ISSUES IN PREPARATION OF EIS/EAI
- CHOICE OF METHODOLOGY
- CHAPTER BASED QUESTIONS

BACKDROP

In part I of Feasibility Studies - an attempt is made in having the essential knowledge and understanding of two important types of feasibility studies. This chapter plans to consider, indepth, the other dimensions or parts of feasibility studies namely, Economic Analysis or Economic feasibility and Environmental appraisal which has caught the attention of all as the process of industrialisation produces good many products and services by making use of the resources of the society and is not free from other products which create environmental problems and threats that challenge the very existence of flora and fauna. This ecological viability or analysis is of top-most importance. The chapter ends with Chapter Based Questions.

A. SOCIAL COST BENEFIT ANALYSIS

WHAT IS COST BENEFIT ANALYSIS ?

Social cost benefit analysis or economic analysis is the methodology designed to evaluate investment projects from the angle of society for which it is being developed and implemented as a part of economic system. It is a tool for evaluating the value of money, particularly in public sector projects. When one thinks of "Social benefits", one can not forget the "Social Costs". Social costs mean all those harmful consequences and damages which a community on the whole sustains as a result of productive processes and for which private entrepreneurs are not held responsible. "Social Costs" concept covers in its fold the social opportunity costs, avoidable wastes and social inefficiencies of different kinds. The implicit assumption is that the main objective of investment decision-making is to maximise the net present value of monetary flow or some variant of it. Though, this social cost benefit analysis is applicable to public investments in most of the countries especially developing countries where government plays significant role In the whole process of economic development, it is equally applicable to private investments as these are subject to approval by governmental and semi-governmental agencies which bring to bear larger national considerations in their decisions.

In the context of developing countries through economic planning, social cost benefit analysis helps in evaluating individual projects within the planned frame-work which spells out national economic objectives for the well being of society and broad allocation of resources of various sectors. Put alternatively, social cost benefit analysis is the process of making tactical decisions within the frame-work of broad strategic choices defined by planning at macro-level. The perspectives and the parameters provided by the macro-level plans serve as the basis of social cost benefit analysis which is a powerful tool for analysing and appraising the individual projects.

Indian economy is undergoing sweeping structural changes since 1991 whereby wide ranging reforms have been introduced in almost all sections through liberalisation, privatisation and globalisation. In this fast emerging scenario of globalisation, the Indian industrial sector requires considerable upgradation in many areas where the survival and success are dictated by the forces of competitiveness and quality. In a resource-scarce economy like India, an effective measuring rod not magic wand, is a must to guage the appropriateness of investments as the process of globalisation is bound to accelerate in the years to come.

RATIONALE BEHIND SOCIAL COST BENEFIT ANALYSIS

The essence of social cost benefit analysis is that it does not accept that the actual receipts of a project adequately measure social benefits and actual expenditures measure social costs. The reason is that actual prices may be inadequate indicator of economic benefits and costs. For instance, in developing countries such as ours, the prices of necessities are set below, in spite of their economic importance, while the prices of less essential goods are set high through a mechanism of taxes and duties. As a result, some projects which appear very promising and profitable when their inputs and outputs are valued at actual prices which, in fact, are unattractive from the focal point of national economy, while other apparently unprofitable projects have high economic returns. However, the theory of social cost benefit analysis accounts that actual receipts and expenditures can be suitably adjusted so that the difference between them, close to ordinary profit, are made to reflect the social gain.

That is, the social cost benefit analysis focusses its attention on social costs and benefits of a given project. These social costs and benefits very often tend to differ from monetary costs and benefits of a given project. The major areas of discrepancy are those which are explained below under six captions.

1. **Market Imperfections :** The market prices, that form the very basis for computing the monetary costs and benefits from the angle of project sponsor, reflect social values only under conditions of perfect competition which hardly prevail in developing countries. Hence, imperfections are present, the market prices do not reflect social values. The most common market imperfections present in developing countries are: (a) rationing (b) prescribed minimum wage rates and (c) foreign exchange regulations. Rationing of a commodity implies control over its price and distribution. The price paid by the consumer under rationing is disproportionately less than the price that would prevail in a competitive market. When minimum wage rates are prescribed, the wages paid to working class are usually higher than what the wages would be in a competitive labour market free from such wage legislations. Again, the official rate of foreign exchange in majority of developing countries is typically less than the rate that would prevail in absence of foreign exchange regulations. This is the root cause as to why the foreign exchange usually commands a high premium in unofficial transactions.

2. **Externalities :** A given project may have beneficial external effects. For instance, it may create certain infra-structural facilities such as roads, and other utilities which are sure to benefit neighbouring areas. Such benefits are considered in social cost

benefit analysis though they are ignored in assessing the monetary benefits to the project sponsors, because they do not receive any monetary compensation from those who enjoy this external benefit created by the project. It is equally true that a given project may have harmful external effects like environment pollution of all kinds. Under social cost benefit analysis, the cost of such environmental pollution is very relevant though the project sponsors may not incur any monetary costs. It is worth emphasizing here that externalities are relevant in social cost benefit analysis, because in such analysis all costs and benefits, irrespective of whom they accrue and whether they are paid for or not, are relevant.

3. **Taxes and Subsidies :** These taxes and subsidies are definitely the monetary costs and gains respectively speaking privately. However socially or publicly taxes and subsidies are treated as mere transfer payments and, hence, considered irrelevant. This game of taxation and subsidisation works on the principle of "steal officially from Paul and give it Peter."

4. **Concern for Savings :** A private firm does not put differential valuation on savings and consumption, not bothered about how the benefits are decided between consumption and savings. However, from social point of view, the division of benefits between consumption and savings that leads to investment is relevant, especially in capital deficient developing countries to rupee of benefits saved is worth more valuable than a rupee of benefits consumed. The concern of society for savings and investment is duly considered in social cost benefit analysis wherein a higher valuation is placed on savings and lower valuation is put on consumption. It is because, a rupee less consumed is a rupee more saved.

5. **Concern for Redistribution :** A private firm is not worried as to how the social benefits are distributed among various groups in the society. However, society is really concerned about the distribution of benefits amongst different segments of it. A rupee of a benefit going to a poor section is considered more valuable than a benefit going to a rich or well-to-do segment. Privately, nobody is bothered about anybody, whereas socially every one is worried about everyone where commonality is common whereas in private, it is uncommon.

6. **Merit Wants :** Merit wants are those goals and preferences which not expressed in the market place but believed by policy makers in the larger interest. For instance, the government of a nation say prefers to promote adult education programme or a balanced nutrition programme for school going children even though these are not sought by consumers in the market place. That is, merit wants are not relevant from the angle of private segment while they are very important from social sector as a whole which believes in maximum social advantage and minimum social disadvantage.

THE OBJECTIVE OF SOCIAL COST BENEFIT ANALYSIS

The objective of SCBA is to secure and achieve the value of money in economic life by simply evaluating the costs and benefits of alternative economic choices and selecting an alternative that offers the maximum net benefit - that is - excess of benefits over costs, in its widest sense.

Broadly, SCBA involves five step choice of a given project :

1. Estimation of social costs and benefits that accrue to the project implementing body.
2. Estimating of costs and benefits which account the individual members of society as consumers or as suppliers of factor input.
3. Estimating of costs and benefits which accrue to the community.
4. Estimating the social cost and benefits that accrue to the National Exchequer and
5. Discounting the social costs and benefits that accure over a period time to determine the feasibility of the project. What is worth remembering is that the non-quantifiable benefits are stated only in descriptive terms and these strategies will work towards the appropriate calculation of profitability ratios. What is described above is general approach to project formulation, implementation and evaluation. However, the same may be modified to suit the specific circumstances.

APPROACHES OF SCBA

The end of 1960s and the early 1970s experts came out with two main approaches towards Social Cost Benefit Analysis. These are UNIDO approach and L-M approach - (Little - Mirrlees approach). An attempt is made to present these two approaches in a palatable way.

1. THE UNIDO APPROACH : UNIDO approach was for the first time presented in the GUIDELINES FOR PROJECT EVALUATION - United Nations 1972 which represents a very comprehensive framework for SCBA in developing countries. It was so rigorous and lengthy that, there was need for more precise and operational guide for project evaluation in practice. With a view to fulfil this need, UNIDO came out with another publication namely, "Guide to Practical Project Appraisal" in 1978.

The UNIDO method or approach of project appraisal contains at least five stages. These logical steps or stages are:

(1) Calculating the financial profitability of the project measured at market prices
(2) Obtaining the net benefit of project measured in terms of economic - efficiency - prices

(3) Adjusting for the impact of the project on savings and investment

(4) Adjusting for the impact of project on income distribution and

(5) Adjusting for the impact of project on merit goods and demerit goods whose social values differ from their economic values. Here, each stage of appraisal measures the desirability of the project from a different dimension. Let us touch these stages to know the implications.

STAGE 1. Calculating of Financial Profitability of the Project Measured at Market Prices : The measurement of financial profitability of the project is almost the same as financial feasibility as discussed at length in the previous chapter. There is no point in just repeating the same here. Hence, it is thought fit to move on to the next stage.

STAGE 2. Obtaining the Net Benefit of Project Measured in Terms of Economic/ Efficiency Prices : The first and the second stages hover round the determination of the net benefit of the project in terms of economic/efficiency prices. These 'economic/efficiency' prices are also called as "shadow prices". In a given situation, market prices represent shadow prices only under conditions of perfect markets that are almost unfulfilled in developing countries invariably. This fact makes it necessary to develop shadow prices and measure the net economic benefit in terms of these prices.

While understanding of shadow prices and prices, there is need to have basic understanding of certain concepts and issues relating these prices. These concepts and issues are narrated as under:

A. CHOICE OF NUMERAIRE :

It is one of the major aspects of shadow-pricing that deals with the determination of the numeraire - the 'unit of account' In which the value of inputs and outputs is expressed. In order to define 'numeraire', certain questions are to be answered. These pertinent questions are:

(1) What unit of currency - domestic or foreign to be used to express benefits and costs ?

(2) Should costs and benefits be measured in current values or constant values ?

(3) With reference to which point-present or future - should costs and benefits be evaluated ?

(4) What use - consumption or investment will be made of the income from the project ?

(5) Should the income of the project be measured in terms of consumption or investment ?

(6) With reference to which group should the income of the projected to be measured ?

"Numeraire" as specified by UNIDO approach stands for the "net present consumption in the hands of people at the base level of consumption in the private sector in terms of constant price in domestic accounting rupees."

B. THE CONCEPT OF TRADABILITY :

One of the key issues in shadow pricing is whether a 'good' is tradable or not. For a 'good' tradable the international price is a measure of its opportunity cost to the country in question. It is so because, for a tradable good, it is possible to substitute import for domestic production and vice versa. Similarly, it is possible to substitute export for domestic consumption and vice versa. Therefore, the international price which is very often referred to as 'border price', represents the 'real' value of the 'good' in terms of economic efficiency.

C. SOURCES OF SHADOW PRICES :

The UNIDO approach has come out with three sources of shadow pricing depending on the impact of the project on national economy. A project, as it uses and produces resources, may for any given input or output *(a)* increase or decrease the total consumption in the economy, *(b)* decrease or increase production in the economy, (c) decrease imports or increase imports, or *(d)* increase exports or decrease exports. If the impact of the project is on consumption in the economy, the basis of shadow pricing is consumer willingness to pay. If the impact of the project is on production in the economy, the basis of shadow pricing is the cost of production. If the impact of project is on international trade, that is, increase in exports, decrease in imports, increase in imports or decrease in exports - the basis of shadow pricing is the foreign exchange value.

D. TAXES :

Taxes generally pose some difficulties when shadow prices are being calculated. Therefore, the UNIDO approach has come out with a set of general guidelines with regard to taxes as follows: *(a)* When a project results in diversion of non-traded inputs which are in fixed supply from other producers or addition to non-traded consumer goods, taxes should be included (b) When a project augments the domestic production by other producers, taxes should be excluded (c) For fully traded goods, taxes should be ignored.

E. CONSUMER WILLINGNESS TO PAY :

In case the impact of the project is on consumption in the economy, as noted earlier, the basis of shadow pricing is consumer willingness to pay. The question is as to how this is measured? Graphically, it can be explained. Look into the below given graph (Fig: 6:1) that helps us to understand about consumer willingness to pay and its measurement. The line DD' represents the demand schedule, SS' the supply schedule, E the equilibrium point, OQ the quantity bought, and OP the price per unit. A glance at demand schedule makes it clear that consumer who buys the first unit is willing to pay OD for the unit and the consumer who buys the last unit is willing to pay OP for that unit. Hence, the consumer willingness to pay for various units is reflected by the schedule DE. Therefore, the total willingness to pay by consumers who buy the product is measured by the area ODEQ. The price paid by them, however, is only OPEQ. The difference between ODEQ and OPEQ, namely, DEP, is referred to as consumer surplus.

Now we are in position to go ahead with the actual work of shadow pricing of specific resources.

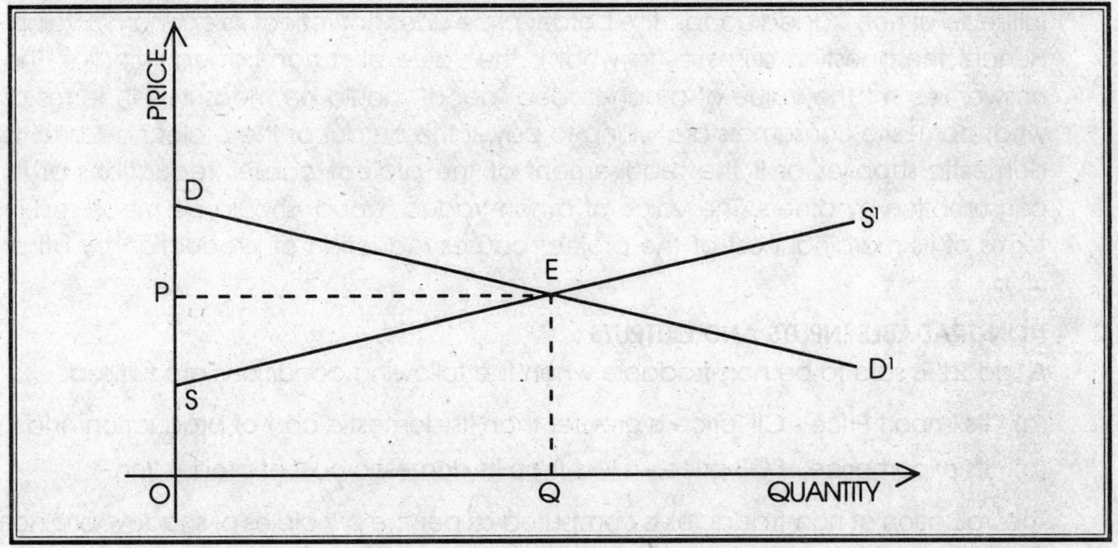

Fig. 6.01

SHADOW PRICING OF SPECIFIC RESOURCES

Under this heading, we discuss in depth those points that come under the umbrella of specific resources. These are:

1. **TRADABLE INPUTS AND OUTPUTS :**
   A 'good' is fully traded when an increase in its consumption results in a corresponding increase in import or decrease in export or when an increase its production results in a corresponding increase in export or decrease in import. For fully traded goods, the shadow price is the border price, translated in domestic currency at the market exchange rate. It means that domestic changes in demand or supply affect just the level of imports of exports. In other words, for an "imported good", the following conditions should be fulfilled: (a) If there is an import quota, it is not restrictive. (b) The import supply is perfectly elastic over the relevant range of import volume. (c) There is no surplus capacity in the domestic industry. That is, all additional supply is imported and if surplus domestic capacity, it can not be utilised for the want of essential inputs. (d) If the additional demand exists in homeland, the imported goods, even after accounting for transport cost from the port of entry to the home land demand cost

is less than the marginal cost of local production. (e) The imported input costs less than the domestic marginal cost of purchase.

Prevailence of above conditions results in meeting additional demand by external trade. Therefore, the input is considered fully traded. Likewise, similar conditions must be satisfied for importable outputs, exportable inputs, and exportable outputs, if they are to be considered fully traded. Underground-reality conditions, it is reasonable to treat tradable inputs and outputs as fully traded, even if the above said conditions are not fully met. A 'good' is not traded if it is tradable but all five conditions are not fulfilled. For non-traded goods, the border price does not reflect its economic value. Hence, the question arises as to what is the value of a non-traded goods ? The answer lies in : The value of a non-traded 'good' should be measured in terms of what domestic consumers are willing to pay, if the output of the project adds to its domestic supplies or if the requirement of the project causes reductions of its consumption by others. The value of a non-traded 'good' should be measured in terms of its marginal cost of the project causes reduction of production by other units.

2. NON-TRADABLE INPUTS AND OUTPUTS :

A 'good' is said to be non-tradable when the following conditions are fulfilled:

(a) Its Import Price - CIF price is greater than its domestic cost of production and

(b) Its export price - FOB price - is less than its domestic cost of production.

The valuation of non-tradables is computed as per the principles of shadow-pricing. On the output side, if the impact of the project is to increase the consumption of the project in the economy, the measure of value is the marginal consumers' willingness to pay; in case, the impact of the project is to substitute other production of the same non-tradable in the economy, the measure of value is the saving in the cost of production. On the input side, if the impact of the project is to reduce the availability of the input to other users their willingness to pay for that input represents the social value; if the projects input requirement is met by additional production of it, the production cost of it is the measure of social value.

3. EXTERNALITIES :

An externality or an external effect is a special class of 'good' which has the features as outlined under: (a) It is not deliberately created by the project sponsor but is an accidental outcome of legitimate economic activity. (b) It is beyond the control of the persons who are affected by it either for better or worse. (c) It is not traded in market place.

An externality or external effect may be beneficial or harmful. The instances of beneficial externalities are say: (1) An oil company drilling in its own fields, may generate useful information about oil potential in the neighbouring fields (2) An approach road or roads built by a company may improve transport system in that area (3) A training programme of a firm may upgrade the skills of its employees resulting in their earning capacity in subsequent employments.

The instances of harmful effects can be: (1) A plant may cause environmental pollution by emitting excessive smoke and poisonous gases, in addition to dust and dirt. The people in the neighbourhood may be exposed to health hazards; even flora of the area might be badly affected. (2) The location of an airport in a particular area may raise noise level beyond tolerance of the people residing around airport. (3) A highway may cut a farmer's land holding into two- separating his grazing land and cow sheds, causing thereby adverse effect on his physical output.

As Social Cost Benefit analysis takes all costs and benefits, external effects of these can not be ignored irrespective of whosoever they accrue to. The valuation of such external effects is rendered difficult because they are often intangible in nature and there is no market price which can be used as a starting point. Hence, their value is estimated by indirect means. For instance, the benefit of information provided by the oil field to neighbouring oil fields may be equated with what the neighbouring oil fields would have spent to get such information; the value of better transport provided by the approach roads may be estimated in terms of increased activities and benefits derived from them; the benefit accruing from training program may be estimated in terms of the increased earning power of employees; the cost of pollution may be estimated in terms of the loss of earnings as a result of damage to the health caused by it and the cost and time spent for fighting unhygienic surroundings; the cost of noise may be calculated from the differences in rent between noisy and noise free zones; the harmful external effect of the highway may be measured by the consumer willingness to pay for the output of farmer which is reduced considerably.

In view of measuring the external effects, some economists have suggested that these effects be ignored. They justify their argument on the count that a project is likely to have both beneficial and harmful external effects, one may not go wrong on the postulate that the net effect would be zero. Though, it is an attempt to rationalise, it has no validity. Hence, external effects must be taken into account wherever and whenever it is possible to do so. If not monetary or quantitative evaluation, at least qualitative evaluation is to be encouraged.

4. LABOUR INPUTS :

The principles of shadow pricing are equally applicable to labour though it is a service whenever a project hires the services of labour, it can have three possible impacts on the rest of the economy namely : (a) It may take labour away from other employments *(b)* It may induce the production of new employees and (c) It may involve import of workers.

When a project takes labour away from other employments, the shadow price of labour is equal to what other employers of labour are willing to pay for this labour. This will be equal to marginal product of such a labour, in case of a relatively free market. In case of social cost associated with inducing additional production of workers consist of the following : *(a)* the marginal product of the worker in the previous employment if the employee is previously unemployed, this would be zero *(b)* the value assigned by the worker on the leisure that he may have to forego as a result of employment in the project, the value of this leisure is reflected in his reservation wage. This reservation wage of a person depends on the factors namely, *(i)* the income he already enjoys through transfer payments *(ii)* his idea of what job is acceptable to him and *(iii)* his preference for work and leisure (c) the additional consumption of food when a worker is fully employed as opposed to when he is idle or only partly employed *(d)* the cost of transport and rehabilitation when a worker is moved from one location to another (e) the increased consumption by the worker and its negative impact on savings and investment in the society when the worker is paid market wage rate by the project and (f) the cost of training a worker to improve his skills.

The social cost associated with import of foreign workers is the wage they command. However, in case a premium should be added on account of foreign exchange remitted abroad by these workers from their savings.

5. CAPITAL INPUTS :

Whenever a capital investment is made in a project, two things take place : *(a)* Financial resources are converted into physical assets and *(b)* Financial resources are withdrawn from the national pool of savings and hence, alternative projects are foregone. Therefore, shadow pricing of capital investment involves two questions namely :

(1) What is the value of physical asset ?

(2) What is the opportunity cost of capital that reflects the benefit foregone by sacrificing alternative project or projects ?

The value or shadow price of physical assets is calculated in the way the value of other resources is calculated. If it is a fully traded good; its shadow price is equal to its border price. If it is non-traded good, its price is measured in terms of cost of production in case the project induces additional domestic production of the asset or consumer willingness to pay if the project takes the asset from other users. Turning to the opportunity cost of the capital, it depends on how the capital required for the project is generated. To the extent that it comes from additional savings, its opportunity cost is measured by the consumption rate of interest that reflects the price the saver must be paid to sacrifice present consumption; to the extent that it comes from the denial of capital alternative projects, its opportunity cost is the rate of return that would be earned from those alternative projects which is also called as the investment rate of interest. In practice, the consumption rate of interest may be used as the discount rate because in STAGE THREE OF UNIDO approach, all inputs and outputs are converted into their consumption equivalents. However, there are problems in determining the consumption rate of interest empirically. Hence, the UNIDO approach recommends a "bottom up" procedure. Under this procedure, the project analyst calculates the internal rate of return of a project and presents the project to the planners or politicians who are the decision- makers. If the project is accepted, the analyst may assume that the planners judge the consumption rate of interest to be more than the interest rate of return. For practical use, the estimated consumption rate of interest can be sufficiently narrowed for practical purpose, provided the planners at the top are consistent.

6. EXCHANGE RATE :

The UNIDO approach uses domestic currency as the numeraire. Hence, the foreign exchange input of the project must be identified and adjusted by an apropriate on price or premium. That is, the valuation of inputs and outputs that were measured in border rupees has to be adjusted upward to reflect the shadow price of foreign exchange.

The question is how exactly the shadow price of foreign exchange established ? There are two possible guidelines or approaches in this regard namely, guideline approach and programming approach.

The guideline approach determines the shadow price of foreign exchange on the basis of marginal social value as revealed by the consumer willingness to pay for the goods that are allowed to be imported at the margin. Hence, the shadow price of a unit of foreign exchange is equal to:

$$\sum_{i=1}^{n} F_i \; Q_i \; P_i$$

Where F_i = fraction of foreign exchange, at margin spent on importing commodity;

Q_i = quantity of commodity *i* that can be bought with one unit foreign exchange.

This will be equal to 1 divided by CIF value of the 'good' in question.

P_i = domestic market clearing price of a commodity *i*.

STAGE 3. Adjustment for Impact of the Project on Savings and Investment : To arrive at Savings Impact and its value, it is essential to know the exact measurement of the value of a project in terms of contribution to savings and income distribution. That is we must measure the income gained or lost by individual groups within the society. Hence, for our analysis, stage 4 comes first and stage 3 follows. Hence, we will skip to stage 4.

STAGE 4. Measurement of the Impact on Distribution : This has two aspects namely, "groups" of society and "Measure of Gain or Loss".

Groups :

The society is divided into six or more groups, as per UNIDO Approach namely, project, other private business, government, workers, consumers and external sector. However, there can be other equally valid groups.

Measure of Gain or Loss :

The gain or loss to an individual group within the society as a result of the project is equal to the difference between the shadow price and the market price of each input or output in case of physical resources or the difference between the price paid and the value received in case of a financial transaction.

To clarify this, let us take two cases. In case one say, farmers in a certain area use 1 million units of electricity generated by a hydro-electric project. The benefit derived by them, measured in terms of willingness to pay, is equal to Rs. 0.40 million. The tariff paid by them to the electricity board is Rs. 0.25 million. Hence, the impact of the project on the farmers is a gain of Rs. 0.15 million (Rs. 0.40 - Rs. 0.25). In case two say, a mining project requires 1000 labourers. These labourers are prepared to offer themselves for work at a daily wage rate of Rs. 4.00 - representing the supply price. The wage rate paid to the labourers, however, is Rs. 10.00 per day. Hence, redistribution benefit enjoyed by the grroup of 1000 labourers is Rs. 6,000. (1000 days/(Rs. 10.00 - Rs. 4.00) per day.

SAVINGS IMAPCT AND ITS VALUE

It is now that we can turn back to STAGE THREE to study the savings impact and its value. It is well established fact that developing countries are capital difficient countries. Therefore, the governments of these countries are more concerned about the impact of project on savings and its value. As said, STAGE THREE OF UNIDO Approach, concerned with this, seeks to answer the following two questions:

(1) Given the income disribution impact of the project what would be its effects on savings ?

(2) What is the value of such savings to the society ?

Impact on Savings :

The savings impact of a project is equal to:

$$\Sigma \Delta Yi\ MPSi$$

Where Δ Yi = Change in income of group i as a result of the project.

MPSi = Marginal propensity to save of the group i.

Value of Savings :

The value of a rupee of savings is the present value of the additional consumption stream produced when that rupee savings is invested at the margin. The additional stream of consumption generated by a rupee of investment depends on the marginal productivity of capital and the rate of reinvestment from additional income. If the marginal productivity of capital is 'g' and the rate of reinvestment from additional income 'a', the additional income stream of consumption generated by a rupee of investment can be worked out as under in the form of a statement.

STATEMENT SHOWING DERIVATION OF ADDITIONAL CONSUMPTION STREAM FROM A RUPEE OF INVESTMENT NOW

Year	0	1	2	3	...n...
Investment (Cumulative)	1	$1 + a\gamma$	$(1 + a\gamma)^2$	$(1 + a\gamma)^3$	$(1 + a\gamma)^n$
Income -	γ	$\gamma(1 + a\gamma)$	$\gamma(1 + a\gamma)^2$	$\gamma(1 + a\gamma)^{n-1}$	
Additional Investment	-	$a\gamma$	$a\gamma(1 + a\gamma)$	$a\gamma(1 + a\gamma)^2$	$a\gamma(1 + a\gamma)^{n-1}$
Consumption	-	$\gamma - (1-a)$	$\gamma(1-a)(1 + a\gamma)$	$\gamma(1-a)(1 + a\gamma)^2$	$\gamma(1-a)(1 + a\gamma)^{n-1}$

From the above statement, it is quite evident that the consumption stream starts with γ (1-a) and grows annually at the rate of *ay* for ever. Its present value, when discounted at the social discount rate *k* is :

$$I = \frac{\gamma(1-a)}{(1+k)} + \frac{\gamma(1-a)\ (1+a\gamma)}{(1+k)^2} + ... +$$

$$\frac{\gamma(1-a)(1+a\gamma)^{n-1}}{(1+k)^n} ....$$

$$= \frac{\frac{\gamma(1-a)}{(1+k)}}{1 - \frac{(1+a\gamma)}{(1+k)}} = \frac{\gamma(1-a)}{k - a\gamma}$$

Where I = Social value of a rupee of savings (investment)

y = marginal productivity of capital

a = reinvestment rate on additional income arising from investment

k = social discount rate

The social value of savings or shadow price of investment for certain values of y, a and k is given in the below stated statement. The formula for social value of savings holds good only when the following conditions are fulfilled :

1. The marginal productivity of capital and the reinvestment rate on additional income - marginal productivity to save - are constant over the time.
2. Savings rate in the society will not become optimum in the foreseeable future. Though these conditions appear quite restrictive, in real ground situations, may have to be accepted for the want of better or verifiable and dependable information.

INCOME DISTRIBUTION IMPACT

It is natural that a prudent government policy of redistribution of income is in favour of economically weaker sections of the society. It is not only desirable socially but essential both socially and economically. Due to practical difficulties in attaining the objective of redistribution totally on through tax, subsidy and transfer measures of the government, investment projects are also considered as investments for income redistribution and their contribution toward this goal is considered in their evaluation. This task is not easy as it calls for giving due weightage to net gain or loss by each group, measured earlier, to reflect the relative value of income for different groups and summing them. The question is how should the relative weights be determined ? Under the guidelines of UNIDO approach, weights which reflect political judgements essentially may be determined by an iterative process involving the interaction between the analyst and the planners. For instance, consider a project with : Project Net present value - Rs. 2 million

Income gain to low income group as out of project Rs. 5 million - Let us take it that the planners, have accepted the project. This means that planners place a premium of at least 40 percent on income going to the poor. In case, the planners reject the project but accept another project that requires a premium of say at least 30 percent on the income, going to the poor, the project analyst might infer that the premium placed by planners on income going to the poor lies between 30 percent and 40 percent.

This iterative process works well if only two groups are involved say poor and others. In cases where more than two groups are involved the procedure breaks down because of several unknown weights that are at work. In situation, the analyst will not be able to figure out the relative weights given by the planners on income of different groups, given the preferenc of the planners. To tackle this problem, a single factor has to be found which determines the income distribution weights so that the 'bottom up' approach becomes workable. This single factor suggested by economists is "the elasticity of marginal utility of income." The marginal utility of income is the value derived from one more unit of income. This depends, obviously, on the present level of income. Elasticity of marginal utility of income is defined by experts as the rate of which the marginal utility of income falls with increase in the level of income. For instance, if the marginal utility of income declines by 5 per cent with 5 per cent increase in income, the elasticity of marginal utility of income is 5 per cent - 5 per cent which works 1 or - 1. Same way, if the marginal utility of income declines by 10 per cent, with a 5 per cent increase in income, the elasticity of marginal utility of income is 10 per cent - 5 per cent = - 2. In case the elasticity of marginal utility is = 1.00, a 1 per cent increase in income of a person say earning Rs. 1,000 a year is socially as valuable as a 1 per cent increase in the income of a person earning Rs. 10,000 a year or Rs. 1,00,000 a year, or for that matter any amount for a year. It implies that from the social point of view the following gains the equally valuable :

A gain of Rs. 10.00 to a person earning Rs. 1,000 = 00 per year.

A gain of Rs. 100.00 to a person earning Rs. 10,000 a year

A gain of Rs. 1,000 to a person earning Rs. 1,00,000 =00 a year.

These things mean that if the weight of Rs. 1,000 = 00 is put at 1, the weight of Rs. 10,000 = 00 is 1/10, and the weight at Rs. 1,00,000 is 1/100.

The formula of the weight attached to an income is given as

$$W_i = \left(\frac{b}{C_i}\right)^n$$

Where, W_i = weight attached to income at C_i level

b = base level of income that has weight of 1

n = elasticity of the marginal utility of income.

Based on this formula, a statement is presented showing relative weights for different levels of income for values *n* varying between 0 and 1.

STAGE 5. Adjustment for the Impact of Project on merit and demerit goods : The analysis of social cost benefit stretches beyond the fourth stage in order to bring home the differences between the economic and social value of resources. This difference exists in merit and demerit goods. As noted earlier, a 'merit good' is one for which the social value exceeds the economic value. For instance, a country may put a higher social value than the economic value on production of oil because it reduces dependence on foreign supplies. The concept of merit goods can be extended to include a socially desirable outcome like creation of employment, encouraging local updated technology. In absence of the project, the government would be able to pay unemployment compensation or provide mere make-work jobs or spend on upgradation of local technology. As opposed to this, in case of a demerit good, the social value of the good is less than economic value. For instance a country may regard alcoholic products and tobacco products as having lesser social value than economic.

The procedure for adjusting for the difference between social value and economic value is outlined step-wise as follows: 1. Estimate the economic value 2. Calculate the adjustment factor as the difference between the ratio of social value to economic value and units. 3. Multiply the economic value by the adjustment factor to obtain the adjustment. 4. Add adjustment to the net present value of the project as calculated in STAGE FOUR.

Taking the following available information, this can be explained illustratively. The information available is: *(a)* The present economic value of the output of the project is Rs. 25 million. *(b)* The output of the project has a social value which exceeds its economic value by 20 per cent. Given this information the adjustment factor would be 0.2 (120 per cent/100 per cent - 1). Multiplying the present economic value by 0.2, one gets an adjustment of Rs. 5 million. This is then added to present economic value of Rs. 25 million thus making it Rs. 30 million. Where the socially valuable output of the project does not appear as an output in the economic analysis is the case where the project generates employment the procedure is some what different. In such a case, the output is treated like an externality and its valuation in social terms is the adjustment.

Though this process of adjusting the difference in social and economic value is a right step in the right direction, is subject to abuse. Once the analyst starts making adjustment for social reasons, the projects which are undesirable economically may be made to appear quite attractive after such adjustment. Since the dividing line between 'political' and 'social' is rather vague, it becomes some what easy to push politically expedient projects, irrespective of their economic merit by investing them with social desirability. Though, there is no way to prevent such manipulation, the stage by stage UNIDO Approach is sure to mitigate its occurrence by bringing it in spot light.

2. LITTLE-MIRRLEES APPROACH : Another approach of Social Cost Benefit Analysis is LM Approach as propounded by **I.M.D. Little** and **J.A. Mirrlees** in their Manual of Industrial Project analysis in Developing Countries, Volume II and Project - An Appraisal and planning for Developing Countries.

There are points of similarities and dis-similarities between the UNIDO Approach and L.M. Approach.

POINTS OF SIMILARITY ARE :

1. Calculating accounting-shadow prices particularly for foreign exchange savings and unskilled labour.

2. Considering the factor of equity.

3. Use of DCF - discounted cash flow analysis.

POINTS OF DISSIMILARITY ARE :

1. **The UNIDO Approach measures costs and benefits in terms of domestic rupees** unlike L-M Approach which measures costs and benefits in terms of international prices which are better known as 'border prices.

2. **The UNIDO Approach measures costs and benefits** in terms of consumption whereas the L-M Approach measures the costs and benefits in terms of uncommitted social income.

3. **The stage by stage analysis recommended by UNIDO Approach** focusses on efficiency, savings and the re-distribution considerations. However, the L-M Approach tends to view these considerations together and not separately.

B. ENVIRONMENTAL APPRAISAL OF PROJECTS

In the decision making process, the planners and the anlysts alongwith promoters should not forget the effects of their actions. They need not go by only commercial success and the project be selected, implemented and controlled. There are other effects than economic which are aweful especially environmental hazards that are produced along with main and subsidiary outputs. These effects are to be identified, assessed and evaluated against the economic benefits arising out of a given action. It goes without saying that economic development is the outcome of the interaction between man and his environment. That is, the interaction between the natural resources and technology supported and designed by people. People are right at the heart of development. No wonder when learned people have expressed that all human activities, be they are economic, social or anything else, are essentially directed to satisfy the 'needs' and 'wants' of mankind through 'altering' and 'using' environmental resources.

World-wide appreciation of the gravity of environmental problems and related issues has been slow and it is much slower in India because we are Indians. Until a problem becomes a serious personal nuisance, Indians tend to ignore it. This, in fact, seems to be a human trait; people act when faced with crises. Take for instance, a question of traffic congestion. When they recognise it as a crisis, people tend to deal with the problem at the same level as that of 'perceived' problem like building flyovers to relieve traffic congestion. People do not, in general, transcend it and deal with it from a higher level where a solution can emerge - in the case of traffic, alternate modes of transportation and methods of work organisation. That can only stem from a deeper understanding of overall system.

TYPES AND DIMENSIONS OF A PROJECT

There can be, broadly, two types of projects, namely 'physical' and 'non-physical'.

Physical projects are those projects that produce physical goods say steel, cement, paper, chemicals, electric, mechanic, electronic goods which may be industrial or consumer goods both durables and non-durables. These projects, in fact, convert the natural resource endowments into exchangeable or sale products. These projects, in fact, inflict a large number of physical changes and discrimptions on environment, and therefore, cause disturbance and imbalance to the environment and ecology. Environmentalists are deeply and greatly concerned with such type of projects. As opposed to physical projects, **non-physical projects** are engaged in producing or rendering various kinds of services such as health, education, transport, energy, defence, law and order and so on. These projects also cover the actions like land reforms, agricultural extension services, sales-promotion campaigns, afforestation, conservation of water resources and so on. These projects are non-physical in nature and they do not directly cause any physical changes in the environment-particularly bad. However, they bring in significant changes of far-reaching consequences on values, attitudes, life-styles, social relations and the like. The net effect of such projects is the creation of new wants and needs in the society. They, in the final analysis, promote consumerism in the society and thereby increase the number of manufacturing projects. Thus, both are inter-related.

Each project has two dimensions namely, (a) the intended, objectives or purposes which can be better called as stated goals or benefits and *(b)* the unintended consequences which are also called as externalities or social costs, are unplanned, unwanted and unanticipated. Environmental management or planning is the study of the unintended consequences of a project. Environment management aims at identifying, examining, assessing and evaluating the likely and probable impacts of a proposed project on environment and, thereby, to work out the remedial action plans to minimise the incidence of adverse impacts. It is not anti-development nor it is against the projects. The goal is to develop or encourage development without damage or with least damage to the environment.

STRESSES ON ENVIRONMENT

Environmentalists or ecologists have identified four different types of stresses or pressures that are being continually inflicted on environment in which human race-along with other species living since the time immemorial. They are:

A. EUTROPHIC STRESS :

This refers to the release of various kinds of wastes into the river and other water bodies and their consequent drying.

B. EXPLOITATIVE STRESS :

It refers to the exploitation of natural resources endowment for production and consumption purposes through agriculture, industry, extraction, fishing and the like. Here, it is significant and relevant to note that the rate of exploitation has a relevance to the natures reproducing capacity.

C. DISRUPTIVE STRESS :

This refers to the physical alterations in nature resulting from such activities like forest clearance, highways, railways, airways, waterways, factory buildings and the like. These changes - both apparent and concealed-cause disturbance to environmental and ecological balance.

D. CHEMICAL AND INDUSTRIAL STRESS :

These are the outcome of science and technology and their applied fields like industry, warfare, space research, agriculture and so on. This comprises of mainly the pollutants and effluents of all types radiation and the like.

Strategies to meet these threats to natural environment through pollution, destruction and overuse can be - both preventive and corrective. It is in this context that environmental appraisal of projects is gaining ground with a hope of attaining sustainable development in harmony with the environment.

ENVIRONMENT AND ITS GAMUT

Environment is very often referred to all those things that are external to a human organism. It encompasses the region, surroundings or circumstances in which anything that exists. It is broadly divided into two components : 1. The abiotic or inorganic millieu, comprising of physical elements like land, water, atmosphere, climate sound, odours and tastes. These are inanimate elements of the habitat systems. Second-the biotic or the organic milieu consisting of animals, plants, bacteria, viruses, all other organisms and the social factors not excluding aesthetics. They are the animate elements.

The more useful and relevant definition of environment in the context of projects which stands for the "surrounding zone-the specific zone to be affected by the project - all natural resources ¾ physical and biological, and the human resources ¾ people, economic development and quality of life. This definition is more suited to organise, quantify and measure environmental impacts of a given action, because this definition is more specific, succinct, focussed and clear. The underlying aspect of this definition is "surrounding zone" or the 'project vicinity". One should distinguish between 'legal' and 'environmental' boundary. Legal boundary refers to the area legally occupied by the project and the 'environmental boundary' that stretches beyond legal boundary. The second one is more relevant to our study because environmental boundary is the area around the project that is likely to be affected environmentally by the project operations. The extent of environmental boundary for a project depends on the diffusion factors like wind speeds, and directions, elevations and the like, among other things. Naturally, it varies from project to project and location to location of some project because no two projects or locations are alike.

There is another definition which is more relevant for our environmental analysis in case of projects. This specific definition runs as :

"The external, natural, physical and residential conditions which affect a man directly and indirectly and which are, in turn, influenced by economic decisions and technological developments."

This definition stands for a complex interactive model between man, environment and science and technology, the outcome of which will be economic development and what is more important is that project facilitates such an interaction.

Environmental management is a phrase encompassing environmental planning, protection, monitoring, assessment, research, education, conservation, and sustainable use of resources, is now accepted as a major guiding factor in all economic decision-making processes on development or otherwise. As government is aware that self regulation alone will not work and therefore, has come out with a wide network of legislation. Hence, environmental clearance for all the major projects on the basis of Environmental Impact Statement (EIS) has been made mandatory in legal terms.

ENVIRONMENTAL RESOURCES OR VALUES

As the word 'environment' is an all-inclusive concept covering within its fold everything external to human race, it is really very difficult to operationalise and apply to particular situations like projects. For the purposes of operationalisation and practical application, the environmentalists have developed a concept called "Environmental Resources or values - well abbriviated as ER/Vs." ER/Vs is defined as an aspect of environment which is of benefit to mankind. The environmentalists have identified and classified various components of environment - that is - ER/Vs into four levels as below :

A. **LEVEL-1.** Physical Resources covering land, water and air.

B. **LEVEL-2.** Ecological Resources consisting of acquatic, terrestrial and endangered or rare species - other than man.

C. **LEVEL-3.** Human Use values, covering transport, agriculture, water supply, recreation, mining, industry, flood control and the like.

D. **LEVEL-4.** Quality life values, covering socio-economic, cultural and aesthetic aspects.

It means that the whole environment is decomposed into several operationally feasible components or elements. These elements can be further sub-divided into good deal of related items. Alternatively, some other environmentalists identify and classify the various elements of environment broadly under eight types namely, (1) Air (2) Water (3) Land (4) Ecology (5) Sound (6) Human aspects (7) Economics and (8) Resources. These are called as Environmental Attributes (EA). Each EA can be further subdivided into different but related elements.

With regard to environmental appraisal of projects, one is expected to follow one of the two classifications namely Environmental Resources/Values (ER/Vs) or the Environmental Attributes (EA). Factually, they can be evaluated assessed individually with respect to the impacts they receive or the changes they undergo due to the proposed project. As there will be a variety of impacts of varying degrees from project to project, the decomposition of environment unit into various quantifiable elements will enable the analyst to give focus and direction to his impact assessment analysis. An environmental effect is considered as an effect of natural or man-made actions which alter environment-as measured by physical, chemical and biological parameters. The project analyst's concern is, however, on man-made actions. The nature and extent of environmental impacts including the magnitude, severity, urgency risk and so on of a project in the final analysis depends on: *(a)* Nature, size and type of the project such as manufacturing, services, agriculture, mining, logging power, harbour, chemicals, sugar and the like, *(b)* technology (c) Location or the eco-region such as urban or rural areas, coastal, river valley, forest or hill areas or any of the eco-system as noted earlier.

WHAT IS ENVIRONMENTAL IMPACT ASSESSMENT EIA ?

Environmental Impact Assessment and **Environmental Impact Statement** are the instruments through which the environmental management tries to accomplish its objective. **Environmental Impact Assessment** is defined as "An activity designed to identify, predict, interpret, and communicate information about the impact of an action on man's health and well-being including the well-being of eco systems on which man's survival depends. In turn, the action is defined to include any engineering project, legislative proposal, policy program, or operational procedure with environmental implications." An **EIA**, therefore, is a study of the probable changes in the various socio-economic and bio-physical attributes of the environment which may result from a proposed action.

WHAT IS ENVIRONMENTAL IMPACT STATEMENT ?

EIS is defined as "A Report, based on studies, disclosing the likely or certain environmental consequences of a proposed action, thus alerting the decision makes, the public and the government to environmental risks involved, the findings enable better informed decisions to be made, perhaps to reject or defer the proposed action or permit it subject to compliance with specific conditions."

It means that the EIS is a document prepared by an expert agency on the environmental impacts of proposed action/project that significantly affects the quality of environment. It is used mainly as a tool for decision-making. Though the words EIA and EIS are freely used interchangeably, both are different inspite of good deal of commonalities and common purposes. The basic difference between the two is that the EIA is carried out by the expert agency while EIS a tool given to decision-makers in different formats. As it is, the EIS is the outcome of EIA. It is better to consider the environmental consequences during the project planning and designing stage in order to avoid higher costs of future remedial actions by a wise-planning and early preventive measures.

OBJECTIVES OF ENVIRONMENTAL IMPACT STATEMENT

EIS has three basic objectives to serve. These are :

1. **To Identify and Describe in as Quantified** manner as possible the environmental resources/values or the environmental attributes which will be affected by the project, under existing or "with or without" conditions.
2. **To describe, measure, and assess the environmental effects** that the proposed project will have on the environmental resources/values in as quantified manner as possible including positive effects which enhance environmental resources/values as well as the negative effects which impair them. Direct or indirect and short-term or long-term effects are to be considered. This also includes the description of the specific ways by which the project plan or design will minimise the adverse effects and maximise positive effects.
3. **To describe the alternatives to the proposed project** which could accomplish the same results but with a different set of environmental effects. Energy generation by thermal, hydel and nuclear modes would explain the case point. Further, alternative locations also are considered.

GUIDELINES ON THE SCOPE AND CONTENTS OF EIS AND EIA

Undermentioned are the commonly accepted points that are to be covered in EIS study or report.

1. **A Description of the Project Proposed Action** : It makes statement of its purpose and description of all relevant technical details to give a complete understanding of the proposed action, including the kinds of materials, man-power/resources involved.
2. **The Relationship of Proposed Action to the Land-Use Plans, Policies and Controls**: The relationship of the proposed action to the land-use plans, policies and controls in the affected area or the project vicinity. It is necessary to gain a complete understanding of the affected environment. What is the nature of bio-physical and socio-economic characteristics that may be changed by the action ?
3. **The Probable Impacts of the Proposed Project on the Environment** : The probable impacts of the proposed project on environment is a very significant aspect to

be considered in detail. It is necessary to project the proposed action into the future and to determine the possible impacts on the environmental attributes. The changes are to be quantified wherever possible.

4. **Alternatives to Proposed Action** : Alternatives to the proposed action, including those not within the existing authority or agency.
5. **Adverse Environmental Effects that can not be Avoided** : Any probable adverse environmental effects that can not be avoided and stating how each avoidable impact will be mitigated.
6. **The Relationship between Short-term Use of Man's Environment and Long term Productivity Improvement** : The relationship between local short-term uses of man's environment and the maintenance of and enhancement of long-term productivity.
7. **Any Irreversible and Irretrievable Commitments of Resources** : Any irreversible and irretrievable commitments of resources including natural, cultural, labour and materials.
8. **Indication of Other Interests and Consideration of Government Policy** : An indication of what other interests and considerations of government policy or programme are thought to off-set the adverse effects identified.

In short, the EIA, is very complex exercise due to the fact that many and varied types of projects are proposed for an equally numerous and varied kinds of environmental settings, by its purpose, scope and contents. Each combination of projects and the complex environmental settings result in a unique cause and effect relationships with regard to their impacts. Hence, combination must be studied individually in order to fairly good and comprehensive analysis.

METHODOLOGY FOR CONDUCTING ENVIRONMENTAL APPRAISAL

There is no one standard method or procedure to conduct EIS mainly because of the difficulties encountered in quantifying the effects which are intangible, complex, and imperceptible in nature. Hence, it is really very difficult to establish meaningful and purposive parameters to portray the effects and their quantification. This difficult task is aggraved by some special factors of which four are worth emphasizing. These are : (1) The diffused nature of impacts in terms of time and space and the gaps in impacts after the cause is worked (2) Any environmental effect is the joint product of several pollutants (3) Inadequacy of techniques to estimate the impacts and costs and (4) Unaware of impacts on the part of people as the impacts are imperceptible.

As intricate and complex problems are involved in identification and quantification of effects, all the sincere efforts to develop quantitive approaches to EIA-including the checklists, matrices, net works, flow-charts-relationships and map overlays, - have been subjective per se as quantification rests on the background and bias of the investigator or the observer.

Despite these hurdles, the generally accepted approach for conducting EIS is one of Item-by Item Review of Effects on the individual environmental resources/values, including both the identification of ER/Vs, and the description and quantification of the effect to the extent it is possible. Such an attempt has series of logical steps which are outlined that make a procedure.

1. **Make Rapid Scanning of Basic Environmental Resources** : These environmental resources are land, water and air, at the macro-level, say the district level where project is to be located. This scanning or appraisal is designed to evaluate the extent of fragility and exploitation of the endowed resource base not excluding the human resources. It is to be followed by relating the project to the regional environment broad terms.

2. **Demarcate the Project Vicinity** : Demarcating the project vicinity or the surrounding zone of the project is done by means of maps as it is a matter of mapping.

3. **Identify, Assess and Describe all the Environmental Attributes** : This is the task of identification, assessing and describing all the environmental attributes to be given in the form of a table that is four levels of environmental resources and values endowed in the vicinity. This gives a total picture of the environment before the start of the project.

4. **Rank the Identified ER/Vs in terms of Dimensions** : Ranking or prioritising the identified ER/Vs by dimensions of fragility, significance, relevance, and quality. This helps in concentrating on the very vital items than thin spread over a large number of items of lesser significance.

5. **Carryout the Item by Item Review** : Next task is to carry out the item-by item review of the effects of the proposed project on the identified ER/Vs embodied in the project vicinity.

6. **Arrange the Effects in a Agreeable Format** : This is the task of rearrangng or grouping the effects in systematic manner for easy grasp preferably in a format.

7. **Prepare Remedial Plans**: The last, but not the least, the step involved is one of preparing remedial plans for mitigating the adverse effects which may be - corrective, compensatory or even enhancing.

MAJOR ISSUES IN PREPARATION OF EIS/EIA

The experts have brought to the surface some major issues that are encountered while preparing EIS/EIA. Some of the issued can not be resolved and, hence, the analyst has to accept these issues as they are. The basic issues are :

1. **Determining the Environmental Impacts** : Determination of environmental impact is the very heart of EIS/EIA. However, it is most complex process. To begin with, it needs drawing of distinction between the environmental impact and the changes in the environmental attributes. Analysts are interested in 'impacts" and not in the "changes" which generally take place between variables even without the project. The process of determining the environmental impacts encompasses specific activities of *(a)* identification of impacts on environmental attributes or the environmental resources/values (b) measurement of impacts on attributes and (c) aggregation of impacts on attributes to project the total impact on environment.

2. **Impact Measurement in Terms of Net Change at a Given Point of Time** : The environmental impacts are the measurement of attributes with and without the project or activity at a given point of time. However, the changes in the attributes take place over the time without the activity. Therefore, the impact must be measured in terms of 'net' change in the attribute at a given point of time.

3. **Identifying the Impacts** : The number of attributes to be evaluated is invariably infinite because any feature of the environment is considered to be an attribute. Hence, they have to be reduced to manageable numbers. That is redundant, duplicative, cumbersome to measure and obscure attributes may be eliminated in favour of those that are more amenable or tractable. This means that some attributes which are very complex to measure or conceptualise may remain to be examined. It is because of this, greater amount of bias and subjectivity are sure to creep in.

4. **Characteristics of Base** : Conditions Prior to the Activity (CPA) need base for computation. The nature of the impact is determined by the condition of the environment existing before the project. The critical factor is the assessment of the characteristics of the base. Take the case of geographical characteristics. The same activity produces different impacts on a particular attribute, say water quality, over different geographical areas. The spatial distribution of different activities introduces one of the difficult entities in comparing one activity and its impact with another. This issue becomes of sinual importance or critical while making choices between projects.

5. **Role of Attributes** : Even though the impacts are considered to be the effects on the definite discrete attributes of the environment, the actual impacts are not correspondingly well bifurcated. Nature, per se, respects man's discrete categories. Speaking strictly, the actual impacts may be the effects of varying severity on a variety of inter-related attributes. The issue is one of identifying and assessing the condition-effect in order to work out the remedial measures.

6. **Measurement of Impact** : Under ideal situations, all impacts must be translated or translable into common units. However, it is not possible because of the difficulty in defining impacts in common units say, for instance, on income and on water quality. Added to this, quantification of some of the impacts may be well beyond the state of the art.

7. **Aggregation Problem** : After the due measurement of the project impacts on various individual attributes or ER/Vs, one faces the problem of aggregating all impacts - both quantitative and qualitative. The issue is how to arrive at a single composite measure to represent the "total activity impact". This entails expressing the various impact-measures in common units which is almost very difficult, if not impossible. Some experts use weighing procedure to attain this which is again subjective. Another associated problem is that of summing up and comparing with the impact of an alternative activity.

8. **Secondary Impacts** : Secondary or indirect impacts on environment should find place in relation to infrastructure investments that stimulate or induce secondary effects in the form of associated investments and the changed patterns of social and economic activity. Such induced growth brings important changes in the natural conditions. Likewise, there can be also important secondary impacts in the bio-physical environment.

9. **Cumulative Impacts** : Cumulative or cumulation stands for the similar activities spread over in an environmental setting like hotels, beach resorts, surface or ground mines, industrial estates and the like. A single individual activity may produce a negligible effect on environment. However, a series of similar activities may produce limping impact or effects on certain aspects of environment. This particular issue raises a question as to how to deal with these significant cumulative effects. Hence, it is suggested to prepare an environmental impact assessment E1A on broad programs than on a series of component actions such as, say, industrial estates mining area, tourism industry and so on. Instead one can prepare an EIA for a particular geographical area where series of similar activities are located like mining areas, coast line for beach resorts and the like.

10. **Reporting of Findings** : The results of the study are to be presented in such a way that it makes easy and clear to understand the total impacts of an activity at one look. Experts are of the opinion that the results are to be portrayed on a summary sheet in a matrix form.

The issues discuss above, howsoever complex they are, are useful in understanding the process of preparing EIS/EIA and the complexities involved. This sort of awareness helps in improving the better understanding of EIS that lead to more objective, well informed and unbiased or less biased decision- making on activities or projects.

CHOICE OF METHODOLOGY

If not in developing countries, at least in advanced nations, the project experts, environmentalists and researchers have come out with good many methodologies to study their overall environmental conditions. It is the choice that decides the depth of analysis carried out in a particular impact assessment. The choice of a particular methodology depends, among other things, on : needs of the user, type of the project, size and technology of project, location - the type of eco-system. It goes without saying that one method is better than other. That is why, the analyst must decide which one will be the best for a given situation and task.

Considerations that Help in Making a choice of Methodology :

1. **Use** : Much depends on the use of EIS. It may be for only information or may be for decision making. If it is for information, there is need for more comprehensive analysis and concentration on interpretation of significance of a broad list of possible impacts. On the other hand, if it is for decision making, it warrants greater emphasis on identification of key issues, qualification and comparisons of alternatives ?

2. **Alternatives** : The question is how the alternatives are different ? Are they fundamentally different ? Or incrementally different ? In fact, both in fundamentals and future variations are important. However, in certain cases, fundamental differences are more important than incremental and vice versa.

3. **Resources** : Availability and the needs have say in this regard. If one speaks of resources - what is the amount of time, money, skills and data are available ? More and more of resources are a must in case if the analyst or user goes in for more indepth and qualitative analysis are needed.

4. **Familiarity** : How far an analyst is familiar with the types of project proposed and actual ground realities under which he is supposed to work. It is a matter of exposure that matters much.

5. **Significance of Issue Involved** : The question is how big is the issue ? There is greater need for explicity, quantification and identification of key issues in case the issue is bigger and bigger. What is big ? how big or small it is - are all comparative concepts which are subjective.

6. **Administrative Constraints** : What methodology is to be used is linked to the extent of governmental or adminstrative restrictions or the framework. In case more restrictions are there on project clearance, then the methodology tends to be more verifiable, amendable to administrative regulatory constraints.

METHODOLOGIES AVAILABLE

The literature on project management, makes available at least six methodologies which are in vogue. Let us know these each with relative merits and demerits in brief.

A. ADHOC :

These methodologies provide a minimum guidance for impact assesment. They merely suggest broad areas of possible impacts say on lakes, forests, instead of defining specific parameters to be investigated. This is given exogenously to the analyst.

The relative merits are :

1. It is simple and no training or skills improvement needed.
2. When no expertise and resources available, this is the best as it goes in for indepth and focussed analysis of few.
3. Gives preliminary understanding.
4. Project effects on environment are given without any weighing and cause and effect relations.

The demerits associated with it are :

1. Restricts to broad areas only.
2. Not all relevant impacts covered.
3. Selective and biased.
4. Lacks consistency due to different criteria to evaluate different groups of factors.

B. OVERLAYS :

These methodologies depend on a set of maps on the environmental characteristics-say physical, social, ecological and aesthetic of the proposed vicinity. These maps are overlaid to produce a composite characterisation of the regional environment. Impacts are then identified by noting the impacted environmental attributes within the project boundaries.

The relative merits of these are :

1. Useful in site and route selection.
2. Effective presentation and display
3. Useful in transport projects and road route alternatives and land and planning.

The relative demerits of these are :

1. Weak quantification and measurement.
2. Not all impacts covered and higher order impacts can not be identified.
3. Social environment not considered and subjective.
4. Self-limiting in scope and coverage.

C. CHECK-LISTS :

These methodologies present a specific list of environmental attributes to be investigated for possible impacts. They need not necessarily attempt to establish the cause and effect links to project activities. They may or may not include guidelines about how attribute data are to be measured and interpreted.

The relative merits of these are :

1. Strong in impact identification.
2. Effective in evolving public attention.
3. Simple and easy to understand and comprehensive.
4. Most useful at the stage of initial environmental examination.

The relative demerits associated with these are :

1. Scaling and weighing are subjective.
2. Leaves interpretation to the decision-makers.
3. Deficiency in measurement.

D. MATRICES :

These methodologies incorporate a list of project activities with check-list of potentially impacted environmental attributes. Then the two lists are related in matrix from which identifies the cause and effect relationships between specific activities. The matrix methodologies may either specify which actions affect which attributes, or may simply list the range of project activities and environmental attributes in an open matrix to be completed by the analyst.

The relative merits of these are :

1. Provides cause and effect relations between activities and impacts on various attributes.
2. Graphic display of impacts gives better understanding.
3. Strong impact identification and their interaction is possible.

The relative demerits associated with these are :

1. Information is lost due to quantification.
2. Scaling and weighing become subjective.

E. NETWORKS :

These methodologies work from a list of project activities to establish cause-condition-effect relationships. It is generally felt that a series of impacts may be triggered by project action. They define set of possible networks and allow the user to identify impacts by selecting and tracing out the appropriate project actions.

The relative merits of these are :

(1) Capable of identifying both direct and indirect effects and their interaction.

(2) Capable of incorporating mitigation and management measures at the planning stage of a project.

The demerits that are in their trait are :

(1) Less useful in considering socio-economic environment.

(2) Display becomes large and unweildy when large industrial complexes or regional plans are considered.

F. COMBINATION COMPUTER AIDED :

These methodologies use a combination of matrices, networks, analytical models, and a computer-aided systematic approach. As it is a combination of different and difficult methodologies, it is a multiple objective approach to: (i) Identify the activities associated with the government policies and programs (ii) identify potential environmental impacts at different levels (iii) provide guidance for abatement and mitigation techniques (iv) provide analytical models to establish cause and effect relationships and to determine quantitatively potential environmental impacts and (iv) provide a methodology and procedure to utilise this comprehensive information in decision-making.

CHAPTER BASED QUSTIONS

A. WRITE SHORT NOTES ON

1. SCBA
2. Rationale behind SCBA
3. Objectives of SCBA
4. Approaches to SCBA
5. UNIDO approach
6. Stages in UNIDO approach
7. Shadow prices
8. Externalities
9. Savings impact and its value
10. Income distribution impact
11. Economic or efficiency prices
12. LM approach
13. Types and dimensions of projects
14. Stresses on environment
15. Environment and its gamut
16. Environmental Resources/values
17. Environmental attributes
18. EIA
19. EIS
20. Major issues in preparing EIA/EIS
21. Choice of methodology.

B. SHORT ANSWER QUESTIONS

1. What is SCBA ?
2. What is the rationale behind SCBA ?
3. What are the approaches to SCBA ?

4. What are shadow prices ?
5. What are externalities ?
6. What is LM approach ?
7. Types of projects. What are they ?
8. What is environment ? What is its gamut ?
9. What are stresses on environment ?
10. What are EIA and EIS ?

C. ESSAY TYPE QUESTIONS

1. What is SCBA ? What is the rationate behind this SCBA ?
2. What is SCBA ? What are its objectives ?
3. What is UNIDO approach and what steps are involved in it ?
4. Explain clearly EIA and EIS ?
5. Clearly explain the scope and contents of EIS and EIA.
6. What is the methodology for conducting environmental appraisal ?
7. What major issues one faces while preparing EIS and EIA ?
8. What methodologies are available for environment evaluation and how does one choose the most appropriate methodology ?
9. What is LM apprach ? What are points of similarities and dis-similarities between UNIDO and LM approaches ?
10. Explain the different stages involved in UNIDO appraoch.

* * * * * *

Chapter 7

PROJECT FEASIBILITY STUDIES PART-3

- WHAT IS MARKET AND DEMAND ANALYSIS ?
- HOW IS MARKET AND DEMAND ANALYSIS CONDUCTED ?
- WHAT IS FORECASTING ?
- TREND EFFECTS IN EXPONENTIAL SMOOTHENING
- CHOOSING A FORECASTING METHOD
- FOCUS FORECASTING
- DEVELOPING A FOCUS FORECASTING SYSTEM
- UNCERTANTIES OF DEMAND FORECASTING
- HOW TO HANDLE THESE UNCERTAINTIES ?
- CHAPTER BASED QUESTIONS

BACKDROP

In a consumer driven market the consumer is the Rex. Hence, the starting point in project analysis is to go by estimating the potential size of the market for the product proposed to be manufactured or the service thought of being offered and to get a clear-cut idea as to market share that is likely to be captured. This is what market and demand analysis does as put in other words. Market and demand analysis is to do with two significant dimensions of market opportunities. In other words, it concentrates on the likely aggregate demand for the product or service and the share of the market the firm is likely to share along with other players. These two dimensions are most difficult yet very important in project analysis. In case the entrepreneur or the project analyser is expected to have indepth study and critical analysis of all those factors that have bearing on demand. These factors are the patterns of consumption, income price elasticity of demand, composition of market, nature and extent of competition, availability of substitutes, reach of supply chain above all political peace and tranquility, environmental changes that have impact on earning and spending. Therefore, this chapter plans to discuss in -depth market and demand analysis in all its dimensions. The chapter ends with Chapter Based Questions.

WHAT IS MARKET AND DEMAND ANALYSIS ?

Market and demand analysis is the management demand - its estimation and determining the extent to which it can be met with satisfaction to consumers and profit to the producers. In other words, whenever a project planning and implementing comes to surface, it begins with two aspects of demand. That is, what is the potential size of the market ? and to what extent the project planner is capable of getting share in the market. In other words, what shall be the probable aggregate demand for a given product or service ? and what will be the market share ? If the total market for mobile phone market size is of the order of 41,000 crores by the end of 2001 and expected to be 81,000 crores in next five years - that is by 2007. Of this very soon, Reliance Infocom which test-launched its cellular telephone on 28th December 2002, will be the leader because of two reasons or competitive advantages, namely : (1) Its ability to price product really cheap and (2) To offer integrated services. Naturally leader's share in the market may range anything between 35 per cent to 45 per cent and remaining market will be shared by both public sector and private sector players each getting share in the range of 15 per cent to even as low as 2 per cent. Thus, market share is important in the aggregate market demand.

HOW IS MARKET AND DEMAND ANALYSIS CONDUCTED ?

Being of key importance, this exercise is carried out very carefully in a systematic manner. There are some logical steps which are to be followed. These are :

(1) Situation analysis and specification of objectives

(2) Collection of secondary information

(3) Conduct of market survey

(4) Characterisation of the market

(5) Demand forecasting and

(6) Market Planning.

These steps are inter-related and not independent of one another. The Fig. 7.01 gives a pictorial presentation for better grasping.

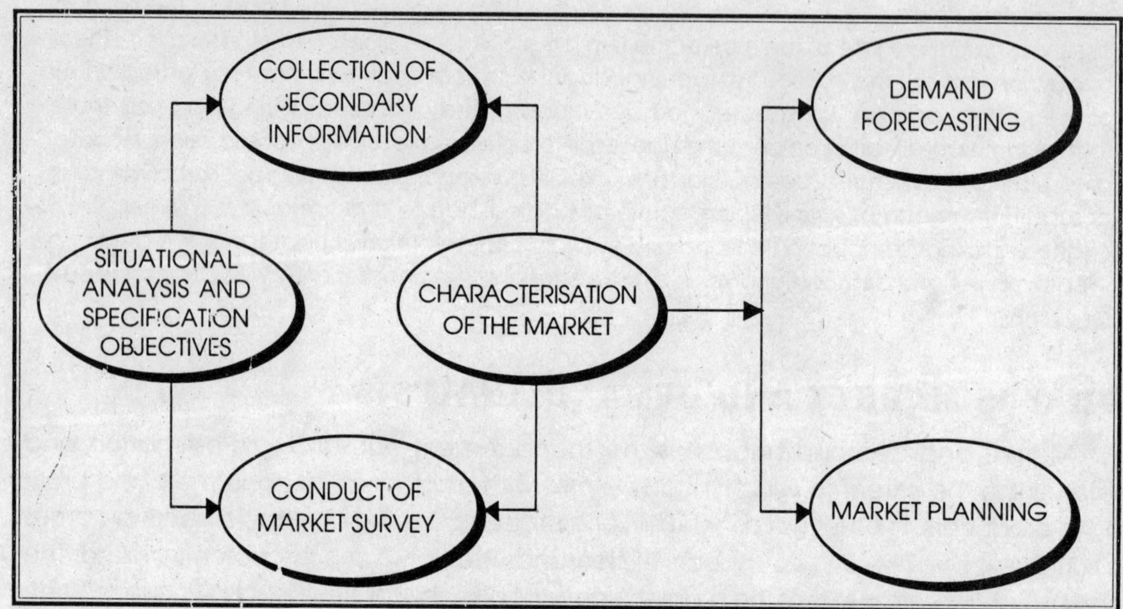

Fig. 7.01 Key Steps in Market and Demand Analysis and their Inter-Relations

1. SITUATIONAL ANALYSIS AND SPECIFICATION OF OBJECTIVES

The project analyst, may be entrepreneur himself, is expected to get relationship between a given product and its market presently available. The work starts with base of an informal chat with customers, competitors, middlemen, dealers and even employees or some one who is related directly or indirectly with the present enterprise or enterprises. The existing company or companies have the past and present which is a rich source of valuable experience. In this regard, the analyst may get good deal of facts relating to consumer preferences, purchasing power of customers, the quantity they buy, where they buy, when they buy and even why they buy ? Equally important are the useful areas of interest are actions and reaction, policies and strategies of the competitors, relating to major four P's of a market mix.

There is no need for formal study that warrants cost and time considerations, in case such a informal situational analysis helps to gather sufficient data to measure the market and get a right grip over projected demand and revenue. However, in majority of cases, there is need for formal study of market and demand, carrying out such formal study there is no escape from spelling out in clear terms and comprehensive span of objectives. It means that the intutive and informal goals that guide and direct the situational analysis are to be expanded and articulated, with utmost degree of clarity. The appropriate approach of spelling out these objectives is to construct them in the form of questions. While doing so, one should bear in mind as to how the information generated will be relevant in forecasting the overall market demand and measuring the market share the project will capture. It is quite evident then that only those questions which are relevant to market and demand analysis will be asked.

To make more clear what has been said in the previous paragraph, let us take a simple case of a small but technologically more competent unit which has developed a home compact flour-mill than the conventional flour-mill which is based on new technology extending more benefits to the users namely, house wife. The immediate problem before the CEO of the firm is how to market it effectively. The objectives of market and demand analysis in this context may be answers to the following questions. Who are the buyers of kitchen flour mills ? What is the present demand for kitchen flour mills ? How is the demand distributed in terms of a span of year and geographically ? What is the break up of demand for flour mills of different capacities ? What price the customers are willing to pay for the improved kitchen flour-mill ? What is the communication or promotion mix that suits the marketing of the product ? How is the firm going to convince the customers of the superiority of the new or improved kitchen flour mill ? What price, warranty and service package will ensure its acceptance ? What channels of distribution are best suited for the kitchen flour mill ? What trade margins and incentives will include the distributors to capture sustained market ? What are the prospects of immediate sales ?

2. COLLECTION OF SECONDARY INFORMATION

To answer the questions designed in the light of the objectives of the market study, the necessary information can be obtained from SECONDARY or PRIMARY sources or both depending on the situation and needs. SECONDARY information is one which is already collected and compiled which may be published or unpublished either by government departments or private bodies and individuals. Secondary information provides us with the base and the starting point for market and demand analysis. It makes available information that is known and gives us leads and cues for gathering primary information needs for further analysis.

SOURCES OF SECONDARY INFORMATION :

The secondary information can be of general and specific type. Let us know about the sources of general and specific type of information. General sources of Secondary Information with specific reference to India, the general sources of information are :

1. **Census of India :** It is a publication of Government of India published every ten years. It provides detailed information of Indian population giving classified information as per demographic features, household size and composition supported by maps, tables, charts and other visual aids.

2. **National Sample Survey Reports :** These reports are released from time to time by the Cabinet Secretary or Secretariat, Government of India detailing information on various economic and social dimensions like patterns of consumption, distribution of households by the size of consumer expenditure, distribution of industries and features of the economically active population. The data presented is representing entire nation by sample survey-interview method.

3. **Plan Reports :** Planning Commission of India releases these plan reports - at definite intervals namely, at commencement at the mid term and end of plan period. These reports and documents and supplements provide a good deal of detailed and authentic information on plan proposals, physical and financial targets, actual outlays, accomplishments - in entirety and cross-section-wise.

4. **Statistical Abstract of the Indian Union :** This is the publication of the Central Statistical Organisation that provides demographic information, estimates of national income, and agricultural and industrial statistics.

5. **India Year Book :** It is the publication of the Ministry of Information and Broadcasting which provides variety of information on socio-economic and other aspects.

6. **Economic Survey :** It is an annual publication of the Ministry of Finance, Government of India, which provides latest data on industrial production, wholesale prices, consumer prices, exports, agricultural production, national income and so on.

7. **Annual Survey of Industries :** It is an annual publication of Central Statistical Organisation portraying information on various aspects of industry, number of units with statewise distribution, average number of working days, employment, materials consumption, quantity of production and the like.

8. **Annual Reports of Development Wing :** This is an annual publication by ministries of Commerce and Industry giving detailed review of industries under the preview of the wing. It does provide information about new items manufactured for the first time in India and the list of protected industries.

9. **Annual Bulletin of Statistics of Exports and Imports :** It is an annual publication of Ministry of Commerce, Government of India. It provides updated data on imports and exports on each sector as formatted on international classification.

10. **Techno-Economic Surveys :** These are conducted and published by NCAER, statewise.

11. **Industry Potential Surveys :** It is the special survey conducted by IDBI alongwith other Financial Institutions giving industrial potential surveys for several backward areas.

12. **The Stock Exchange Directory :** This Directory is published by Bombay Stock Exchange giving a full-length a decade of performance and financial statements for listed companies and other known companies. Naturally, it is rich source of comparative analysis which is updated periodically.

13. **Monthly Studies of Production of Selected Industries :** It is a monthly publication of Central Statistical Organisation. It provides all-India data on production, number of units installed, capacity, statewise break-up, stock level and so on for several selected industries.

14. **Monthly Bulletin of RBI :** This publication gives details of production indices, prices, balance of payment position, exchange rates and the like.

15. **Publications of Advertising Agencies :** The ad agencies of India which are to the forefront like Clarion, McCann and Thompson have been publishing test markets, marketing rating indices of major firms of India, consumer index of markets and other studies which focus spot light on Indian markets.

16. **Statistical Year Book :** It is an annual publication of the U.N. that provides world statistics relating to various aspects like population, demographics, gross domestic production, industrial production, international trade and the like.

17. **Manorama Year Book :** It is an annual publication that gives the information on the same lines as **India**. It is a private publication.

18. **Other Publications :** The other important publications worth noting are (1) Weekly Bulletin of indusrtrial Licenses, Import Licences and Export Licenses published by Government of India. Studies of Economic Division of State Trading Corporation; Commodity reports and other studies of the Indian Institute of Foreign Trade: Studies and Reports of Export Promotion Councils and Commodity Boards and Annual Report on Currency and Finance published by R.B.I.

Specific sources of secondary information are the publications by private sector manufacturers' associations and other bodies. Even government publications are there that give detailed information with reference to a particular industry. Some of these are given as under :

(i) **Automobiles :** (1) Annual Reports of Association of Automobile Manufacturers (2) Automobile Ancillary Industry which has Annual Publication. We have monthly Magazines namely Auto India and Over Drive.

(ii) **Chemicals :** Chemical industrial publications include other related products such as fertilisers, drugs and pharmaceuticals. (1) Annual Reports of Organisation of Pharmaceutical Producers of India (2) Indian Drugs and Pharmaceutical Industries (3) Chemical Age of India.

(iii) **Electrical and Electronics :** (1) Annual Electric Power Survey of India (2) Annual Report of Indian Electrical Manufactures' Association (3) Electric India-a fortnightly (4) Electronic Digest (5) Electronic Information and Planning-a monthly publication. With the onslaught of electronics in information technology, large number of monthlies and fortnightlies are being - giving case studies and new arrivals.

(iv) **Industrial Machinery :** (1) Build Machine - Build India (2) Textile, Machinery Accessories and Stores Journal (3) Annual Report of Indian Machine Tool Manufacturers Association (4) Search.

(v) **Metallurgical :** (1) Iron and Steel Control Bulletin-Quarterly (2) Steel Furnace monthly (3) Annual Reports of Steel Wire Manufacturers Association of India (4) Minerals and Metals Review (5) Annual Reports of Steel Re-rolling Mills Association.

(vi) **Textiles :** (1) Indian Textile Bulletin (2) Silk and Rayon Industries of India (3) Wool and Woollens of India (4) Man-made Fibres (5) Synthetic Fibre (6) Jute Chronicle (7) Monthly Summary of Jute and Gunny Statistics (8) Annual Reports of Indian Cotton Mills Federation.

(vii) **Other Industries :** (a) Cement (b) Glass Udyog (c) Hotel Guide India (d) Indian Packaging Directory (e) Packaging India (f) Rubber India (g) Statistics of Marine Products Exports (h) Year Book of Fishery Statistics (i) Poultry Year Book.

In addition, we have good many monthly journals and periodicals which cover all aspects of business. The examples of this kind are: Business India, Business Today, Advertising and Management, Indian Journal of marketing, Indian Management. One can not ignore dailies especially, Economic Times of India, Financial Express and so on. Further, Internet surfing is an endless source.

EVALUATING THE SECONDARY INFORMATION

Though secondary information is available readily and at least cost, its reliability, authenticity and relevance for the purpose of meeting the requirements of a project analyst is to be checked. Therefore, the market analyst has to know thoroughly regarding the following points of critical importance. These are : 1. Who has gathered the information ? What were the objectives ? 2. When was the information gathered and when was it published ? 3. The extent of representativeness of the period for which information was gathered 4. Whether the terms in study been carefully and clearly defined ? 5. What was the target population ? 6. How was the sample chosen ? 7. How far is the sample representative ? 8. The extent of relevance and suitability of gathering of information ? 9. The degree of sampling bias and non-response bias in the gathered information ? 10. What is the extent of misrepresentation by respondents ? 11. How accurately is the collected information edited, tabulated and analysed ? 12. Whether the statistical analysis is properly applied or not ?

3. CONDUCT OF MARKET SURVEY

Though useful and authentic, the secondary information may not be able to meet the requirement that is very comprehensive and is needed for scientific market and demand analysis. In fact, secondary data is supporting in giving a start. Therefore, the individual information needs differ widely, there is need for collecting primary data through a market survey that matches perfectly with the project in question which is subject to appraisal.

There are two basic approaches as to conduct of survey-namely, census and sample survey. In case of census survey approach, the entire population or the universe is covered. Here, the term 'population' or 'universe' is taken as collecting information from each and every respondent may be an individual or an organisation. Thus, we took the case of estimating demand and market share for the improved kitchen flour mill. To conduct the survey by census method, we will have to cover the entire potential customers say in a state, or a region or all India on one hand and the existing units that are manufacturing the conventional kitchen flour mills, dealers, and others. Instead, sample survey can be resorted the firms concerned. Each approach has its own merits and limitations. Census approach is time consuming, costly in terms of associated expenses say field survey method. However, the information got is quite adequate and reliable and accurate. On the other hand, sample survey is less expensive, less time consuming. However, in terms of results, census approach is more dependable than sample survey.

The information sought in a market survey relates to one or more of the following aspects namely, (a) total demand and the growth rate of demand (b) demand in different segments of the market (c) Income and price elasticities of demand (d) Motives of buying (e) purchasing plans and intentions (f) Satisfaction with the existing products (g) Unsatisfied needs (h) Attitudes towards different products (i) Practices and preferences in the area of distribution (j) Socio-economic features of buyers.

STEPS IN CONDUCTING SAMPLE SURVEY :

At least seven steps are involved in conducting a sample survey as suggested by research experts. These steps are logical in that, they are to be meticulously and carefully congruated series of steps. These steps are :

1. **Define the Target Population :** Defining of target population is of utmost importance in clear and carefully studied manner as it is the first step. The target population may be divided into certain segments with their unique features. If you are considering case of owners of cellular telephones, there can be four to five groups of income brakets or three and four categories of vocation, occupation or profession. The total demand ultimately depends on these demographic features.

2. **Select the Sampling scheme and Size :** Sampling schemes imply the types of sampling say simple random sampling, cluster sampling, sequential sampling, stratified sampling, systematic sampling non-probability sampling and so on. It is worth noting

here that each scheme of sampling has its own merits and demerits. Another important aspect of sampling is, size of it which has greater and deeper bearing on the reliability and accuracy of estimates. It goes without saying that larger the size of sample better it is because it assures greater reliability and accuracy.

3. **Design the Questionnaire :** To collect the information from the respondents, the main instrument is the questionnaire. The effectiveness of the questionnaire as a device for getting the much needed information from respondents rests on its length, the types of questions asked, above all wording of or framing of questions. To develop all acceptable questionnaire the surveyor should have a thorough understanding of the product or service, its usage, fertile imagination and clear insights into the human behaviour, appreciation of linguistic differences, familiarity with the tools and techniques of descriptive and inferential statistics to be used at later stage of analysis. It also calls for the knowledge of psychological scaling techniques where qualitative information is sought of say-attitudes, motivations, psychological traits, level of satisfaction and so on. Industry and trade surveys are more dependable on technical and specialised questions than in case of consumer surveys. Since questionnaire is the very base, a pilot survey of questions is to be tested and modified if need there be.

4. **Recruit and Train the Field Investigators :** Collection of data from respondents is done through field investigators. This is being crucial, a plan of recruitment and training is to be prepared and implemented. Minimum qualifications covering the skills of collecting data are to be laid down and to bring standardisation and congruity in this work they are to be trained in proper directors as what is expected of them. The training programme should cover-imparting of knowledge, developing communication skills and bringing about attitude change. Basically product, company and customer knowledge is must.

5. **Get Information as per the Questionnaire from the Target Respondents :** The respondents can be interviewed personally, or through mail or telephone. Each means is having its own merits and demerits. What is suitable and feasible for the investigating form is to be followed.

6. **Scruitinise the Information Collected :** A thorough scrutiny of collected information needs to be done in order to do away with inconsistent and invalid information that does not serve any purpose. For instance, never do we get correct information about women's age and men's income. That is why some wise gentleman has said "Never ask the age of a woman and salary or earning of a man."

7. **Analyse and Interpret the Information :** This is the vital aspect of conducting sample survey. The gathered information has no meaning unless, it is minutely analysed and interpreted threadbare with due care and fertile imagination. The data are to be tabulated as per the plan of analysis followed by strict statistical investigation wherever possible and needed. The analyst has a variety of statistical tools and methods which

broadly classed into two categories namely 'parametric' and non-parametric. Parametric methods assume that the variable or the attribute under study conforms to some known distribution. Non-parametric methods do not have such presumption as to any particular distribution. The results of data-based on sample Survey are to be extrapolated to the target population. This warrants use of appropriate inflationary factors based on the ratio of the size of the target population to that of the size of the sample studied. This is not an easy job. Therefore, the task of statistical analysis of data should be done by a person who has mastery in econometrics or statistics as well as economics. Instead, an assistant should work under the guidance of an experienced econometrician.

One should note that the results arrived of the market survey can be futile and vitiated by factors like - non-representativeness of the sample, lack of precision and inadequacies in the questions, failure of comprehending questions by respondents, deliberate distortions in the answers given by the respondents, inapt and careless handling of the interviews by the investigators, cheating on the part of investigators, careless or slip-shod scrutiny of data and incorrect and inappropriate analysis and interpretation of data.

SOME SPECIFIC PROBLEMS :

A market researcher or surveyor has to face some specific problems with special reference to Indian conditions.

1. **Heterogeneity of the Country :** Unity in diversity is the key feature of Indian economy. That is why,foreign experts have dared to call India as not a 'country' but a 'continent' featured by multiplicity of cultures, sub culture, languages, ethnic groups and other diversities in religion, rituals and practices and so on. If one goes in for all-India survey, it is impossible which needs division of country into broad based territories crossing the state boundaries. This unavoidable heterogeneity of the nation renders the task much difficult. No two researchers have one way of dividing the country for the purpose of study. It is their Individual line of thinking and judgement that decide the division. This heterogeneity in heterogeneity creates problems in comparing the findings of different research agencies.

2. **Multiplicity of Languages :** Multiplicity of languages faced by the surveyor or the researcher adds fuel to the fire of heterogeneity - particularly when an all-India survey is expected. Indians have 2,000 languages and dialects of which 20 are officially recognised. India presently has 28 states each state having people from all over the country further accentuating the problems created by heterogeneity.

3. **Framing of Questionnaire :** The scaling techniques, very commonly recommeded in marketing research literature, involve a Five Point scale or Seven Point Scale. These accepted and refined scales are not easily possible in regional languages. What is more important is that they are not comprehensible to a vast majority of respondents

who lack the minimum education and refinement to understand them. Therefore, whenever the refined or sophisticated scaling techniques are used, answers given by respondents are more erratic and inconsistent. However, a possible solution lies in asking the respondent more open-ended questions and less pre-coded question on definite scales.

4. CHARACTERISATION OF THE MARKET

The market for the product or service can be described in terms of clear cut characteristics based on the information gathered from secondary sources and through the market survey or primary sources. At least one can think of seven market features as outlined below.

1. **Past and Present Effective Demand :** To measure the effective demand of the past and present, the starting point is consumption which is spelled out in equation as : Production + Imports - Exports - Changes in Stock level.
   The figure of consumption or apparent consumption is to be adjusted for consumption of the product by the producers and effect of abnormal factors. After such due adjustments, the consumptions series may be arrived at for several years. In a competitive market, both effective demand and apparent consumption are equal. In countries where competitive markets do not exist for a variety of products because of exchange restriction controls on production and distribution, the figure of apparent consumption has to be ironed out of market imperfections. It is the normal feature in case of underdeveloped or developing countries. Such warranted adjustment is the most difficult task, if not impossible.

2. **Break Down of Total Demand :** The aggregate or the total demand needs to be broken down into demand for different segments of the market. Market segments are defined in terms of (a) nature of product (b) consumer group and (c) geographical area. Each base of market segment leads further sub-division. In case of NATURE OF PRODUCTS - the phrase "commercial vehicles" may be buses or trucks, six wheelers, four wheelers, three wheelers and even two wheelers of different capacities and nature of fuel consumption say petrol, diesel, gas, electricity and so on.

   Taking CONSUMERS as basis of segmentation, these products may be for industrial consumers and domestic consumers. Industrial consumers can be divided industrywise while domestic consumers may be derived further as durables and non-durables for different income groups. Coming to GEOGRAPHICAL DIVISION, consumers for products can be of various of types say value to weight relationship, after sales services will be of much use.

   Such segmental analysis is needed for the simple reason that the nature of demand tends to vary from segment to segment. Nature of demand here stands for dimensions of demand, quantity, quality, price, time and so on. This helps in designing specific and matching marketing strategies that work in each segment. It is because, one blanket pack of marketing strategies for the total market is neither feasible nor fructifying. .

3. **The Price :** Price is one of the major components of market mix. Therefore, price statistics are to be gathered along with the statistics relating to physical quantities. The prices charged for products can be broadly of three levels namely, manufacturer, wholesaler and retailer. The price quoted by manufacture can be FOB - Free on Board price or CIF - Cost Insurance and Freight - Price. Landed prices are appliable in case of imported goods; average, wholesale price by wholesalers and average retail price by retailers.

4. **Methods of Distribution and Sales-Promotion :** It is the nature of product that decides the method of distribution. Basically, industrial goods and consumer goods have different distribution methods. Again, industrial goods classed into raw-materials, supplies, fabricated parts, installations and machineries and services: the consumer goods are so classed as to commence goods, shopping goods and speciality goods; these subdivisions need different methods of distribution arrangement or supply chain arrangements. Again, methods of sales-promotion - advertising, salesmanship and promotions- dealer-consumer-sales force widely differ. Both the methods of distribution and sales-promotion employed at present and their justification should be specified. Such a blended and classified study helps to a greater extent in explaining definite patterns of consumption and bring to the surface the difficulties and barriers that are likely to be encountered while marketing the proposed product or products.

5. **The Consumers :** The entire circus of market and demand analysis is for consumers. Market and demand mean consumers. Experts have classified consumers in two ways namely, demographic and psychographic. Demographic classification encompasses, age group, sex, income group, profession or vocation or occupational group, residence group, social back-drop group. In case of psychographics, classification is done by preferences, intentions, habits, attitudes, responses, life styles and so on.

6. **Supply and Competition :** It is essential to know the existing sources of supply as to whether they are foreign or domestic. In case of domestic supply, information is collected in terms of location, present production capacity, planned expansion, capacity utilisation level, hurdles in production and above all cost structure. In case of foreign supply - location, adequacy, regularity, dependability, cost and time of delivery. Equally important is competition - competition from substitutes or near substitutes. Such specification is a must because practically each product is replaced by other product because relative changes in prices, quality standards, extent of availability, promotional input and so on.

7. **The Government Policy :** Government of every nation plays a significant role in influencing the demand and the market for a product. Government as a custodian of society has its own plans, priorities, policies, legislations and rules and regulations

having deep impact on market and the demand for a product in question. Hence, these implications are to be spelled out clearly. These implications are reflected in production targets in national plans; import and export trade controls; import duties; export incentives, excise duties, sales tax, industrial licensing, preferential purchases, credit controls, financial regulations and substitutes or penalties of variety types. Each is to be studied with reference to the product that is going to be manufactured and marketed.

5. DEMAND FORECASTING

Next step is one of estimating or forecasting the future demand, once the information about various aspects of market and demand from the primary and secondary sources. This stage of demand forecasting covers meaning and methods of demand forecasting.

WHAT IS FORECASTING ?

In operations management aspects of operations are important, but not as important as forecasting. Good many managers wonder how they can predict with certainty as to what will happen in the future. The answer is pure and simple. They cannot do so. Instead, managers must work with probabilities or the likelihood that certain events will occur. In planning processes, managers use forecasts and must accept the fact that forecasting involves errors.

A 'forecast' is a prediction of future events. Such predections are rarely perfect, regardless of the quantity of historical data and the extent of the managerial experience. Fortunately, forecasting methods have been improved to the point where they provide useful estimates for planning purposes. Thus, 'forecast' is an 'estimate' or 'conjecture regarding future event'. The word 'conjecture' is the 'inference based on evidence which is not complete' or 'a guess, the truth of which is yet to be confirmed.' 'Forecast' represents a commitment on the part of sales department and each of its divisions of expected sales which becomes a goal against which the effectiveness of the sales department will be measured. Forecasting is, therefore, prognastication of future with certain amount of accuracy. Forecasting means estimation of types, quantity and quality of future work say, sales and, therefore, production. Forecasting is that exercise that gives rise to plans for dealing with future. It is a systematic attempt to predict the future with the greatest possible accuracy based on the past or known events. It is.to probe the future that holds for a particular organisation. Put alternatively, forecasting is predicting future events by the best possible means. Forecasting is not a guess work. It is the inference based on large mass of data on past performance. It is a sort of calculated error. Therefore, forecasting may be looked upon as the projection based activity on past data.

Forecasts and forecasting are so closely akin to production and operations management so that this activity can not be thrown away, for it is of senewal importance. It is because, the problems before a manufacturing organisation are what to produce?

How much to produce ? For whom to produce ? When to produce ? At what cost to produce ? Where to produce ? And how best to produce? These answers can be found for each question on what customers need and want. Thus, estimating sales or predicting the sales gives the base for the quantity and quality of production and base production figures are predicted, estimation can be made for each operations and the timely and sound decisions can be taken. Therefore, forecasting means, demand forecast and indirectly the sales forecast.

FORECASTING AND PROJECT MANAGEMENT

The forecaster has at his command several different types of forecasting methods because demand exhibits good many different characteristics. The aim of forecaster is to develop an useful forecast from the information available to him. In order to achieve his objective, the forecaster must select the most appropriate technique. This, being very important, involves trade-offs between forecast accuracy and cost. Though one can have four methods, they are very fundamental namely, time series analysis, causal methods and qualitative techniques. The other one is simulation. The method or technique used is based on the time horizon and application with its dimensions such as forecast quantity, decision area and forecasting technique.

This can be better explained with the help of a table 7.1 and Fig. 7.02. on the page 239 (next). Both are used for the benefit of readers. It is left to the discretion of the readers whether they go in for a diagram or a chart. The aim of the author is to produce sufficient food presented in a palatable way.

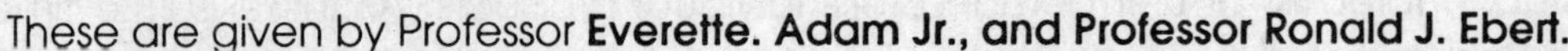
These are given by Professor **Everette. Adam Jr., and Professor Ronald J. Ebert.**

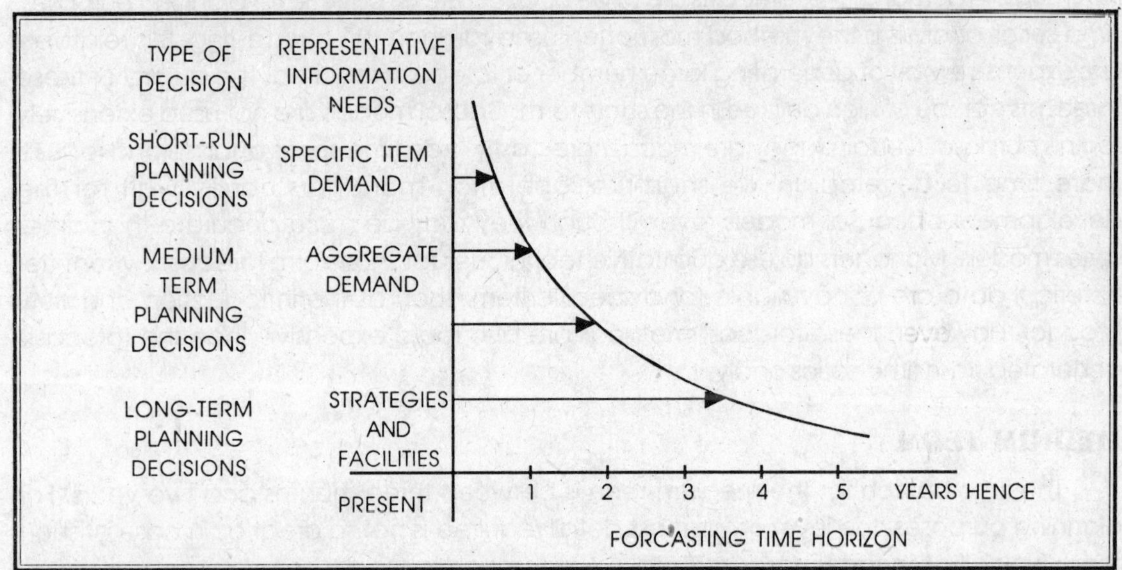

Fig. 7.02 Demand Forecasting Horizon and type of decision with Representative Information Needed

Following is the Table 7.1 as given by Professor Lee J. Krajewski and Professor Larry. P. Ritzman, from Ohio University of America.

TABLE 7.1
TABLE SHOWING DEMAND FORECAST APPLICATIONS

APPLICATION	TIME HORIZON		
	SHORT-TERM (0 - 3 months)	MEDIUM-TERM (3 months -2 years)	LONG-TERM (More than 2 years)
Forecast Quantity	Individual products	Total sales group or families of products	Total sales
Decision Area	Inventory management- Final Assembly Scheduling Work-force scheduling Master Production Scheduling	Staff planning production planning Master Production Scheduling Purchasing Distribution	Facility Location Capacity Planning Process Design
Forecasting Technique	Time-Series Causal Qualitative	Causal Qualitative	Causal Qualitative

It will not be out of place if each time horizon is explained with reference to three variables of forecast quantity, decision area and forecasting technique.

SHORT TERM :

In the short run-between zero and three months in future, managers are typically interested in forecast of unit demand for individual products. As there is little time for satisfying the demand, the forecasts are to be as accurate as possible for planning purposes. Time-series analysis is the method most often used for short-run forecasting. It is relatively less expensive way of generating large number of forecasts required. The quality of these forecasts can be of high degree in the short-term. Causal models are not used extensively for this purpose. Certainly they are much more costly than time-series analysis and require more time to develop. In the short-run, operation managers hardly wait for the development of causal models, even though they may be more accurate than time-series models. Managers do use qualitative techniques for short-term forecasts whenever historical data are not available for a specific item, such as the introduction of a new product. However, these forecast methods are also more expensive than the forecasts generated from time-series analysis.

MEDIUM TERM :

The time horizon for the medium-term is between three months and two years. For planning purposes, the level of forecast detail required is not so great as in case of short term. Typically, managers forecast total sales demand in rupees or number of units of an aggregation of goods or services into groups or families of similar products. The need for medium-term forecasts arises from planning problems related to issues of capacity, such as those given in chart 4. Causal models are very commonly used for medium term forecasts. Typically, these models do a good job of identifying periods. When the growth rate of demand will change, as when slow sales growth will turn into rapid decline. Determination of these 'turning points' is very important for the operations manager, particularly in the medium and long-term. Some of the qualitative methods of forecasting are also helpful in identifying the 'turning points'. However, as noted earlier, they are most often used in situations where no historical data exist. Time-series analysis does not typically yield accurate results in the medium and long-term basically because it is assumed that existing patterns will continue in the future. This assumption may be valid for the short-term, but is less accurate over longer time horizons.

LONG TERM :

Long term time horizon ranges over or beyond two years. For such long term, forecasts are usually developed for total sales demand in rupees or same other common units of measurement such as barrels, kgs, pounds, kilograms, or tons and so on. Accurate forecasts of demand for individual products not only are very difficult to make but they are also too detailed for long-range planning purposes. As indicated in Table 4. Three decision areas - facility location, capacity planning and process design require market demand estimates for an extended period into future. Causal models and qualitative methods are the fundamental techniques used for long-term forecasting. However, even mathematically derived causal model forecasts have to be tempered by managerial experience and judgement because of the time horizon involved and the potential consequences of decisions based on them.

FORECASTING TECHNIQUES

Let us take up discussion of various forecasting techniques and common models. The Table 7.02. clearly exhibits these forecasting techniques and common models.

TABLE 7.02
FORECASTING TECHNIQUES & MODELS

CLASSIFICATION OF TECHNIQUES AND MODELS	NATURE
I. QUALITATIVE :	**Subjective, judgemental. Based on estimates and opinions.**
A. Grass-roots :	Derives a forecast by compiling input from those at the end of hierarchy who deal with what is being forecast. For instance, an overall sales- forecast may be derived by combining inputs from each sales-person, who is closest to his or her own territory.

B. Market Research :	Sits out to collect data in a variety of ways Survey-interviews to test hypothesis about the market. This is typically used to forecast long-range and new-product sales.
C. Panel Consensus :	Free and open exchange at meetings. The idea is that discussion by the group will produce better forecasts than any one individual. Participants may be executives, sales people or customers.
D. Historical Analogy :	Ties what is being forecast to a similar item. Important in planning new products where a forecast may be derived by using the history of similar product.
E. Delphi Method :	Group of experts respond to questionnaire. A moderator compiles results and formulates a new questionnaire which is submitted to the group. Thus, there is learning process for the group as it receives new information and there is no influence of group pressure or dominating individual.
II. TIME SERIES ANALYSIS	**Based on the idea that the history of occurrences over time can be used to predict the future.**
A. Simple Moving Average :	A time period containing a number of data points is averaged by dividing the sum of the point values by the number of points. Each, therefore, has equal influence.
B. Weighted Moving Average :	Specific points may be weighted more or less than the others, as deem fit by experience.
C. Exponential Smoothening :	Recent data points are weighted more with weighting declining exponential as data become in order.
D. Regression Analysis :	Fits a straight line to past data generally relating the data value to time. Most common fitting technique is least squares.
E. Box Jenkins Technique :	Very complicated but apparently the most accurate statistical technique available. Relates a class of statistical models to data and fits the model to the time series by using **Bayesian Posterior distributions.**
F. Shinkin Time Series :	It is also called X-11 technique developed by Julius Shinkins of the Census Bureau. An effective method to decompose a time-series into seasonals trends and irregular. It needs atleast three years of history. Very good in identifying 'turning points'. For example, in company sales.

G. Trend Projections :	Fits a mathematical trend line to the data points and projects it into the future.
III. CAUSAL	**Tries to understand the system underlying and surrounding the item being forecast. For example, sales may be affected by advertising, quality and competitors.**
A. Regression Analysis :	Similar to least squares method in time series but may contain multiple variables. Basis is that forecast is caused by the occurrence of other events.
B. Econometric Models :	Attempt to describe some sector of the economy by a series of interdependent equations.
C. Input/Output Models :	Focus on sales of each industry to other firms, and governments. Indicate the changes in the sales that a producer industry might expect because of purchasing changes by another industry.
D. Leading Indicators :	Statistics that move in the same direction as the series being forecast but move before the series such as an increase in the price of petrol indicating a future drop in the sale of large cars.
E. End Use Method :	It is also called as consumption coefficient method-which is comparatively simple.
F. Consumption Level Method :	It is issued in case products for direct.
IV. SIMULATION MODELS :	**Dynamic models, usually computer-based, that allow the forecaster to make assumptions about the interval variables and external environment in the model.** Depending on the variables in the model, the forecaster may ask such questions as : what would happen to my forecast if price increased by 10 percent ? What effect would a mild national recession have on my forecast ?

SOURCE : Production and Operations Management - **Professors Richard, B. Chase, Nicholas J. Aquilano and F. Robert Jacobs**, page 502-Published by Tata MacGraw Hill, 8th Edition.

A. QUALITATIVE TECHNIQUES

The five qualitative techniques are well recognised and an attempt is made to touch upon these with view to acquaint the students the gist of these as future forecasters.

I. GRASSROOTS :

'Grassroots' forecasting builds the forecast by adding successively from the bottom. The assumption underlying here is that the person closest to the customer or end user of the product knows its future needs best. Though this is not always true, in many instances, it is valid and it is the basis for this method. Forecasts at this bottom level are summed and given to the next higher level. This is usually a distrist warehouse, which then adds in safety stocks and any effects of ordering quantity sizes. This amount is then fed to the next level, which may be a regional warehouse. The procedure repeats until it becomes an input at the top level, which, in the case of a manufacturing unit, would be the input to the production system.

II. MARKET RESEARCH :

Very often the firms hire outside companies that specialise in market research to conduct this kind of forecasting. As a supporting system, you yourself may have been, involved in market surveys through a marketing class. Certainly you might not have escaped phone calls asking you about product preferences, your income, habits and so on. Market research is used mostly for product research in the sense of looking for new product ideas, likes and dislikes about the existing products which competitive products, within a particular class are preferred, and so on. Again, the data collection methods are primarily surveys and interviews.

III. PANEL CONSENSUS :

The underlying idea behind 'panel consensus' is 'two heads are better than one'. This point is extrapolated to the idea that a panel of people from a variety of positions can develop more reliable forecast than a narrower group. Panel forecasts are developed through open meetings with free exchange of ideas from all levels of management and individuals. The difficulty with this open style is that lower employee levels are intimidated by higher levels of management. For instance, a salesman in a particular product line may have a good estimate of future product demand but may not speak up to refute a much different estimate given by the vice-president of maketing. This defect is corrected by Delphi method. When decisions in forecasting are at a broader and higher level, the term 'Executive Judgement' is generally used. The term is self-explanatory for, a higher level of management is involved.

IV. HISTORICAL ANALOGY :

An ideal situation would be where existing product or generic product could be used as model, while attempting to forecast demand for a new product. There are good many ways to classify such analogies - for instance, complementary products, substitutes, or competitive products and products as a function of income. It is also more clear in mail-order or catalogs. It is but natural when you buy a CD, through the mail order, you are sure to receive more and more mails containing information about CDs and CD players. A causal relationship is that the demand for compact dics is caused by the demand for CD players. An anology would be forecasting the demand for digital video-disk players by analysing the historic demand for Stereos, VCRs. The products that are in the same general category of electronics may be bought by consumers at similar prices. A still simpler example can be of toasters and coffee-pots. A firm that has already in production of toasters and wants to produce coffee-pots can very well use the toaster history as a likely growth model.

V. **DELPHI METHOD :**

As said earlier the limitation of Panel Consensus method is set right by Delphi Method in that a statement or opinion held by the higher level employees is valued as more important than low ever level employees though it may not be true always. The worst side is that lower level people feel threatened and do not contribute their true feelings or beliefs. Delphi method does away with this by concealing the identity of individuals participating in the study. Under this program each one has equal weightage. Particularly, a moderator creates a questionnaire and distributes it to the participants. Their reponses are summed and given back to the entire group along with a new set of questions. Delphi method was developed by the Rand Corporation of America in the 1950s.

PROCEDURE INVOLVED IN DELPHI METHOD :

The step by step procedure involved in Delphi method is consisting of five steps :

Firstly, choose the experts to participate. There should be a variety of knowledgeable people in different areas.

Secondly, through a questionnaire or E-mail, get forecasts or any premises or qualifications for the forecasts from all participants.

Thirdly, summarize the results and redistribute them to the participants along with appropriate new question.

Fourth, summarize again, refining forecasts and conditions, and again develop new questions.

Fifth, repeat step four if necessary. Distribute the final results to all the participants.

Delphi technique can usually achieve satisfactory results in three rounds. What is required is a function of the number of participants, how much work is involved for them to develop their forecasts, and their speed of responding.

The Delphi method is a process of gaining consensus from group of experts while maintaining their anonymity. This form of forecasting is very much useful when there are no historical data from which to develop statistical models-when judgement or opinion, based on experience and study of market, industry or scientific developments, are the only bases for making informed projections. Delphi method can be used to develop long-range forecasts of product demand and new product sales projections. It is fair to good in identifying the turning points in demand. One of the most useful applications for Delphi method is that of technological forecasting. The rate technological change is increasing much more rapidly than ever before. Medical science and computer science are just the two fields that are experiencing explosive technological change. Replacing human heart and liver with a mechanical heart and artificial liver have become an accepted medical procedure. Computers become obsolete soon after they are produced. In addition, an almost completely automated factory is possible. Therefore, question is what is next ? Attempting to answer that question is the focus of technological forecasting. The Delphi method can be used to get a consensus answer from a panel of experts. The panel members may be asked to specify the scientific advances that they envision, as well as changes in environmental and social forces such as quality of life, governmental regulations and the actions of competitors. The result of such a process can provide a definite direction for firm's research and development staff.

The key to the Delphi technique lies in the coordinator and experts. The experts frequently have diverse backgrounds. Thus, two physicians, a chemist, an electrical engineer, a cost-accountant and financial expert and marketing wizard might make a very effective panel. The coordinator must be talented enough to synthesize diverse and wide-spread statements and arrive at both structured set of questions and forecast.

In short, Delphi method has a very good ranage of accuracy both for short-term and long-term forecasting, though it takes a minimum of two months to develop a forecast and a fine coordination of participants and group coordinator.

B. TIME SERIES ANALYSIS

The time-series forecasting models attempt to predict the future based on past data. For instance, sales figures collected for each of the past say six weeks can be used for the seventh week. Similarly, quarterly sales figures collected for the past several years can be used to forecast the future quarters. Here, in both the cases sales figures are common but different forecasting time series models are likely to be used as time interval differs. That is, in the simplest form of time series analysis, the only information used is the historical record of demand. The analyst is not concerned with changes in the external and internal factors as noted earlier and assumes that what had occurred in the past will continue to occur in the future. The methods of time-series analysis focus on average, trend and seasonal influence characteristics of time series. The task of analyst is to try to replicate these characteristics while projecting the future demand. The techniques of time series are explained with an example along with graphical presentation.

I. SIMPLE MOVING AVERAGE :

Though moving averages are centred, it is most convenient to use past data to predict the following period directly. To take a simple case, a centered five month average of January, February, March, April and May gives an average centered on March. However, all five months of data must be existing. If our aim is to forecast for June, we must project moving average-by some means from March to June. If the average is not centered but is at the forward end, one can forecast more easily, though one may lose some amount of accuracy. Thus, if one wants to forecast June with a five month moving average, out can take average of January, February, March, April and May. When June passes, the forecast for July would be the average of February, March, April, May and June.

The FORMULA for a Simple Moving Average is= $F_t = \dfrac{A_{t-1} + A_{t-2} + A_{t-3} + A_{t-n}}{n}$

where : F_t = Forecast for the coming period

n = Number of periods to be averaged

A_{t-1} = Actual occurrence in the past period

A_{t-2}, A_{t-3}, and A_{t-n} = Actual Occurrences to periods, ago, three periods ago and so on up to n periods ago.

II. WEIGHTED MOVING AVERAGE :

In case of simple moving average, it gives equal weight to each component of the moving average data-base. As against this, weighted moving average allows any weights to be placed on each element of course, providing that the sum of all weights is equal to I. For instance, a departmental store may find that a four month period, the best forecast is derived by using 40 per cent of the actual sales for the most recent month, 30 per cent of two months ago, 20 per cent of three months ago and 10 percent of four months ago.

Therefore, Formula for Weighted Moving Average is :

$$F_t = W_1 A_{t-1} + W_2 A_{1-2} + \ldots + W_n A_{t-n}$$

Where : W_1 = Weight to be given to the actual occurrence for the period t - 1

W_2 = Weight to be given to the actual occurrence for the period t - 2

W_n = Weight to be given to the actual occurrence for the period t - n

n = Total number of periods in the forecast.

What is important to note is, the SUM of all the WEIGHTS MUST BE EQUAL TO 1, While many periods may be ignored and the weightage scheme may be in any order.

That is : $\sum_{i-1}^{n} W_i = 1$

How to Choose Weights ?

The Simplest ways to choose weights are rich experience and good trial and error. As a general rule, the most recent past is the most important indicator of what to expect in the future, and therefore, it should get higher weightage. The past month's revenue or plant capacity, for example, would be a better estimate for the coming moth than the revenue or plant capacity of several months ago. However, if the data are seasonal, weights should be established accordingly. For instance, bathing suit sales in July of last year should be weighted more heavily than bathing suits in December in the northen part of India. That is, the weighted moving average has a definite advantage over the simple moving average in being able to vary the effects of the past data. However, it is more inconvenient and costly to use than the exponential smoothening method.

III. EXPONENTIAL SMOOTHENING :

The major drawback in case of both simple moving average and weighted moving average is the need to carry continuously a large amount of historical data. This is equally true in case of regression analysis techniques. As each piece of new data is added in these methods, the oldest observation is dropped and the new forecast is calculated. In many applications, the most recent occurrences are more indicative of the future than those in the most distant past. If this premise is valid - that the importance of data diminishes as the past becomes more distant then EXPONENTIAL SMOOTHENING may be the most logical and the easiest method to use. The reason as to why it is called "exponential Smoothening" is because, each increment in the past is decreased by (1- a).

For at least SIX REASONS, exponential smoothening techniques have become most trust worthy. These are :

1. Exponential models are very accurate.
2. Formulating an exponential model is relatively easy.
3. The user can understand how the model works.
4. A little computation is needed to use the model.
5. Computer storage requirements are small because of limited use of historical data and,
6. Tests for accuracy as to how well the model is performing are easy to compute.

Under the method of Exponential Smoothening, only three items of data are needed to forecast the future namely, the most recent forecast, the actual demand that occurred for that forecast period and a smoothening constant alpha (a). This smoothening constant determines the level of smoothening and the speed of reaction to differences between forecasts and the actual occurrences. The value for the constant is determined both by the nature of the product and by the manager's sense of what constitutes good response rate. For instance, if a firm produced a standard item with relatively stable demand, the reaction rate to differences between actual and forecast demand would tend to be small say just 5 to 10 percentage points. However, if the firm is experiencing growth, it would be desirable to have a higher rate say 15 to 30 percentage points, to give greater importance to recent growth experience. The more rapid the growth, the higher the reaction rate should be. Sometimes, users of the simple moving average switch to exponential smoothening but like to keep the forecasts about the same as the simple moving average. In this case, the alpha (a) is approximated by 2 (n + 1), where the 'n' is the number of time periods.

The Equation for a single Exponential Smoothening forecast is :

$F_1 = F_{t-1} + a(A_{t-1} - F_{t-1})$

Where : F_t = The Exponentially smoothed forecast for period t

F_{t-1} = The Exponentially Smoothed forecast made for the prior period

A_{t-1} = The actual demand in the prior period

α = The desired response rate or smoothening constant.

This equation states clearly that the new forecast is equal to the old forecast plus a portion of the error which is the difference between the previous forecast and what actually occurred which some authors express "F_t" a smoothened average.

TREND EFFECTS IN EXPONENTIAL SMOOTHENING

It is worth while to remember that an upward or downward trend in the data collected over a sequence of time periods causes the exponential forecast to always lag behind may above or below-the actual occurrence. Exponential smoothend forecasts can be corrected somewhat by adding in a trend adjustment. To correct the trend, the trend equation uses a "smoothening constant" delta (δ). The delta reduces the impact of the error that occurs between the actual and the forecast. If both the alfa and delta are not included, the trend would overreact to errors. To get the trend equation going, the first time it is used the trend value must be entered mannually. This initial trend value can be calculated on the basis of observed past data.

The equation to compute the forecast including trend (FIT) is :

$FIT_t = F_t + T_t$

$F_t = FIV_{t-1} + a\ (A_{t-1})$

$T_t = T_{t-1} + a\ \ (A_{t-1})$

Where :

F_t = The exponentially Smoothened Forecast for the period t.

T_t = The exponentially smoothened trend for the period t.

FIT_t = The forecast including trend for the period t.

FIT_1 = The forecast including trend made for the prior period

A_{t-1} = The actual demand for the prior period.

α = Smoothening constant.

= Smoothening constant.

Choosing the Appropriate Value of Alpha :

Exponential smoothening requires that the smoothening constant alpha ( ) be given a value between 0 and 1. If the real demand is stable - as is normally found in case of food and electricity - one would like a small alpha to lessen the effects of short-term or random changes. On the contrary, if the real demand is rapidly increasing or decreasing - as in case of fashion wares and small appliances - one likes to take large alpha in trying to keep up with the change. It would be ideal if one could predict which alpha one should use. In this regard, two things, unfortunately go against one who is trying. First, it would take some passage of time to determine the alpha that would best fit one's data. This would be too tedious to follow and revise. Second, the one picks this week may need to be revised in the near future because, demands do change. Therefore, one needs some automatic method to track and change one's alpha values.

Adaptive Forecasting :

There are two approaches to control the value of alpha. One uses various values of alpha; the other uses a tracking signal.

1. **Two or more predetermined values of alpha.** The amount of error between the forecast and the actual demand is measured. Depending on the degree of error, the different values of alpha are used. If the error is large, alpha is 0.8, if the error is small, alpha is 0.2.

2. **Computed values for alpha.** A tracking alpha computes whether the forecast is keeping pace with genuine upward or downward changes in demand as opposed to random changes. In this application, the tracking alpha is defined as the exponentially smoothened actual error divided by the exponentially smoothened absolute error. Alpha changes from period to period within the possible range of zero to one.

Forecast Errors :

When one is using the word 'error', one refers to the difference between the forecast value and what has actually occurred. In statistics, these 'errors' are called 'residuals'. As long as the forecast value is within the confidence limits, this is not really an error. However, common usage refers to the difference as an error. It is well known that demands for a product is generated through the interaction of a number of factors which are too complex to describe accurately in a given model. Therefore, all forecasts certainly contain some error. While discussing forecast errors, it is convenient to distinguish between "sources of error" and the "measurement of error".

Sources of Error :

Errors can stem from variety of sources. One most common source that many forecasters are unaware of its projecting past trends into the future. Errors can be classified as bias or 'random'. Bias errors occur when a consistent mistake is made. Sources of bias include failing to include the right variables; using the wrong relationships among the variables; employing wrong trend line; mistakenly shifting the seasonal demand from where it normally occurs, and the existence of some undetected secular trend. Random errors can be defined as those that can not be explained by the forecast model being used.

Measurement of Error :

The degree of an error is expressed in various alternative terms such as "standard error", "mean squared error" "variance" and "mean deviation-absolute" or "mean absolute deviation". In addition, tracking signals may be used to indicate any positive or negative bias in the forecast, because, the standard error is the square-root of a function, it is often more convenient to use the function itself. This is called the mean square error or variance. We will consider Mean Absolute Deviation and Tracking signal.

MAD

The MEAN ABSOLUTE DEVIATION (MAD) was in vogue in the past but subsequently was ignored in favour of standard deviation and standard error measures. In recent years, MAD has made a comeback purely because of its simplicity and utility in getting tracking signals. MAD is the average error in the forecasts, using absolute values. MAD is valuable because, it measures the dispersion of some observed value from some expected value, like that of standard deviation.

MAD is computed by using the differences between the actual demand and the forecast demand without regard to sign. It is equal to the sum of the absolute deviations divided by the number of data points. The equation of MAD is :

$$MAD = \frac{\sum_{t=1}^{n} \left| A_t - F_1 \right|}{n}$$

Where : t = Period of number

A = Actual demand for the period

F = Forecast demand for the period

n = Total number of periods

| | = A symbol used to indicate the absolute value disregarding positive and negative signs.

Tracking Signal :

A "tracking signal" is a measurement that indicates whether the forecast average is keeping pace with any genuine upward or downward changes in demand. As used in forecasting, the tracking signal is the number of mean absolute deviations that the forecast value is above or below the actual occurrence. The following figure exhibits a normal distribution with a mean of zero and MAD equal to 1. Thus, if one computes the tracking signal and finds it equal to minus 2, one can see that the forecast model is providing forecasts that are quite a bit above the mean of the actual occurrences. A tracking signal (TS) can be calculated by using the arithmetic sum forecast deviations divided by the mean absolute deviation :

$$TS = \frac{RSFE}{MAD}$$

Where :

RSFE is the running sum of forecast errors, considering the nature of the error. For instance, negative errors cancel positive errors and vice versa.

MAD is the average of all forecast errors disregarding whether the deviation are positive or negative. It is the average of the absolute deviations.

Let us take one practical case that clears the procedure for computing the MAD and the tracking signal for a six month period. Where the forecast has been set at a constant 1,000 and the actual demand that occurred are shown.

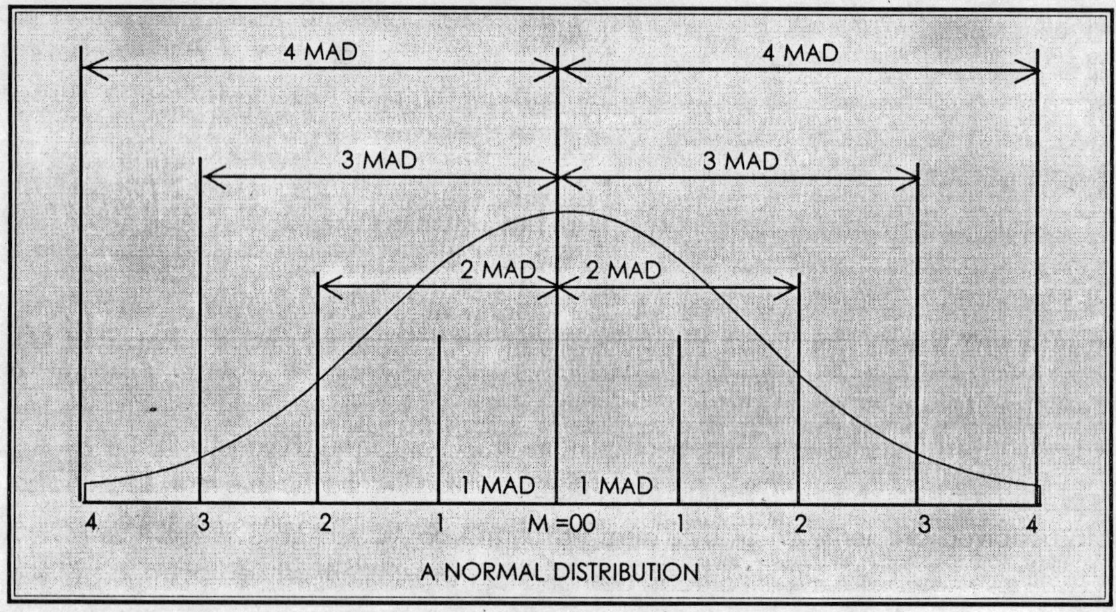

Fig. 7.03 A NORMAL DISTRIBUTION WITH MEAN = 0 and MAD = 1

IV. LINEAR REGRESSION ANALYSIS :

Regression is the functional relationship between two or more correlated variables. It is used to predict one variable given in the other. The relationship is usually developed from an observed data. Under the method, the data should be plotted first to see if they appear linear or if at least parts of the data are linear. Linear Regression refers to the special class of regression where the relationship between variables forms a straight line.

The linear regression line of form Y = a + bX, where Y is the value of the dependent variable, a is the intercept, b is the slope and X is the dependent variable. In time series analysis, X is units of time. Linear regression is very useful for long-term forecasting of major occurrences and aggregate planning. There can not be better example than that of forecasting demand for product families. Even though the demand for individual products within a family may vary during a time period, the demand for the total product family is smooth beyond ones expectations.

The basic restriction in using linear regression forecasting is, as the name suggests, that past data and future projections are assumed to fall about a straight line. While this limits its application, Sometimes, one uses a shorter period of time, linear regression can still be used. For instance, there may be short segments of longer period that are approximately linear.

Linear regression is used for both time series and for causal relationship forecasting. When the dependent variable, it is the time series analysis. If one variable changes because of the change in another variable this is the causal relationship. To explain the concept, the following example is used to compare forecasting models and types of analysis say for hand fitting a line, for the least squares analsysis.

It is very essential to note here that these forecasts are based on the line only and do not identify or adjust for elements such as seasonal or cyclical elements.

The best line to use is the one that minimises this total. As before, the straight line equation is :

$$Y = a + bx$$

From the graph it was determined both 'a and 'b'. In the least squares method, the equation for a and b' are :

$$a = \bar{y} = b\bar{x}$$

$$b = \frac{\sum xy - n\bar{x}.\bar{y}}{\sum x^2 - n\bar{x}^2}$$

Where :

a = Y intercept

b = Slope of the line

$\bar{Y}$ = Average of all ys X = Average of all xs

X = x value at each data point

y = y value at each data point

n = Number of data points

Y = Value of the dependent variable computed with the regression equation.

C. CAUSAL RELATIONSHIP FORECASTING

Causal methods provide us the most sophsticated forecasting tools. They are used when the historical data are available and the relationship between the factor to be forecasted and other external and internal factors can be identified. These relationships are expressed in mathematical terms can be very complex. Causal methods are by far the best for predicting turning points in demand and preparing long range forecasts. In other words to be of value for the purpose of forecasting, any independent variable must be a leading indicator. For instance, one can expect that an extended period of rainy days in the increase sales of umbrellas and raincoats. The rain causes the sale of rain wear or gear. This is a causal relationship, where one occurrence causes another. If the causing element is far enough in advance, it can be used as a basis for forecasting. A number of causal methods are used. However, the most widely used method is linear regression which is explained below.

I. Linear Regression Method :

Linear regression is one of the best known causal methods of forecasting. This approach uses two variables namely dependent and "independent". The dependent variable such as demand or cost, is the variable that the forecaster wants to forecast. The independent variables are assumed to have affected the dependent variable and thereby 'caused' the results observed in the past. Time also can be an independent variable as a surrogate representing an unspecified group of variables contributing to trends or seasonal patterns in the data.

To explain the use of linear regression, here I have used the simplest model in which the dependent variable is a function of only one independent variable. Any linear regression method requires that we hypothesize a relationship between the dependent variable and the independent variable. In the simplest case, we hypothesize that relationship would be a straight line. Accordingly the formula is :

$$Y_i = a + \beta X_i + u_i$$

Where :

Y_i = the dependent variable value for the observation i.

X_i = the independent variable value for observation i.

a = the Y intercept of the line.

β = the slope of the line.

u_i = random error.

Here, we do not know the '*a*' and 'β' values, so we must estimate them from a sample data. These data are used to calculate '*a*', the estimate of '*a*' and '*b*' estimate of β', using a technique of least squares. The objective is to find values of '*a*' and '*b*' that minimize the sum of squared deviations of the actual 'Y_i values from the estimated values, or

$$\text{Minimise} \sum_{i=1}^{n} \left[Y_i - (a + bX_i)\right]$$

where n is the number of data points in the sample.

The process of finding the values of a and b that minimize the sum of squared deviations is complex; so we will state the equation only as under :

Where : a = $\bar{Y} - b\bar{X}$ and $b = \dfrac{\sum XY - n\overline{XY}}{\sum X^2 - n\bar{X}^2}$

a = the estimate of the Y intercept.

b = the estimate of the slope of the line.

$\bar{Y}$ = the average of the Y values.

= the average of X values.

It is worthwhile to note here that the values of a and b also minimise the cumulative sum of forecast errors, the average error (bias), and the standard deviation of forecast errors. However, they do not minimise mean absolute deviation, popularly called as MAD.

II. Multiple Regression Analysis :

Another forecasting method is multiple Regression analysis in which a number of variables are considered, together with effects of each on the item of forecaset. For instance, in case of house furnishings field, the effects of the number of marriages, housing starts, disposable income and the trend can be expressed in a multiple regression equation, as :

$$S = B + B_m (M) + B_h(H) + B_t(T)$$

Where :

S = Gross sales for the year

B = Base sales, a starting point from which other factors have influence

M = Marriages during the year

H = Housing starts during the year

I = Annual disposable income

T = Time trend (first year = 1, second = 2, third = 3 and so forth) B_m, B_h and B_t represent the influence on expected sales of the members of marriages and housing starts, income and trend.

Forecasting by multiple regression is an appropriate approach when a number of factors influence a variable of interest in this case, sales. Its difficulty lies with the mathematical computation. Fortunately standard computer programmes for multiple regression analysis are available, relieving the need for tedious manual calculation.

III. Chain Ratio Method :

The potential sales of a product may be estimated by applying a series of factors to a measure of aggregate demand. Let us take a case of an Indian Company planning to manufacture triple edge blade cartridges. In the light of it, the company used chain ratio method to estimate potential sales - step by step.

- Estimated male (adult) population in the country by 2003 = 175 million
- Proportion of adult male population using single, double triple edge blade cartridges = 0.80
- Adult male population using single, double, triple cartridges = 140 million
- Number of times in a year a person, who use triple edge cartridges, shares = 100
- Total shavings done per year = 14,000 millions
- Proportion of shavings done with triple edge cartridges = 0.35
- Average.number of savings per triple edge cartridge = 10
- Average number of savings using triple edge cartridges = 49000 million
- Total number of blades used per year triple edged cartridge = 4900 million
- Proportion of triple edge, cartridge market = 0.25
- Potential sales of tripe edge cartridges. = 1125 million

This chain ratio method uses very simple analytical approach to estimate potential demand. Its reliability, precision are largely dependent on the ratios and rates used in the process of determing the sales potential. These ratios and rates can be both objective and subjective which make results challenging.

IV. Consumption Level Method :

In case of products which are directly consumed, this method is perfectly suiting. Under this methods estimates of consumption level on the basis of elasticity coefficients - particularly income elasticity of demand and price elasticity of demand.

Income Elasticity of Demand

The income elasticity of demand signifies the responsiveness of demand to variations in income. It is measured as follows :

$$E_1 = \frac{Q_2 - Q_2}{I_2 - I_1} \times \frac{I_1 + I_2}{Q_2 + Q_1}$$

Where : E_1 = Income elasticity of demand

Q_1 = Quantity demanded in the base year

Q_2 = Quantity demanded in the following year

I_1 = Income level in the base year

I_2 = Income level in the following year.

Price Elasticity of Demand

The price elasticity of demand measures the responsiveness of demand to variations in price. It is defined as :

$$Ep = \frac{Q_2 - Q_1}{P_2 - P_1} \times \frac{P_1 - P_2}{Q_2 - Q_1}$$

Where :

E_p = Price elasticity of demand

Q_1 = Quantity demanded in base year

Q_2 = Quantity demanded in following year

P_1 = Price per unit in the base year

P_2 = Price per unit in the following year

This price elasticity of demand is useful tool in demand analysis. The future volume of demand may be estimated on the basis of price elasticity co-efficient and expected price change. The price elasticity coefficient may also be used to study the effect of variable prices that may be obtained in future on economic viability of the project. However, while using price elasticity measure, two points must be borne in mind :

(1) The price elasticity co-efficient is applicable to only small variations.

(2) The price elasticity measure is based on the postulation that the structure and behaviour remain cosntant.

V. End Use Method :

End use method is also called as consumption co-efficient method and is very suitable in estimating the demand for intermediate products. This method is made up of four logical steps :

(1) Identification of the possible uses of the product

(2) Defining the consumptions co- efficient of the product for various uses

(3) Projecting the output levels for consuming industries and

(4) Derving at the demand for the product.

VI. Leading Indicator Method :

Statistic that move in the same direction as the series being forecast but move before the series such as an increase in the price of petrol indicating a future drop in the sale of large cars. That is leading indicators are variables which change ahead of other variables, the lagging variables. Therefore, observed changes in leading indicators may be used to predict the changes in lagging variables. For instance, the change in the level of urbanisation - a leading indicator -may be used to predict the change in the demand for white goods like airconditions or aircoolers, audio-visual products - a lagging variable.

Two basic steps are called for in using the leading indicator method.

(1) Identify the appropriate leading indicator or indicators

(2) Establish the relationship between the leading indicator or indicators and the variable to be forecast.

The main merit of this method is that it does not require a forecast of an explanatory variable.

However, the problems associated are :

(1) It may be difficult to find an appropriate leading indicator or indicators

(2) The lead-lag relationship may not remain stable over a period of time.

VII. Econometric Models :

An econometric model is a mathematical expression of economic relationship or relationships derived from an economic theory. The fundamental objective of econometric analysis is to forecast the future behaviour of the economic variables incorporated in the model. There can be two types of econometric models which are in use namely single equation model and simultaneous equation model. It means that single equation model assumes that one variable the dependent variable or explained variable, is influenced by one or more independent variables or explanatory variables. The instance of single equation model can be :

$$Dt = ao + aj + Pt + az\ Nt$$

Where :

Dt = Demand for a certain product in year 't'

Pt = Price for the product in year 't'

Nt = Income in year 't'.

In case of simultaneous equation models, the relationship or relationships are expression in two or more equations. A simple case of simultaneous equation model taking three equations can be :

$$GNPt = Gt + It + Ct \quad \text{...(i)}$$

$$It = ao + a1\ GNPt \quad \text{...(ii)}$$

$$Ct = bo + b1\ GNPt \quad \text{...(iii)}$$

Where :

GNPt = Gross National Product for year 't'

G t = Governmental purchases for year 't'

It = Gross Invetment for year 't'

Ct = Consumption of year 't'

Construction of such econometric models involves four steps namely : (1) Specification (2) Estimation (3) Verification (4) Production.

Econometric models have certain merits and limitations.

The merits are :

(1) The proces of economic analysis sharpens the understanding of complex cause, and effect relationships

(2) They provide basis for testing assumptions and for judging the extent of sensitivity results vis-a-vis changes in assumptions.

The limitations are :

(1) These are data demanding and expensive

(2) There is need for projected values of independent variables to fore-cast the behaviour of the dependable variable.

CHOOSING A FORECASTING METHOD

In this context, the first question arises as to whether you need a forecasting system? The system can range from simple inexpensive tools to extensive programs requiring extensive commitments of time, treasure and talent.

A business uses forecasting in planning its inventory and production levels as well as for new product development staffing and budgets. At the product level, it is inexpensive to develop forecasts to develop forecasts using simple moving average, weighted moving average or exponential smoothening. These methods would apply to large bulk of standard inventory items carried by a firm. The choice of which of these three methods to use is based on market conditions. Moving averages weight each period the same, exponential smoothening weights the recent past more, and weighted moving average allows the weights to be determined by the forecaster. Which is better ? One test would be to use each method on sample data and measure the errors using the MAD and RSFE as we did. In any case, all forecasts should be passed on to the appropriate area to someone familiar with the product to adjust or modify the forecast. In using regression analysis, it is critical to assure that the data fit the model. If they donot, explorations will create serious errors.

Executive opinion, sales force and customer survey near the top of the list because of marketing emphasis and valuable forecast indicators are trends and market share. Comparing manufacturing and service firms, manufacturing firms tend to be more thorough and provide more interactions in circulating and adjusting the forecast. The most significant forecasts are by-product lines and product-life cycles. Manufacturers tend to use more quantitative techniques and are more satisfied with the forecasting process. They also tend to rate the forecasting as well as the level of accuracy more important than service firms rate them.

Service firms tend to involve more people in forecasting and have a higher percentage of executive involvement. Service firms also tend to :

(1) view the weighted moving average as an important technique and

(2) use subjective forecasting much more than manufacturers. Because of different techniques each uses, service firms also reported that their forecasting process is more cumbersome than manufacturers'. Additionally, service firms are less satisfied with the forecast.

FOCUS FORECASTING

Focus forecasting is the brain child of **Berine Smith. B. Smith** uses it primarily in finished goods inventory management. **Mr. B. Smith** substantiates strong arguments that statistical approches used in forecasting do not give the best results. He states that simple techniques that work well on past data also prove the best in forecasting the furture.

What is it and Its Methodology ?

"Focus forecasting" simply tries several rules that seem logical and easy to understand to project past data into the future. Each of these rules is used in a computer simulation program to actually project demand and then measure how well that rule performed when compared to actually happened. Therefore, the two components of the focus forecasting system are :

(1) Several simple forecasting rules and

(2) Computer simulation of these rules on past data.

These are simple, common sense rules made up of and then tested to see whether they should be kept. The examples of simple forecasting rules could include:

(a) Whatever we sold in the past three months is what we will probably sell in the next three months.

(b) What are sold in the same three month period last year, with probably sell in that three month period this year.

(c) We will probably sell 10 percent more in the next three months than we sold in the past three months.

(d) We will probably sell 50 percent more over the next three months than we sold for the same three months of last year.

(e) Whatever percentage change we had for the past three months this year compared to the same three months last year will probably be the same peprcentage change that we will have for next three months of this year.

One thing is sure that these forecasting rules are not hard and fast. If a new rule seems to work well, it is added. If it does not, it is deleted.

The second part of the process is computer simulation. To use the system, a data history should be available for at least 18 to 24 months period. The simulation process, then uses each of the forecasting rules to predict some recent past data. The rule that did best in predicting the past is the rule used to predict the future.

DEVELOPING A FOCUS FORECASTING SYSTEM

How to develop a focus forecasting system? Here are certain suggestions or guidelines that help in designing focus forecast system. These are :

1. **Do not Try to Add Seasonality Index :**
   One should not add a seasonality index. Let the forecasting system findout seasonality by itself, especially with new items because, seasonality may not apply until the pipe-line is filled and the system is stable. The forecasting rules can handle it.

2. **Do not just Unregard Unusual Demands :**
   When a forecast is usually high or low say, two or three times the previous period, or the previous year if there is seasonality, print out an indicator such as the letter 'R' telling the person affected by this demand to review it. Do not just disregard unusual demands because they may, infact, be valid changes in the demand pattern.

3. **Encourage Participation by Forecasters :**
   Let the people who will be using the forecasts namely buyers or inventory planners participate in creating rules. **B. Smith** plays his game with all the company buyers because, "one cannot and out guess focus forecasting." Using two years data and 2000 items, focus forecasting makes forecasts for the past six months. Buyers are asked to forecast the past six months using any rule they prefer. If they are consistently better than the existing forecasting rules, their rules are added to the list.

4. **Keep the Rules Simple :**
   By keeping the rules simple, they will be easily understood and trustéd by the users of the forecast which increases the value of focus forecasting.

   In a nutshell, it appears that focus forecasting has significant merit when demand is generated outside the system, such as in forecasting end-item demand, spare-parts and materials and supplies used in a variety of products. It is economical also as B. Smith reports that computer tune apparently is not very large since 1,00,000 items forecasts every month using the golden rules of focus forecasting.

D. SIMULATION MODELS :

As said earlier, dynamic models, usually computer based, allow the forecaster to make assumptions about the internal variables and external environment in the model. Many commerical forecasting programs are available. Most are available for micro-computers and use shared net work data bases. Major companies of America like Wal-Mart are now using programs that work over internet. The future is to improve the standards of performance and packages will be standardized meeting specific needs of manufacturers and traders in forecasting. All but most sophisticated forecasting formulae are quite easy to understand. Any one who can use a spread sheet such as Microsoft Excel can create a forecasting program on personal computer. Depending on one's knowledge of the spreadsheet, a simple program çan be written anywhere from a few minutes to a couple of hours. How this forecast is to be used by the firm could be the bigger challenge. If demand for many items is to be forecast, this becomes a data handling problem, not a problem in the forecasting logic.

DESIGNING THE FORECASTING SYSTEM :

The contents of this chapter brought to the surface number of forecasting methods and techniques. The problem before manager is to select one best and suitable method so that he can make forecasts and proceed to the next stage of analysing operations management problems. Unfortunately, it is not that easy as one says. The choice rather correct choice of a particular method is certainly a significant aspect of designing a forecasting system, but there are some other important considerations. While designing a forecasting system, the manager must decide on :

(1) What to forecast ?

(2) What software package to use for a computerised programme ?

(3) How the system can assist managerial decision making? Let us touch these three key points.

I. Deciding What to Forecast :

It is quite common to hear operations managers saying that forecasts of demand should be made for all goods or services produced by their companies. Through some sort of demand estimate is needed for all items, it may be easier to forecast some aggregation of the products and then derive individual product forecasts. Selecting the correct unit of measurement is also important for, the forecasts can be as important as choosing the best method. This should consider two points namely, level of aggregation and units of measurement.

1. Level of Aggregation :

In actual practice, very few companies have errors of more than 5 percent in their forecasts of total demand for all products. However, errors in forecasts for individual items range from 100 percent to + 300 percent or more. Thus, the greater the aggregation is, the more accurate are the forecasts. Many companies employ a two tier forecasting system in which forecasts are first made for 'product families", a group of goods or services that have similar demand requirements and common processing, labour and materials requirements. Forecasts for individual items are divided in such a way that their sum equals to the total forecast for the family. Such approach maintains consistency between planning for the final stages of manufacturing and long-term planning for sales, profit and capacity.

II. Units of Measurement :

The forecasts that serve as input to planning and the analysis of operations problems are most useful if they are based on product units rather than rupee values. Forecasts of sales revenue are not very much helpful because, prices can and often do fluctuate. Thus, even though the total sales in rupees might be the same from month to month, the actual number of units of demand will vary widely. Forecasting the number of units of demand and then translating them into sales revenue estimates by multiplication is often much better method. It may, however, so happen that forecasting the number of units of demand for a product may not be possible. The companies producing goods or services to customer order, face this problem. In such cases, it is better, to forecast the standard labour or machine hours required of each of the critical resources, based on historical patterns. For such companies, estimates of labour or machine hours are important for scheduling and capacity planning.

2. Selecting a Software Package :

This being the age of computer technology and sweeping revolution of information, many forecasting software packages are available for all sizes of computers. These package are available for all sizes of computers. These packages offer a wide variety of forecasting capabilities and report formats. Packages such as General Electric's Time Service Forecasting System (GETSFS) and IBMs Consumer Goods System (COGS) and Inventory Management Program and Control Technique (IMPACT) contain forecasting modules used by many firms that have large computer facilities. Since the introduction of microcomputers, scores of software packages have been developed for virtually all of the popular personal computers. The applications range from simple to very sophisticated programs. These micro-computer packages are priced to make them attractive alternatives to traditional main-frame packages. Taking cost effectivences of techniques, some are preferred in short range while others in long range. Therefore, selection of forecasting software package is the joint decision by marketing manager and operations manager. Or, a team may be there representing important departments. The final selection of the package is based on :

(1) How well the package satisfies the needs and wants?

(2) The cost of buying or leasing the package

(3) the level of clerical support required and

(4) the amount of programmer maintenance period required.

3. Managerial Use of the System :

There are two important aspects that are to be mentioned in regard to the use of computerised forecasting system :

(1) Single number forecasts are rarely useful because, forecasts are almost always wrong. Resultantly, managers know that if there is single number of forecasted product demand, actual demand will be any thing but that figure. Therefore, a far more useful approach is to provide the manager with a forecasted value and an error range, which can be done by using MAD. This adjusted information gives the manager a better feel for the uncertainty in the forecast and allows the manager to better plan inventories, staffing levels and the like.

(2) It concerns itself with the expected amount of managerial interface with the system. Tracking signals should be computed for each forecast, and the messages should be generated when the signals exceed the range selected. The managers should have the authority to override a computer generated forecast with a forecast of their own or modify the method used when changes in the demand pattern dictate. That is managers should exercise full freedom to use forecast which helps them to gain confidence in the forecasting system.

Thus, in conclusion one can say that developing a breakthrough in forecasting system is not easy. However it must be done because, forecasting is fundamental to any planning effort.

UNCERTANTIES OF DEMAND FORECASTING

The efforts to forecast the demand are marred by possible errors and uncertainties which will blunt the results. These errors and uncertainties stem from three major sources which are outlined as under.

1. **Data About Past and Present Market :** The analysis of past and present market is the very foundation of the exercise of projection. This can be damaged by the inadequacies in data. These inadequacies are : (a) Lack of standardisation : Data relating to market features like product, price, quantity, cost, income and the like, may not reflect uniform concepts and measures, (b) Few observations : observations available to conduct purposive and meaningful analysis may not be enough (c) Impact of Abnormal Factors : Some of the observations are likely to be influenced by abnormal factors like war or natural calamity.

2. **Methods of Forecasting :** The methods used for demand forecasting are not free from the following stated limitations. (a) Inability to handle unquantifiable factors. The methods that are quantitative are not capable of handling unquantifiable factors which, at times can be of great importance. (b) Unrealistic assumptions : Each forecasting method works on certain assumptions. For instance the trend projection method is founded on the "mutually compensating effects" premise and the end use method is based on the constancy of technical co-efficients. Uncertainties arise when the assumptions underlying the chosen method tend to be unrealistic and wrong, (c)

Excessive data requirement : Normally, the more advanced a method, the greater the data requirement. For instance, use of an econometric model or simulation models have to forecast values of not single variable but good many variables. It is neither easy not very accurate unless computer programming is resorted to.

3. **Environmental Changes :** Any business unit is a sub-system of a supra system namely environment. Each business which functions in this volatile uncertain environment having the combined influence of variant forces. These only add to uncertainty of a greater degree. These changes are : (a) Technological : Technological advancement or changes result in improved product, cheaper product rendering existing product or products obsolete. Digital technology has thrown analog technology in case of many products, (b) Governmental policies : whether there is stable government or unstable : the governmental policies change whereby some lines of activity gain and others lose. In case government gives extra concessions to herbal products, non-herbal products lose business. Small scale units gain much under the umbrella of packages of concessions or sops (c) International : The economies of the world will be influenced badly or favourably depending on sudden change in international economy. Thus, all countries with soft currencies are bound to suffer when a country or countries with hard currencies bring about change in their policies in various fields. (d) Sources of New Raw- materials : Whenever new sources of raw-materials or their substitutes are brought to surface, the market position of several products are affected favourably or unfavourably. (e) Unpredictable Monsoons: Meteorological predictions are not very uncertain because of impossibility of exact productions. Each year India on one side faces flood conditions and on the other draught conditions. This situation virtually affects majority of economic and non-economic activities.

HOW TO HANDLE THESE UNCERTAINTIES ?

There is dire need for adequate and effective efforts to cope up with these uncertainties. The possible solutions lie in : (a) Conduct analysis with databased on uniform and standard definitions (b) Ignore the abnormal or uncontrollable observations while identifying trends co-efficients and relations. (c) Critical evaluation of assumptions of forecasting methods and choice of most appropriate method. (d) Adjustment of the projections derived from quantitative analysis in the background of a due consideration on quantifiable influences which are significant. (e) Continuous and close monitoring of enviornmental forces for identification of acceptable significant changes. (f) Consider likely alternative scenarios and their impact on the market and competition. (g) Conduct sensitivity analysis to measure the impact on the size of demand for both unfavourable and favourable variations of the determining factors from their most likely levels.

6. MARKET PLANNING :

The terminal part of the market and demand analysis exercise is that of market planning. All these logical steps culminate into a suitable marketing plan that enables the product to reach the desired level of market penetration. A marketing planning is to design a market mix to various target markets or market segments. A suitable market-mix covers the four dimensions namely Product - Price - Place and Promotion.

A "Product Mix" is the composite of products offered for sale by the firm over a period of learn. The product mix variables are - (a) The product line and product range (b) Product design (c) Product Package (d) Product quality (e) Product labelling (f) Product branding (g) After sale services - such as installation, user education, warranties, repairs, replacements.

A "Place Mix" or "Distribution Mix" stands for matching arrangements for the smooth flow of goods and services from producers to consumers. The place mix variables are (1) Transporation (2) Warehousing (3) Inventory levels (4) Channels of distribution - consisting of wholesalers and retailers.

A "Price Mix" signifies the pricing of a products taking into all factors. The price mix variables are (1) pricing policies and strategies (2) the terms of credit (3) Terms of delivery (4) Margin (5) Resale price maintenance.

A 'Promotion Mix' or 'Communication Mix' deals with creating and maintaining marketing communication between all those that come in contact with marketing activity. The promotion mix variables are (1) Personal selling (2) Advertising (3) Sales promotion (4) Trade fairs and exhibitions (5) Public relations and (6) publicity.

CHAPTER BASED QUESTIONS

A. WRITE SHORT NOTES ON

1. Market and Demand analysis
2. Steps in conducting market and demand analysis
3. Situation analysis
4. Secondary data 5. Market survey
6. Census survey
7. Sample survey
8. Characterisation of market
9. Demand forecasting
10. Market planning
11. Qualitative methods of forecasting
12. Time series techniques
13. Causal methods
14. Simulation method
15. Focus forecasting.

B. SHORT ANSWER QUESTIONS

1. What is market and demand analysis ?
2. What is situational analysis ?
3. What is collection secondary data ?
4. What is conduct of market survey ?
5. What is sample survey ?
6. What is focus forcasting ?
7. What are qualitative methods of forecasting ?
8. What are causal methods of forecasting ?
9. What problems are associated with forecasting ?
10. What are lime series ?

C. ESSAY TYPE QUESTIONS

1. What is market and demand analysis ? What steps are involved in it ?
2. What is demand forecasting ? What are the different methods of forecasting ?
3. What is conduct of market survey ? What steps are involved in its conduct ?
4. What is characterisation of market ? What are its features that are spelled out ?
5. What is demand forecasting ? What are its merits and limits ?
6. Explain causal forecasting in brief.
7. Explain qualitative techniques of forecasting.
8. What is a econometric model ? What is it consist of ?
9. How can you develop a sound forecasting method ?
10. Forecasting is not free from serious limitations. How do you do away with these hurdles?

* * * * *

Chapter 8

PROJECT FEASIBILITY STUDIES PART-4

- WHAT IS "RISK" AND "UNCERTAINTY" ?
- RISK COMPONENTS
- TYPES OF PROJECT RISKS
- MEASURES OF RISK
- ANALYTICAL DERIVATION OR SIMPLE ESTIMATION
- STANDARDISATION OF THE DISTRIBUTION
- SENSITIVITY ANALYSIS
- EVALUATION
- SCENARIO ANALYSIS
- SIMULATION
- APPLICATION ISSUES ASSOCIATED WITH MONTE CARLO SIMULATION
- DECISION-TREE ANALYSIS
- CHAPTER BASED QUESTIONS
- CHAPTER BASED PRACTICAL QUESTIONS

BACKDROP

After scanning through technical financial, economic and social dimensions, the top management is to deliver its decision on projects viability or otherwise. Hence, managerial appraisal is the apex point that paves the way for final judgment or managerial decision as "go ahead" or "Stop". Decision-making is the prerogative of every management. This managerial decision, the toughest of all, is going to decide the future of a project and its results. Hence, managerial appraisal is basically concerned with risks associated with the project in question. That is why, managerial feasibility is having the paramount position and comes last to decide the drums of the destiny. Hence, this chapter is reserved to discuss in detail risks and risk-management. The chapter ends with Chapter Based Questions.

WHAT IS 'RISK' AND 'UNCERTAINTY' ?

The techniques that are used in capital budgeting call for the estimation of future cash-inflows and cash-outflows by taking into account the factors namely, expected economic life span of the project, the salvage value of the asset at the end of economic life, capacity of the project in terms of technology, selling prices of its output, production cost, future demand for the output, rate of depreciation and the rate of taxation, among other things. However, due to uncertainties about future, the estimates of demand, production, sales, costs, selling prices and other variables can not be exact. All these elements of uncertainty have to be taken into account in the form of forcible risk while taking decision on investment proposals. Risk management is the toughest task even for the managers of high calibre. Before going into the details, let us know what these two terms mean namely 'risk' and 'uncertainty'.

In practice, these terms "risk" and "uncertainty" are interchangeably used. However, they have different meanings in different contexts. 'Risk' is that uncertainty which is predictable, and to which probability can be assigned. According to this statement, two conditions should be fulfilled: (i) the decision-maker is aware of possible outcomes which may occur and affect his decision and (ii) the decision-maker is in a position to assign a probability to each possible outcome envisaged by him. In case these conditions are absent, it can be called as uncertainty. That is, "uncertainty" is that event which can not be predicted and therefore, there is no question of assigning probability to it.

From the angle of an ordinary thinker or a layman, "risk" and 'uncertainty' have difftrent meanings. Let us take that there are two projects namely, Alpha and Beta. Project Alpha is likely to offer an IRR in the range of 25 and 45 percentage and Beta in the range of 15 and 35 per cent. If the cut-off rate of the firm is 20 per cent, one is very likely to say the project Beta is riskier than project Alpha, though in both the cases the uncertainty (difference between 20 per cent between the highest and lowest IRR) level is the same. That is, an understanding of a common man of the two terms is quite different from statisticians' definitions. A common man looks at the down side risk (a possibility of earning an IRR less than the minimum acceptable rate of return). For our analysis, uncertainty and risks are so closely interlinked that they are interchageably used. That is, 'Uncertainty' also denotes 'risk'.

RISK TAKING AND GAMBLING

Some people have a wrong notion that 'risk-taking' is equal to 'chance taking, that is, gamblers also take risks or chances. However, blind and thoughtless chance taking is the mainstay of gambling. Gambling can not be risk-taking for risk-taking involves informed and calculated risks within the limits. That is two elements, distinguish 'risk-taking' from 'gambling' or chance taking (a) information or knowledge and (b) awareness about the ability to survive (absorb) the ill-fated outcome of a decision. The former lays emphasis on building a data-base and skill to interpret data while the latter works as a constraint on greed. The ability to absorb an adverse result, if any, also means the attitude towards risk. Let us see these two aspects or elements.

KNOWLEDGE BASE

The knowledge base or information base speaks that there is need for a sound data base for sound decision-making. The root cause of risk is, therefore, data and their interpretations. There can be four types of data namely, known-known, known-unknown, unknown-known and unknown-unknown that help as in ranging certainty and uncertainty in absolute terms. The Fig. 8.01 makes it very clear.

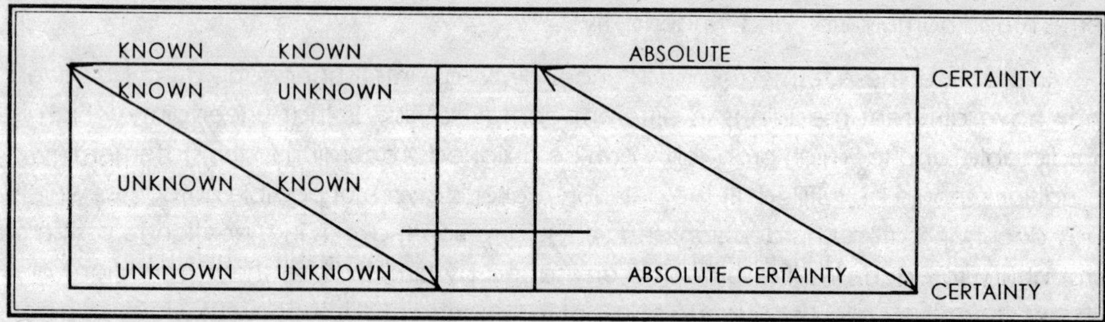

Fig. 8.01 THE KNOWLEDGE BASE

The above classification is based on two factors namely, the need for information and the availability of required and reliable information. If a manager knows about the need for information and that required information is available and very reliable that gives absolute confidence to the manager, then it can be called as "known known". The "known unknown" category implies that the manager is aware of the need for some information, but information is not available or even if available not fully reliable, it may infuse in him a high degree of confidence. The third category "unknown-known" implies that the manager does not know about the need of it and is available and is not reliable can be giving lower confidence. The "unknown-unknown" category implies that manager is neither aware of the need for information, nor that information is available at all. The best examples of these can be divine acts of Almighty - that are "unknown-unknown".

This helps us to develop a decision-making grid in case of projects involving projects involving risks and uncertainties. This decision-making grid can be configured as given in Fig. 8.02.

From the above "decision-grid" the projects with very little or no information base in the initial point - point A - where very little logic is available and the proposal is based on very high intuition - that will pass through many stages like project feasibility, market-survey, test-marketing and finally the project report stage. Building information at minimum additional cost before moving over to the next stage is the prime purpose behind the stages. A project is seriously considered for adoption only at a stage when confidence is attained, by the management. It is natural that some decision-makers feel more confident about reaching at early stage whereas others opt to wait and do good deal of homework before arriving at a decision for mounting the funds.

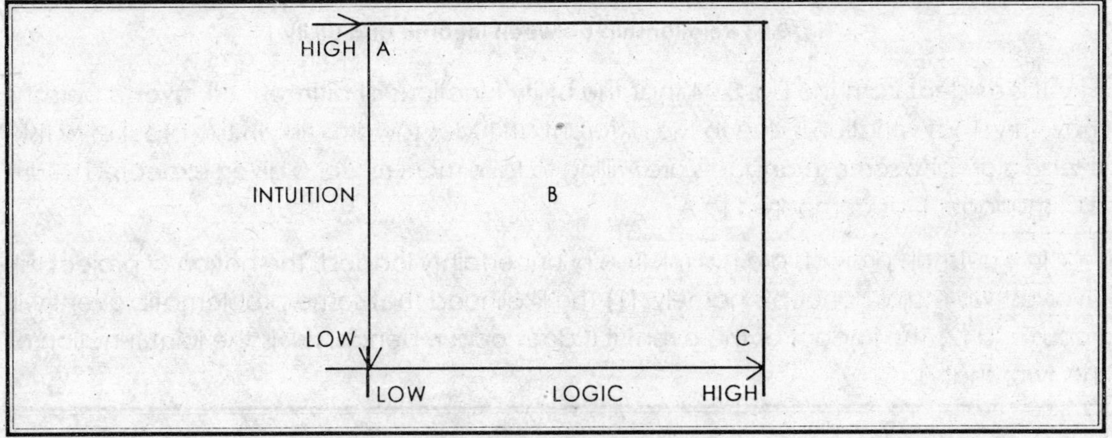

Fig. 8.02 Dicision-making Grid

ATTITUDE TOWARDS RISKS

Basically, risk is a perception. Hence, the managerial decision is guided by the attitude of the decision-maker towards risk. Risk is an attitude or a mindset. Based on this "attitude towards risk", decision-makers can be of three types as depicted in the Fig. 8.03 which is constructed on the two variables namely, utility and income and their relationship.

All those who take risk are doing so if the corresponding returns expected by them are high enough to justify the degree of risk taken. That is, a manager likes to take every additional dose of risk if the corresponding additional returns satisfy him. This means that a different amount of risk premium is attached to different degrees of risk. Hence, risk premium is the function of the utility of returns. A rational business manager is expected to be "risk-averse" whose utility curve is concave. His marginal utility of additional income is lower. Consequently, a rational manager is risk lover who expects higher marginal return for every additional dose of risk showing his curve as convex. The relationship between the risk and expected return which can be amply clarified if one goes through the Fig. 8.04.

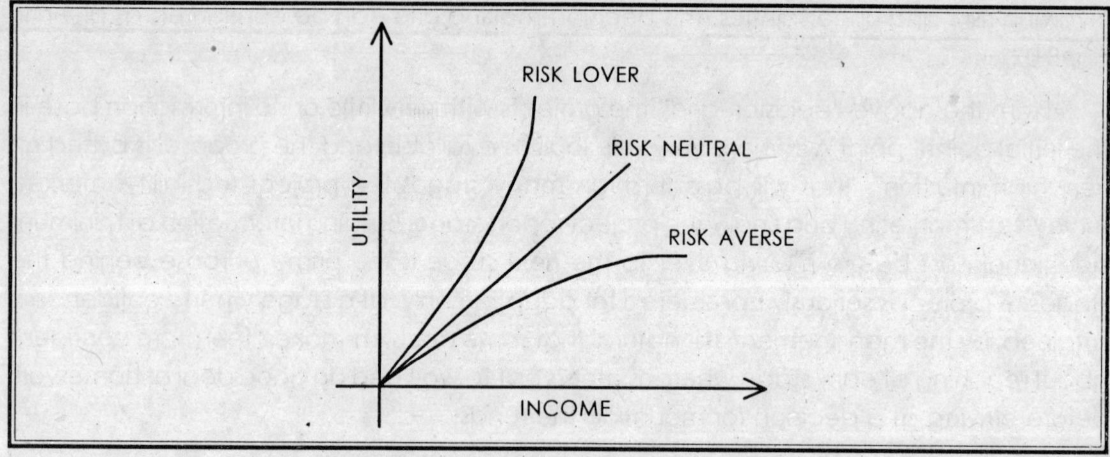

Fig. 8.03 Relationship between Income and Utility

It is evident from the Fig. 8.04 that the utility functions of different risk averse persons may vary. That variation is due to the different attitudes towards risk. In the bracket of risk-averse class also some managers are willing to take more risk for a given expected return like manager B as compared to A.

In a nutshell, projects are not risk free or uncertainty loaded. The notion of project risk involves two major concepts namely: (1) The likelihood that some problematic event will occur and (2) The impact of the event if it does occur. Hence, risk is the joint function of the two; that is,

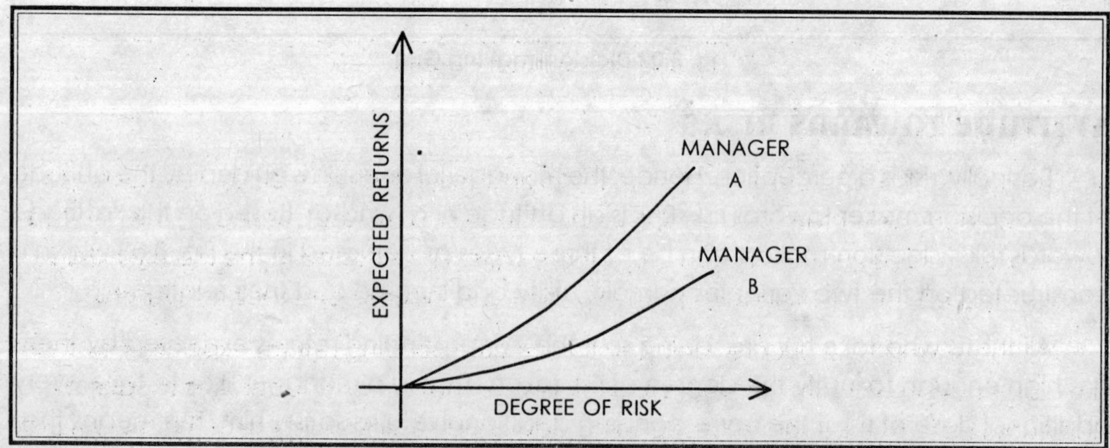

Fig. 8.04 Different Utility functions of risk averse managers

Risk =f (liklihood, impact)

It means that given that risk involves both liklihood and impact, a project will be ordinarily considered risky whenever at least one factor-either the likelihood or the impact- is large. For instance, a project is considered risky where the potential impact is human-fatality or massive financial loss even when the likelihood of either is small.

RISK COMPONENTS

The component of risk-management is an affair that goes on from the birth of a project till its death and even after its death are the identification of the risk event, the assessment of the probability of the identified risk and the impact of the risk. These components are:

RISK IDENTIFICATION

The identification of the risk is very important, the risk must be described, in detail so that it will not be confused with any other risk or project task that must be done. Each risk should be given an identification number. During the course of project, as more information is gathered about the risk all of this information can be consolidated.

RISK PROBABILITY

Since all risks have a probability of greater than zero and lees than 100 per cent, the probability of risk occurring is essential to the assessment of the risk. Any risk event that has probability of zero can not occur and need not be considered as risk. A risk event that has probability of 100 per cent is not a risk. It has a certainty of occurring and must be planned for in the project plan.

RISK IMPACT

Risk impact is the cost of the risk, if it occurs. This, in its qualitative measure, is the pain level of the risk. Quantitative measures include the impact of the identified risk in terms of schedule days, effort man-hours, money and so on.

STEPS IN RISK MANAGEMENT

It is generally thought that the risk management process is done in four steps- 1) Risk identification 2) Risk evaluation 3) Risk mitigation 4) Risk control and evaluation.

RISK IDENTIFICATION

The risk identification process consists of identifying the risks and documenting them so that they will not be forgotten and they have been identified.

RISK EVALUATION

The risk evaluation process consists of evaluating each risk so that the ones that will have the most severe effect on the project will receive the most attention.

RISK MITIGATION

Risk mitigation consist of determining a plan to reduce, limit, or even, ignore the risk and its effect on the project.

RISK CONTROL AND EVALUATION

Risk control and evaluation consists of observations and reporting on the risks as time goes by. Some risks will prove to have not occurred, while others will have occurred and the mitigate strategies will be observed to have worked or not worked.

TYPES OF PROJECT RISKS

Project risks are classified by different academicians and experts in a different way. Here, two such cases of classification are taken.

One group classifies them as Internal and External or Controllable and uncontrollable risks.

I. INTERNAL RISKS

Internal risks stem inside the project or project organisation. The project managers and stake holders usually have a measure of control over these. These internal risks are broadly classified as (A) Market Risks and (B) Technical Risks.

A. MARKET RISKS :

Market risk is the risk of not fulfilling either market needs or the requirements of particular consumer. The sources of market risk include:

- Incompletely or inadequately defined market or customer needs and requirements.
- Failure to identify changing needs and requirements.
- Failure to identify newly introduced products by competitors. Market risk can be reduced by thoroughly and accurately defining needs and requirements right at the start of the project, and continuously monitoring and updating the requirements as needed throughout the project.

B. TECNICAL RISKS :

Technical risk is the risk of not meeting time, cost or performance requirements due to technical problems with the end-item or project activities. Technical risk tends to be high in projects involving activities that are unfamiliar or require new ways of integration. It is especially high in projects that involve new and untried technical applications. Technical risk is low in projects that involve mostly familiar activities done in customary ways. One way of expressing these technical risks by rating the risk of the project end-item or primary process as being high, medium or low in terms of maturity, complexity, quality, concurrency or dependency.

II. EXTERNAL RISKS

External risks are those that are external to the project or project organisation. Being external, the project managers and stakeholders do have either very little control or no control over these. External risk hazards include changes in :

- Market conditions
- Customer needs and behaviour
- Competitors' actions
- Supplier relations
- Government Regulations
- Adverse weather conditions
- Interest rates
- Labour availability Strikes and walk outs
- Decisions made by senior management or the customer regarding project priorities, staffing budgets
- External control by customers or sub-contractors over project work and resources.

Another group of experts has different way of classifying project risks as (1) Stand Alone Risk (2) Firm Risk and (3) Systematic risk.

1. **Stand Alone Risk :** This signifies the risk of a project when it is viewed in isolation. When individual project in taken into account independently for its sources of risks which can be both internal and external.

2. **Firm Risk :** Firm Risk is also called as corporate risk which reflects the contribution of project risk of the firm where there are good many projects and total impact is counted.

3. **Systematic Risk :** Systematic risk is nothing but market risk which is internal in nature which represents the risk of a project in the context of market portfolio.

MEASURES OF RISK

Risk is a variable factor and, therefore, there are several measures. The most important one are at least six which are all statistical techniques. These are :

1. Range
2. Mean Absolute Deviation - MAD

3. Variance
4. Semi-Variance
5. Standard Deviation
6. Co-efficient of Variation.

Before we take the illustrations, let us look into the definitions in terms of formulae.

1. RANGE

Range is the difference between the highest value of the outcome and the lowest value of the outcome. Symbolically it can be :

$$R_g = R_h - R_l$$

Where R_g = Range

R_h = highest value

R_l = Lowest value

The RANGE does not consider probabilities, nor does it pay attention to other possible outcomes between the highest and the lowest value. The sensitivity analysis uses RANGE value in its application.

2. MEAN ABSOLUTE DEVIATION

The phrase '**mean absolute deviation**' is self-explanatory. The deviation of each observation from their mean is added up to get mean absolute deviation. While adding up the difference, the signs are ignored. It is called absolute because negative sign is ignored. Symbolically, it is :

$$MAD = \sum_{i=1}^{n} P_i \left| R_i - \bar{R} \right|$$

Where :

P_i = the probability of the ith possible value.

R_i = the ith possible value of the variable.

$\bar{R}$ = the expected value of the distribution.

$R_i - \bar{R}$ = Only the absolute value is considered; a negative value is ignored.

3. VARIANCE

Variance is the difference of the value from the mean of distribution is squared to avoid negative sign. By squaring the difference the values which are far away from the mean are given more weightage. Due to squaring, however, the variance can not be compared with the expected (mean) return. Symbolically, variance stands for :

$$\text{Variance} = V = \sum_{i=1}^{n} P_i \left(R_i - \bar{R}\right)^2$$

Where : P_i = the probability of the ith possible value.

R_i = the ith possible value of the variable.

$R_i - \bar{R}$ = Only the absolute value is considered.

4. SEMI-VARIANCE

It is the same as variance but it considers R values only if $R_i < \bar{R}$ (that is, only if there is a chance of getting less than the expected result). If $R_i > \bar{R}$, then zero value is taken for $(R_i - \bar{R})$. Symbolically, SV can be :

$$SV = \sum_{i=1}^{n} P_i \left(R_i - \bar{R}\right)^2$$

Where : SV = Semi - variance

$(R_i - \bar{R})$ is always positive.

Negative $(R_i - \bar{R})$ is taken as zero.

5. STANDARD DEVIATION

Standard deviation is needed because the variance can not be compared with the expected (mean) return. Therefore, its root is taken and standard deviation is calculated so that it can be compared with return. However, it ignores the size of the project, and therefore, the comparison of two projects becomes difficult. Symbolically, standard deviation is projected as :

$$SD = \sigma \text{ (Sigma)} = \sqrt{\text{Variance}} = \sqrt{\sum_{i=1}^{n} P_i (R_i - \bar{R})^2}$$

Where SD/ σ = Standard deviation

P_i = Probability of the ith possible value.

R_i = the ith possible value of the variable.

$\bar{R}$ = the expected value of the distribution.

6. CO-EFFICIENT OF VARIATION

When the standard deviation (σ) is divided by expected returns (that is, mean or $\bar{R}$) one gets the **coefficient of variation**. It is, therefore, useful in comparing risks of the two projects of different sizes. Lower Coefficient of Variation is considered good. This rule "lower coefficient of variation is better" assumes that the decision maker is risk- neutral. That means that the utility curve of the decision-maker is neither convex nor concave, but it is a straight slope-line. Risk neutral feature implies that the rate of risk- premium is constant for every unit of incremental risk. Symbolically, Co-efficient variation is :

$$CV = \sigma \div \bar{R}$$

Where : CV = Coefficient Variation

σ = Standard deviation

$\bar{R}$ = expected return/mean

In order to understand these measures, one illustration can be used giving all six values or results. You are provided with two variables namely, 'outcome' and the probability in respect of an investment :

Outcome Rs.	Probability
1,100	0.2
700	0.5
600	0.3

1. **Range :**

$R_g = R_h - R_i$

Range = Rs. 1,100 - Rs; 600 = Rs. 500.

2. **Mean absolute deviation :**

$$MAD = \sum_{i=1}^{n} P_i \left| R_i - \bar{R} \right|^2$$

$\therefore$ MAD : Expected Value =

$\bar{R}$ = [(Rs. 1,100 $\times$ 0.2) + (Rs. 700 x 0.5) + (Rs. 600 $\times$ 0.3)]

= Rs. 750

MAD = 0.2 $\times$ (1,100-750) + 0.5 (700-750) + 0.3 (600-750)

= 70 + 25 + 45

= 140

In case the mean absolute deviation is calculated on the basis of arithmetic mean (170) rather than the expected value then, answer will be 170.

For calculating the results of other remaining measures, there is need for certain calculations which are inter-related and are given in the form of a table.

P	R	P x R	$(R - \bar{R})$	$(R - \bar{R})^2$	$P(R - \bar{R})^2$
0.2	Rs. 1,100	220	350	1,22,500	24,500
0.5	Rs. 700	350	- 50	2,500	1,250
0.3	Rs. 600	180	- 150	22,500	6,750
		$\bar{R}$ 750			σ^2 32,500
					σ 180

3. Variance :

$$V = \sum_{i=1}^{n} P_i (R_i - \bar{R})^2$$

$$V = 0.2 \times 350^2 + 0.5 \times 50^2 + 0.3 \times 150^2$$

$$V = 32{,}500$$

4. Semi-Variance :

$$SV = \sum_{i=1}^{n} P_i (R_i - \bar{R})^2$$

Where SV or Semi-variance $(R_i - \bar{R})$ is always positive.

Hence Negative $(R_i - \bar{R})$ is taken as zero.

$$SV = 0.2 \times 350^2 + 0.5 \times 0^2 + 03 \times 0^2$$

$$SV = 24{,}500$$

5. Standard Deviation :

$$SD = \sigma \text{ (Sigma)} = \sqrt{\text{Variance}} = \sqrt{\sum_{i=1}^{n} P_i (R_i - \bar{R})^2}$$

$$SD = \sqrt{32,500} = 180 \text{ (Using Variance)}$$

$$\text{OR} = \sqrt{24,500} = 156.5 \text{ (Using semi-variance)}$$

6. Co-efficient of Variation :

$$CV = \sigma \div \bar{R}$$

$$CV = 180 \div 750 = 0.24 \text{ (Using Variance)}$$

$$\text{Or } CV = 156.5 \div 750 = 0.209 \text{ (Using semi-variance)}$$

Of all the above measures of risk, STANDARD DEVIATION is the most commonly used measure of risk in the area of finance. The basic reasons for using SD are :

1. If a variability is normally distributed, its mean and SD contain all the information about its probability distribution.

2. If the utility of money is represented by a quadratic function - a function commonly suggested to represent diminishing marginal utility of wealth - then the expected utility is the function of mean and SD.

3. SD is analytically easily tractable.

For measuring the expected value and dispersion of a variable, its probability distribution is needed. In some cases, the probability distribution can be defined with a fairly high degree of objectivity on the basis of past evidence. For instance, a tribesman may be able to define with a high degree of objectivity, the probabilities associated with certain states of nature in case he has facts recorded or not for similar ventures - say bird or an animal of a particular specie. Since such a probability distribution is substantially based on observations that are objective facts, it may be called as an "objective" probability distribution. However, there are situations in real-life where objective evidence may not be available for defining the probability distributions. In such cases knowledgeable persons may share their individual experiences and judgement to define the probability distribution. As there is a high degree of subjectivity in these distributions, such distributions can be referred to as 'subjective' probability distributions. Thus, a meteorologist's probability distributions are objective than a farmer or a person working in the field.

ANALYTICAL DERIVATION OR SIMPLE ESTIMATION

Back to investment proposals, the expected say NPV and the standard deviation of NPV may be obtained through analytical derivation or simple estimation, under certain circumstances. One is free to take other criterion than NPV. Based on the nature of cash-flows, one can think of three possible analyses namely, (1) Uncorrelated cash-flows (2) Perfectly correlated cash-flows and (3) Moderately correlated cash-flows.

1. UNCORRELATED CASH-FLOWS :

In a situation where the cash-flows of different years are uncorrelated, the cash-flows for year t is independent of the cash-flow for year t-r. To put the same thing in different way, there is no relationship between cash flows from one period to another. In such a situation, the expected NPV and SD of NPV can be defined as under :

$$NPV = \overline{NPV} = \sum_{t=1}^{n} \frac{\overline{A_t}}{(1+i)^t} \quad \text{...(1)}$$

$$\sigma\ (NPV) = \left[\sum_{t=1}^{n} \frac{\sigma t^2}{(1+t)^{2t}}\right]^{\frac{1}{2}} \frac{n!}{r!(n-r)!} \qquad ...(2)$$

Where: NPV = expected net present value

$\overline{A}_t$ = expected cash-flow for year t

i = risk - free interest rate

I = initial outlay

σ (NPV) = Standard deviation of net present value

σ_t = Standard deviation of the cash-flow for year t

It is worth emphasizing at this point that in above formulae the discount rate is the risk-free interest rate because one is to separate the time value of money and the risk-factor. The risk of the project, reflected in the σ (NPV), is considered in conjunction with NPV computed with the risk free discount rate. If the NPV is computed using risk adjusted discount rate and then if this is seen alongwith σ (NPV), the risk factor would be double counted.

ILLUSTRATION:

Project X involves an initial investment of Rs. 20,000 and the benefits associated with the project are :

Year 1st		Year 2nd		Year 3rd	
Net Cashflow	Probability	Net Cashflow	Probability	Net Cashflow	Probability
Rs. 6,000	0.3	Rs. 4,000	0.2	Rs. 6,000	0.3
Rs, 10,000	0.4	Rs. 8,000	0.6	Rs. 10,000	0.4
Rs. 14,000	0.3	Rs. 12,000	0.2	Rs. 1,40,000	0.3

You are required to calculate $\overline{NPV}$ and σ (NPV) assuming that i = 6 per cent.

SOLUTION:

$$\overline{NPV} = \sum_{t=1}^{n} \frac{\overline{A}_t}{(1+i)^t} - I$$

$$= \frac{10,000}{(1.06)^1} + \frac{8,000}{(1.06)^2} + \frac{10,000}{(1.06)^3} - 20,000$$

$$= \text{Rs. } 4,950$$

$$\sigma\,(NPV) = \left[\Sigma \frac{\sigma_t^2}{(1+i)^{2t}} - 1\right]^{\frac{1}{2}}$$

$$= \left[\frac{48,00,000}{(1.06)^2} + \frac{32,00,000}{(1.06)^4} + \frac{48,00,000}{(1.06)^6}\right]^{\frac{1}{2}}$$

$$= \text{Rs. } 4,516$$

2. PERFECTLY CORRELATED CASH-FLOWS :

The behaviour of cash-flows in periods is similar if cash-flows are perfectly correlated. That is, the actual cash-flow in a year is a standard deviation to the left of its expected value, cash-flows in other years will also be a standard deviation to the left of their respective expected values. In other words cash-flows of all years are linearly related to one another. Hence, the expected value and the standard, deviation of NPV are as indicated below when cash-flows are perfectly correlated.

$$\overline{NPV} = \sum_{t=1}^{n} \frac{\overline{A}_t}{(1+i)^t} - I \quad \text{...(i)}$$

$$\sigma(NPV) = \sum_{t=1}^{n} \frac{\sigma_t}{(1+i)^t} \quad \text{...(ii)}$$

ILLUSTRATION:

An industrial project calls for an investment of Rs. 10,000. The mean and standard deviation of cashflows, which are perfectly correlated, are as follows :

Year	$\overline{A}_t$	σ_t
1	Rs. 5,000	1,500
2	Rs. 3,000	1,000
3	Rs: 4,000	2,000
4	Rs. 3,000	1,200

You are required to calculate $\overline{NPV}$ and σ (NPV), taking a risk-free interest rate of 6 per cent.

SOLUTION:

$$\overline{NPV} = \sum_{t=1}^{n} \frac{\overline{A_t}}{(1+i)^t} - I$$

$$= \frac{5,000}{(1.06)^1} + \frac{3,000}{(1.06)^2} + \frac{4,000}{(1.06)^3} + \frac{3,000}{(1.06)^4} - 10,000$$

$$= \text{Rs. } 3,121$$

$$\sigma(NPV) = \sum_{t=1}^{4} \frac{\sigma_t}{(1+i)^t}$$

$$= \frac{1,500}{(1.06)^1} + \frac{1,000}{(1.06)^2} + \frac{2,000}{(1.06)^3} + \frac{1,200}{(1.06)^4}$$

$$= \text{Rs. } 4,935$$

3. MODERATELY CORRELATED CASHFLOWS :

When cash-flows are moderately correlated and, therefore, do not conform to the two patterns - independent and perfect correlation - as seen earlier, a simple and handy formulae can not be employed for assessing return and risk. Moderately correlated cash-flows may be evaluated with the help of CONDITIONAL PROBABILITY DISTRIBUTIONS.

ILLUSTRATION:

An industrial investment involves an initial capital expenditure of say Rs. 1,00,000. The cashflows the patterns of cash flows for 1st year, 2nd year, 3rd year have the figures alongwith initial and conditional probabilities.

1st Year

Cash-flows	Initial Probability
Rs. 30,000	0.5
Rs. 50,000	0.5

2nd Year

Cash-flows	Conditional Probabilities
Rs. 30,000	0.8
Rs. 40,000	0.2
Rs. 50,000	0.6
Rs. 60,000	0.4

3rd Year

Cash-flows	Conditional Probabilities
Rs, 35,000	0.6
Rs. 40,000	0.4
Rs. 45,000	0.5
Rs. 50,000	0.5
Rs. 60,000	0.7
Rs. 70,000	0.3
Rs. 75,000	0.8
Rs. 90,000	0.2

Calculate the $\overline{NPV}$ and (NPV) taking a risk free interest rate of 6 percent.

SOLUTION:

It is worthwhile to note that the probability with which a cash-flow stream occurs is nothing but the probability of individual elements in that cashflow stream. The general rule for calculating the joint probability is given as under:

$P = (A_i, A_2 ..., A_n) = P(A_1)\ P(A_2/A_1) \times P(A_3/A_1,A_2) \times ...P(A_n/A_1, A_2 ..., A_n - 1)$

By following this general rule, the joint probability for cash flow streams will be as under:

Stream of Cashflow	NET PRESENT VALUE	JOINT Probability
1.	$\frac{30,000}{(1.06)}+\frac{30,000}{(1.06)^2}+\frac{35,000}{(1.06)^3}-1,00,000=15612$	0.24
2.	$\frac{30,000}{(1.06)}+\frac{30,000}{(1.06)^2}+\frac{40,000}{(1.06)^3}-1,00,000=11414$	0.16
3.	$\frac{30,000}{(1.06)}+\frac{40,000}{(1.06)^2}+\frac{45,000}{(1.06)^3}-1,00,000=1684$	0.05
4.	$\frac{30,000}{(1.06)}+\frac{40,000}{(1.06)^2}+\frac{50,000}{(1.06)^3}-1,00,000=5882$	0.05
5.	$\frac{50,000}{(1.06)}+\frac{50,000}{(1.06)^2}+\frac{50,000}{(1.06)^3}-1,00,000=42046$	0.21
6.	$\frac{50,000}{(1.06)}+\frac{50,000}{(1.06)^2}+\frac{70,000}{(1.06)^3}-1,00,000=50442$	0.09

7.	$\frac{50,000}{(1.06)}+\frac{60,000}{(1.06)^2}+\frac{75,000}{(1.06)^3}-1,00,000=63540$	0.16
8.	$\frac{50,000}{(1.06)}+\frac{60,000}{(1.06)^2}+\frac{90,000}{(1.06)^3}-1,00,000=71134$	0.04

Now that we got joint probability of NPV, the information can be presented in the following table that helps in calculating $\overline{NPV}$ and σ (NPV) based on conditional probability approach.

1st Year		2nd Year		3rd Year			
Net Cashflow	Initial Probability P(1)	Net Cash-flow	Conditional Probability P (2/1)	Net Cashflow	Conditional Probability P (3/2, 1)	Cash flow Stream	Joint Probability (P 1, 2, 3)
				35,000	0.6	1	0.24
		30,000	0.8	40,000	0.4	2	0.16
30,000	0.5	40,000	0.2	45,000	0.5	3	0.05
				50,000	0.5	4	0.05
				60,000	0.7	5	0.21
50,000	0.5	50,000	0.6	70,000	0.3	6	0.09
		60,000	0.4	75,000	0.8	7	0.16
				90,000	0.2	8	0.04

Hence: NPV = 21186

σ (NPV) = 33647

STANDARDISATION OF THE DISTRIBUTION

No doubt, thorough knowledge of $\overline{NPV}$ and σ (NPV) is very much useful in evaluating the risk features of a project. If the NPV of a project is approximately normally distributed, one can calculate the probability of NPV being less than or more than a certain specified value. This probability is obtained by finding the area under the probability distribution curve to the left or right of the specified value. Take for instance, the probability distribution of NPV is given as under, if one wants to calculate the probability of NPV being less than as specified value, say 0, one has to obtain the area under 'probability' distribution curve to the left of 0 - which is a shaded region. If one is interested in finding the probability that NPV exceeds a certain value, say Rs. 2 lakhs, it is possible to calculate the area under the probability distribution curve to the right of Rs. 2 lakhs - this area is shown as the shaded region. The graph thus configures is as shown in Fig. 8.06.

PROCEDURE FOR CALCULATING THE AREA TO THE LEFT OR RIGHT OF A SPECIFIED POINT

This can be done by following a definite procedure containing two steps:

Step 1 :

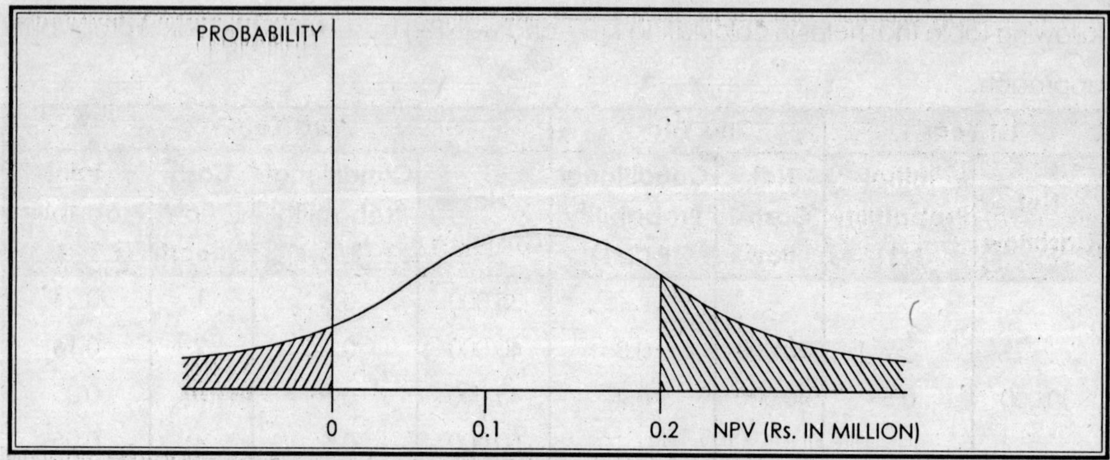

Fig. 8.05 Areas under Normal Distribution Curve

Standardise the difference between the specified point and NPV. To do this, the difference between the specified point and NPV is divided by σ (NPV). The standardised difference may be referred to as Z. The purpose of standardisation is to transform the actual distribution of NPV into a standard normal distribution. The standard normal distribution has a mean of 0 and standard deviation of 1.

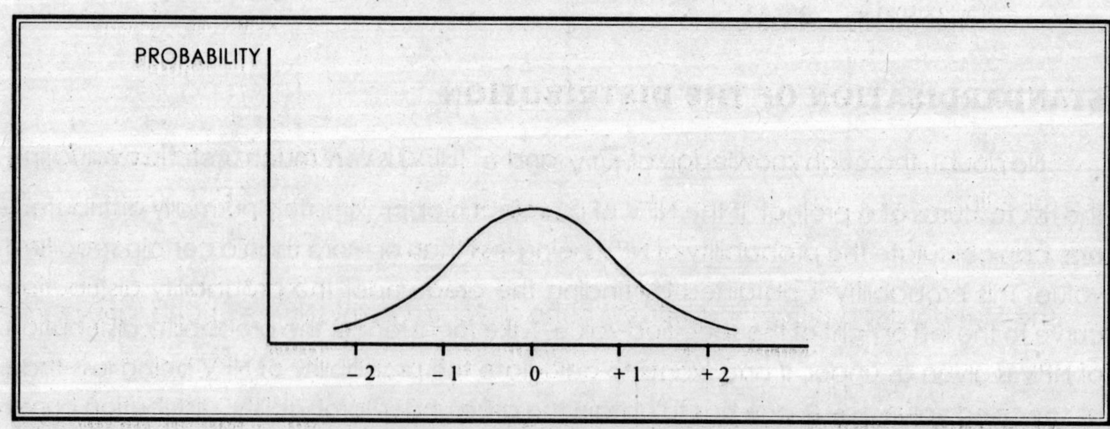

Fig. 8.06 Standard Normal Distribution

Step 2 :

Refer to the standard normal distribution table and locate the probability to the left or right the need of the Z value obtained in step 1.

To demonstrate the above procedure, take for instance that a project's NPV and $\overline{NPV}$ are Rs. 96,000 and Rs. 60,000 respectively and one wants to find the probability that NPV will be less than 0. This is presented as under the caption CUMULATIVE PROBABILITY UP TO Z FOR STANDARD NORMAL DISTRIBUTION.

Z	Cumulative Probability	Z	Cumulative Probability
-3.0	0.001	0.2	0.579
-2.8	0.003	0.4	0.655
-2.6	0.005	0.6	0.726
-2.4	0.008	0.8	0.788
-2.2	0.014	1.0	0.841
-2.0	0.023	1.2	0.885
-1.8	0.036	1.4	0.919
-1.6	0.055	1.6	0.945
-1.4	0.081	1.8	0.964
-1.2	0.115	2.0	0.977
-1.0	0.159	2.2	0.986
-0.8	0.212	2.4	0.992
-0.6	0.274	2.6	0.995
-0.4	0.345	2.8	0.997
-0.2	0.421	3.0	0.999
-0.0	0.500	–	–

By evaluation :

Step 1 :

The Standardised difference between the specified point (NPV = 0) and $\overline{NPV}$ = Rs. 96,000 is $\frac{0 - 96,000}{60,000} = -1.6$

Step 2 :

The cumulative probability up to Z = - 1.6 is equal to .055. It means that there is 5.5 per cent chance that NPV will be equal to or less than 0.

For further clear understanding, one more case can be taken up. Say, that a project's $\overline{NPV}$ and σ (NPV) are Rs. 2,00,000 and Rs. 1,50,000. Prove that the probability is greater than Rs. 3,80,000 - at what point ?

SOLUTION:

Step 1 :

The standardised difference between the specified point (NPV = 3,80,000)

$$\text{and } \overline{NPV} : \frac{3,80,000 - 20,00,000}{1,50,000} = 1.2$$

Step 2 :

Referring the cumulative probability chart upto Z = 1.2 is 0.885. Hence, the probability to the right of Z = 1.2 is:

1 - 0.885 = 0.115

That is, the probability that NPV will be greater than Rs. 3,80,000 is 0.115.

SENSITIVITY ANALYSIS

Sensitivity analysis has been largely accepted as a method of risk analysis. As the term clearly indicates, the Sensitivity Analysis is a technique in which sensitivity of profit or NPV or IRR to the change in one particular factor is checked. The philosophy that "only a few factors may warrant management attention" is embedded in the Sensitivity Analysis. The vital few have to be identified, as they make a difference to the success of the project. It is an attempt to highlight the impact of adverse variations in each of the significant variables that affect the cash-flow in a given project. Sensitivity analysis is otherwise called as 'what if' analysis explain the relationship between the profit - net present value of return - with a change in a particular variable or variables. In other words, it involves a process of recalculating the net present value if a particular factor turns out to be a different level than originally estimated. It follows very simplistic analysis tools. Only one variable is considered at a time and the question of what the profit will be? if that variable is changed to another level is addressed. Then the second variable is selected and so on. Thus, it analyses as to what is going to happen to the net present value or cash-flow if sales value is reduced ? or sales price is reduced. It equally takes serious note if the effective life of plant is reduced due to external or internal factors. It is because economic life span of an investment is shortened because of superior technology or changes in fashion or style movement.

OBJECTIVES OF SENSITIVITY ANALYSIS

In relation to a given project, the objectives of sensitivity analysis are threefold:

1. To Find the Answers to the Questions such as What would happen to Net present value. If there is change in any one parameter of project such as: (i) Increase or decrease in the value of variable or variables, (ii) Increase or decrease in economic life of the project. (iii) Increase or decrease in cash-flows (iv) Increase or decrease of Sales Volume or Sales price.
2. To Identify those Variables in the Model which are highly sensitive such as change in economic, political and environmental forces. Any sudden decision by the government might affect adversely or favourably the industry of which a firm is only a unit.
3. To Trace the Variables About Which further information is Needed before a decision is taken on project. The Project decision is a long-term decision having many dimensions - economic, social, ecological, cultural, political, which are to be given due weightage. A hurry is always a cause of worry.

PROCEDURE INVOLVED IN SENSITIVITY ANALYSIS

Sensitivity analysis is made up of three steps which are quite simple. These steps are:

1. Setting Relationship Between Basic Factors: It is to do with setting up of relationship between the basic underlying factors such as quantity sold, unit selling price, life of the project and so on and the net present value or any other parameter.
2. Estimating the Range of Variation: It estimates the range or extent of variation and the most likely value of each of the basic underlying factor. Say, if cash-flow is going to come down by fall in the sales or sales price, then its extent and impact.
3. Studying the Effect on Net Present Value of Variation: It concludes the effect or impact study of the variations in basic variables particularly one at a time.

ASSUMPTIONS OF SENSITIVITY ANALYSIS

The sensitivity model works on two assumptions namely, (1) Only one variable changes at a time, while other variables of the project remain constant. (2) There is absence of correlation between any two variables or among the groups of variables under consideration in the project.

METHODS OF SENSITIVITY ANALYSIS

Among other possible tools or methods, four are very commonly used. These are (1) Percentage change approach (2) Accounting Break Even approach (3) NPV Break-even approach and (4) Pass-off matrix.

1. PERCENTAGE CHANGE APPROACH IN SENSITIVITY ANALYSIS

In a situation where there is no initial information about the possibility of variation in different factors, the percentage change method of sensitivity analysis becomes a must.

ILLUSTRATION:

World Cup Makers limited has a project cost of Rs. 10 lakhs. The additional information available is :

Sales units per year	15,000	
Sales price per unit	Rs. 100	= 00
Material cost per unit	Rs. 40	= 00
Labour cost per unit	Rs. 15	= 00
Power cost per unit	Rs. 20	= 00
Other expenses per unit	Rs. 5	= 00

The expected project life is six years and the break up value at the end of project life is zero. Ignore working capital and taxation. Consider a 15 per cent discount rate and assume that there are no non-cash items of expenses.

You are required to :

1. Construct a table showing net present values at 5%, 10% and 15% change on either side in one variable at a time for all variables.
2. Select the two most crucial factors and construct a NPV table for various level changes in both the variables.

SOLUTION:

Table Showing NPV for Different Percentage changes in Different Factors.

Percentage Change	Sales Units	Sales Value Rs.	Materials Cost Rs.	Labour Cost Rs.	Power Cost Rs.	Other Expenses (Cost) Rs.	Investment Value
- 15 %	(2,05,360)	(7,16,200)	(2,05,360)	7,490	(35,080)	92,630	(14,800)
- 10 %	(91,840)	(4,32,400)	(91,840)	50,060	21,680	1,06,820	35,200
- 05 %	21,680	(1,48,600)	21,680	62,630	78,440	1,21,010	85,200
0 %	1,35,200	1,35,200	1,35,200	1,35,200	1,35,200	1,35,200	1,35,200

05 %	2,48,720	4,19,000	2,48,720	1,77,770	1,91,960	1,49,390	1,85,200
10 %	3,62,240	7,02,800	3,62,240	2,20,340	2,48,720	1,63,580	2,35,200
15 %	4,75,760	9,86,600	4,75,760	2,62,910	3,05,408	1,77,770	2,85,200

NOTE : (1) Negative Values are bracketed.

(2) Negative changes are unfavourable.

(3) Positive changes are favourable.

From the above table, it is observed that the fluctuation in NPV is highest in case of sales price, followed by material cost followed by power costs and sales quantity respectively. Investment overseen is also a matter of concern at the last stage.

The above calculations, if presented in the form of graph, the configuration of graph will be :

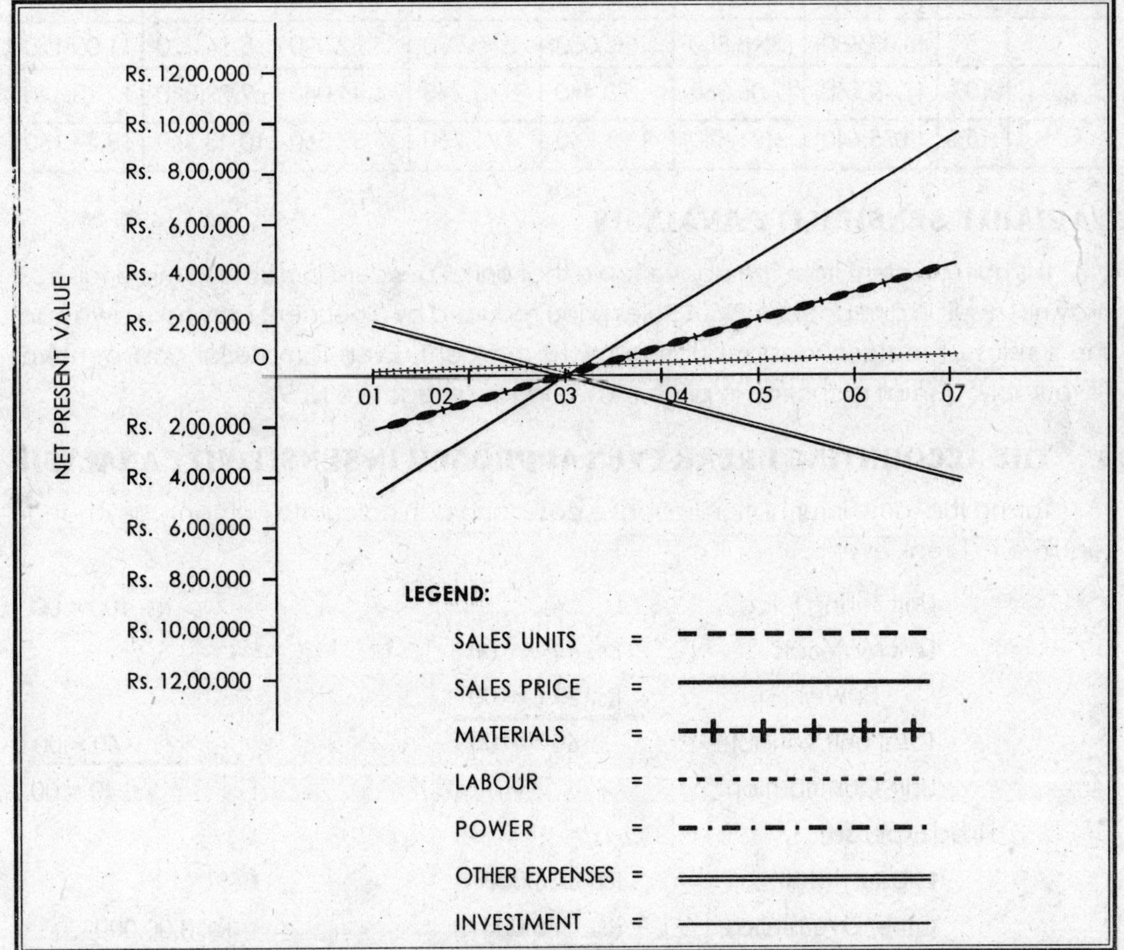

Fig. 8.07 Graphic Presentation of NPV Sensitivity of various Factors

It is possible to have two-variable Sensitivity Analysis. Taking the above data of the company one can take two variables say 'Sales Price' and 'Material Cost' considered together.

In case these two variables are taken, the calculations that configure will be as shown in the following Table :

		SALES PRICE						
		- 15%	- 10%	- 05%	0%	05%	10%	15%
	-15%	(10,56,700)	(7,72,960)	(4,89,160)	(2,05,360)	78,441	3,62,240	6,46,040
	-10%	(9,43,240)	(6,59,440)	(3,75,640)	(91,840)	1,91,960	4,75,760	7,59,560
	-05%	(29,720)	(5,45,920)	(2,62,128)	21,680	3,05,480	5,89,280	8,73,080
Material Cost	0%	(7,16,200)	(4,32,400)	(1,48,600)	1,35,200	4,19,000	7,02,800	9,86,600
	5%	(6,02,680)	(3,18,880)	(35,080)	2,48,720	5,32,520	8,16,320	11,00,120
	10%	(1,48,160)	(2,05,360)	78,440	3,62,240	6,46,040	9,29,840	12,13,640
	15%	(3,75,640)	(91,840)	1,91,960	4,75,760	7,59,560	10,43,360	13,27,160

VARIABLE SENSIBILITY ANALYSIS

It is quite evident from the above table that only 5 per cent increase in materials cost may not result in a negative NPV. A Sales price reduced by 5 per cent may take away act the surplus of material cost reduction by 10 per cent. Even if material cost behaves favourably, a small reduction in price may bring in a negative NPV.

2. THE ACCOUNTING BREAK EVEN APPROACH IN SENSITIVITY ANALYSIS

Taking the same information in above case, one can calculate percentage change required to break even.

Unit Selling Price		Rs. 100 = 00
Less Materials	Rs. 40 = 00	
Power	Rs. 20 = 00	
Total unit variable	60 = 00	60 = 00
Unit Contribution		Rs. 40 = 00
Fixed Expenses:		
Labour total	Rs. 2,25,000	
Other Overheads	Rs. 75,000	Rs. 3,00,000

Hence, Break even Sales Rs. $= \dfrac{\text{Total Fixed Costs}}{\text{Unit Contribution}}$

$= \dfrac{\text{Rs. }3,00,000}{\text{Rs. }40} = 7,500 \text{ units}$

Reduction in Sales quantity =

Total Units = 15,000 - Break even

Units = 7500 = 7500 units

It means reduction by 50%.

∴ Break Even Sales Price:

$\dfrac{\text{Total Sales Revenue}}{\text{Total Output}} = \dfrac{\text{Rs. }3,00,000}{15,000 \text{ units}}$

= Rs. 20 per cent required contribution + Rs. 60

Variable cost = Rs. 80 price

20 ÷ = 20% reduction

The Break even materials cost :

Required contribution Rs. 20

Rs. 20 reduction in contribution means Rs. 20 increase in material cost

∴ Rs. 60 new material cost

∴ 20 ÷ 40 = 50 per cent increase

The break even power cost : should go up by Rs. 20 per unit which is equal to reduction in unit contribution.

∴ New energy cost Rs. 20 + Rs. 20 = 40

∴ 20 ÷ 20 = 100% increase

Break even Labour Cost :

Total contribution now	Rs. 6,00,000
Less total fixed costs now	Rs. 3,00,000
Profit	Rs. 3,00,000

In case labour cost increases by Rs. 3,00,000 to Rs. 5,25,000 then zero profit is being earned.

∴ Rs. 5,25,000

∴ Rs. 3,00,000 ÷ 5,25,000 = 133.33% increase.

Break Even Other Expenses :

Other expenses should go up by Rs. 3,00,000 - which is equal to profit - from Rs. 75,000.

∴ Rs. 3,75,000.

∴ Rs. 3,00,000 ÷ Rs. 75,000 = 400% increase.

All the above calculations can be presented in a table form.

SUMMARY OF ITEMWISE % CHANGE NEEDED FOR BEP

Sales Factor	Quantity	Values of Break even	Change	Percentage change needed to break even
Sales Quantity	15000 units	7500 units	7500 units lower	50% R
Sales Price	Rs. 100 p. unit	Rs. 80 per unit	Rs. 20 less	20% R
Material Costs	Rs. 40 p. unit	Rs. 60 per Unit	Rs. 20 more	50% I
Larsons Costs	Rs. 2,25,000 (T)	Rs. 5,25,000	Rs. 3,00,000 more	133.33% I
Power Costs	Rs. 20 per unit	Rs. 40 per unit	Rs. 20 more	100% I
Other Costs	Rs. 75,000 total	Rs. 3,75,000	Rs. 3,00,000 more	400% I

NOTE = R = Reduction (P) = Per

I = Increase (T) = Total

3. NPV BREAK EVEN APPROACH IN SENSITIVITY ANALYSIS

Taking the same information, it is presented annually:

Unit Variable			Annual Value
Sales Quantity			15,000 Units
Sales Price	Rs. 100 =00		Rs. 15,00,000
Materials	Rs. 40 =00		
Power	Rs. 20 = 00		Rs. 9,00,000
Contribution	Rs. 40 = 00		Rs. 6,00,000
Less Fixed Costs:			
Labour		Rs. 2,25,000	
Other Expenses		Rs. 75,000	Rs. 3,00,000
Profit/Cash-flow			Rs. 3,00,000
Initial Investment Cost			Rs. 10,00,000
Rate of discount:			15%

By Using Annuity Table, value of Rs. 3,00,000 @ 3.784 factor the NPV = Rs. 11.35 200 Rs. 10,00,000

NPV = Rs. 1,35,000

On Calculating Breakeven NPVs :

1. **If investment outlay increases by Rs. 1,35,000, the project will generate :**

Zero NPV $\because \dfrac{\text{Rs. }1,35,000}{10,00,000} \times 100 = 13.52\%$

Annual Cash-Inflow for BEP $\dfrac{\text{Rs. }10,00,000}{\text{Rs. }3.784}$

= Rs. 2,64,270

$\therefore$ 11.9 percent reduction (Rs. 3,00,000 - $\dfrac{2,64,270}{3,00,000}$)

in Out Cash-flow to breakeven

2. **Annual sales units for zero NPV :**

Break even annual contribution

Rs. 2,64,270 + 3,00,000

= Rs. 5,64,270

Rs. 5,64,270 ÷ 40 (unit contribution)

= Rs. 14106

$\therefore$ 6% reduction $\left(\dfrac{\text{Rs. }15,000-14,106}{\text{Rs. }15,000}\right)$ in Sales quantity, will mean zero NPV.

3. **Unit Sales Price for Zero NPV :**

Present Contribution	Rs. 6,00,000
Less Contribution needed	Rs. 5,64,270
Cushion in Contribution	Rs. 35,730
Number of units ÷	15,000
∴ Reduction in Selling Price =	$\dfrac{35,730}{15,000}$
= Rs. 2.382 (Rounded Rs. 2.38)	

If the sales price is reduced by Rs. 2.35 (2.38%) the NPV will be zero.

4. Material Costs :

Reduction in contribution of Rs. 2.38 per unit for zero NPV will be:

The present material cost per unit Rs. 40 + 2.38. Therefore, new material cost per unit will be Rs. 42.38, or by about 6% zero NPV will be earned.

5. Power Costs :

Power costs increased by Rs. 2,38 over the existing (Rs. 20 per unit) will lead to Rs. 22.38 or about 12 per cent for zero NPV.

6. Labour Cost :

Annual OCF for breakeven	Rs. 2,64,270
Present OCF	Rs. 3,00,000
Reduction in OCF to BE	Rs. 35,730

∴ labour cost should increase by Rs. 35,730 or by 15.9% to get zero NPV.

7. Other Expenses :

Increase in other expenses by Rs. 35,750 or by 47.7% to break even :

All these seven points can be summarised in the table below :

Table Showing NPV, BE Points in a Summary Form

Factor	New Value to Breakeven	Percentage Change Needed to
Sales, Quantity	Units 14,106	6.08% reduction
Sales Price	Rs. 97.62	2.40% reduction
Material Costs	Rs. 42.38	6.00% increase
Labour Costs	Rs. 2,60,750	15.90% increase
Power Costs	Rs. 22.38	12.00 increase
Other Expenses	Rs. 1,10,750	47.70% increase
Proiect Cost	Rs. 11.35.200	13.50% increase

4. PAY-OFF MATRIX IN SENSITIVITY ANALYSIS

This pay off matrix approach gives the changing impacts under given or likely situation as business conditions are subject to change. However, what exactly will be the change and its effect on NPV ?

Taking same variables, let us consider three possible changes as most unfavourable, most likely and most favourable taking investment as the same figure. These alternative situational changes expected are given by the company.

Variables	Most Unfavourable	Most Likely	Most Favourable
Sales Quantity units	12,800	15,000	16,000
Sales Price per unit	Rs. 93	Rs. 100	Rs. 115
Material cost unit	Rs. 42	Rs. 40	Rs. 39
Labour Rupees total	Rs. 3,50,000	Rs. 2,25,000	Rs. 2,00,000
Power cost per unit	Rs. 25/-	Rs. 20/-	Rs. 17/-
Other Expenses	Rs. 85,000	Rs. 75,000	Rs. 70,000

You are asked to frame pay-off matrix and find the variables that have greater influence on the net present value of the project.

SOLUTION:

Pay off Matrix for Various Outcomes (NPVs in Rupees)

Factor/Variable	Most Unfavourable	Most Likely	Most Favourable
Sales Units	- 1,97,792	1,35,200	2,86,560
Sales Price	- 2,62,120	1,35,200	9,86,600
Material Cost	21,680	1,35,200	1,91,960
Labour Cost	- 3,37,800	1,35,200	2,29,800
Power Cost	- 1,48,600	1,35,200	3,05,480
Other Expenses	97,360	1,35,200	1,54,120

The above pay-off matrix can be reconfigured to show the percentage deviation from the midpoint. The changed percentage deviation in pay-off will appear as under :

Table Showing Percentage Deviation Pay-off

Variable	Most unfavourable (Interms of Percentage)	Most Likely (In terms of percentage)	Most Favourable (In terms of percentage)
Sales Units	- 246.30	0	112.00
Sales Price	- 293.90	0	629.70
Material Cost	- 84.00	0	41.30
Labour Cost	- 349.90	0	68.00
Power Cost	- 210.00	0	126.00
Other Expenses	-28.00	0	14.00

It is evident from the two tables that deviation is the least in other expenses and then materials cost. Labour, sales price and sales units have a greater impact on the NPV.

EVALUATION

Sensitivity analysis, as a tool of assessing risk, has certain merits and demerits.

MERITS :

1. **Identifies the Variables and their Relationships :** Sensitivity analysis forces the management to identify the underlying variables and their relationships in assessing impact on N.P.V. of project.

2. **It assesses the Strength or Weakness of a given Project :** The sensitivity analysis exposes clearly how strong or how weak or vulnterable a project is to the changes in the underlying variables.

3. **It hints the need for Further Task :** In case the net present value or the IRR is highly sensitive to changes in some variable, it warrants further investigation or collect futher information to have correct results.

LIMITATIONS :

1. **It Studies Impact of One variable at a Time :** Sensitivity analysis studies the impact of variation in one of the factors at a time, holding other factors constant. This is not true and meaningful when the underlying factors are to have interrelationship. For instance, with a change in the selling price, there may be change in the quantity sold which are closely interrelated. Such situations are not considered in sensitivity analysis.

2. **Sensitivity Analysis is merely Indicative Providing no Remedy :** Sensitivity analysis presents merely a complicated set of switching values without throwing light on them. That is, it indicates merely the likely variation in results in case of change in a variable. It does not provide any remedy. A decision in the matter depends on the judgement of the management for which not only sensitivity analysis but also other information may be taken into consideration.

SCENARIO ANALYSIS

As noted earlier, one of the serious limitations of sensitivity analysis is that one variable is varying and the rest are taken as constant. As variables are interrelated, it is very essential to measure the impact of more variables and their interrelationships. Hence the kaleidoscopic Impact rather the overall impact of changes in variables is blended in on the project's NPV. One can think of different situations under which each variable is varied to study the impact and measure the risk under multidimensional conditions. Such an attempt is nothing but scenario analysis. Let us take three situations or scenarios namely;

(1) the base scenario where the demand and the price are expected to be normal

(2) the scenario where the demand is high, but the price is low.

(3) the scenario where the demand is low but the price is high.

ILLUSTRATION:

Calculate the NPV for the three possible scenarios from the following information.

Details	Scenario I	Scenario II	Scenario III
Original Investment	Rs. 20,00,000	20,00,000	20,00,000
Unit selling price	Rs. 30.00	Rs. 15.00	Rs. 35.00
Demand in units	1 lakh	4 lakh	1.5 lakh
Unit variable costs	Rs. 20 = 00	Rs. 10 = 00	Rs. 25 = 00
Fixed costs Rs. per unit	Rs. 5 = 00	Rs. 3 = 00	Rs. 8 = 00
Depreciation straight line	✓	✓	✓
Rate of Tax 55%	✓	✓	✓
Annual cash flow	Rs. 2,36,000	Rs. 45,000	Rs. 1,25,000
Project life-10 years	✓	✓	✓
Scrap value zero	✓	✓	✓
Rate of Discount 15%	✓	✓	✓

You are required to calculate NPV of project in case of cash scenario and see what factors contribute for-and related in influencing the NPV. You are free to make any assumption.

SOLUTION:

Calculating the NPV of project under scenario I, II and III.

I. Calculations Under Scenario I

Annual Sales: 2,00,000 units × Rs. 30 =		Rs. 60,00,000
Less Variable Costs: 2,00,000 units × Rs. 20 =		Rs. 40,00,000
Contribution: Rs. =		Rs. 20,00,000
Less Fixed Costs: 2,00,000 x Rs. 5 = Rs. 10,00,000		
Add Depreciation	Rs. 2,00,000	= Rs. 12,00,000
Profit Before Tax		= Rs. 8,00,000
Less Tax @ 55%		= Rs. 44,000
Profit After Tax		= Rs. 36,000
Annual Cash flow:		
PAT + Depreciation:	Rs. 36,000	
	Rs. 2,00,000	= Rs. 2,36,000

Discounting the Cash flows : (TOTAL and Average)

Year	Cash flows	Factor Discount 15%	Discounted Cash-flows
1	Rs. 2,36,000	0.89,957	Rs. 2,05,218.52
2	Rs. 2,36,000	0.75,614	Rs. 1,78,448.04
3	Rs. 2,36,000	0.65,752	Rs. 1,55,170.00
4	Rs. 2,36,000	0.57,175	Rs. 1,34,933.00
5	Rs. 2,36,000	0.49,718	Rs. 1,17,334.00
6	Rs. 2,36,000	0.43,233	Rs. 1,02,029.88
7	Rs. 2,36,000	0.37,549	Rs. 88,721.84
8	Rs. 2,36,000	0.32,690	Rs. 77,148.40
9	Rs. 2,36,000	0.28,426	Rs. 67,085.36
10	Rs. 2,36,000	0.24,718	Rs. 58,325.04
Total	Rs. 23,60,000		Rs.11,84,415.56
Average	Rs. 2,36,000		Rs. 11,856.56

NPV = Rs. 11,84,415.56 – 20,00,000 = (Rs. 8,15,584.44)

II. Calculations Under SCENARIO II

Discounting the cash flows:

Annual sales 4,00,000 units × Rs. 15.00 =		Rs. 60,00,000
Less variable cost 4,00,000 units × Rs. 10.00 =		Rs. 40,00,000
Contribution		Rs. 20,00,000
Less Fixed Costs		
Given 4,00,000 x Rs. 3.00	= 12,00,000	
Add depreciation $\frac{20,00,000}{10}$	= 2,00,000	= 14,00,000
Profit before tax		Rs. 6,00,000
Less Tax a 55%		Rs. 3,30,000
Profit After Two		Rs. 2,70,000
Add depreciation Rs. $\frac{20,00,000}{10 \text{ years}}$ =		Rs. 2,00,000
Annual Cash-flow:		4,70,000

Statement showing discounted cash flows and net present value

Year	Annual cash flow	Discount factor 15%	Discounted cash flows
1st	Rs. 4,70,000	0.86957	Rs. 4,08,697.90
2nd	Rs. 4,70,000	0.75614	Rs. 3,55,385.80
3rd	Rs. 4,70,000	0.65752	Rs. 3,09,034.40
4th	Rs. 4,70,000	0.57175	Rs. 2,68,722.50
5th	Rs. 4,70,000	0.49718	Rs. 2,33,674.60
6th	Rs. 4,70,000	0.43233	Rs. 2,03,195.10
7th	Rs. 4,70,000	0.37594	Rs. 1,76,691.80
8th	Rs. 4,70,000	0.32690	Rs. 1,53,643.00
9th	Rs. 4,70,000	0.28426	Rs. 1,33,602.20
10th	Rs. 4,70,000	0.24718	Rs. 1,16,174.60
Total	Rs. 47,00,000		Rs. 23,58,821.90

Average	Rs. 4,70,000	Rs. 2,35,882.19
NPV		Rs. 23,58,821.90
Less original cost		Rs. 20,00,000.00
NPV =		Rs. 3,58,821.90

III. Calculations Under Scenario III

Annual Sales: 1,50,000 x units @ Rs. 35.00		Rs. 52,50,000
Less Value Costs 1,50,000 x Unit Cost 25.00		Rs. 37,50,000
Contribution		Rs. 15,00,000
Less Fixed costs : 1,50,000 units × units cost 8.00	= Rs. 12,00,000	
Add depreciation	= Rs. 2,00,000	Rs. 14,00,000
Profit Before Tax		Rs. 1,00,000
Less Tax @ 55%		Rs. 55,000
Profit Ater Tax		Rs. 45,000
Annual Cash flow: Profit	= 45,000	
Add Depreciation	= 2,00,000	Rs. 2,45,000

Statement showing discounted cash flows and Net Present Value

Year	Cash In flow	Discount factor @15%	Discounted cash flows
1st	Rs. 2,45,000	0.86957	Rs. 2,13,044.65
2nd	Rs. 2,45,000	0.75614	Rs. 1,85,254.30
3rd	Rs. 2,45,000	0.65752	Rs. 1,61,092.40
4th	Rs. 2,45,000	0.57175	Rs. 1,40,078.75
5th	Rs. 2,45,000	0.49718	Rs. 1,21,809.10
6th	Rs. 2,45,000	0.43233	Rs. 1,05,920.85
7th	Rs. 2,45,000	0.37594	Rs. 92,105.30
8th	Rs. 2,45,000	0.32690	Rs. 80,090.50
9th	Rs. 2,45,000	0.28426	Rs. 69,643.70
10th	Rs. 2,45,000	0.24718	Rs. 60,559.10
Total	Rs. 24,50,000		Rs.12,29,598.60

Average	Rs. 12,29,598.60 ÷ 10	Rs. 1,22,959.86
Net Present Value		Rs. 12,29,598 = 60
Less Original Cost		Rs. 20,00,000 = 00
NPV		Rs. (7,70,401.40)

From the above three scenarios, both scenarios I & III give negative present value due to low demand and reduced selling price. Though, it is against the general relation "Lower demand caused by higher prices" or higher demand caused by lower prices" because other factors remaining same having great impact.

Scenario analysis differs from company to company. Very often three scale scenarios are considered as optimistic, normal, pessimistic. Optimistic scenario is featured by high demand, high selling price, low variable cost, and so on.

Normal scenario is characterised by average demand, average selling price, average variable cost and so on.

Pessimistic scenario is featured by low demand, low selling price, high variable cost and so on.

The prime objective of such a scenario analysis is to get a projection or reflection of what happens under the most favourable or the most unfavourable configuration of key variables, without caring much about the internal consistency of such configurations. It is like a flexible budgeting giving the changing impact on the profitability and profit working at different levels. The aim is to keep abreast even "if some thing happens" - as business is situational are dynamism is the key feature of it.

SIMULATION

Simulation gives the probability distribution of outcomes, which can be used to determine the probability or likelihood of a particular outcome a completion time or cost. For instance, simulation of project completion time can establish an appropriate target completion date or to prepare contingency plans. Simulation goes beyond sensitivity analysis and grants more perfection to the decision-maker. Sensitivity analysis clarifies the sensitivity of the criterion of the merit - NPV or IRR - to variation in basic factors and provides information of the following type. In case the quantity produced and sold decreases by 2 per cent, the NPV falls by say 8 per cent other things remaining the same. Such information, however, useful is insufficient to sound decision-making. A sound decision-maker seeks to know the likelihood of such occurences and such information can be generated by computer based Monte Carlo Simulation for developing the profile of criterion merit by randomly continuing the values which have bearing on the chosen criterion. Thus, simulation tool is used for developing probabilties and a useful profile there-from.

PROCEDURE INVOLVED IN SIMULATION

The basic steps involved in simulation are:

1. **Project Model :** The model of the project projects as to how the net present value is related to the "parameters" and the "exogenous variables". These "introgenous variables" are "parameters" that are input variables specified by the decision-maker and held constant over all simulation runs. On the other hand, "exogenous variables" are input variables which are stochastic in nature and wide outside the control of the decision-maker. In simple sense parameters are controllable and extrogenous variables are uncontrollable.
2. **Specification of Values :** The decision-maker is to specify the values of parameters and the probability distribution of exogenous variables.
3. **Selection Value at Random :** Next, the decision-maker is to select a value, at random, from the probability distribution of each of the exogenous variables.
4. **Determination of NPV :** The decision-maker is to go ahead with determining the net present value corresponding to the randomly generated values of exogenous variables and pre-spelled out parameter values.
5. **Repetition of Steps Three and Four :** The analyst or the decision-maker is to repeat steps three and four for a number of times to get a large number of simulated net present values.
6. **Plotting the Frequency Distribution :** The process ends with plotting of frequency distribution of the net present value.

ILLUSTRATION

To acquaint ourselves with the exact nature of simulation, a simple imaginary case can be taken up. Say Bell and Company is evaluating the given investment proposals. The two aspects of this project face uncertainty namely, annual cash flow and the life of the project. The Net Present Value Model for the project is:

$$NPV = \sum_{t=1}^{n} \frac{CF_t}{(1+i)^t} - I$$

Where: i = the risk free interest rate (10%)

I = the initial investment (Rs. 15,000)

CF_t = Exogenous variables with the below given distributions.

n = (It varies from 3 to 10 years as given)

Annual Value	Cash-flows Probability	Project-life value	Probability
Rs. 1,000	0.02	Years 3	0.05
Rs. 1,500	0.03	4	0.10
Rs. 2,000	0.15	5	0.30
Rs. 2,500	0.15	6	0.25
Rs. 3,000	0.30	7	0.15
Rs. 3,500	0.20	8	0.10
Rs. 4,000	0.15	9	0.03
		10	0.02

Let us presume that the company wants to have 10 manual simulation runs for this project. This exercise calls for generating values, at random, for the two extrogenous variables namely, annual cash-flow and the project life. For this purpose, there is need for:

(1) Setting up the correspondence between the values of exogenous variables and random numbers and

(2) Choosing random number generating device.

For this purpose Random Numbers are extracted from Rand Corporation, "A MILLION RANDOM DIGITS WITH 1,00,000 NORMAL DEVIATES" Glencoe, Illinois-The Free Press, 1955. The extracted Random Numbers are:

53479	81115	98036	12217	59526
97344	70328	58116	91964	26240
66023	38277	74523	71118	84892
99776	75123	03172	43112	83086

30176	48979	92153	38416	42436
81874	83339	14988	99937	13213
19839	90630	71863	95053	55532
09337	33435	53869	52769	18801
31151	58295	40823	41330	21093
67619	52515	03037	81699	17106

THE STATEMENT SHOWING CORRESPONDENCE BETWEEN VALUES OF EXOGENOUS VARIABLES AND TWO-DIGIT RANDOM NUMBERS

Annual Cash-flows				Project-Life			
Value	Probability	Cumulative Probability	Two digit random Numbers	Value	probability	Cum. probability	Digit Random numbers
Rs. 1,000	0.02	0.02	00 to 01	Years 3	0.05	0.05	00 to 04
Rs. 1,500	0.03	0.05	02 to 04	4	0.10	0.15	05 to 14
Rs. 2,000	0.15	0.20	05 to 19	5	0.30	0.45	15 to 44
Rs. 2,500	0.15	0.35	20 to 34	6	0.25	0.70	45 to 69
Rs. 3,000	0.30	0.65	35 to 65	7	0.15	0.85	70 to 84
Rs. 3,500	0.20	0.85	65 to 85	8	0.10	0.95	85 to 94
Rs. 4,000	0.15	1.00	86 to 99	9	0.03	0.98	95 to 97
				10	0.02	1.00	98 to 99

It is worth emphasizing here that one can pick any random number upto any digits. In the above case, the first two digit random numbers are picked from top up to 1st and 2nd groupings. Two numbers are needed one for the annual cash-flow and another for the project-life 53 and 97 and the corresponding values for cash-flow and project-life are Rs. 3,000 and 6 years respectively.

GETTING PROBABILITY DISTRIBUTIONS OF BASIC VALUES

The most significant step in simulation is that of defining the probability distributions of basic variables. One must remember that it is very often impossible to find the true distributions, in defining these distributions. Those distributions that are defined are based on judgement, in practice, by experts. Hence, great deal of care and caution is expected to be exercised while translating the judgement of experts into probability distributions.

There are two approaches in obtaining probability distributions namely, 'portrait' and "building block" approaches. The first approach is similar to the portrait method used for identifying suspects. Under this approach, a standard probability distribution -

normal, beta, chi-square, poisson, uniform, exponential, or any other - is drawn up, usually by a statistician, on the basis of the judgement expressed by the expert - the informant. This is shown to the expert for his comments. The expert may suggest changes, if any, in case the distribution does not fit in his frame work of judgement. For instance, he may suggest that the probabilities at the tails should be greater or the probability of the nodal value should be higher. The statistician modifies the earlier distribution to incorporate the changes suggested by the expert and presents it back to the expert again. This process goes on till the expert is satisfied with the probability distribution and represents his judgement in perfect match. The major limitation of this method is that the expert may accept smooth distribution for he may be charmed by the appearance of smooth curves and conned by the complicated formulae. In case of second approach the probability distribution is defined by the expert where he tries to quantify his judgement by a procedure having **FIVE steps :** (1) he chooses the range encompassing the possible values (2) he divides the range into intervals which he thinks have different probabilities associated with them (3) he assigns probabilities to these intervals such that Σ pi = 1 (4) he may divide intervals into sub-intervals, if he feels that the probabilities within an interval are different and (5) he continues the process till he arrives at distribution which represents his judgement perfectly. This method has two merits namely, (1) the expert has complete freedom in expressing his judgement and (2) it goes well with the principle of using all the available information.

To finish the task, the results of simulation can be presented as under in the form of a table.

Table Showing Simulation Results

Annual Cash-flow			Project-Life		
Run	**Random number**	**Corresponding value of annual cash-flow**	**Random number**	**Corresponding value of project life**	**Net Present Value**
1	53	Rs. 3,000	97	9	Rs. 4277
2	66	Rs. 3,500	99	10	Rs. 8506
3	30	Rs. 2,500	81	7	Rs. (829)
4	19	Rs. 2,000	09	4	Rs. (7660)
5	31	Rs. 2,500	67	6	Rs. (2112)
6	81	Rs. 3,500	70	7	Rs. 4039
7	38	Rs. 3,000	75	7	Rs. 1605
8	48	Rs. 3,000	83	7	Rs. 1605
9	90	Rs. 4,000	33	5	Rs. 2163
10	58	Rs. 3,000	52	6	Rs. 66

PROBLEM OF CORRELATION

The example considered earlier is based on the assumption that the probabity distributions of various factors influencing NPV are independent. However, in actual practice, correlations may exist among the distribution of several factors. For instance, the number of units sold may be correlated with the price per unit. Or the input costs with the output or level of activity and so on. If this is the case, the dependences of factors which are correlated should be considered together. Such an attempt calls for joint probability distribution of co-related factors which aggravates the problem of estimation. At this juncture, one must consider the choice relating to the level of disaggregation. The exact nature of this choice may be highlighted with an instance of investment project whose cost of production may be considered at different levels. These levels can be configured as under:

Chart Showing Levels of Details

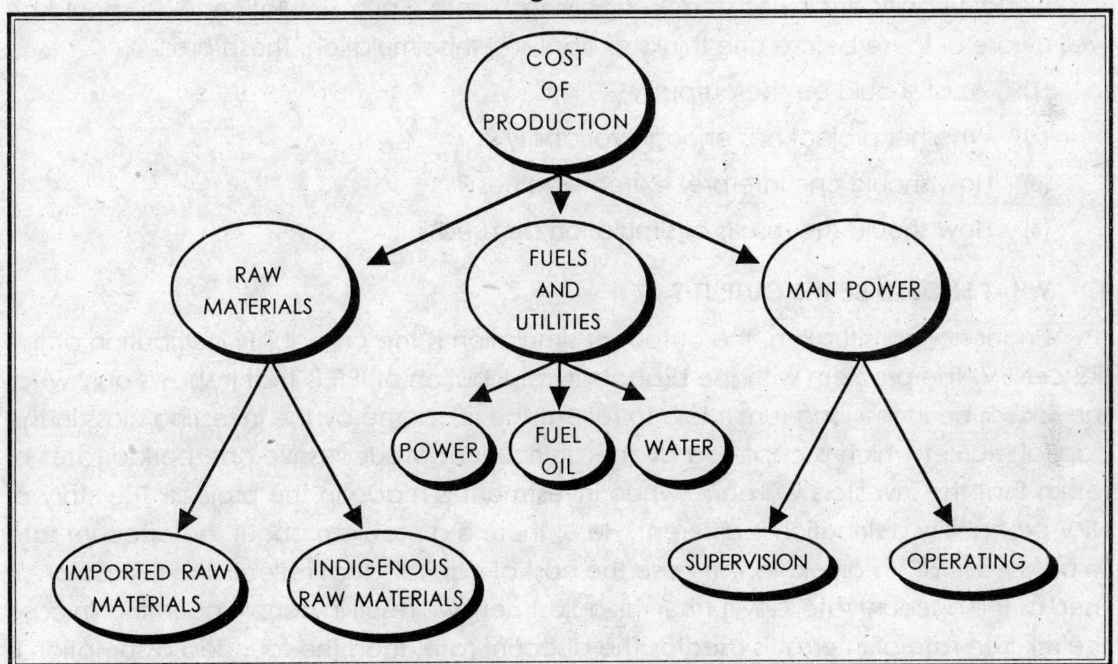

Fig. 8.08 Levels of details

The emergent immediate problem is "To what level of detail should-one go ?" In other words, whether one should define the probability distribution of cost of production without explicitly considering the probability distribution of various elements like cost of raw-materials, fuels and utilities, man power ? Or should one consider explicitly the distributions of these elements ? Or should one go further and consider explicitly the distributions of sub-elements like cost of imported raw materials, cost of indigenous raw-materials and so on ?

Speaking ideally, the greater the degree of disaggregation, the better it is because it contributes to clarity of judgement. However, disaggregated analysis calls for considering correlations explicitly, which is often a very difficult task, if not impossible. By limiting the degree of disaggregation, one can consider correlations implicitly. If one chooses to define the probability distribution of cost of production, without doing disaggregated analysis, one need not consider explicitly the correlations between say cost of raw materials and cost of fund. The distribution of cost of production would implicitly consider this. In the final analysis, the choice of the level of aggregation or disaggregation would be based on the trade off between the merits of clarity of judgement and the complexities of disaggregated analysis. As the influence of correlations is more significant than that of the shape of any particular distribution, it is preferable to limit disaggregation.

APPLICATION ISSUES ASSOCIATED WITH MONTE CARLO SIMULATION

Certain significant issues stem in applying Monte Carlo Simulation. One should be well aware of these before one thinks of applying this simulation. These are:

(1) What should be the output ?

(2) Whether project has enough variability ?

(3) How should one interpret extreme values ?

(4) How should the results of simulation be used ?

1. WHAT SHOULD BE THE OUTPUT ?

Under normal situation, the output of simulation is the probability distribution of the IRR or NPV. The problem with the probability distribution of IRR is that it shows only what the risk will be in the long-run. It fails to reflect the risk borne by the investing class in the capital market which is captured by the distributions of successive one period rates of return that the investors will earn, when investment is made in the project. The story of NPV probability distribution is different. Here, there is a problem about the discount rate to be used in NPV calculation. In case the cost of capital - that reflects the risk factor - is used as the discount rate, any further risk adjustment will result in double counting. In case the risk free rate of interest is used as the discount rate, than the founded assumption is that the uncertainty about the project's cash-flows would be resolved almost immediately. Since uncertainty is not resolved, the meaning of simulated probability distribution is not very clear. Under these circumstances, it pays to look at the distributions of cash-flows or the earnings. In case a project has an expected economic life of say eight years, the project evaluator may examine eight separate cash-flow distributions. These distributions may be scaled by their respective expected values for comparisons to be made between the projects.

2. WHETHER PROJECT HAS ENOUGH VARIABILITY ?

According to the "Capital Asset Pricing Model the thrust is on the systematic non-diversifiable-risk of an investment and not its unsystematic-diversifiable-risk. Simulation can provide information on the total risk - that is-systematic risk and unsystematic risk, but fails to give separately systematic risk. Therefore, a person using simulation should take into account total risk as a proxy for systematic risk. Though it is a strong assumption, it is reasonable because empirical studies have clearly demonstrated a fairly reliable association between systematic and different measures of earnings volatility. Added to this, systematic risk tends to be proporational to total risk for firms that operate in a single homogeneous industry.

3. HOW EXTREME VALUES SHOULD BE INTERPRETED ?

Those who argue in favour of simulation, are of the opinion that it helps in answering questions like "What is the probability that NPV would be less than zero?" or "What probability that IRR would be less than x per cent?" These questions can be answered quite satisfactorily when the 'tails' of the simulated distribution are reliable. However, the 'tails' tend to be the least reliable part of simulated distribution. Another and more important problem in interpreting the 'tails' of the simulated distribution is one that is associated with the assumption that management follows a strategy based on general business conditions which it is likely to face. This sounds theoretically well. However, under real life situations, managements modify their strategies to cope up with likely suprises that follow. It is but natural that whenever adverse developments occur, new actions are likely to be taken. In extreme cases, the project may be abandoned due to same future losses. Thus, the 'tails' of the simulated distribution are likely to project more unrealistic strategies which are important in risk assessment.

4. HOW THE RESULTS OF SIMULATION SHOULD BE USED ?

Professor Hertz D.B. strongly recommended simulation as is clear from his articles "Investment Policies that payoff" and "Risk Analysis of Capital Investments" - both the articles published by Harvard Business Review - Vol - 46 and 42 respectively, on the basis that probability distribution of the criterion of merit namely - NPV or IRR - leads to better decisions. It means that a decision-maker is able to reach a decision on the basis of the probability distribution In practice, however, not many business executives capable of reviewing the probability distribution of a project's NPV or IRR and deciding with full confidence as to whether the project is worthwhile or not. By very nature, some projects which will be sure winners and some sure losers whereby making simulation redundant exercise. Hence, a better approach to use the results of simulation involves two stage decision-making process. Stage ONE: Reviewing the probability distributions of the project–probability distributions of cash-flows IRR and the like – along with other factors and make an assessment. Stage TWO: Defining the appropriate discount rate to be employed on the basis of the business risk assessment in stage ONE.

EVALUATION

MERITS :

1. **It is the Most Versatile Tool :** Simulation can handle the problems featured by (a) numerous exogenous variables following any kind of distribution and (b) complex inter- relationships among the parameters, exogenous variables, and endogenous variables. Such problems defy the capabilities of analytical methods.
2. **It Provides for Explicit Consideration :** Simulation compels the decision-maker to explicitly consider the inter-dependencies and uncertainties that characterise the project.

DEMERITS :

1. **Simulation is Imprecise Tool :** By experience, most of the experts have found this tool as most controversial. It is difficult to model the project and specify the probability distributions of exogenous variables. As a tool, it is inherently imprecise for, it provides a rough approximation of the probability distribution of NPV or IRR or any other criterion of merit. Because of its imprecision, simulated probability distribution is likely to mislead when a tail of the distribution is critical.
2. **A Realistic Simulation Model is Complex :** A realistic simulation model is bound to be more complex designed by a management scientist or expert which is beyond the reach of practical application of a decision-maker. A decision-maker who lacks total understanding of the model will not toy with the model.
3. **Difficulty of Interpretation :** In a simulation run, risk-free discount rate is used to determine the NPV or IRR. This is done to avoid prejudging the risk which is supposed to be reflected in the dispersion of the distribution of NPV. Hence, the measure of NPV takes a meaning which is very much different from its usual one. It is this fact that it makes it very difficult to interpret.

DECISION-TREE ANALYSIS

In the modern ultra-dynamic world of business, there are complex investment decisions which involve a sequence of decision over the time. Infact, decision-making process, itself is non ending because one decision leads to another. Some investment options involve a set of decision, from alternatives in the future point of time. A future decision would be dependent on today's decision. Many decision nods in the future make a tree of decisions. A "decision tree" is a diagram wherein the 'branches' represent different chances or chance events or decision strategies. Decision-trees can be used to assess which risk responses among the alternatives yield the best to be expected consequence. Thus, a decision-tree is a graphic representation of relationship between present decision and future events, future decisions and their consequences. The sequence of events is mapped out over the time in a format that resembles to branches of a tree and, hence, it is called as decision-tree analysis.

STEPS IN DECISION-TREE ANALYSIS:

The decision-tree analysis, involves four basic steps which are explained as under:

1. **Identifying the Problem and Alternatives :** Tapping of good deal of relevant information from different sources is the starting point to understand the problem involved and the possible alternatives. These sources can be-marketing research, engineering studies, economic forecasting, financial analysis and so on. Fertile imaginative effort must be made to identify the nature of alternatives that arise as the decision situation opens up itself and assess the kinds of uncertainties that lie ahead with respect to market size, market share, prices, cost-structure, availability of inputs such as raw-materials, power and other related aspects such as technological changes, competitive actions and government regulations. Persons associated with analysing the situation must be encouraged to express freely their doubts, uncertainties and reservations and motivated to suggest contingency plans and identifying promising opportunities in the emerging environment recognising that risk and uncertainty are inherent features of investment proposals.

2. **Designing the Decision-Tree :** A decision-tree exhibits the anatomy of the decision situation in terms of "decision points" and "chance points". The "dicision points" - also called as "decisions forks" – and the alternative options available for experimentation and action at these decision points. The "chance points" - also called - "chance forks" where outcomes are dependent on chance process and the likely outcomes at these points. The decision-tree portrays in a diagrammatic form the nature of the decision situation in terms of alternative causes of action and chance outcomes which have been identified in the first step of the analysis. A decision-tree can take complex and cumbersome proposition if an attempt is made to consider widest possible future events and decisions. However, such a decision-tree is not useful especially when it is over elaborated. Hence, every effort should be made to keep decision tree more simple so that the decision-makers can focus their attention on major future alternatives without being engrossed in a mass of moss. That is why, experts like Breaky and Myers said rightly "Decision trees are like grapevines; they are productive only if vigorously pruned."

3. **Specifying Probabilities and Monetary Values for Outcomes :** Once the team comes out with decision-tree, the following data are to be gathered namely (1) probabilities

associated with each of the possible outcomes at various chance forces and (2) monetary value of each combination of decision alternative and chance outcome. The probabilities of various outcomes may, sometime be, defined objectively. For instance, the probability of a good monsoon may be based on objective, historical data. However, under real life situations, the possible outcomes encountered in real life are such that objective probabilities for these can be hardly got. For instance, how one can define objectively the probability that a new product like "water run car" will be successful in the market ? In such cases, probabilities have to be necessarily defined subjectively. Such subjective probabilities, to be very useful, they are to be based on the experience, judgement, intuition, and considered opinions. Equally difficult task is that of assessing the cash-flows associated with various possible outcomes where judgement of experts has a high role to play.

4. Evaluating the Alternatives : Once the decision-tree is projected and data about probabilities and monetary values are gathered, the terminal task is that of evaluation of alternatives. The decision alternatives may be evaluated as under:

(1) Commence at the right-head end of the tree and calculate the expected monetary value at various chance points that come first as are proceeds leftwise.

(2) Evaluate the alternatives at the final stage decision points in terms of their expected monetary values based on the expected monetary values of chance points as seen in step 1.

(3) Select the alternative which has the highest expected money value and short cut or truncate the other alternatives, at each of the final stage decision points. Each decision point is assigned a value equal to the expected monetary value of the alternative selected at the decision point.

(4) Proceed backward-that is-left ward-in the same manner, calculating the expected monetary value at chance points, selecting the decision alternative which has the highest expected monetary value at various decision points, cutting short or truncating inferior decision alternatives and assigning values to decision points, till the first decision point is reached.

ILLUSTRATION

Orient Oil Company owns drilling rights in given area and the company is faced with a problem of whether or not make seismic test which helps in indicating the chances of finding oil in that area. This decision has to be made at stage 1. There are two alternatives at stage 2. They are either to sell its drilling rights or to drill. This decision contains sets of alternative decisions at different points of time, and that the decision taken today has a bearing on decisions to be taken in future.

SOLUTION:

Decision-tree approach is one application of EV Rule-EV rule is the expected return and variance or standard deviation are compared for taking decision. It is also called as "mean- variance rule". As per the mean variance rule, the decision is taken by evaluating investment in the basis of expected return and variance. Standard deviation is also used in place of variance. Since, EV Rule ignores the size of the project, in decision-tree analysis mere EV Rule will not be enough. Following is the decision-tree analysis of above case. The following will be the configuration of Decision-Tree Model for oil drill problem with decision nods and possible outcome:

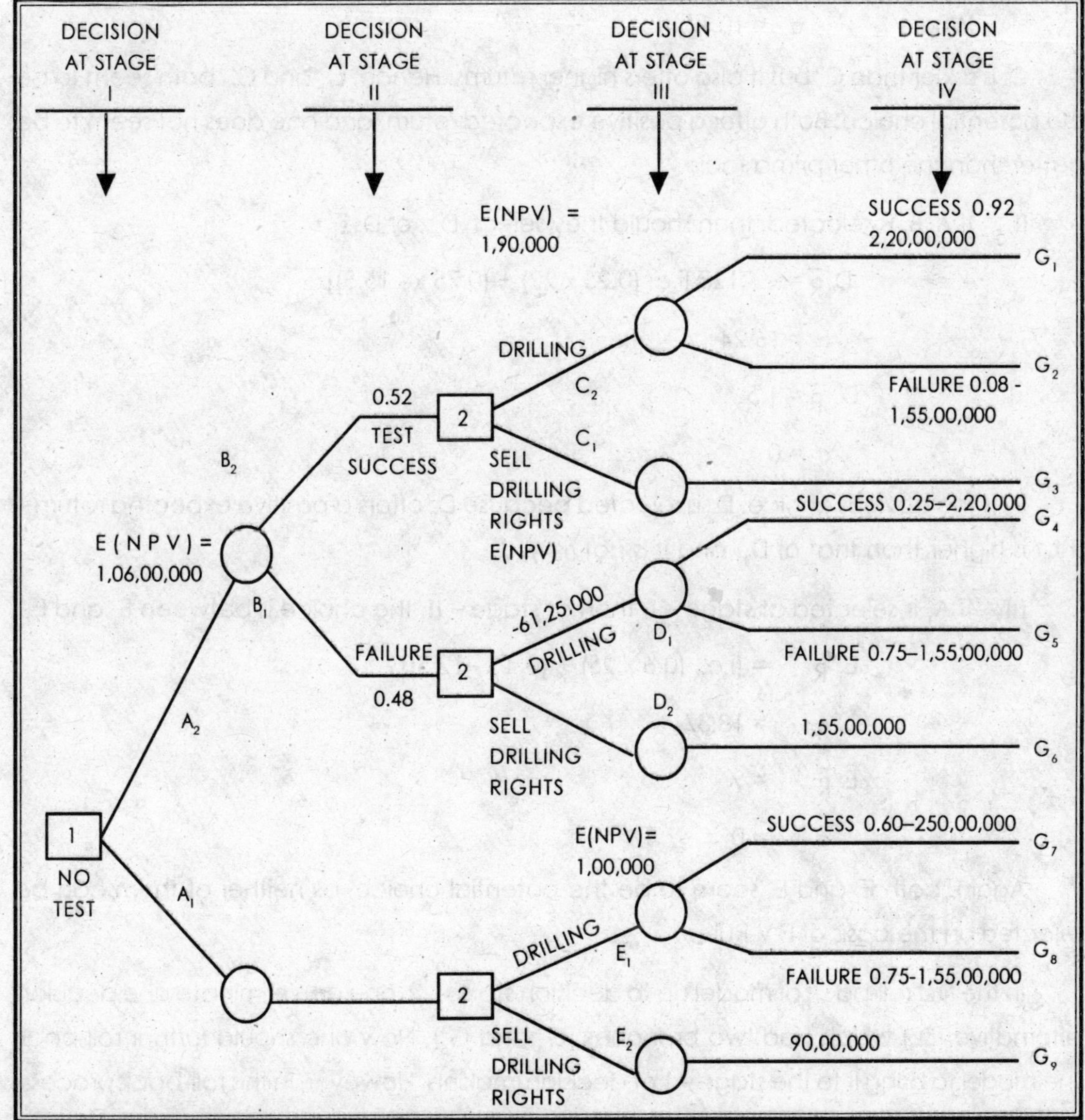

Fig. 8.09 Decision-Tree Presentation

To read and interpret, we will have to start from right to left or roll back the tree from the end and eliminate those branches which are not acceptable. At stage 2, the decision-maker, will be confronted with any one of the following three sets of decisions:

I. If he selects A_2 and B_2, then should they select C_2 or C_2?

C_1 $\bar{R}$ = 15 where $\sigma = 0$

C_2 $\bar{R}$ = 19 [i.e. (0.92 x 22) + (0.8 x 15.5)]

Where σ = 10.17

C_2 is riskier than C_1 but it also offers higher returns. Hence, C_1 and C_2, both seem to be the potential choice. Both offer a positive expected return, and one does not seem to be better than the other prima facie.

II. If A_2B_1 is selected, then should they select D_1, or D_2?

$D_1\bar{R}$ = – 6.125 [i.e. (0.25 x 22) + (0.75 x - 15.5)]

σ = 16.24

D_2 $\bar{R}$ = 1.5

σ = 0

D_2 is the obvious choice. D_2 is rejected because D_2 offers a positive expected return – that is higher than that of D_1, and it is not risky.

III. If A_1 is selected at stage – I, then at stage – II, the choice is between E_1 and E_2.

E_1 $\bar{R}$ = [i.e., (0.6 x 25) + (0.4 x –12.5)]

σ = 18.37

$E_2\bar{R}$ = 9

σ = 0

Again, both E_1 and E_2 seem to be the potential choice, as neither of them can be rejected on the basis of E-V Rule.

In the first roll-back of model up to decision stage – 2, one can eliminate one decision alternative (D_2) which had two branches (G_4 and G_5). Now one should further roll-back the model to bring it to the stage – 1 of decision-making. However, in this roll-back process, alternative D_1 and branches G_4 and G_5, should not be considered.

At decision stage – 1, the following decision alternatives are available:

(a) Strategy 1

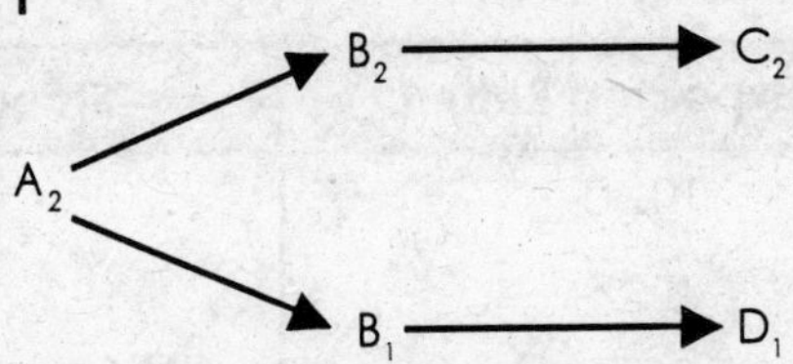

The expected return and standard deviation of strategy 1 are:

$\bar{R}$ = 0.52 x 0.92 x 22

+ .52 x 0.08 x (15.5)

+ 0.48 — 1.5

= 10.6

σ = root of 0.52 x 0.92 (22 - 10.6)²

+ 0.52 X 0.08 (–15.5 –10.6)²

+ 0.48 X (1.5 –10.6)²

= 11.41

(b) Strategy 2 :

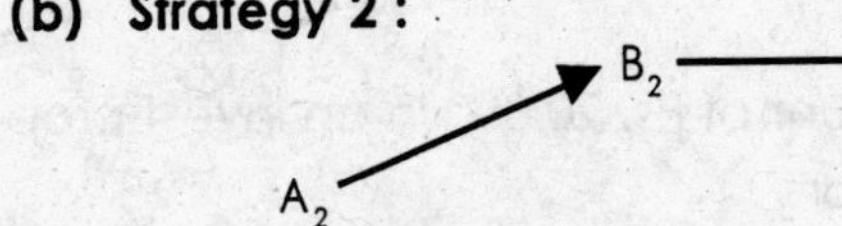

The expected return and standard deviations of strategy 2 are:

$\bar{R}$ = 8.52

σ = 6.74

(c) Strategy 3 :

$A_1 \longrightarrow E_1$

$\bar{R}$ = 10

σ = 18.37

(d) Strategy 4 :

$A_1 \longrightarrow E_2$

The expected return and the standard deviation of strategy 4 are:

$\bar{R}$ = 9

σ = 0

The above matter can be presented in the form of a Table Strategywise — in terms of Expected returns and Standard deviation as under:

Strategy	$\overline{R}$ = Expected Return	σ = Standard deviation
1	10.60	11.41
2	8.52	6.74
3	10.00	18.37
4	9.00	0

From the above, it is quite evident that strategy-2 is eliminated against strategy-4 and strategy-3 is eliminated against strategy-1 by applying E-V Rule. This decision-tree roll-back model now has reduced the alternatives to only two, namely, strategy-1 and strategy-4. If the additional return of 1.6 (i.e., 10.60 – 9.00) million is considered justified for the additional risk of 11.41 standard deviation, then strategy- 1 will be selected, else strategy-4 will be selected. Here, weighing returns against risk is significant. When complex sequential decisions are involved in a problem, the application of E-V Rule to the roll-back model of the decision tree becomes almost mandatory.

ILLUSTRATION:

Mr. Jolly good is thinking of investing an amount of Rs. 20,000 in an invest proposal. The expected returns during the life of investment are :

1st year :

Event	Cash inflows	Probability
I	Rs. 8,000	0.30
II	Rs. 12,000	0.50
III	Rs. 10,000	0.20

2nd year :

Cash inflows in year 1st are :

Event	Cash inflows	Probability	Cash Inflow	Probability	Cash Inflow	Probability
I	Rs. 15,000	0.20	Rs. 20,000	0.10	Rs. 25,000	0.20
II	Rs. 20,000	0.60	Rs. 30,000	0.80	Rs. 40,000	0.50
III	Rs. 25,000	0.20	Rs. 40,000	0.10	Rs. 60,000	0.30

You are to take cost of capital at 10 per cent and calculate for Mr. Jollygood the option that is best under Decision-Tree Analysis:

SOLUTION:

Statement Showing NPV of Cash-Inflows

Options	Cash-flows		Discount Factor		Present Values		Total Rs.	Net Present Value
A	1st year	2nd year	1st Year	2nd year	1st Year	2nd year		
(i)	Rs. 8,000	Rs. 15,000	0.909	0.826	Rs. 7272	Rs. 12390	Rs. 19,662	Rs. 338
(ii)	Rs. 8,000	Rs. 20,000	0.909	0.826	Rs. 7272	Rs. 16520	Rs. 23,792	Rs. 3,792
(iii)	Rs. 8,000	Rs. 25,000	0.909	0.826	Rs. 7272	Rs. 20650	Rs. 27,922	Rs. 7,922
B								
(i)	Rs, 12,000	Rs. 20,000	0.909	0.826	Rs. 10,908	Rs. 16,520	Rs. 24,428	Rs. 7,428
(ii)	Rs. 12,000	Rs. 30,000	0.909	0.826	Rs. 10,908	Rs. 24,780	Rs. 35,688	Rs. 15,688
(iii)	Rs. 12,000	Rs. 40,000	0.909	0.826	Rs. 10,908	Rs. 33,040	Rs. 43,948	Rs. 23,948
C								
(i)	Rs. 10,000	Rs. 25,000	0.909	0.826	Rs. 9,090	Rs. 20,650	Rs. 29,740	Rs. 9,740
(ii)	Rs. 10,000	Rs. 40,000	0.909	0.826	Rs. 9,090	Rs. 33,040	Rs. 42,130	Rs. 22,130
(iii)	Rs. 10,000	Rs. 60,000	0.909	0.826	Rs. 9,090	Rs. 49,560	Rs. 58,650	Rs. 38,650

Col. 1	Col. 2	Col. 3	Col 4.	Col. 5	Col. 6
Year 0	Year 1st	Year II	Net Present Value of Inflows	Joint probability	Expected Net Present Values
		Rs. 15,000	Rs. – 338	0.06	Rs. – 20.28
0.3	Rs. 8,000	Rs. 20,000	Rs. 3,792	0.18	Rs. 682.56
		Rs. 25,000	Rs. 7,922	0.06	Rs. 475.32
		Rs. 20,000	Rs. 7,428	0.05	Rs. 371.40
CASH OUTFLOW Rs. 20,000 — 0.5	Rs. 12,000	Rs. 30,000	Rs. 15,688	0.40	Rs. 6275.20
		Rs. 40,000	Rs. 23,948	0.05	Rs. 1197.40
		Rs. 25,000	Rs. 9,740	0.04	Rs. 389.60
0.2	Rs. 10,000	Rs. 40,000	Rs. 22,130	0.10	Rs. 221.30
		Rs. 60,000	Rs. 38,650	0.06	Rs. 2319.00
				1.00	Rs. 11911.50

As the investment proposal has a net present value of Rs. 11911.50 at a discount factor of 10%, the proposal may be accepted.

SELECTION OF A PROJECT

Once the project analyst has obtained the reliable information regarding "expected return" – NPV or IRR or any other criterion of merit-and "Variability of return" measured in terms of standard deviation or any other dispersion index-the next immediate question before the analyst is whether the project is to be accepted or rejected ?

To reach a definite cut off point, experts have come out with three methods namely Risk Profile Method, the Certainty Equivalent Method and the Risk Adjusted Discount Rate method. An understanding of each is a must for reaching a decision.

1. **Risk Profile Method :** In order to use this method, there is need for transforming probability distribution of NPV, an absolute measure, into the probability distribution of profitability index, a relative measure. To understand such transformation, let us consider the probability distribution of NPV of a project, which calls for an investment of Rs. 1,00,000 and the NPVs are 20,000, 40,000. These are plotted graphically in Fig. 8.11 as shown.

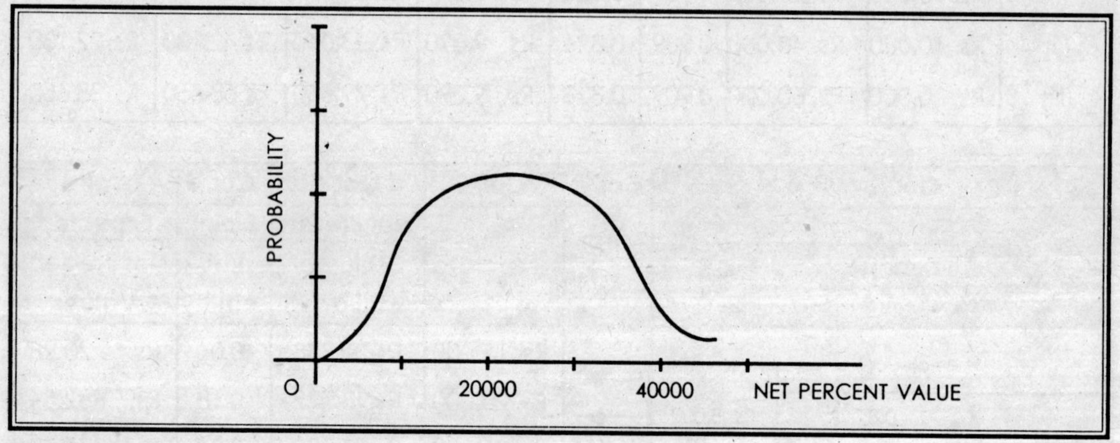

Fig. 8.10 Probability Distribution of Net Present Value

Coming to profitability index, it is a linear transformation of NPV, which is calculated by applying the formula :

$$\text{Probability Index} = \frac{\text{Net Present Value} + \text{Investment}}{\text{Invest ment}}$$

$$= \frac{\text{Net Present Value}}{\text{Invest ment}} + 1$$

Accordingly the shape of its probability distribution is identical to that of the probability distribution of NPV. The configuration of the probability distribution profitability index for above project is graphically portrayed as under Fig. 8.12.

After having transformed the probability distribution of NPV into the probability distribution of profitability Index, one can compare the dispersion of profitability index of the project with maximum risk-profile acceptable to management for the expected profitability index of the project. Let us take a case that maximum risk-profile acceptable to management when the expected profitability index is 1.20, the configuration in Fig. 8.13.

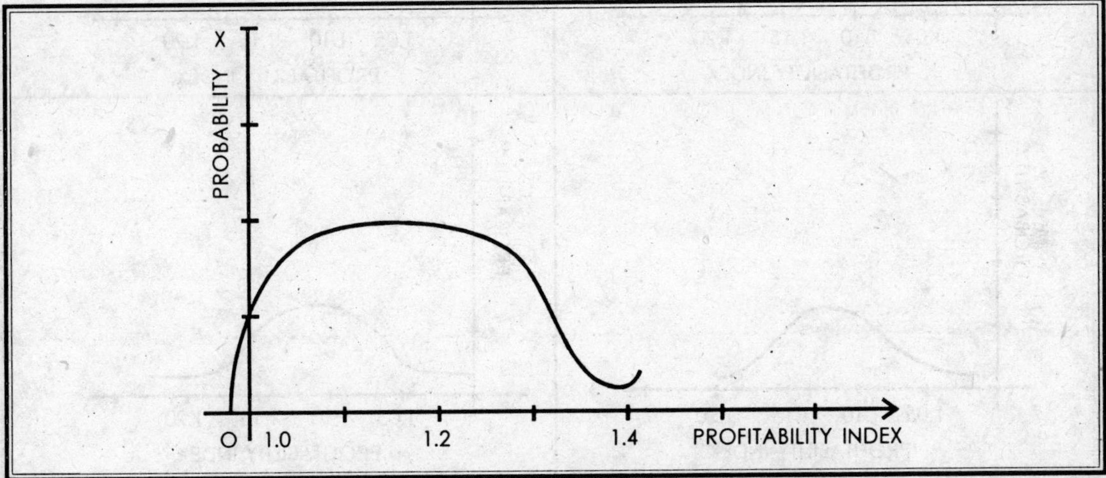

Fig. 8.11 Probability Distribution of Profitability Index

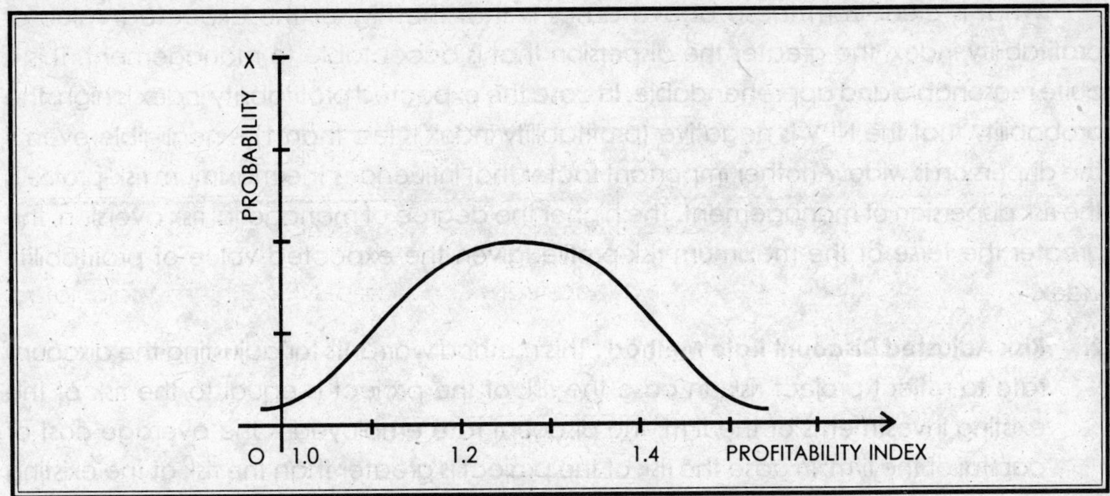

Fig. 8.12 Normal Probability Distribution of Profitability Index

Maximum Risk-Profile Acceptable when Expected Profitability Index is 1.2.

These maximum risk-profiles can take different shapes as shown under:

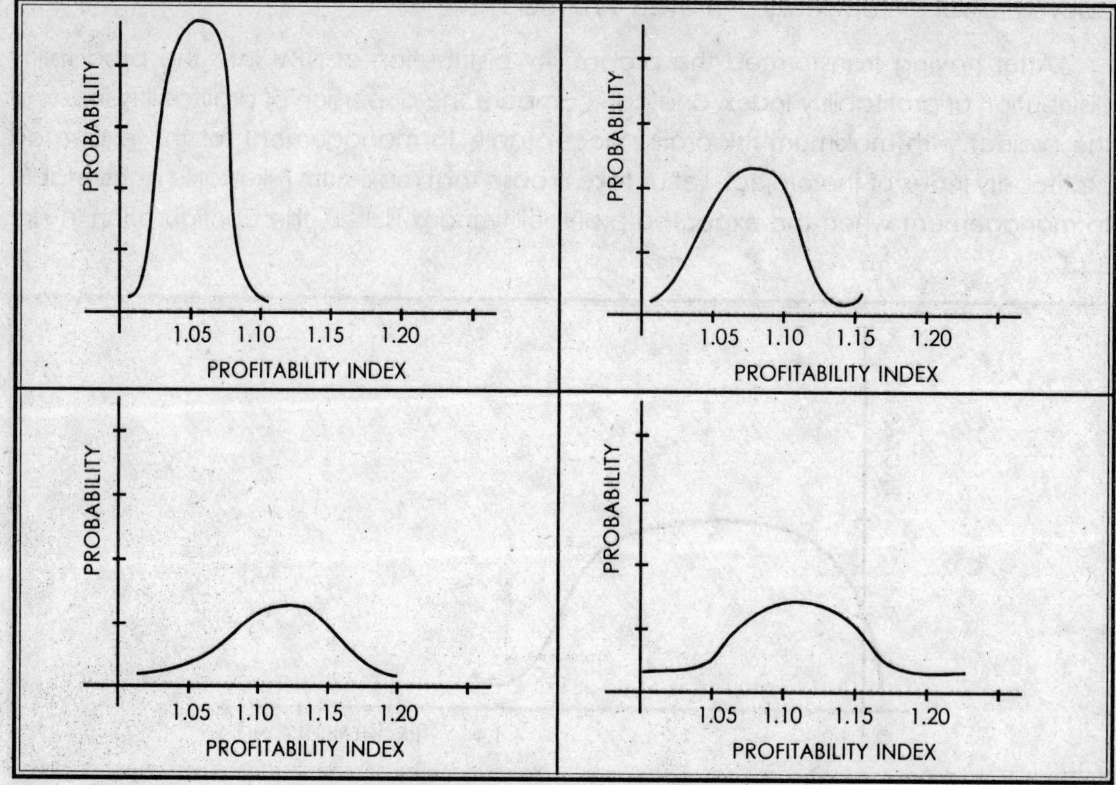

Fig. 8.13 Varieties of Maximum acceptable risk profiles

What is clear from these above cases is that the higher the expected value of profitability index, the greater the dispersion that is acceptable to management. This is quite reasonable and apprehendable. In case the expected profitability index is high, the probability that the NPV is negative (profitability index is less than 1) is negligible even if the dispersion is wide. Another important factor that influences the maximum risk-profile is the risk dispersion of management. The higher the degree of managerial risk aversion, the greater the terse of the maximum risk-profile, given the expected value of profitability index.

2. **Risk Adjusted Discount Rate Method :** This method warrants for adjusting the discount rate to reflect project risk. In case the risk of the project is equal to the risk of the existing investments of the firm, the discount rate employed is the average cost of capital of the firm; in case the risk of the project is greater than the risk of the existing investments of the firm, the discount rate used is higher than the average cost of capital of the firm; in case, the risk of the project is less than the risk of the existing

investments of the firm, the discount rate employed is less than the average cost of capital of the firm.

The Risk-adjusted Discount Rate =

$$\gamma_k = 1 + n + d_k$$

Where :

γ_k = Risk adjusted discount rate for project k

i = risk-free rate of interest

n = adjustment for the firm's normal risk

d_k = adjustment for the differential risk of project k.

It is worthwhile to note that (i + n) measures the firm's cost of capital dk which may be positive or negative depending on how the risk of the project under consideration compares with the existing risk of the form. The adjustment for the differential risk of project k, depends on the management's perception of the project risk and the attitude of management towards risk or risk-return preference.

ILLUSTRATION:

Cipla Ltd. – a well known pharmaceutical company uses the following risk-adjusted discount rates for different types of investments.

INVESTMENT CATEGORY	RISK ADJUSTED DISCOUNT RATE
1. Replacement Investment	Cost of Capital
2. Expansion Investment	Cost of Capital + 30%
3. Investments in Related Lines	Cost of Capital + 6%
4. Investment in New Lines	Cost of Capital + 10%

Once the project's risk-adjusted discount rate - γ_k- is spelled out, the project is accepted provided its NPV is positive by calculating with the formula =

$$NPV = \sum_{i=1}^{n} \frac{\overline{A}_t}{(1+\gamma_k)^t} - 1$$

Where NPV = Net Present Value of k

$\overline{A}_t$ = Expected Cashflow of Year t

γ_k = Risk-adjusted rate for project k

Let us prove it with an illustration of Cipla Ltd :

The Original Investment Rs. 10,00,000. Annual Cash-flows

1st year	Rs. 2,00,000
2nd year	Rs. 3,00,000
3rd year	Rs. 4,00,000
4th year	Rs. 3,00,000
5th year	Rs. 2,00,000

The risk-adjusted rate for this project is say 18 per cent.

Required :

State whether the investment in this project is worthwhile.

SOLUTION:

By using the above formula, the NPV can be calculated as under:

$$\frac{\text{Rs. } 2,00,000}{(1.18)} + \frac{\text{Rs. } 3,00,000}{(1.18)^2} + \frac{\text{Rs. } 4,00,000}{(1.18)^3} + \frac{\text{Rs. } 3,00,000}{(1.18)^4} + \frac{\text{Rs. } 2,00,000}{(1.18)^5}$$

$$- \text{Rs. } 10,00,000 - \text{Rs. } 1,29,440$$

As the NPV is negative, it goes without saying that investment in this proposal is not worthwhile.

Risk-adjusted discount rate is a very common method employed. As noted earlier, different rates of discounts are employed the depending on the nature of investments. In case of entirely new investments - it is the highest; moderate in case of expansion programmes, lower in case of similar investment lines and least in case of replacement investments. Though widely used method, it has its own limitations namely, (1) It is difficult to estimate d_k very consistently-where arbitrary or adhoc ways may be used (2) The underlying assumption is that the risk increases with time at a constant rate-which is something not really acceptable.

3. **Certainty Equivalent Method :** Unless one understands the concept of "certainty equivalent coefficient" it is difficult to understand this certainty equivalent method. Certainty equivalent coefficient is the ratio of certain cash-flows to risky cash flows. The co-efficient varies between 0 and 1 depending upon the risky cash-flow figure being equal to or less than the certain cash-flow. The certainty equivalent co-efficient is determined by the use of formula:

$$CF = \frac{CCF}{RCF}$$

Where CE = Certainty Equivalent Coefficient

CCF = Certain Cash-Flow

RCF = Risky Cash-Flow

This reflects basically two things : (1) Variability of the outcomes and (2) One's attitude towards risk. Certainty equivalent co-efficients transform expected values of uncertain flows into their certainty equivalents.

Under the certainty equivalent method, the NPV is calculated as under:

$$NPV = \sum_{i=1}^{n} \frac{a_t \bar{A}_t}{(1+i)^t} - 1$$

Where: NPV = Net Present Value

$\bar{A}_t$ = expected Cashflow for year t

t = Certainty equivalent coefficient for the cash flow of year t

i = risk free interest rate

I = initial investment (about which it is assumed that there is no uncertainty)

ILLUSTRATION:

Bharat Forge Ltd. is planning to invest in a machinery that does moulding work calling for an initial investment of Rs. 50,00,000. The expected cash-flows and certainty equivalent coefficients are configured as under.

Year	Expected Cash flow	Certainty equivalent co-efficient
1	Rs. 12,00,000	0.90
2	Rs. 15,00,000	0.85
3	Rs. 22,00,000	0.82
4	Rs. 25,00,000	0.78
5	Rs. 30,00,000	0.76

The risk free interest rate is 5 per cent. You are required to calculate the NPV of the proposal under consideration.

The NPV is equal to :

$$\frac{\text{Rs. }12,00,000\,(9.90)}{(1.05)}+\frac{\text{Rs. }15,00,000\,(0.85)}{(1.05)^2}+\frac{(\text{Rs. }22,00,000\,(0.82)}{(1.05)^3}+$$

$$\frac{\text{Rs. }25,00,000\,(0.78)}{(1.05)^4}+\frac{(\text{Rs. }30,00,000\,(0.76)}{(1.05)^5}-50,00,000$$

= Rs. 10,28,571+Rs. 17,56,463+Rs. 15,58,363+Rs. 16,04,270+Rs. 17,86,440 – Rs. 50,00,000

= Rs. 71,34,107 – Rs. 50,00,000

= Rs. 21,34,107

As said earlier, the value of the certainty equivalent coefficient usually ranges between 0 and 1. A value of 1 means that the cash-flow is certain or the management is risk neutral. However, in industrial situation, cash-flows are generally uncertain and managements are usually risk averse. Therefore, the certainty equivalent co-efficients are typically less than 1. Following is the table illustrating certainty equivalent co-efficients for different types of investments. This gives a practical view of the situation.

TABLE INDICATING TYPICAL CERTAINTY EQUIVALENT COEFICIENT FOR DIFFERENT TYPES OF INVESTMENTS

Types of Investments	Certainty Equivalent Coefficients				
	1st Year	2nd Year	3rd Year	4th Year	5th Year
Replacement Investments:	0.92	0.87	0.84	0.80	0.76
Expansion Type of Investments:	0.89	0.85	0.80	0.75	0.69
New Product Line Investments:	0.85	0.80	0.74	0.68	0.61
Reserach and Development Type Investments:	0.75	0.70	0.64	0.58	0.52

In a nutshell, certainty equivalent method is superior method to risk adjusted discount rate method conceptually because, it does not assume that risk increases with time at a constant rate. Each year's certainty equivalent co-efficient is based on the level of risk characterising its cash-flow. Though, it is conceptually superior to that of risk adjusted method, it is not popular because of inconvennience and difficulties encountered in specifying a series of certainty equivalent co-efficients which appear simple to adjust the discount rate. Because of cumbersomeness, this certainty equivalent method should not be given up.

CHAPTER BASED QUESTIONS

WRITE SHORT NOTES ON

1. Risk and uncertainity
2. Risk taking and gambling
3. Types of project risks
4. Measures of risk
5. Sensitivity analysis
6. Scenario analysis
7. Objectives and assumptions of Sensitivity analysis
8. Simulation
9. Problems associated with applicates of Simulation
10. Decision-tree analysis

SHORT ANSWER QUESTIONS

1. What is risk and uncertanity ?
2. How is risk taking different from gambling ?
3. What are different types of project risks ?
4. What is sensitivity analysis ?
5. What are measures of risk ?
6. What is scenario analysis ?
7. What is simulation ?
8. What problems are associated with application of Monte Carlo Simulation ?
9. What is standard deviation ?
10. What is probability distribution ?

ESSAY TYPE QUESTIONS

1. Define clearly the terms 'risk' and 'uncertainty'. What classification do you follow in classifying risks ?
2. What are different measures of risk ? Give equations of each and meaning and the purpose.
3. What is Sensitivity analysis ? What are its objectives and the procedure involved in it ?
4. What is Sensitivity Analysis ? What different methods are used in this approach ?
5. What is Scenario approach ? How is it superior to sensitivity analysis ?
6. What is simulation ? What procedure is involved in it ?
7. What is Monte Carlo Simulation? What practical difficulties do you face in applying it ?
8. What is decision-tree approach ? Explain the steps involved in this analysis.
9. What are the different methods of selecting or rejecting a proposal ?
10. Critically evaluate the simulation as a approach in decision-making.

* * * * * * *

CHAPTER BASED PRACTICAL QUESTIONS

1. Calculate the measures of risk from the given information in case of project X. The two variables available are :

Outcome	Probability
Rs. 2,500	0.2
Rs. 1,200	0.6
Rs. 800	0.3

Find out the expected value under each measure.

2. J K Limited has to offer you two variables in terms of outcome and probability in respect of project X.

You are to calculate expected value. Give formula of each measure.

Outcome	Probability
Rs. 5,000	0.3
Rs. 3,000	0.5
Rs. 1,500	0.4
Rs. 750	0.2

3. An industrial unit is planning to invest Rs. 2,00,000. The cash-flow for 3 years and the conditional probabilities are as follows :

1st Year	Initial Probability
Rs. 60,000	0.5
Rs. 1,50,000	0.5
Rs. 3,00,000	0.4
Rs. 4,50,000	0.3
Rs. 5,00,000	0.2

2nd year	Conditional probability
Rs. 75,000	0.8
Rs. 80,000	0.2
Rs. 90,000	0.6
Rs. 1,20,000	0.4
Rs. 1,60,000	0.3
Rs. 2,00,000	0.3
Rs. 4,00,000	0.2

3rd year	Conditional probabilities
Rs. 75,000	0.6
Rs. 1,00,000	0.4
Rs. 1,20,000	0.5
Rs. 1,10,000	0.6
Rs. 1,00,000	0.7
Rs. 80,000	0.8
Rs. 70,000	0.2

Calculate the $\overline{NPV}$ and σ (NPV) – taking a risk-free interest rate of 7%.

4. Calculate NPV and σ (NPV) taking a risk free rate of interest of 10 per cent with the following details is respect of a project that needs an investment of 5,00,000.

1st year	Initial probabilities
Rs. 1,00,000	0.2
Rs. 1,50,000	0.6
Rs. 1,75,000	0.5
Rs. 2,00,000	0.3
Rs. 3,00,000	0.4
2nd year	
Cash-flows	Conditional probabilities
Rs. 1,20,000	0.3
Rs. 1,20,000	0.3
Rs. 1,30,000	0.5
Rs. 1,35,000	0.5
Rs. 1,40,000	0.2
Rs. 1,50,000	0.8
3rd year	
Cash-flows	Conditional probabilities
Rs. 1,15,000	0.2
Rs. 1,20,000	0.8
Rs. 1,30,000	0.5

Rs. 1,50,000	0.7
Rs. 1,75,000	0.2
Rs. 1,25,000	0.3
Rs. 1,20,000	0.7
Rs. 1,80,000	0.3

5. Victory Flag Ltd. has a project that costs 15 lakhs. The additional information available is :

Sales units per year	10,000
Sales price per unit	Rs. 2,00.00
Material cost per unit	80.00
Labour cost per unit	40.00
Overheads per unit	90.00
Expected life span of project	5 years
Break up value at end	zero
Rate of discount	10%

You are required to :

1. Construct a table showing net present values at 5%, 8%, 10% change on either side in one variable at a time for all variables.
2. Select the most crucial factors (at least two) and construct a NPV table for various level changes in both the variables.

You may assume that there is no need to take into account working capital and taxation and non-cash expenses.

6. TRUE limited is interested in an investment proposal of 20,00,000 in respect of which the following information is made available.

Annual production and sales units	Rs. 15,000
Selling price per unit	Rs. 500.00
Total variable cost per unit is made up of D. Materials	Rs. 150.00
D.Labour	Rs. 200.00
Overheads	Rs. 75.00

The investment in machinery has a total economic life of 6 years having no scrap value at the end of life. Company follows 12 per cent rate of discount. You are required to prepare two tasks of framing the statements on the assumptions that there is no need to account for working capital needs, and tax and non cash items are excluded from the calculations.

1. Design a table projecting NPV at 5%, 12% and 15% changes is in either side in one variable at a time for all the variables.
2. Select two most crucial factors and frame a statement showing NPV for various levels of change in the variables.

7. Take the information given in problem 5 and calculate the percentage required to break even under the Accounting Break Even Approach in case of each variable. Give results in a sequential pattern.

8. Use the details of problem 6 given above and calculate percentage needed to break even under the Accounting Break Even Approach for each variable. Calculations are to be made in a logical sequence.

9. Calculate Break even N V V S for each variables under NPV Break Even Approach under sensitivity analysis. Stepwise calculations are expected. The data can be used as given in problem 5 above. Tabulate the matter at the end.

10. Use the data given in problem to above for calculating NPV Break Even for each of the variable. You have the freedom of presenting the data as you deem fit. Present findings in a statement.

11. Design the pay-off matrix using the information given in problem 5. The additional information given is:

Statement detailing situational changes

Variables	Most Unfavourable	Most Likely	Most Favourable
Sales units	8,000	10,000	15,000
Sales price	Rs. 160/-	Rs. 200/-	Rs. 225/-
Material cost	Rs. 90/-	Rs. 80/-	Rs. 75/-
Labour cost	Rs. 45/-	Rs. 40/-	Rs. 35/-
Overheads	Rs. 92/-	Rs. 90/-	Rs. 80/-
Total Fixed Expenses	Rs. 3,50,000/-	Rs. 3,00,000/-	Rs. 2,25,000

12. Design pay-off matrices with the following information in case of Up Sunrise Industries Ltd.

Initial investment	Rs. 12,00,000
Rate of discount	15 per cent
Annual production and sales:	20,000

Sales Price per unit		Rs. 150/-
Variable Costs:		
Unit D.Material	Rs. 75/-	
Unit D Labour	Rs. 40/-	
Unit Overheads	Rs. 10/-	

Total annual fixed costs:	
Manufacturing	Rs. 1,50,000
Administration	Rs. 1,50,000
Selling and Distribution	Rs. 50,000
Total	Rs. 3,50,000

The three possible situations anticipated are :

Variables	Most Unfavourable	Most Likely	Most Favourable
Units produced & sold	14,000	20,000	28,000
Sales price per unit	Rs. 120/-	Rs. 150	Rs. 175/-
Variable costs			
D. Material	Rs. 80/-	Rs. 75/-	Rs. 70/-
D.Labour	Rs. 50/-	Rs. 40/-	Rs. 30/-
Overhead	Rs. 20/-	Rs. 10/-	Rs. 81/-
Fixed Costs:			
Total Manufacturing	Rs. 1,75,000/-	Rs. 1,50,000/-	Rs. 1,40,000/-
Total Administration	Rs. 1,70,000/-	Rs. 1,50,000/-	Rs. 1,45,000/-
Total Selling & Distribution	Rs. 65,000/-	Rs. 50,000/-	Rs. 35,000/-

13. Calculate the NPV for three possible scenarios from the following data.

Details	Scenario I	Scenario II	Scenario III
Original Investment:	Rs. 5,00,000	Rs. 50,00,000	Rs. 5,00,000
Unit Selling price:	Rs. 40/-	16/-	45/-
Units decided: Units	1,50,000	3,00,000	1,00,000
Unit Variable Costs:	Rs. 12/-	Rs. 10/-	Rs. 15/-
Fixed Costs per unit:	Rs. 7/-	Rs. 5/-	Rs. 20/-
Depreciation-Straightline	✓	✓	✓
Rate of Tax 60%	✓	✓	✓

Annual Cash-flow	Rs. 25,000/-	Rs. 40,000/-	Rs. 18,000
Project Life 7 years	✓	✓	✓
Junk value Nil	✓	✓	✓
Rate of discount 10%	✓	✓	✓

After calculating NPV of project in each scenario, find out what factors have contributed for and related in influencing the NPV. You have the freedom of making reasonable assumptions.

14. (a) What is scenario analysis ? (b) With the given information in connection with King Kong Limited, calcuate the NPV for three possible scenarios. After finding out the NPV of project in each situation, trace out what factors have contributed for and related in influencing the NPV. You have the freedom of making any acceptable presumptions which you consider a must. The details made available under three scenarios are as under :

Details	Scenario 1	Scenario 2	Scenario 3
1. Initial Investment	Rs. 4,00,000	Rs. 4,00,000	Rs. 4,00,000
2. Units produced & sold	3,500	5,000	6,500
3. Unit selling price	Rs. 125/-	Rs. 150/-	Rs. 200/-
4. Variable Costs:			
Direct Material	Rs. 65/-	Rs. 60/-	Rs. 50/-
Direct Labour	Rs. 45/-	Rs. 40/-	Rs. 35/-
Direct Expenses	Rs. 15/-	Rs. 10/-	Rs. 7/-
Overheads	Rs. 22/-	Rs. 20/-	Rs. 15/-
5. Total Fixed Costs: (per unit)			
Depreciation	Rs. 5/-	Rs. 6/-	Rs. 8/-
Others:	Rs. 11/-	Rs. 2/-	Rs. 4/-
6. Annual Cash-flows:	Rs. 25,000/	Rs. 35,000	Rs. 20,000
7. Junk Value	Nil	Nil	Nil
8. Life of project:	6 years	6 years	6 years
9. Rate of discount	12%	12%	12%
10. Installation Charges	Rs. 5,000	Rs. 5,000	Rs. 5,000

15. You are required to plot a decision tree after calculating the NPV of cash flows in case of Terry Go Round Company that supplies you with the following relevant information :

1. Initial Investment Rs. 50,000 having the Life of two years.

1st year

Event	Cash Inflows	Probability
I	Rs. 10,000	0.20
II	Rs. 15,000	0.50
III	Rs. 12.000	0.30

2nd year cashflows 10,000 cashflows 1,50,000 cashflows 12,000

Event	Cashflows	Probability	Cashflows	Probability	Cashflows	Probability
I	Rs. 10,000	0.15	Rs. 15,000	0.10	Rs. 25,000	0.20
II	Rs. 12,000	0.60	Rs. 20,000	0.75	Rs. 15,000	0.50
III	Rs. 15,000	0.25	Rs. 25,000	0.15	Rs. 30,000	0.30

Take a cost of capital equal to 10.00 per cent and work out best option for the unit.

16. Make Achievers Limited is considering an investment of Rs. 1,20,000. The expected returns during the First Year of investment proposal are given as under :

Event	Cash Inflows	Probability
A	40,000	0.4
B	80,000	0.5
C	1,00,000	0.1

Year SECOND

Cash inflows in year ONE are :

	Rs. 40,000		Rs. 80,000		Rs. 1,00,000	
	Cash inflows	Probability	Cash inflows	Probability	Cash inflows	Probability
A	Rs. 80,000	0.3	Rs. 55,000	0.1	Rs. 60,000	0.3
B	Rs. 1,00,000	0.6	Rs. 75,000	0.7	Rs. 80,000	0.5
C	Rs. 1,20,000	0.1	Rs. 1,05,000	0.2	Rs. 1,20,000	0.2

You are required to take cost of capital as 15% and advise about the advisibility or otherwise of the accepting the proposal finding NPV and presenting the information in the form of a decision tree.

* * * * * *

Chapter 9

PROJECT EVALUATION AND REVIEW TECHNIQUES

- BASIC STEPS IN PROJECT MANAGEMENT
- NETWORK MODELING WITH PERT/CPM
- COST AND RESOURCE CONSIDERATIONS
- COMMENTS ON PERT/CPM SYSTEMS
- CHAPTER APPENDIX
- CHAPTER BASED QUESTIONS
- CHAPTER BASED PRACTICAL PROBLEMS

BACKDROP

You might have watched the pagentaries and competitions especially Olympic Games, World Cup Soccer held every four years. But have you ever tried imagined the myraid of interrelates activities that go on behind the scenes at such events. Try to picture the planning that took place before, during and after the games. The committees responsible for managing 55 to 85 sports of which held simultaneous in different locations, each consisting of several tasks that have to be carried out in a logical sequence. The committees are to care for housing and security for the athletes during their play at the Olympic venue or venues. The other activities include setting up transportation and housing accommodations for approximately 2.5 million spectators, arranging press and TV coverage, planning contingencies for bad weathers and even scheduling post-game clean up. Like these Olympic Games, projects are unique operations with a finite span. Generally, many interrelated activities must be scheduled and monitored within strict time, cost, and performance guidelines. Hence, this chapter is designed to consider the methods for managing such complex projects. This chapter starts with basic steps involved in project management and continues with exposing the two best known net-work planning methods namely PERT and CPM ending with an assessment of their limitations. The chapter ends with Chapter Based Questions.

BASIC STEPS IN PROJECT MANAGEMENT

As we have noted earlier, project is an interrelated set of activities that has a definite starting and ending point and that results in a unique product. The standard examples of projects can be : Construction of a building or an amusement park. Construction of road, a dam or an oil pipeline. Renovating blighted urban area. Developing a prototype for a new ocean lines or an plane. Installing a large computer system. Introducing a new product. Organising a state fair. Registering eligible recipients for a health -care program. Redesigning the layout of a plant or office and so on.

Managing a project, irrespective of its size and complexity requires identifying every activity to be undertaken and planning when each activity must begin and end in order to complete the overall project on time. To achieve that goal, the project manager needs an effective method for organizing a net-work of interrelated activities and personnel. The degree of difficulty in such scheduling is a function of the numbers of activities, their required sequence, and their timing. Typically, all projects involve the following:

1. Describing the project
2. Developing a network model
3. Inserting time estimates
4. Analysing the model
5. Developing the project plan and
6. Assessing periodically the progress of the project and repeat steps 2-6, as needed.

1. DESCRIBING THE PROJECT

The project manger is to describe first the project in terms that everyone involved in it will easily understand. This description should include a clear statement of the project's end point. In addition, the project manager must carefully define all project activities and precedent relationships. An 'activity' is the smallest unit of work effort consuming both time and resources that the project manager can schedule and control. A "Precedence relationship" is a sequencing constraint between related activities. That is, it determines that one activity can not start until a preceding activity has been completed. For our purpose let the project be "Relocation of Appolo Hospital" and let Mr. James Kindley be the "project manager". Mr. James Kindley has defined the project and project activities as under:

"In the interest of better serving the public in Chennai the Appolo Hospital has decided to relocate from Chennai of a large suburb which at present has no major medical facility. The move to Anna Nagar would mean constructing a new hospital and making it operational. Mr. James Kindley-the executive director of the board of Appolo Hospitals, must prepare a hearing before the Central Appolo Hospitals Board, scheduled for next week on the proposed project. Part of the hearing will address the specifics of the total project, including time and cost estimates for its completion.

With the help of his staff, Mr. James Kindley has identified 11 major project activities. He has also specified the immediate predecessors (those activities that must be completed before a given activity can begin) for each activity. The results are as under :

Activity	Description	Immediate Predecessor (s)
A	Select administrative and medical Staff	–
B	Select site and do site survey	–
C	Select equipment	A
D	Prepare final construction plans and layout	B
E	Bring utilities to the site	B
F	Interview applicants and fill positions in nursing, support staff, maintenance, and security	C
H	Construct the hospital	D
I	Develop an information system	A
J	Instal the equipment	E, G, H
K	Train the nurses and staff	F, I, J

PRECEDENCE RELATIONSHIPS CHART 9.01

Mr. James Kindley realizes that he could break down each activity into more detailed elements. However, the upcoming hearing does not require that level of detail. He also knows that he will have to supply time and cost estimates for each activity. Then he will have to use this information to answers questions such as :

- Can the project be completed in 72 weeks ?
- Which activities are crucial to completing the project on scheduled ?
- Considering the total project cost, what is the minimum - cost schedule ?

From the above description, it is clear that activity H_1 construct the hospital, reflects the fact that completion of constructions will have a major bearing on when the hospital becomes operational. However, he has not bothered to list the many activities included in the construction process. That will be the responsibility of the construction supervisor that Mr. James Kindley will hire. In general, a manager's project description should reflect only the level of detail the he or she needs in order to make scheduling and resource allocation decisions.

2. DEVELOPING NET-WORK MODEL

The network model is represented by a "network diagram," consisting of nodes (circles) and arcs (arrows) that depict the relationships between activities. Interpretation of the graphic symbols will differ depending on the specific modelling technique used as illustrated in Fig. 9.01. There are two approaches - Activity on Arc (AOA) network and activity on node (AON) network.

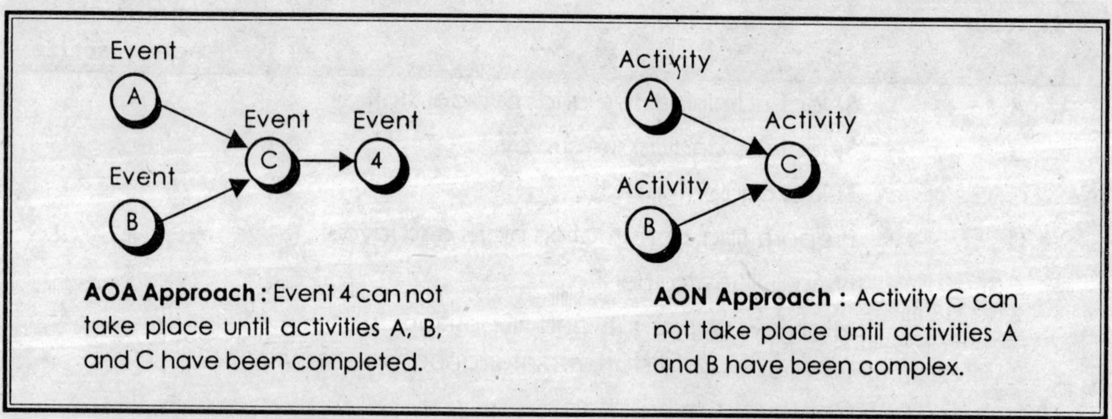

Fig. 9.01 AOA and AON Approaches to Activity Relationships

The AOA network, uses arcs to represent activities and nodes to represent events. An 'event' is the point at which one or more activities are to be completed and one or more other activities are to begin. An event consumes neither time nor resources. Since the AOA approach emphasis activity connection points, one can say that it is event-oriented. As figure 09:01 shows, precedence relationships require that an event not occurs until all preceding activities have been completed. A second approach is the AON network in which the nodes represent activities and the arcs indicate the sequence in which they are performed. This approach is activity-oriented. The precedence relationships require that an activity can not began until all preceding activities have been completed. In our explanation, we will use AON networks in all the examples that we will encounter because they are easier to construct than AOA networks. One can also go in for AON network.

3. INSERTING TIME ESTIMATES

Regardless of the modelling method selected, project manager is to decide whether to use probabilistic (Uncertain) or deterministic (certain) time estimates for activities. This decision historically led to a choice of one of the two different network planning methods namely program evaluation and review technique (PERT) or the Critical Path Method (CPM).

Originally, PERT was designed to cope up with uncertainty in activity times. The US NAVY sponsored the development of this planning & scheduling method during the 1950s to help manage the Polaris Missile Project. The project involved 3,000 separate contractors and suppliers. Because of many of the project activities had never been performed before, time estimates were uncertain. In retrospect, PERT is generally created with reducing the projects completion time by at least 18 months. During the late 1950s, **Mr. J.E. Kelly** of Ramington-Rond and **Mr. M.R. Walker** of Du Pont developed CPM as a means of scheduling maintenance shutdowns at chemical processing plants. Since maintenance projects were routine, reasonably accurate time estimates for activities were available. Thus, CPM was based on the assumption that project activity times can be estimated accurately and do not vary.

Before PERT and CPM, project managers used Gannt charts to schedule and control projects. However, for large projects. Gannt charts become difficult to work with because: (1.) they do not directly recognize precedence relationships between activities (2.) they do not indicate which activities are crucial to completing the project on time. Today, the differences between PERT and CPM are minor. Basically, either approach can cope with uncertainly, and both can use AOA or AON networks. In our discussion, we do not make arbitrary distinctions between these methods. Instead we refer to them collectively as PERT/CPM.

4. ANALYZING THE MODEL

The project manager can use the network models to identify activities that are crucial to project completion and to estimate the probability of completing a project on time. By identifying those activities that, if expedited, could reduce the time needed to complete the project, the manager may be able to reduce total costs. Since this requires a practical explanations it is taken up later.

5. DEVELOPING PROJECT PLAN

Having created a network model, the project manager can then develop a schedule for each activity within the project. Activities crucial to on time project completion will receive preference subject to resource availability. After the project actually begins, periodic reports will show the current status of all activities relative to their planned completion dates.

6. UPDATING THE PROJECT PLAN

Periodically, the project manager will have to adjust the schedule on the basis of additional information. Perhaps an activity took longer than expected new activities were identified, or precedence relationships among several activities changed. This information may call for changes in the network or the time estimates and, ultimately, in the overall project schedule itself.

NETWORK MODELING WITH PERT/CPM

Back to Appolo Hospital project Mr. James Kindley has identified the various activities and their precedence relationships. In this area of discussion, we use the following PERT/CPM procedures to analyse those activities of :

1. Diagramming the AON network
2. Estimating activity times
3. Calculating time statistics
4. Determining the critical path
5. Analyzing the probabilities.

1. DIAGRAMMING THE ACTIVITY ON NODE NETWORK

Diagramming a project as a network first requires establishing the precedence relationships between activities, as Mr. James Kindley did in chart 9.01. For complex projects this task can be really tedious. However, it is essential because incorrect or omitted procedure relationships will result in costly delays.

An AON network for the Appolo Hospital project, based on 11 activities as described by James kindley and their precedence relationships, is given in Figure 9.02.

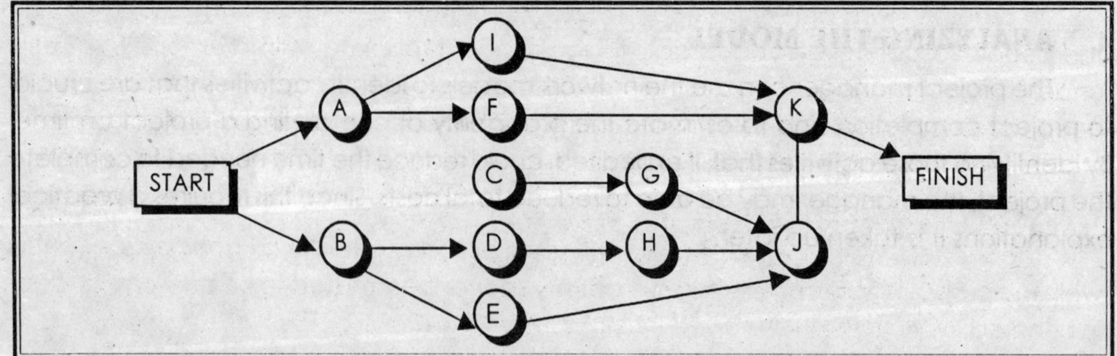

Fig. 9.02 AON Network Diagram for the Appolo Hospital Project.

Activity	Description
A	Select administrative and medical staff
B	Select site and do site survey
C	Select equipment
D	Prepare final construction plans and layout
E	Bring utilities to the site
F	Interview applicants and fill positions is nursing, supporting staff, maintenance, and security
G	Purchase and take delivery of the equipment
H	Construct the hospital
I	develop an information system
J	Install the equipment
K	Train the nurses and staff

The above diagram depicts activities an circles, with arrows indicating the sequence in which they are to be performed. Activities A and B emanate from the start node because they have no immediate predecessors. The arrows connecting activity A to activities, C, F and I indicate that all three require completion of activity A before they can begin. Similarly, activity B must be completed before activities D and E can begin. The rest of the diagram follows the same logical sequence. Start and finish nodes do not actually represent activities. They merely provide the beginning and ending points for the network.

The network diagram provides the basis for project analysis. Thus, the diagram must accurately represent all the activities and precedence relationships. For instance, having a loop in the network where activity B preceded activity D, D preceded E, and E preceded B would make sense. Modelling a large project as a network is a useful process in itself because, at the very least, it forces the management to identify necessary activities and recognize the precedence relationships between them.

2. ESTIMATING ACTIVITY TIMES

In order to overcome the uncertainty inherent in time-estimates, the manager asks the people responsible for each activity to provide three time estimates for all activities under their control. They should base their estimates on the assumption that all resources needed to complete an activity within its most likely time are available during a normal work period. These three estimates are.

1. MOST OPTIMISTIC TIME : (a)

The shortest time in which the activity can be completed, if all goes exceptionally well. The probability of completing the activity sooner is estimated to be only one chance in hundred.

2. MOST LIKELY TIME : (m)

The best estimate of the average time required to perform an activity if the activity could be repeated many times under similar circumstances (no learning factor)

3. MOST PESSIMISTIC TIME : (b)

The longer estimated time required to perform an activity, assuming that everything that could go wrong does go wrong. The probability that it will take more time to complete the activity is estimated to be only one chance in hundred.

3. CALCULATING THE TIME STATISTICS

These time estimates give the project manager enough information to estimate the mean and variance of a probability distribution for each activity. In PERT/CPM each activity time is treated as though it were random number derived from a beta probability distribution. The primary reason for choosing this distribution is that it can take on a variety of shapes, allowing the most likely time estimates to fall anywhere between the most pessimistic and most optimistic end points. This condition is not possible with just any distribution. For instance, the normal distribution is symmetrical, requiring the mode to be equidistant from the end points. This condition would be unduly restrictive.

The estimate for the mean of the beta distribution is given by the following weightage average of the three time estimates. Note that the most likely time is weighted four times greater than most pessimistic or most optimistic estimates.

$$t_e = \frac{a+4m+b}{6}$$

The variance of the beta distribution for each activity is: $\sigma^2 = \left(\frac{b-a}{6}\right)^2$

The Variance increases as the difference between the more pessimistic and most optimistic time estimates increases. This result means that less certain a person is an estimating the actual time for an activity, the greater will be the variance.

ILLUSTRATION:

Suppose Mr. James Kindley has arrived at the following time estimates for activity B (Site selection and survey) of the hospital project :

a = 7 weeks m = 8 weeks b = 15 weeks Calculate the expected time for activity B and the variable.

SOLUTION:

The expected time for activity B is

$$t_e = \frac{7 + 4(8) + 15}{6} = \frac{54}{6} = 9 \text{ weeks}$$

Note that the expected time (9 weeks) does not equal the most likely time (8 weeks) for this activity. These times will be equal only when the most likely time is equidistant from the mostoptimistic and most pessimistic times. Now, let us calculate the variance for activity B as follows:

$$\sigma^2 = \left(\frac{15-7}{6}\right)^2 = \left(\frac{8}{6}\right)^2 = 1.78$$

The accompanying table shows expected activity times and variances for the activities listed in James Kindley's project description. Note that the greater uncertainty lies with the time estimate for activity I, followed by the estimates for activities E and G. The expected times for each activity will prove in determining the critical path.

Time Estimates and Activity Statistics for Appolo H. Project

	Time Estimates (Weeks)			Activity statistics	
Activity	Most Optimistic (a)	Most Likely (m)	Most Pessimistic (b)	Expected Time (t_e)	Variance (σ^2)
A	11	12	13	12	0.11
B	7	8	15	9	1.78
C	5	10	15	10	2.78
D	8	9	16	10	1.78
E	14	25	30	24	7.11
F	6	9	18	10	4.00
G	25	36	41	35	7.11
H	35	40	45	40	2.78
I	10	13	28	15	9.00
J	1	2	15	4	5.44
K	5	6	7	6	0.11

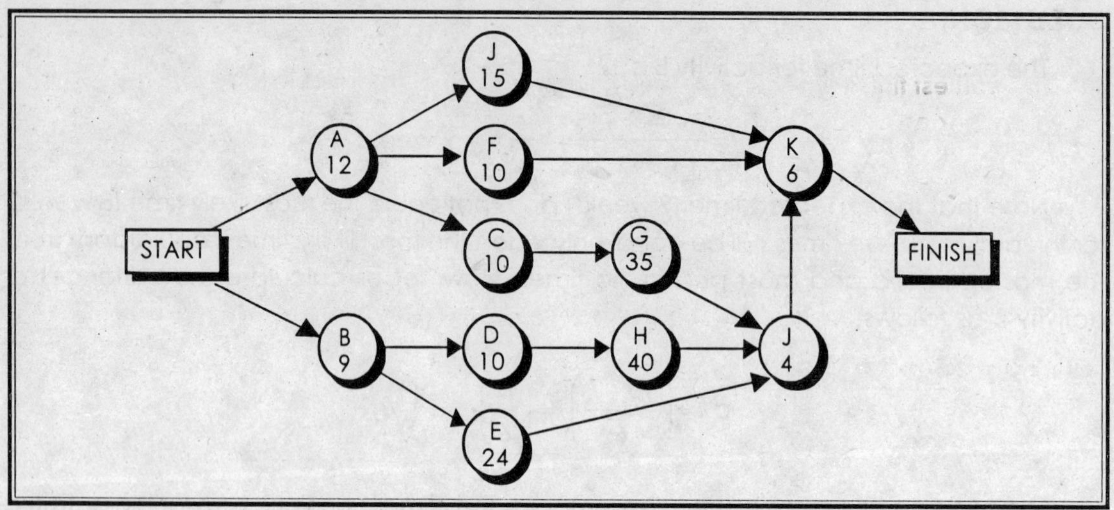

Fig. 9.03 AON Network showing activity times

4. DETERMINING THE CRITICAL PATH

A crucial aspect of project management is time of completion. The sum of all the expected times for each activity in the earlier table is 175 weeks. This estimate reflects strictly sequential work. That is, work proceeding on only one activity at a time. However, PERT/CPM is based on the assumption that the resources are available to proceed on various activities simultaneously. Thus the project manager at this stage - must consider only the precedence relationships and the expected times in scheduling activities. In fact, the figure 09:03 indicates that the project can be finished in much less than 175 weeks.

In order to determine the earliest completion time of a project, the project manager, must first find the critical path. The **critical path** is the sequence of activities between a projects start and finish that takes the longest time to complete. Put in other words, all activities along the critical path must be completed before the overall project is completed. The critical path also has zero slack time at each activity along the path. "Activity Slack" is the maximum time an activity can be delayed without delaying the entire project. One calculates the slack using four time values for each activity.

1. **Earliest start time** is the earliest possible beginning time for an activity.
2. **Latest start time** is the latest possible beginning time for an activity that will allow project to be compute on schedule.
3. **Earliest finish time** is the earliest start time plus the time needed for an activity.
4. **Latest finish time** is the latest possible completion time for an activity that will not delay the entire project.

EARLIEST START AND EARLIEST FINISH TIMES

To calculate the earliest start and finish times, one can make use of two simple rules:

1. **The earliest finish time** (EF_i) for an activity is equal to its earliest start plus its expected duration, or

$$EF_i = ES_i + t_e$$

2. **The earliest start time** (ES_i) for an activity i is equal to the latest of the earliest finish times of the immediately preceding activities. That is,

$$ES_i = \max [\text{EF times of all activities immediately preceding activity i}]$$

For instance, let us calculate the earliest start and finish times for the activities in the hospital project. Figure 9.03 contains the expected activity times for the table 9.01

Let us begin at the start node at time zero. Activities A and B have no predecessors, so the earliest start times for these activities are also zero. The earliest finish times for these activities are :

$$EF_A = 0 + 12 = 12 \text{ and}$$

$$EF_B = 0 + 9 = 9$$

Thus, EF_A becomes the earliest start time for activities I F and C; EF_B becomes the earliest start time for activities D and E. Consequently,

$$EF_I = 12 + 15 = 27$$

$$EF_D = 9 + 10 = 19$$

$$EF_F = 12 + 10 = 22$$

$$EF_E = 9 + 24 = 33$$

$$EF_C = 12 + 10 = 22$$

Similarly, $EF_G = 22 + 35 = 57$ and $EF_H = 19 + 40 = 59$. Activity J has several predecessors, so $ES_J = \max [EF_G, EF_H, EF_E] = 59$. Thus, $EF_J = 59 + 4 = 63$. Finally, $ES_K = \max [EF_I, EF_F, EF_J] = 63$ and $EF_K = 63 + 6 = 69$. This result means that the earliest the project can be completed is 69 weeks. The earliest start and earliest finish times for all activities are shown in figure 9.04.

LATEST START AND LATEST FINISH TIMES

To calculate the latest start and latest finish times, one is to start at finish node and assume that project is to be completed at the maximum of the earliest finish times of all activities immediately preceding it. Alternatively, the negotiated contract due date could be used. In that case, the activity slack on the critical path may not be zero. The other two rules are :

1. **The Latest Start Time** (LS_i) for an activity i is equal to its latest finish time minus its expected duration or :

$$LSi = LFi - te$$

2. **The Latest Finish Time** (LF_i) for an activity i is equal to the earliest of the latest start times of all activities immediately following it. That is,

LF_i = min [LS times of all activities immediately following activity i]

For the hospital project, one can calculate the latest start and latest finish times for each activity using Fig. 9.03. One can begin by setting the latest finish activity time of activity K at week 69, its early finish time. Thus,

$LS_K = 69 - 6 = 63$

If activity K is to start not later than week 63, all its predecessors must finish not later than that time. Consequently,

$LF_I = LF_F = LF_J = 63$

The latest start times for these activities are :

$LS_I = 63 - 15 = 48$

$LS_F = 63 - 10 = 53$

$LS_J = 63 - 4 = 59$

Once we have calculated LS_J, we can calculate the latest start times for the immediate predecessors of activity J :

$LS_G = 59 - 35 = 24$

$LS_H = 59 - 40 = 19$

$LS_E = 59 - 24 = 35$

Similarly, one can now calculate latest start times for activities C and D.

$LS_C = 24 - 10 = 14$ and

$LS_D = 19 - 10 = 9$

Activities A and B have more than one predecessor. LF_A = min [LS_I, LS_F, LS_C] = 14, and LS_A = 14 -12 = 2i LF_B = min [LS_D, LS_E] = 9, and LS_B = 9 - 9 = 0. This result means that activity B must be started immediately if the project is to be completed by week 69. The latest start and latest finish times for all activities are shown in figure 9.04 as below.

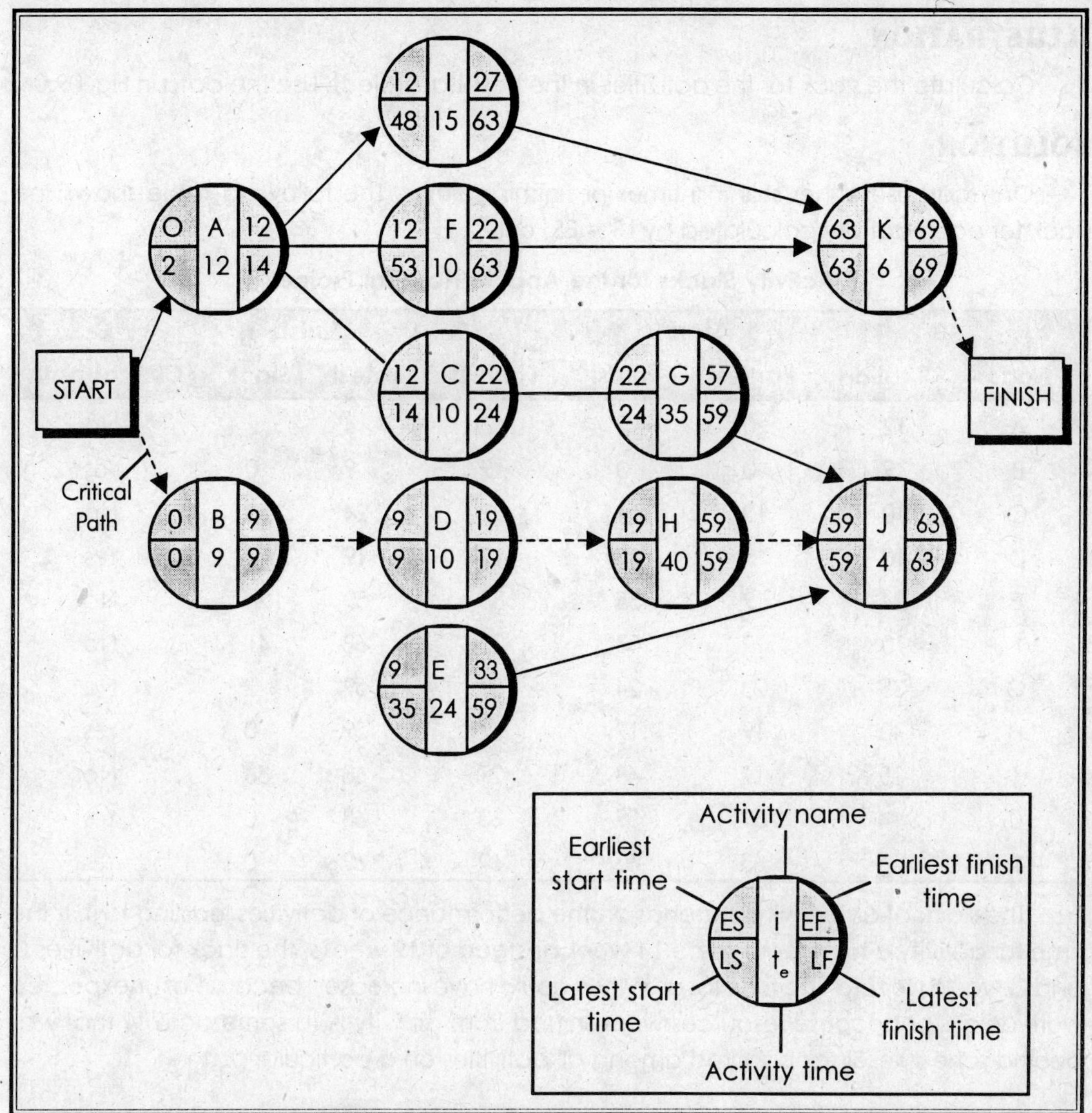

Fig. 9.04 Network Showing Data Needed for Activity Statistics

ACTIVITY SLACK

Slack information is useful to project managers because it helps them to make decision regarding reallocation of resources. Resources could be taken from activities with slack and given to other activities that are behind schedule until the slack is used up. One can calculate activity slack in one of the two ways :

$$S_i = LS_i - ES_i \text{ or } S_i = LF_i - EF_i$$

ILLUSTRATION:

Calculate the slack for the activities in the hospital project. Use the data in Fig. 09.04.

SOLUTION:

One can use either starting times or finishing times. The following table shows the slack for each activity calculated by $LS_i = ES_i$, or $LF_i - EF_i$.

Activity Slacks for the Appolo Hospital Project

Node	Duration	Start		Finish		Slack	Critical path
		Earliest	Latest	Earliest	Latest		
A	12	0	2	12	14	2	No
B	9	0	0	9	9	0	Yes
C	10	12	14	22	24	2	No
D	10	9	9	19	19	0	Yes
E	24	9	35	33	59	26	No
F	10	12	53	22	63	41	No
G	35	22	24	57	59	2	No
H	40	19	19	59	59	0	Yes
I	15	12	48	27	63	36	No
J	4	59	59	63	63	0	Yes
K	6	63	63	69	69	0	Yes

The slack at an activity depends on the performance of activities leading to it. If the time for activity a turned out to be 14 weeks instead of 12 weeks, the slack for activities C and G would be zero. The time for activity A could have increased because of unexpected work delays or because resources were shifted from activity A to some activity that was behind schedule. Slack is shared among all activities on a particular path.

CRITICAL PATH

Now one can identify the critical path. All activities on the critical path have zero slack. The activity string B - D - H - J - K constitutes the critical path for the hospital project. The dotted or dashed line in Fig. 9.04 denotes the critical path graphically, and the preceding table shows how it can be identified in report form.

The critical path is important because it defines the completion time of the project. Any delay in activities along the critical path delay project completion. Adding the expected times for each activity along the critical path, one can determine that the expected time to complete the hospital project is 69 weeks. Thus, Mr. James Kindley should focus more attention on these activities in managing the project although if activity A or C were to fall behind by two weeks, they and activity G would be as on the critical path as well. Using up slack can result in more than one critical path for a project.

Rather than calculating activity slack first, one could have found the critical path by enumerating all the activity paths in the network and identifying the one having the longest cumulative time. Table 9.01 shows this solution, mainly to demonstrate that the path having the minimum slack is also the longest path in the network. Although manually finding the critical path is this way is easier for small projects computers must be used to find it for large, complex projects. Computer routines normally compute activities slack because project managers want this information any way. Identifications of the critical path is the byproduct of that information.

Path	Expected Time (Weeks)
A - F - K	28
A - I - K	33
A - C - G - J - K	67
B - D - H - J - K	69 (Critical)
B - E - J - K	43

TABLE 9.1 Network paths for the Appolo Hospital Project

5. ANALYZING PROBABILITIES

In the process of calculations, it is assumed that the time estimates for activities involve some uncertainly. Knowing the probability of activities any activity in a specific amount of time, therefore, would be useful. To obtain it, one must define the probability distribution of achievement dates for an activity. Managers focus most often on the projects completion date, so here one can use the finish node as an example.

In order to specify the probability distribution of achievement dates for the finish node, one must determine a mean and variance. If one assumes that the activity times along the critical path are independent of each other, it seems reasonable to use the sum of the expected activity times on the critical path as the mean of the distributions. For the Appolo Hospital project, the easier expected finish time for activity K (and, therefore, the finish node) is 69 weeks.

Similarly, because of the assumption of activity time independence, one uses the sum of the variances of the activities on the critical path as the variance of the project time distribution. From the table 09:01, one finds that variable of the critical path B - D - H - J - K counted be 1.78 + 1.78 + 2.78 + 5.44 + 0.11 = 11.89.

Consequently, the central limit theorem allows one to use the normal probability distribution to find the probability of achieving a particular due date for the project. One can use the Z - transformation formula as follows :

$$Z = \frac{T' - TE}{\sqrt{\Sigma \sigma^2_{\varphi}}}$$

Where

T' = due date for the project

TE = earliest expected completion date of the project

□□$^2_{cp}$ = Sum of the variances on the critical path.

The procedure for assessing the probability of completing any activity in a project by a given date is similar to the one it is discussed just now. However, instead of critical path, one would use the longest time path of activities from the start node activity node in question.

ILLUSTRATION:

Calculate the probability that the hospital will become operational in 72 weeks.

SOLUTION:

With a critical path length of 69 weeks and a variance of 11.89 one can calculate the 3-value as follows :

$$Z = \frac{72 - 69}{\sqrt{11 - 89}} = \frac{3}{3.45} = 0.87$$

Using the normal distribution table in Appendix 1 given at the end of this chapter, one finds that the probability is about 0.20 that the project will exceed 72 weeks. This probability is presented graphically as under in Fig. 9.05.

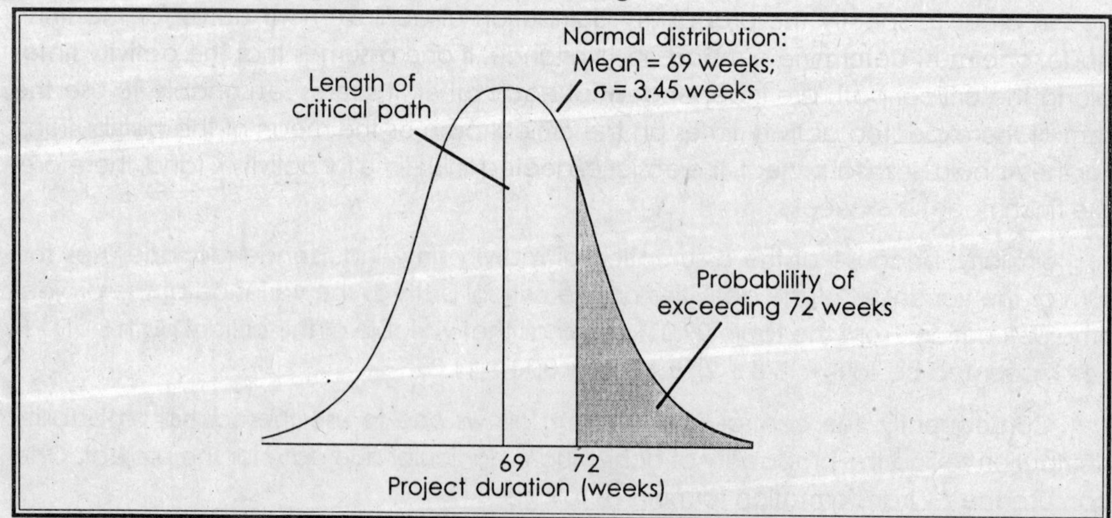

Fig. 9.05 Probability of Exceeding 72 Weeks

Thus, one can use the uncertainty in activity time estimates to make statements about the chances of completing a project on schedule. The analyses hinges on the identifications of the critical path. It is seen that one calculated the critical path on the basis of the expected times for each activity and disregarded the variances. Conceivably, one or more network paths for a project may be shorter than the critical path, but have enough variance in activity time estimates to actually become the critical path sometime during the project. Such is the case in Appolo Hospital project. In table 9.01, one finds that path A - C - G - J - K is 67 weeks long, or only two weeks shorter than the critical path. The sum of the variances along that path is 15.55. Thus, close attention to activities A, C, and G, in addition to activities B, D, H, J and K seems warranted.

Also the critical path with the largest variance should be used in denominator of the 3-transfromation formula if the project has multiple critical paths. Thus, approach allows the probability estimate to reflect the correct amount of uncertainty in the project duration.

6. MONITORING PROJECT PROGRESS

Even the best possible project plans can go wrong. Therefore, progress must be monitored so that delays can be readily identified. A slack-sorted report on a weekly basis is helpful in this respect. Take that in the Appolo Hospital project, 16 weeks have passed and activity A has just been completed. Consequently, activity A was completed 4 week late (Check Fig.: 09:04). Also take that activities B took 10 weeks instead of the expected 9 weeks. Table 09:02 shows a slack sorted report as of 16th week of the project. Activities A and B are not shown because they have already been completed.

It is worth noting that activities C, G, J and K now have negative slack and replace activities D and H on the critical path. The activities at the top of the report are more critical then those at the bottom. If the original completion target of week 69 is still valid, the project manager would try to make up two weeks of time somewhere along path C - G - J - K. However, to make the deadline, one week will also have to be made up along path D - H. If that time is made up, there will be two critical paths : C - G - J - K and D - H - J - K.

Activity	Duration	Earliest Start	Latest Start	Slack	Critical path
C	10	16	14	−2	Yes
G	35	26	24	−2	Yes
J	4	61	59	−2	Yes
K	6	65	63	−2	Yes
D	10	10	9	−1	No
H	40	20	19	−1	No
E	24	10	35	25	No
I	15	16	48	32	No
F	10	16	53	37	No

TABLE 9.2 Slack - Sorted Computer Report

Manager can use slack-sorted reports such as this one more conveniently than a network diagram. Most project managers work with this type of computer report and never see network diagram.

COST AND RESOURCE CONSIDERATIONS

So far, our discussion has focused on managing project time. The implicit assumption is that if the project can be kept on schedule, total project costs will be acceptable. The reality of project management, however, is that there are always time-cost trade-offs. Total project costs are the sum of the direct costs, indirect costs, and penalty costs. Direct costs cover labour, materials, and any other costs directly related to project activities. Indirect costs cover administration and other variable overhead costs that can be avoided by reducing the total project time. Penalty costs may be incurred if the project exceeds beyond some specific date. Conversely, in some cases a bonus may be provided for the early completion. Thus when a project manager considers total project costs, or total profits, the best schedule may require expediting some activities to reduce over all project completion time. This is done by use of PERT/CPM methods.

DIRECT COSTS AND TIMES

Direct costs can be subdivided into normal costs and crash costs for each activity. Associated with these costs are a normal time and crash time.

1. **Normal Time (NT)**

   The time to complete the activity under normal conditions. This time is analogues to the expected time, te, noted earlier.

2. **Normal Cost (NC)**

   The activity cost associated with the normal time

3. **Crash Time (CT)**

   The shortest possible time to complete the activity

4. **Crash Cost (CC)**

   The activity cost associated with the crash time.

COST ASSUMPTIONS

In making a cost analysis, one assumes that costs increase linearly as activity time is reduced from its normal time. For instance, take that normal time for activity C in case of Appolo Hospital project is 10 weeks at a direct cost Rs. 4,000 lakhs. If the crash time is 5 weeks at a crash cost of Rs. 7,000 lakhs, the net time reduces is 5 weeks at a net cost increase of Rs. 3,000 lakhs. One assumes that it costs Rs. 600 lakhs (or Rs. 3000/5 lakhs) per week to crash activity C. This assumption of linear marginal cost is illustrated in fig. 09:06. Including a hypothetical actual cost curve. Thus, if activity C were expedited by two weeks the estimated direct cost would work out Rs. 5,200 lakhs eventhough the actual cost would be much less. PERT/CPM methods do not require the assumption of linear cost increases. Non-linear relationships can be used, but the linear assumption is usually more than enough.

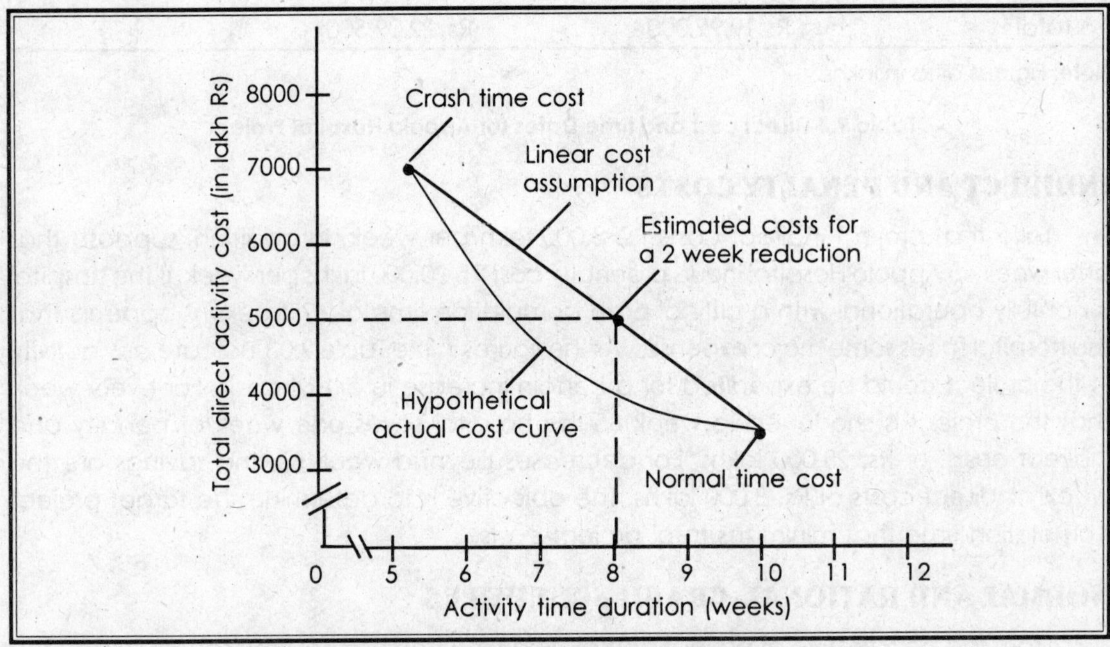

Fig. 9.06 COST-TIME RELATIONSHIP IN COST ANALYSIS

Table 9.03 contains direct cost and time data for the Appolo Hospital Project. The amount in the last column were calculated as follows :

$$\text{Cost to crash per week} = \frac{CC - NC}{NT - CT}$$

Activity	Normal Time (NT)	Normal Cost (NC)	Crash Time (CT)	Crash Cost (CC)	Time Reduction (Week/s)	Cost to Crash Per week
A	12	Rs. 12,000	11	Rs. 13,000	1	Rs. 1,000
B	9	Rs. 50,000	7	Rs. 64,000	2	Rs. 7,000
C	10	Rs. 4,000	5	Rs. 7,000	5	Rs. 600
D	10	Rs. 16,000	8	Rs. 20,000	2	Rs. 2,000
E	24	Rs. 1,20,000	14	Rs. 2,00,000	10	Rs. 8,000
F	10	Rs. 10,000	6	Rs. 16,000	4	Rs. 1,500
G	35	Rs. 5,00,000	25	Rs. 5,30,000	10	Rs. 3,000
H	40	Rs.12,00,000	35	Rs. 12,60,000	5	Rs.12,000

I	15	Rs. 40,000	10	Rs. 52,500	5	Rs. 2,500
J	4	Rs. 10,000	1	Rs. 13,000	3	Rs. 1,000
K	6	Rs. 30,000	5	Rs. 34,000	1	Rs. 4,000
Total		Rs.19,92,000		Rs. 22,09,500		

Note: Figures of Rs in lakhs.

Table 9.3 Direct cost and time Dates for Appolo Hospital Project

INDIRECT AND PENALTY COSTS

Take that project indirect costs Rs. 8,000 lakh per week. In addition, suppose that after week 65 Appolo Hospital incurs a penalty cost Rs. 20,000 lakhs per week, if the hospital is not fully operational with a critical path completion time of 69 weeks, it appears that the hospital faces some major expenses. As the figures in the Table 9.03 indicate,any activity in the project could be expedited for a certain increase in direct costs. For every week that the project is shortened-to week 65-the hospital saves one week of penalty and indirect costs, or Rs. 28,000 lakhs. For decreases beyond week 65, the savings are the weekly indirect costs of Rs. 8,000 lakhs. The objective is to determine the target project completion time that minimizes total project costs.

NORMAL AND RATIONAL CRASH SCHEDULES

From the perspective of project completion time, the normal time schedule and the minimum-time-schedule provide the limits for the minimum-cost-schedule search. Finding the cost for normal time schedule is straight forward. Table 9.03 shows that total direct cost is Rs. 19,92,000 lakhs. Indirect costs are Rs. 8,000 lakhs per week, or Rs. 5,52,000. Four weeks of penalty costs come to Rs. 80,000 lakhs. Thus, the total costs for a 69-week projects Rs. 26,24,000 lakhs.

The first step in finding the cost of the minimum-time schedule is to find the minimum project duration by crashing all the activities in the project and finding the length of the critical path. Figure 9.07 on the next page shows the CPM network with the crash times (in weeks) for each activity. The critical path B-D-H-J-K, with a total completion time of 56 weeks. Total direct cost for this expedited schedule as shown in the Table 9.03 is Rs. 22,09,500 lakhs. Indirect costs would be Rs. 4,48,000 lakhs [or 56(Rs. 8,000 lakhs)]. As there are no penalty costs, the total project cost would be Rs. 26,57,500 lakhs.

The minimum-time schedule that we just evaluated crashed all activities to their limits. However, the minimum time of 56 weeks can be achieved without crashing all the activities. Table 9.04 shows how to derive the **Rational Cash Schedule** for the hospital project.

Noncritical Activity	Cost of crash Per week	Crash Time (week)	Maximum Relax Time (week)	Adjusted Time (week)	Savings relative to total crash schedule
E	Rs. 8,000	14	10	24	Rs. 80,000
G	Rs. 3,000	25	9	34	Rs. 27,000
I	Rs. 2,500	10	5	15	Rs. 12,500
F	Rs. 1,500	6	4	10	Rs. 6,000
Total					Rs. 1,25,500

Note: Rs in lakhs.

TABLE 9.03 Deriving the Rational crash schedule

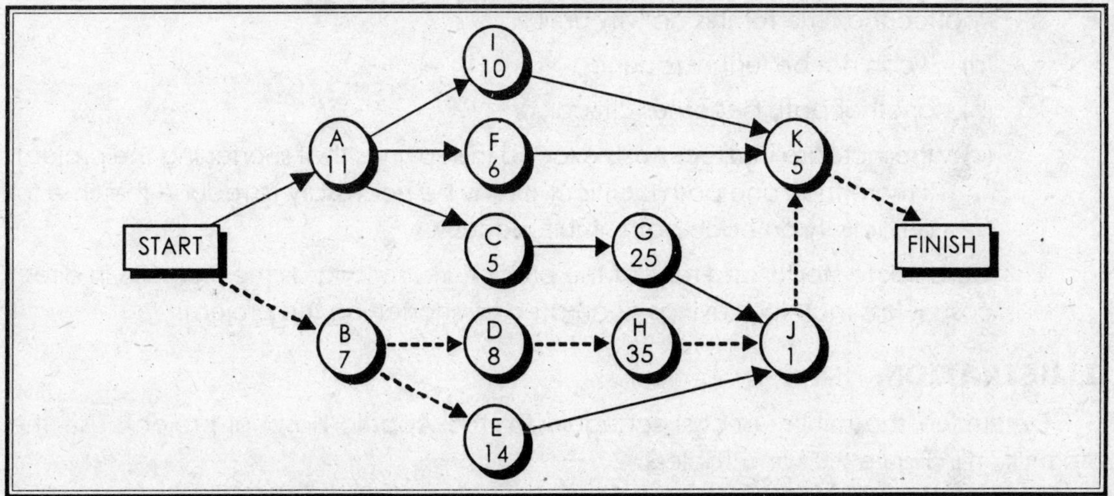

Fig. 9.07 Network showing crash times and the critical path.

No one begins by finding the activity not on the critical path that is the most expensive to crash. Then one can relax it as much as possible, without exceeding its normal time or increasing the length of the total project. This activity is E. One can return it to its normal time and save Rs. 80,000 lakhs relative to the total crash schedule. The next most expensive non-critical activity is G. Its normal time is 35 weeks; however, one can relax it only 9 weeks because at an adjusted time of 34 weeks, path A-C-G-J-K is also 56 weeks long. Activities I and F can both be returned to their normal times, but all other activities remain at their crash times. The total savings to the total crash schedule is Rs. 1,25,500 lakhs. Consequently, the total project cost for the rational crash schedule is Rs 25,32,000 lakhs (for Rs. 26,57,500_Rs. 1,25,500 lakhs).

FINDING THE MINIMUM-COST SCHEDULE

So far we have established a total project cost upper limit of Rs 25,32,000 for the rational crash schedule. Thus, Mr James Kindley should not accept an intermediate schedule between 56 and 69 weeks that costs more than Rs. 25,32,000 lakhs. In evaluating intermediate schedules, one can start with normal time schedule and crash activities along the critical path in such a way that the added crash costs are less than the savings in indirect and penalty costs. This same procedure could be used for AOA networks. The procedure involves the following steps:

1. Determine the critical path(s) in the project
2. Find the activity or activities on the critical path(s) that is(are) cheapest to crash per week
3. Reduce the time for this activity until
   (a) it can not be further reduced
   (b) another path becomes critical, or
   (c) the increase in direct costs exceed the savings that shortening the project. If more than one path is critical, it may be necessary to reduce the time for an activity on each path simultaneously.
4. Go back to step 1 and repeat the procedure, so long as the increase in direct costs is less than the savings generated by shortening the project.

ILLUSTRATION:

Determine the minimum-cost schedule for the Appolo hospital project. Use the information in Figure 9.07 and Table 9.4.

SOLUTION:

Trial 1 :

1. The critical path is B-D-H-J-K
2. The cheaper activity to crash per week is J at Rs. 1,000 lakhs, which is much less than the savings in indirect and penalty costs of Rs. 28,000 lakhs per week.
3. Crash activity J to its limit of 3 weeks because the critical path remains unchanged. This action affects three paths in the network. The new expected times for each path are :

A-I-K	33 weeks
A-F-K	28 weeks
A-C-G-J-K	64 weeks
B-D-H-J-K	66 weeks
B-E-J-K	40 weeks

Compare these times to those in table 9.1

Trial 2 :

1. The critical path is still B-D-H-J-K.
2. The cheapest activity to crash per week is now D at Rs. 2,000 lakhs.
3. The first week of reduction in activity D saves Rs. 28,000 lakhs but second saves only Rs. 8,000 lakhs. However, these savings still exceed the cost of crashing D by two weeks. After week 65, there are no more penalty costs. Note that after crashing D, one now has two critical paths.

Trial 3 :

1. The critical paths are B-D-H-J-K and A-C-G-J-K. Both paths must now be shorterned to realize any savings in indirect costs of project. If one is shortened and another is not, the length of the project remains unchanged.
2. The alternatives available are to crash one of the following combinations of activities (A,B), (A,H), (C,B), (C,H),(G,B), (G,H) or to crash actively K which is on both critical paths. Jointly crashing (A,B) costs Rs. 8,000 lakhs; (A,H) Rs. 13,000 lakhs; (C,B) Rs. 7,600 lakhs; (C,H) Rs. 12,600 lakhs; (G,B) Rs. 10,000 lakhs; and (G,H) Rs. 15,000 lakhs. The cheapest alternative is activity K at Rs. 4,000 lakhs per week.
3. Crash activity K to its limit of fine weeks. The critical paths remain unchanged.

COST ANALYSIS FOR THE APPOLO HOSPITAL PROJECT

Crash Trial Activity	Resulting Critical Path*	Time Reduction (weeks)	Project Duration (weeks)	Total Project Direct Cost at last Trial	Crash Costs Added This Trial	Total Indirect costs	Total penalty costs	Total project costs
0 -	B-D-H- J - K	–	69	Rs. 19,92,000	Rs. –	Rs.5,52,000	Rs. 80,000	Rs.26,24,000
1. J	B-D-H-[J]- K	3	66	Rs. 19,92,000	Rs. 3,000	Rs.5,28,000	Rs. 20,000	Rs.25,43,000
2. D	A-C-G-[J]- K B-[D]-H-[J]- K	2	64	Rs. 19,95,000	Rs. 4,000	Rs. 52,000	Rs. 0	Rs.25,11,000
3. K	A- C -G-[J]-[K] B-[D]-H-[J]-[K]	1	63	Rs. 19,99,000	Rs. 4,000	Rs.5,04,000	Rs. 0	Rs.25,07,000
4. B,C	A- C -G-[J]-[K] B-[D]-H-[J]-[K]	2	61	Rs. 20,03,000	Rs.15,200	Rs.4,88,000	Rs. 0	Rs.25,06,200

* A ☐ indicates that activity has been crashed to its limits Rs in lakhs.

Trial 4 :

1. The critical paths are B-D-H-J-K and A-C-G-J-K.
2. The least expensive alternative at this stage is to simultaneously crash activities B and C at a cost of Rs. 7,600 lakhs per week. This amount is still less than the savings of Rs. 8,000 lakhs per week.

3. Crash activities B and C by two weeks, the limit for activity B.

Any other combination of activities will result in a net increase in total project costs because the crash costs exceed weekly indirect costs. The following table contains a summary of the COST ANALYSIS FOR THE APPOLO HOSPITAL PROJECT.

It is evident from the above summary of the cost analysis that minimum-cost schedule is 61 weeks, with a total cost of Rs. 25,06,700 lakhs. To get this schedule it was to crash activities B, D, J, and K to their limits and actually C to 8 weeks. The other activities remain at their normal times. This schedule costs about Rs. 25,800 lakhs less than the rational crash schedule.

The Figure 9.08 given below shows the cost curves for the hospital project.

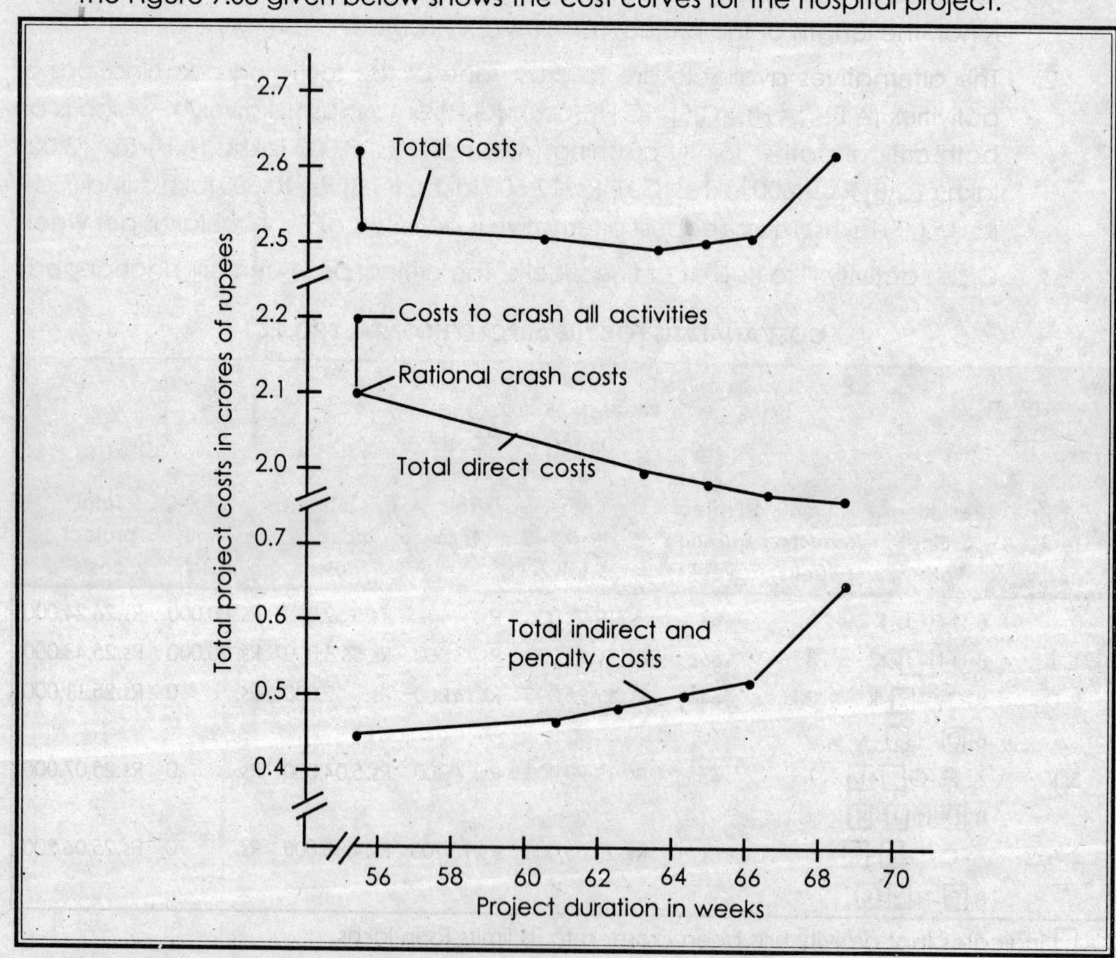

Fig. 9.08 Cost curves for the Appolo Hospital Project.

The curves consist of a series of straight-line segments because of the basic assumption that marginal costs are linear. In the analysis we stopped at 61 weeks, but one could continue crashing more activities (even though, total costs would have increased) until week 56 and plotted the costs along the way to get a better approximation of the cost curves in the range. Of course, one has no guarantee that the schedule so developed is the optional minimum-cost schedule.

RESOURCE LIMITATIONS

The project management models that we have faced so far consider only activity times in determining overall project duration and the critical path. Please recall yourself that an underlying assumption in the use of PERT/CPM is that sufficient resources will be available when needed to complete all project activities on schedule. However, developing schedules without considering the load placed on the resources use and even cause project delays if capacity limitations are exceeded.

For the purpose of our discussion, take into account the project represented by the project diagram in Fig. 9.09. Each of the fine activities involves a certain amount of the time and has a resource requirement. The critical path is A-B-E, and the total time to complete the project, ignoring resource limitations, is nine days.

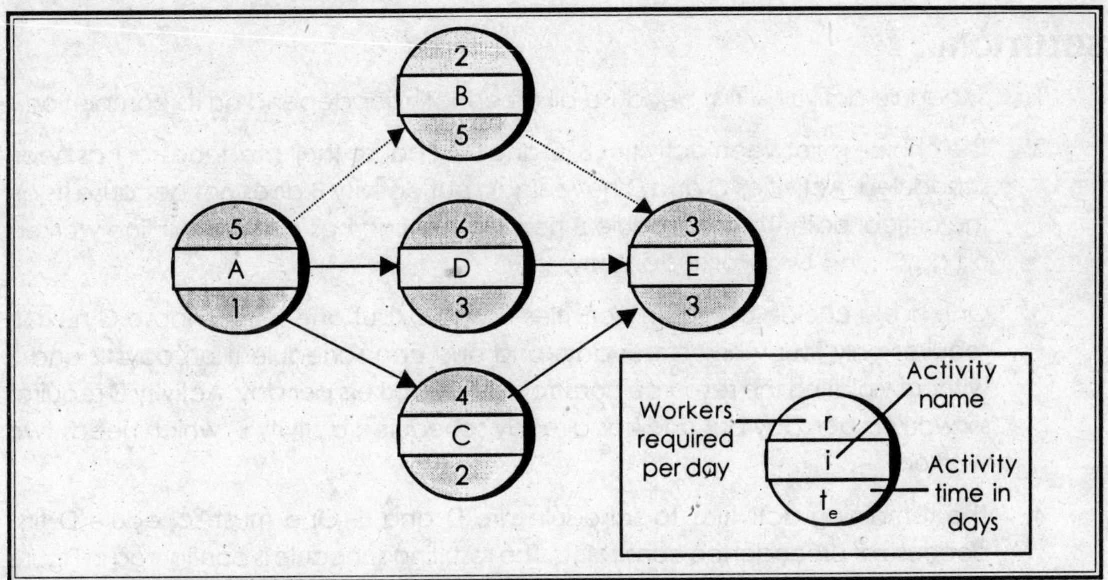

Fig. 9.09 Project Diagram showing Resource requirements and the critical path.

Although AON network diagrams are used for displaying an entire project and showing the precedence relationships between activities, they are not very useful for showing the implications of resource requirements for a schedule of activities. Gantt charts are more useful in this regard.

Since it is to generate a schedule that recognizes resource constraints, as well as the precedence relationships between activities, it is taken that the discussion is limited to a small number of workers per day. Although one could use an optimizing approach, such as linear programming to derive a schedule under these conditions a more useful approach in practice is to use a procedure such as one developed by **Mr. Weist** :

1. Start with the first day of the project and schedule as many activities as possible, considering precedence relationship and resource limitations. Continue with the second day and so on, until all activities are scheduled.
2. When several activities compete for the same resources give preference to the activities with the least slack as calculated using standard PERT/CPM methods.
3. Reschedule non-critical activities, if possible to free resources for critical or non-slack activities.

The intent of this procedure is to minimize total project time, subject to resource constraints.

ILLUSTRATION:

Generate a resource-constrained schedule for the project depicted in Fig 9:09. Assume that we have only six workers per day.

SOLUTION:

1. Schedule activity A first because all other activities depend on its completion.
2. The choice is between activities B, C and D because their predecessor has been scheduled. Activities C and D have slack, but activity B does not because its on the critical path. Thus, schedule B next. So far, one has committed fine workers on day 1 and two workers on days 2-6.
3. One has a choice between activities C and D, but one must choose C next. It requires only four workers per day, and one can schedule it on days 2 and 3 without violating the resource constraint of six workers per day. Activity D requires six workers per day but one has already scheduled activity B, which needs two workers.
4. The remaining activities to schedule are D and E. One must schedule D first because of precedence constraints. The resulting schedule is configured in Figure 9:10 as under.

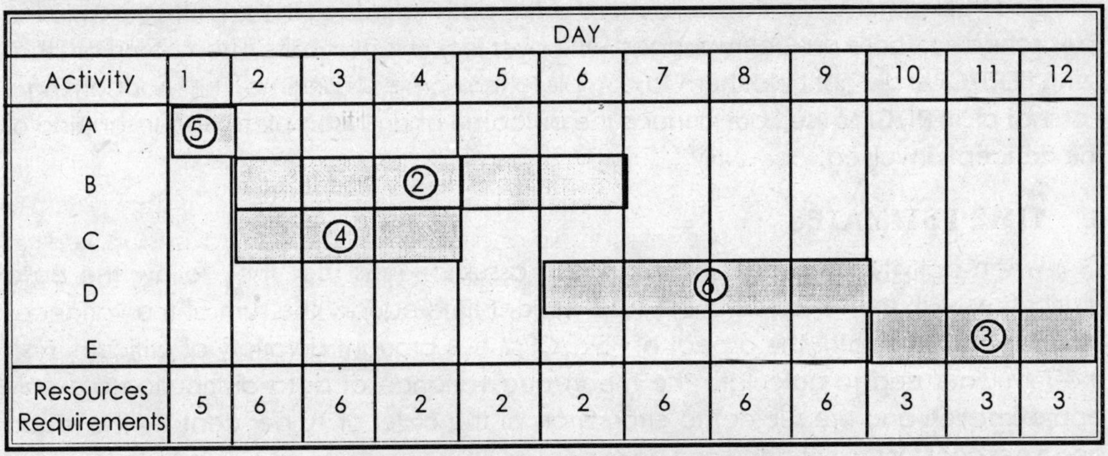

	DAY											
Activity	1	2	3	4	5	6	7	8	9	10	11	12
A	(5)											
B				(2)								
C			(4)									
D								(6)				
E											(3)	
Resources Requirements	5	6	6	2	2	2	6	6	6	3	3	3

Fig. 9.10 Resource-Constraint Schedule

This schedule results in the shortest project time possible under the resource constraints; however, the use of the procedure will not always be so successful. One can only say that it will generally produce solutions close to, but not necessarily, the optimum.

COMMENTS ON PERT/CPM SYSTEMS

Through out this chapter, an attempt has been made to highlight the benefits of PERT/CPM systems grant to the project managers. However, the limitations are also worth while to note before coming to a definite conclusion. The serious limitations are:

1. NETWORK DIAGRAMS

The methods used in PERT/CPM are founded on the assumption that the project activities having clear beginning and ending points can be identified. It is also assumed that activity sequence relationships can be identified at the start of the project and specified in a network diagram. However, these assumptions are very often too restrictive. For instance, one, one activity must be shown to precede the other in the PERT/CPM network diagram. In reality, two activities, where one must precede the other, often can be overlapped and worked on simultaneously upto a certain point. Further, project content can change, and a network diagram developed at the start of a project may later limit the project manager's flexibility to handle changing situations. At times, the actual precedence relationships can not be specified beforehand. That is, the sequences of some activities is contingent on the results of certain other activities, which cannot always be anticipated. In such situations, PERT/CPM methods may not be very useful.

2. CONTROL

The major underlying assumption in PERT/CPM methods is that the managers should focus on the activities along the critical path. However, the managers should also pay attention to near-critical paths as noted earlier. The reason is that these near-critical paths could easily become critical if one or more of the activities along these paths slips relative to its schedule. Those project managers who over look this possibility often complain that using PERT/CPM did not help them to complete their projects on time. This shortcoming is not that of PERT/CPM itself but rather is the outcome of an incomplete understanding of the concepts involved.

3. TIME ESTIMATES

When activity times are uncertain, the assumption is that they follow the beta distribution, with the variance of the total project time equally the sum of the variances along the critical path. This aspect of PERT/CPM has brought a variety of criticism. First, the formulae used to calculate the mean and variance of beta distribution are only approximation and are subject to error. Errors of the order of 10 per cent for the mean and 5 per cent for the variance can be expected. These errors could give incorrect critical paths. Secondly arriving at a single, accurate time estimate, let alone three, for any activity that has never been performed before, is very difficult. A single time-estimate-the most-likely time-is preferred by most of the project managers. They believe that pessimistic time estimates are often inflated and vary much more from the most-likely time estimate than do the optimistic time estimates. They argue strongly that some managers use these pessimistic time estimates as an excuse for failure perhaps, a more harmful by-product of inflated pessimistic time estimates is the inflation of expected activity times, which builds a cushion of slack into the schedule. Thirdly and finally, the choice of the beta distribution is somewhat arbitrary, and the use of another distribution would result in different expected times and variances for each activity.

In conclusion it can be said that though applications of PERT/CPM to project management has shortcomings, managers who have recognized these limitations of these methods have used them effectively. In fact, their shortcomings have not precluded widespread use of PERT/CPM methods all over the world.

CHAPTER APPENDIX

NORMAL DISTRIBUTION

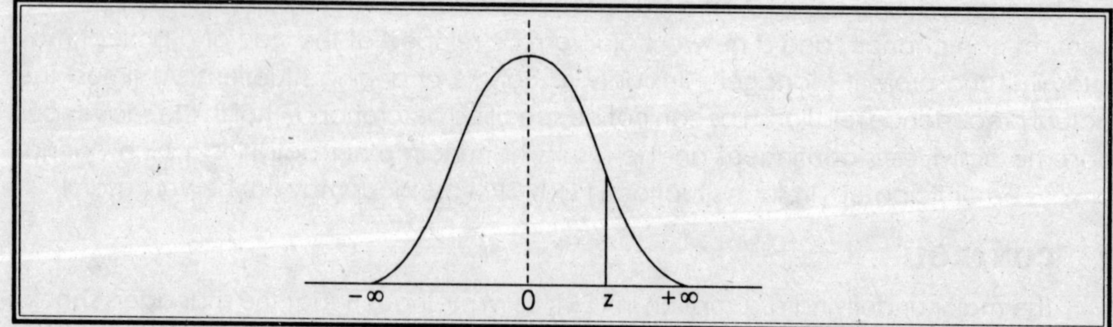

	.00	.01	.02	.03	.04	.05	.06	.07	.08	.09
.0	.5000	.5040	.5080	.5120	.5160	.5199	.5239	.5279	.5319	.5359
.1	.5398	.5438	.5478	.5517	.5557	.5596	.5636	.5675	.5714	.5753
.2	.5793	.5832	.5871	.5910	.5948	.5987	.6026	.6064	.6103	.6141
.3	.6179	.6217	.6255	.6293	.6331	.6368	.6406	.6443	.6480	.6517
.4	.6554	.6591	.6628	.6664	.6700	.6736	.6772	.6808	.6844	.6879
.5	.6915	.6950	.6985	.7019	.7054	.7088	.7123	.7157	.7190	.7224
.6	.7257	.7291	.7324	.7357	.7389	.7422	.7454	.7486	.7517	.7549
.7	.7580	.7611	.7642	.7673	.7704	.7734	.7764	.7794	.7823	.7852
.8	.7881	.7910	.7939	.7967	.7995	.8023	.8051	.8078	.8106	.8133
.9	.8159	.8186	.8212	.8238	.8264	.8289	.8315	.8340	.8365	.8389
1.0	.8413	.8438	.8461	.8485	.8508	.8531	.8554	.8577	.8599	.8621
1.1	.8643	.8665	.8686	.8708	.8729	.8749	.8770	.8790	.8810	.8830
1.2	.8849	.8869	.8888	.8907	.8925	.8944	.8962	.8980	.8997	.9015
1.3	.9032	.9049	.9066	.9082	.9099	.9115	.9131	.9147	.9162	.9177
1.4	.9192	.9207	.9222	.9236	.9251	.9265	.9279	.9292	.9306	.9319
1.5	.9332	.9345	.9357	.9370	.9382	.9394	.9406	.9418	.9429	.9441
1.6	.9452	.9463	.9474	.9484	.9495	.9505	.9515	.9525	.9535	.9545
1.7	.9554	.9564	.9573	.9582	.9591	.9599	.9608	.9616	.9625	.9633
1.8	.9641	.9649	.9656	.9664	.9671	.9678	.9686	.9693	.9699	.9706
1.9	.9713	.9719	.9726	.9732	.9738	.9744	.9750	.9756	.9761	.9767
2.0	.9772	.9778	.9783	.9788	.9793	.9798	.9803	.9808	.9812	.9817
2.1	.9321	.9826	.9830	.9834	.9838	.9842	.9846	.9850	.9854	.9857
2.2	.9861	.9864	.9868	.9871	.9875	.9878	.9881	.9884	.9887	.9890
2.3	.9893	.9896	.9898	.9901	.9904	.9906	.9909	.9911	.9913	.9916
2.4	.9918	.9920	.9922	.9925	.9927	.9929	.9931	.9932	.9934	.9936
2.5	.9938	.9940	.9941	.9943	.9945	.9946	.9948	.9949	.9951	.9952
2.6	.9953	.9955	.9956	.9957	.9959	.9960	.9961	.9962	.9963	.9964
2.7	.9965	.9966	.9967	.9968	.9969	.9970	.9971	.9972	.9973	.9974
2.8	.9974	.9975	.9976	.9977	.9977	.9978	.9979	.9979	.9980	.9981
2.9	.9981	.9982	.9982	.9983	.9984	.9984	.9985	.9985	.9986	.9986
3.0	.9987	.9987	.9987	.9988	.9988	.9989	.9989	.9989	.9990	.9990
3.1	.9990	.9991	.9991	.9991	.9992	.9992	.9992	.9992	.9993	.9993
3.2	.9993	.9993	.9994	.9994	.9994	.9994	.9994	.9995	.9995	.9995
3.3	.9995	.9995	.9995	.9996	.9996	.9996	.9996	.9996	.9996	.9997
3.4	.9997	.9997	.9997	.9997	.9997	.9997	.9997	.9997	.9997	.9998

CHAPTER BASED QUESTIONS

A. WRITE SHORT NOTES ON

1. Steps in project management
2. AOA approach
3. AON approach
4. PERT
5. CPM
6. Activity
7. Activity time
8. Critical path
9. Slack
10. Crash time
11. Normal distribution
12. Project costs

B. SHORT ANSWER QUESTIONS

1. what is describing a project ?
2. What is developing network mode ?
3. What is AON approach ?
4. What is AOA approach ?
5. What is critical path ?
6. What is activity slack ?
7. What is analyzing probabilities ?
8. What is normal distribution ?
9. What are cost and rescue considerations ?
10. What is crash times ?

C. ESSAY TYPE OF QUESTIONS

1. What are the steps in project management ?
2. What are AOA and AON approaches to networking ?
3. What is networking with PERT/CPM ?
4. What is scheduling? What are the ways of time scheduling ?
5. What are the merits and limitations of PERT/CPM methods ?

CHAPTER BASED PRACTICAL PROBLEMS

1. The following information is available about project 'Anta'

Activity	Immediate Predecessor/s	Time (Days)
A	–	2
B	–	5
C	A	3
D	A	4
E	B	4
F	B	3
G	C, D	2
H	D, E, F	6
I	G, H	4

Required : (a) Draw the network diagram for this project 'Anta'.

(b) Find the critical path.

2. The following information has been gathered for project 'Aadi'.

Activity	Time (week/s)	Immediate Predecessor/s
A	5	–
B	10	A
C	3	A
D	6	A, C
E	10	B, C
F	2	E, D

Required : (a) Draw the network diagram

(b) Calculate the slack for each activity and determine the critical path. How long will the project 'Aadi' take ?

3. Consider the following information in case of project 'Quit'

Activity	Time (week/s)	Immediate Predecessor/s
A	2	–
B	3	–
C	6	–

D	1	A, B
E	3	B
F	7	D, C
G	7	E, C
H	11	F, G

Required : (a) Draw the network diagram for this project

(b) Specify the critical path/s

(c) Calculate the total slack for activities A and D

(d) What happens to the slack for D if A takes five weeks ?

(4) The construction crew of Fine Builders must frame in a new house. The following data are available for the project.

Activity	Immediate Predecessor/s	Time (Days)	Workers Required (Per day)
A	–	2	2
B	–	3	6
C	A	2	4
D	B	4	3
E	C, D	3	5

Required : (a) Draw the network diagram for the project.

(b) Disregarding capacity limitations, determine the projects critical path and duration.

(c) What is the slack for each activity ?

(d) Only six construction workers are available each day. Use the Weist's procedure to find a new schedule and draw a Gantt chart for it.

(i) What is the critical path in this schedule ?

(ii) How long will the project take now ?

(5) A crew of linemen for Bell Telephone Company must install some cable in a rural area. The following data are available for the project.

Activity	Immediate Predecessor/s	Time (Days)	Crew-members required (Per day)
A	–	2	9
B	A	3	6

C	A	5	3
D	A	3	5
E	D	4	4
F	B, C, E	1	7

Required : (a) Disregarding capacity informations, determine the critical path and calculate slack for each activity. How long will the project take ?

(b) Suppose that there are only nine crew members. Use Weists' procedure to find a schedule that does not exceed nine workers per day on the project. Draw a chart for your schedule.

(i) What is the critical path now ?

(ii) What are the slack's for each activity ?

(iii) How long will it take to complete the project now ?

(6) Your company has just received an order for a specially designed electric motor from a good customer. Nonetheless, the contract states that starting on the thirteenth day from now your firm will experience a penalty of Rs. 100 per day if the job is not completed. Indirect project cost amount to Rs. 200 per day. The data on direct costs and activity precedence relationships are given below:

Activity	Normal Time (days)	Normal Cost	Crash Time (days)	Crash Cost	Immediate Predecessor/s
A	4	Rs.1,000	3	Rs.1,300	None
B	7	Rs.1,400	4	Rs.2,000	None
C	5	Rs.2,000	4	Rs.2,700	None
D	6	Rs.1,200	5	Rs.1,400	A
E	3	Rs. 900	2	Rs.1,100	B
F	11	Rs.2,500	6	Rs.3,750	C
G	4	Rs. 800	3	Rs.1,450	D, E
H	3	Rs. 300	1	Rs. 500	F, G

Required : (a) Draw the project network diagram.

(b) What completion date would you recommend?

(7) The following information relates to a new project your company is undertaking.

Activity	Immediate Predecessor/s	Time (Days)
A	–	11
B	–	10
C	A, B	8
D	A, B	6
E	A, B	7
F	C, E	15
G	C, D	4
H	G	9
I	F, G	5
J	E, G	8
K	I, J	10

Required : (a) Draw the network diagram for the project

(b) Determine the critical path and project completion time

* * * * *

Chapter 10

PROJECT MANAGEMENT FUNCTIONS PART-1

- WHAT IS A 'SYSTEM' AND 'PROCEDURE'
- FEATURES OF A SYSTEM
- DESIGN OF SYSTEMS
- SYSTEMS AND PROCEDURE PLAN
- PROJECT DIRECTION
- PROJECT INITIATION / STARTUP PERIOD
- DURING PRODUCTION PERIOD
- PROJECT CONTROL
- CHAPTER BASED QUESTIONS

BACKDROP

In project planning and organization, there are thousands of variables both human and non-human. The only way to fight the large uncertainties generated by such a large varieties is to develop sound systems and procedures. These sound systems and procedures reduce not only enormous varieties but also regulate largely themselves helping to reduce the manager's task. Absence systems would only lead to further chaos and unwanted results. The main task of manager to design systems and procedures and to manage through them for his benefit and the benefit of the organization. Hence, this chapter is reserved to cover the discussion on systems and procedures as a part of project management and the functions of project direction and control. The chapter ends with the Chapter Based Questions.

WHAT IS A 'SYSTEM' AND 'PROCEDURE'

A business 'system' refers to the total picture of men, machines, materials and paperwork involved in implementing any phase of a project. For instance, purchasing system of an organization involves purchase officers, vendors or suppliers, materials, specification, general purpose conditions and purchase order. On the other hand, 'procedure' is a planned sequence of operations for carrying out a recovering work involved in a system uniformly and consistently. In the purchase system, procedures need to be developed for short-listing suppliers, issuing an enquiry to them, evaluation of offer, and finally placing an order.

Procedure is a sequence of operations in performing a particular business activity. Procedures are plans in that they establish a customary method of handling the business activities. A procedure is one prescribing manner or method by which the work is to be performed. It is a planned sequence of operations for handling recurring business activities uniformly and consistently.

FEATURES OF A SYSTEM

Any system to be called so has its own features. These are:

1. IT IS A COMPLEX OF ELEMENTS :

A system is made up of number of parts or elements. A system constitutes a finite number of elements. If a particular system repeats; the occurrence of its elements will also be repeated.

2. WELL ORGANIZED ELEMENTS :

The arrangement of elements is so scientific, the orderliness of arrangement or pattern is obvious. The pattern is likely to be repeated if the system is repeated.

3. INTERRELATED ELEMENTS :

Each element has its own individual function to perform yet it makes other elements to perform because of interrelation. That is, absence of one element in a system disables another if the latter depends for its input on the output of the former.

4. **SELF-SUFFICIENT ORGANIC WHOLE :**

A system has an output with a use value. The constituent elements do produce outputs and they have no any use value outside the system and cannot stand on their own. That is, only a system produces an output that can serve as an output to another system. When a system serves as an input to another system, it can be considered to be the sub-system of a bigger system.

5. **OWN BEHAVIOUR PATTERN :**

In a system, individual elements lose their identity and seek to adjust, cooperate and act or react with the environment collectively in pursuance of a common goal.

6. **IT IS HIERARCHICAL :**

An individual human being who is the embodiment of a bio-logical system belongs to a family, the family belongs to a society and the society belongs to a nation. Thus while at a micro-level a system consists of elements, at a macro-level a system maybe only an elemental system of a larger system constituted by several such systems.

DESIGN OF SYSTEMS

There are three important steps involved in designing any business system namely

1. Conceive the total physical system and its natural modules
2. Identifications of connection between the modules
3. Development of control system using information as the media has been developed for self control as well as forced control of the total project. The points to be borne in mind are: (a) The system must be natural as possible (b) The system must be information bound (c) The system should accommodate for external intervention because a system works when there is least outside interference.

Hence, project management system consists of "Project work system" and "Project control system".

SYSTEMS AND PROCEDURE PLAN

The last phase of the project of the project execution plan deals with the systems and the procedures. As project management calls for organizations of disorganized work forces, a heavy emphasis is placed on routine systems and procedures so that no intervention is required in the day-to-day operation of a system. Hence, there are atleast eight routine sub-systems of project management for which appropriate procedures can be thought of right at the start of the project implementation. These are: contract management, configuration management, time management, cost management, fund management, materials management, man management and communications management.

1. CONTRACTS MANAGEMENT

Contracts provide us with a way of making agreements that can be depended upon. Contracts are binding agreements between two or more parties. The terms of contract are not only binding but enforceable by the legal system and the courts of law. The management of contracts needs a definite procedure.

1. Prequalification procedure.
2. General conditions of contract.
3. Tendering procedure.
4. Procedure for tender evaluation and award of a contract.
5. Procedure for signing an agreement.
6. Measurement procedure for completed work.
7. Billing and payment procedure.
8. Free issue materials reconciliation procedure.
9. Change order procedure.
10. Work inspection and acceptance procedure.
11. Completed work-take-over procedure.

2. CONFIGURATION MANAGEMENT

Configuration management stands for the efforts made to maintain the integrity of the project in terms of aims, objectives and physical configuration as finalized before the zero date of the project. In this connection the following procedure may be developed.

1. Procedure for finalization of project scope in terms of work breakdown structure.
2. Procedure for the finalization of basic engineering packages.
3. Procedure for finalization on engineering design basis.
4. Equipment numbering and control procedure.
5. Drawing numbering and control procedure.
6. Design revision procedure.
7. Value engineering procedure.
8. Design change control procedure.
9. Vendor drawing approval procedure.
10. Quality assurance and inspection procedure.
11. Technical audit procedure for the completed plant.

3. COMMUNICATION MANAGEMENT

Perhaps, communication is the most vital link in the whole scheme of project management. The procedures related to communication do not refer to mere correspondence; instead the entire package of interaction between the different agencies and individual is encompassed. Speaking managerially, communication refers to the information flow that leads to control, self-control. The procedure concerning communication management can be:

1. Procedure for correspondence and distribution of mail.
2. Filing procedure
3. Reporting procedure.
4. Procedure for meeting and recording minutes of meetings.
5. Procedure for data logging
6. Project newsletter and general information procedure.
7. Procedure for making presentations
8. Procedure for project workshops.
9. Control-room maintenance procedure .
10. Suggestion scheme.

4. MAN MANAGEMENT SYSTEM

Rather the most complex sub-system is that of man management system. Man management covers the vast area of man power selection and till the retaining the party for a longer time in the organization for mutual benefit. The procedures for this sub-system can be:

1. Man power requirement forecasting procedure.
2. Procedure for requisitioning man-power
3. Recruiting or recruitment procedure.
4. Procedure for training or organization of project staff.
5. Procedure for role analysis and goal setting
6. Procedure for performance evaluation.
7. Procedure for delegation of authority
8. Counselling procedure.
9. Procedure for staff mobilization and demobilization.
10. Procedure for establishing a new site.

5. TIME MANAGEMENT

Time management is management of project time. The procedures for time management do not refer only to schedule development. Planning, scheduling, monitoring and control together constitute the total system of time management. Hence, procedures for time management are to address to all these areas. Such procedures can be:

1. Procedure for preparation of WBS, work load assessment and numbering of work packages.
2. Procedure for development of project schedules including estimation of resources.
3. Procedure for progress measurement.
4. Procedure for project review.
5. Procedure for revision of project schedules.
6. Procedure for obtaining feedback and updating of schedules.
7. Procedure for reporting.
8. Procedure for management evaluation of bids to assess capability of vendors/ contractors to adhere to schedules.
9. Procedure for management audit.
10. Procedure for work tracking and day-to-day follow-up.

6. MATERIALS MANAGEMENT

Material management is very significant sub-system for any industrial project. The aim is to supply the right type of materials, in right quantity, in right time, from right source at right price. The procedures required for effective material management are many. A standard set of procedures can be:

1. Equipment numbering procedure.
2. Vendor qualification procedure.
3. Procedure for obtaining DGTD clearance and import licence.
4. General conditions of purchase.
5. Obtaining procedure includes repeat orders and change orders.
6. Purchase order numbering procedure.
7. Quality assurance and inspection procedure.
8. Vendors evaluation procedure.
9. Custom clearance procedure.
10. Packing, marking and dispatching procedures.
11. Insurance and claims procedure
12. Warehouse management procedure.

13. Billing and payment procedure.
14. Material status reporting procedure.
15. Bulk material control procedure.
16. Expediting procedure.

7. COST MANAGEMENT

Cost management is the completion of project management triple constraint of cost, schedule and the scope. The objective of this sub-system is to ensure that the project is complete within the original cost approved. Effective cost management needs a set of procedures which is given below.

1. Project cost estimation procedure.
2. Cost coding and cost accumulation procedure.
3. Procedure for cost updating and revision.
4. Procedure for man-hour control.
5. Procedure for value engineering and ongoing cost reductions.
6. Procedure for price evaluation of bids.
7. Procedure for commitment control.
8. Procedure for change control.
9. Procedure for cost reporting.
10. Procedure for project cost review.
11 Procedure for expenditure control.
12 Procedure for cost and production audits.

8. FUND MANAGEMENT

This sub-system is of top importance to vendors and contractors who have problem with working capital. They need a meticulous planning, monitoring and controlling cash-flow to avoid project coming to a halt and weakening of it. Effective management of funds needs a definite set of procedures that guarantees easy, smooth and even flow of cash in the organization. These are:

1. Procedure for the finalization of expenditure budget.
2. Procedure for forecasting fund requirement.
3. Procedure for mobilization of funds.
4. Procedure for opening letter of credit.
5. Procedure for securing advance payments.
6. General terms of payment.
7. Procedure for processing payment requests.

8. Fund control procedure.
9. Procedure for expenditure audits.
10. Procedure for requisition and approval of additional funds.

PROJECT DIRECTION

In fact, a project faces a rough weather in the beginning and it loses a sufficiently long time before the project reaches any sign of stability. The project execution system should depend more on external intervention for its survival than its internal self-regulating capability, till it acquires stability. As the project enters the area of stability, the need for external intervention reduces or may be therein weakened position. The external intervention takes three forms namely, direction, coordination and control. Here, we are to touch only project direction and project control. However, a reference to coordination cannot be ruled out because these direction, coordination and control are not independent but inter-dependent managerial functions. To have exact picture of these functions, one should have the management efforts schedule given in fig. 10.01

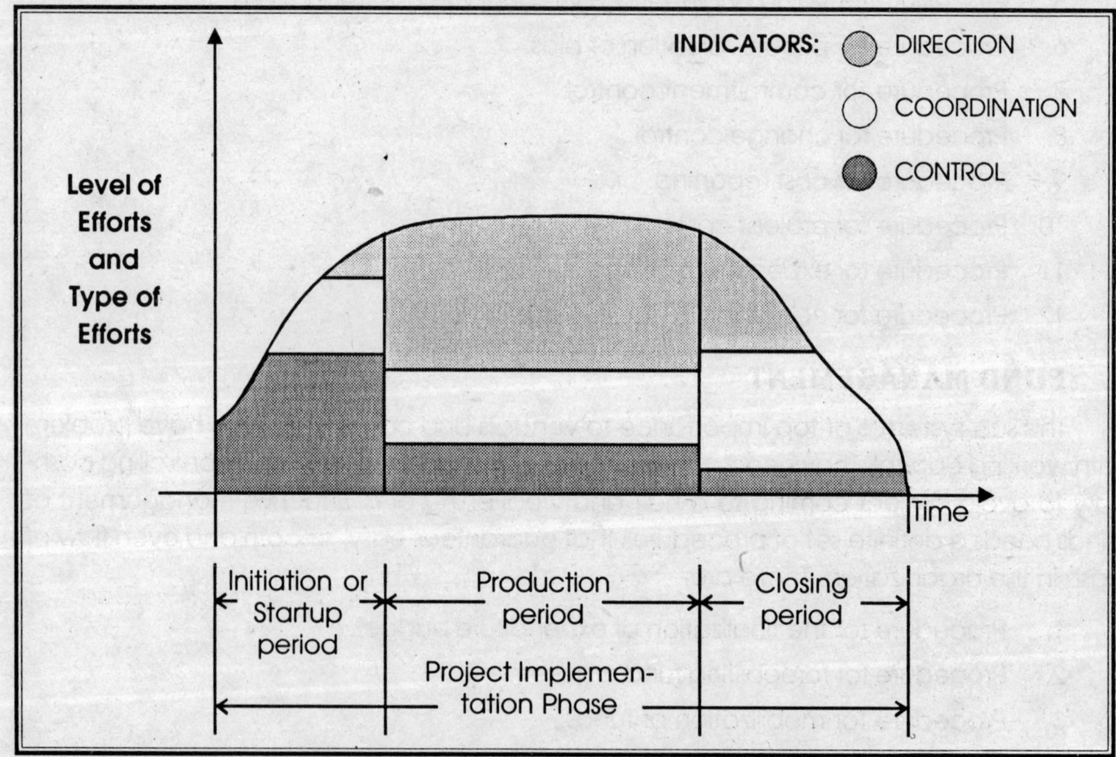

Fig. 10.01 Management Effort Schedule

From the above diagram three different periods during the implementation phase of a project. Initiation or startup period, production period and closing period. The initiation period requires good deal of direction and coordination with little or no control. However, when project enters stable production period, the need for direction reduces considerably and the coordination and control aspects of management gain good ground over direction. The direction dimension of management leans into insignificance during the closing period of the implementation phase. Similarly, the need for control reduces sizeably during that period, thus leaving coordination to play a leading role heading towards results. It means that though each function is important, each has its own role to play at different stages of the implementation phase.

PROJECT DIRECTION stands for the use of the authority to channelize the activities of the project on desired lines. As plans and schedules prescribe what is desirable for time control of project authorizing them for implementation constitutes project direction towards time control. When schedules are so authorized, they become working documents and depending on the importance attached to them, can even become work orders. The executive agencies or the individuals will be then compelled to strictly follow the plans and schedules. Plans and schedules may not go into work and scheduling system may change into superfluous paper-work. That is, mere development of plans, systems and procedures, will not produce better results unless they are authorized for implementation. Let us examine the role of direction at each stage of implementation phase.

PROJECT INITIATION / STARTUP PERIOD

The need for project direction is the maximum possible at this period. This period starts soon after the issue of the project charter. During this period, the project manager has to take actions for successful launching of the project. Since project charter is one that gives broad scope lacking meticulous details, everything is hazy at startup point. Therefore, every one turns to project manager for his direction. Hence, a project manager has to provide directions relating to :

1. The scope of work.
2. Specification of results of the completed work.
3. Basis of work.
4. Division of work- as to imported versus indigenous, departmental versus contract.
5. Schedule of work.
6. Budget for work.
7. Systems and procedures for work.
8. Coordination of work.
9. Authority and accountability for work.
10. Control of work.

These can be given a 'formal' and 'informal' way. 'Formal' way takes the shape of project manual while the second one the project kick of meeting or project workshop.

Project kick-off meeting is preferable as it is participative than authoritative because process success depends on team-work. The finalization of the gamut of work, budgets, schedule and other relevant items is generally initiated at a project kick-off meeting. This meeting with the participants provides project manager to present what he wants and clears the doubts of the participants and the team members have. Once clarifications are made, the participants are asked to draw up a detailed workout and assess information inputs, resources and the efforts needed for completing the work under their focus. This kick-off meeting may be followed by a workshop where the overall project schedule, project execution plan and the systems and the procedures may be finalized after a thorough examination of the plus and minus points. A document distribution matrix may be prepared listing all the key control documents and their review, approval and distribution. These documents are the directions for work when issued through project managers memo. In short, kick-off meeting and startup workshop activities includes:

1. Coordination of the project requirements and that of participating agencies
2. Establishment of directives and controls
3. Team building and
4. Communication

During the project initiation period, direction means not simply giving a push to the project. In fact, the directions shape the destiny of the project. It is so because direction is at this stage are really crucial for the success of the project. Hence, only experienced and pretty senior managers are asked to handle this phase of project. The reason is if the project receives good guidance during its infancy, it can stand on its own at later stage. Even the outside consultants are approached. However, it is better to think twice before going for consultants.

DURING PRODUCTION PERIOD

Direction during the last phase mostly concentrates on establishing the baselines for the project performance. Here after the form of direction undergoes a change. This becomes one of administrative direction because the direction is provided on case to case basis, through formal documents or personal contacts, even group meetings are held. This direction refers to the approval of work schedule, detailed budgets, specification, purchase orders, work orders, construction drawings tranets, miscellaneous expenses, changes in baselines and so on.

Project start up, design reviews, purchase order and work orders, are one time directions. However, a project requires continuous directions till its completion. In case the system and procedure work well, then the directions are required only when unforeseen events occur. Otherwise, directions are required as and when the problems arise during the project execution. In either case, a decision has to be made as to what should be done, and same should be authorized for implementation. That is, decision-makings and directions are part of day-to-day functions of a Project manager. The routine decision involves five steps:

1. Understanding the decision environment.
2. Establishing the decision alternatives.
3. Evaluation of alternatives and selection of course of action
4. Communicating the decision to the individual or the agency who is to implement the decision.
5. Checking up if the decision is working so that the decision could be steered by the consequence.

The identification of problems and providing direction by following the five steps is done through **project review meetings** which are half weekly or monthly on regular basis. To get the best, it is essential to fix up the agenda and the frequency well achieved to facilitate good deal of homework on the part of the participants. A project review meeting is for the project team. Engineers, vendors, contractors, could all participate in these meetings. However, every one cannot participate in the same meeting for the known reasons. It is because contractors meet at site, vendors at vendor's work site, engineers meet at owner's office. That is why, the agenda in various review meetings will be different. Generally, a review meeting discusses:

1. Status of implementation of the decisions taken in the previous meeting.
2. Progress attained during the review period vis-a-vis agreed targets.
3. Problems.
4. Decisions regarding the problems.
5. Agreed action programme and progress target upto the next review meeting.

The minutes issued after the meeting are the direction till next review meeting. Those who have not attended the meeting for one reason or the other, the next day they get the instructions in writing. To get much of these meetings, there is need for effective communication system.

PROJECT CONTROL

If one looks at the chart of management efforts schedule (Fig. 10.01) it is clear that role of control is least in the startup period, while it is maximum in the production period and goes on diminishing in the this period of closing period of implementation. The project control consists of two parts namely, 1. Establishment of controls and 2. Ongoing controlling activities using the controls so established.

The first part is done using WBS, organization, contracts, schedules, budgets systems, and procedures and authorizing their implementation. This is completed during the initiation period of the project. Now we need to concentrate on how one should control a project. When it enters, the production period using the controls so established during the initiation period.

The fundamental objective with those involved in execution of the project or the work volume, that is it should get completed in time, within the cost and performance as per specifications which can be called as collateral objectives. The secondary objectives are sometimes looked after by persons other than those who are directly involved in execution. This necessitates multi-level control to control the project. How controls could be exercised during the production period is our immediate concern. This can be progress or scope control, schedule control and cost control. All these need four steps namely,

1. Setting targets for what is expected to be achieved.
2. Measurement of what is happening, anticipation of what may happen.
3. Comparison between what should happen and what is happening or likely to happen.
4. Taking corrective actions to make things happen as they are expected.

I PROGRESS/ SCOPE CONTROL

As the fundamental aim is to complete the project, a given project must be completed cent-percent not less nor more. However, it happens rarely. Hence, deviations are found in terms of time, cost and performance. Hence there is need for control. The basis of progress control is the control of the task which occur at the last level of the work breakdown structure. It goes without saying that completion of tasks lead to next higher level of work and finally the whole project. By ensuring completion of the tasks, the completion of the project can be ensured.

Progress control commences with the establishment of a task list. Every agency is asked to submit a task list in a standard format. The total quantum of work and efforts to be put in will be arrived at once the tasks are closed to complete the project. This list acts as a means of functional control scope control to take stock of what has been completed and yet to be completed. The list is used to prevent inclusions of unauthorized work that affects the progress of the work, cost and time of completion. This is done through "work order" or "change order procedure". A task list spells out the scope of the work which has to be approved and approved list becomes a work-order.

Not all the tasks can be measured by the same unit of measure as tasks have different milestones of advancement. This brings in complexity for measuring as to how much should be done and how much has been done. Individually for each task and for tasks of similar type there is no problem. The problem crops up when one attempts to aggregate the progress of tasks of different types, trades and complexities. One easy way to overcome this problem is to ease WBS as the overall frame-work for progress aggregation and assign weightage to each WBS level in proportion to cost contribution each level has towards the total installed cost of the project. Thus, the actual percentage of progress indicates whether a task has been completed in full or how much of it is yet to be completed. A comparison of progress figures of successive months will indicate whether a task is making any progress or not. Further, comparison between scheduled progress and actual progress will reveal what the gap is and how much effort is needed to make up the gap by a given date. The rate of progress enables one to forecast the probable date of task completion with or without additional resources.

The process through which program is ensured in expediting or follow up. To expedite is to help the progress of something. However, progress does not flow by merely asking for it or putting pressure to hasten things. Formal expediting of a project is done through project review or coordination meetings. These are weekly meetings, reviewing the reasons for the gaps in progress expected, to take stock of future work and resource availability for ensuring expected progress. Though expediting is a project management function and is required in all phases of project and for all aspects of work, one group of people which engages in expediting vendors for timely manufacture and supply of requirements are alone designated as expediting engineers.

Progressing of equipment and materials requires a knowledge of the construction requirements. Supply progress must be adequate to support construction progress. Same way processing of drawings requires knowledge of the procurement and construction requirements and engineering progress should support procurement and construction progress. Thus, for progressing any phase the requirement of the subsequent phases must be known so that the progress attained in the preceding phases can support the progress required in the succeeding phases. In alternative words, the progress in each phase is to be in balance. Thus, requirement for balance in progress is not so clear, while progressing a project at a lower level. However, when the progress of the entire project is viewed, this balance or lack of it, becomes, the main issue for progressing a project. Again, progress control at lower levels concentrates on the gaps between progress committed and program actually attained, the same has no meaning at higher levels. A higher levels what would cause concern at any time is the case where the actual progress in any phase of the project falls short of the minimum required to support the current feasible progress at the down stream phases and the project as a whole.

Thus, for progress review at higher levels of management, it is but essential to know as to what progress is required in a particular phase of a project to keep the project moving at the desired rate of progress. This is achieved through line of balance (LOB). Thus, progress control is not merely demanding and persuading for progress. It requires setting of progress targets, identification of problems, review for solutions and eventual implementation of the solution evolved. That is, the aim is to achieve not only scheduled progress but much wanted balanced progress.

II PERFORMANCE CONTROL

Any project on completion must perform. Failure of the project to come up in time or budget get may be condoned, but failure to perform will never be tolerated. That is why, project management people are criticised not only, for time and cost overrun, but also for non- performance. Performance control, like progress control, requires continuous monitoring during the production phase. This is preceded by right specifications, selection of right vendors or contractors and above all right contractual stipulations regarding warranties and guarantees. The warranty, specifies in this regard, the quality of performance, the purchases has a right to rely on. The guarantee concerns as to what will be done by the seller, controller or manufacturer in the event when goods are found defective or do not meet certain standards of performance. The warranty normally deals with a of specific period of time and performance and this is what the purchaser bargains and pays for. The guarantee is what the contractors or vendors are obligated to do when they do not live up to the warranty's specifications. Put in other words, a guarantee is liquidated damage clause that refers to broken warranties. A guarantee costs the seller or the contractor or the manufacturer money or its equivalent in material parts or services. However, a project can not simply depend on the supplier's warranties and guarantees. Because of project slippage, the warranty period may expire before project completion. What the owner may get in terms of liquidated damages would be a poor compensation for the perpetual headache caused by a non performing plant. Therefore, ongoing performance control is a must.

Performance control starts with the identification of performance parameters. The performance parameters which are critical for viability of the project must be established first in clear terms. Then, output is one performance parameter. Hence, raw materials and power consumption per unit can be others. The design and specification must be made to meet these performance requirements. The subsequent stages of project execution- such as ordering and manufacturer- must ensure that these requirements are not traded off for some other short-term benefits. That is, a single performance parameter runs through the stages of project execution till the final performance guarantees and confirms the achievement of performance. The concept of line of balance is used with advantage of performance control. It is understood that if production falls short of the line of balance, the equipment or the unit in question will limit production of the entire plant. Such an equipment or unit is a bottle-neck and any attempt to remove this after the plant is commissioned is double bottle-necking operation. Contrary to this, if the equipment has the capacity above the line of balance it adds unwants only to the cost of plant without improving the overall performance of the plant.

One can impose control limits like upper control limit (UCL) and lower control limit (LCL) on releasing that it is not possible to stay exactly on the line of balance. The line of balance for performance may again be upset during the ordering stage. It is known that the item could not be purchased unless its minimum guaranteed performance matches with the line of balance. However, when standard items having performance in excess of minimum requirement are only available in the market, it is natural that stringent inspection and guarantee clauses are responsible for increase the cost in purchase of such items. Thus, performance control may lead to reduced cost of purchase contrary to the general apprehension of increase in cost for giving attention to performance.

Though the line of balance keeps track of perform of individual pieces of equipment the performance of the whole project is dependent on the integrated performance of the whole performance all these individual equipment. Put in other words, it is the system of equipment or the configuration as a whole whose performance is important for the project. Hence, any minor change in pieces of equipment reduces the entire configuration irrelevant or reduce its performance. Any change in specification by engineering or any request for change in the same during ordering or manufacture is to be reserved from all angles well before clearance is given. The first basic principle for control of change is that all changes must be notified. None should be allowed to make any change without prior notice. Such unauthorized changes can be traced through quality assurance plan. This plan ensures faithful translation of designs and specifications of the product. On the other hand, quality control rejects a product that fails to confirm to the specification. At design stage, however it is the periodic design review meeting that are to check and ensure that no changes have been made. Sometimes, however changes for better. Hence, change system or change control system should record these changes, examine them from all possible angles - time, cost and performance and later on authorize them for implementation. A formal change control system needs that a written change notices are eased to all those who are affected or likely to be affected by such changes. It is also necessary that all changed orders are logged properly. This enables identification of the source of change, assess cumulative cost of changes incurred on the project. Change orders can also serve as defence records to save the skin of a project manager.

Performance finally has to be built into a product during manufacturing stage. In addition to guarantee, vendors are asked to submit a detailed quality assurance plan at the building stage itself. Such a plan with the activities to be examined by the quality control group of the vendor and other documentation to be maintained for reason by the owner's inspectors or their party inspection agencies. The owner's quality control agency visits the vendor's shop on the vendor's call for inspection of equipment and machinery at its various stages of manufacture according to the agreed quality assuarance plan. The inspection agency cheers for adequecy of technical documentats, adherence to prescribed qualification procedure, adoption of good manufacturing practices and compliance with emerging standards and specifications during visits. The inspection agency has the authority to stop execution in case of non-performance. The inspection agency releases an item for despatch only when all the necessary condition for performance are fulfilled.

III SCHEDULE CONTROL

Schedule control ensures adherence to the greed time schedule for the project. Schedule has to be used as the basis for direction, communication, coordination and progress control. In other words, schedule and scheduling systems are inseparable part of project execution. Progress control is possible through use of input schedules and scheduling system. The emphasis is on converting all available inputs into outputs by taking commitments from the working groups. As input for one working group is to come from another output group, all the groups have to progress in a desired way in an integrated manner. Uneven or imbalanced process will be the cause for project delay. It is also possible that working group might achieve say 99 per cent progress and the project completion gets delayed just because a single input is not ready. Hence, monitoring and the control of project and its time becomes a must in addition to the progress control to ensure adherence to project schedule. There can be two types of schedule control.

Schedule control starts with the forecast of project completion activity In case the forecast indicates that project completion requirements are going to be met, no action is initiated. This forecast is to be provided to the controlling authority in the form of a feedback report. In case the forecast indicates that the project completion date may not be met, immediate investigations are ordered to trace out the ways and means of bringing the project back to schedule. Completion forecasts, unless mathematically worked by an independent and competent monitoring staff, tend to give a rosy picture. In such cases, it is good thing to keep close watch on areas which generally delay a project and take all possible steps to make sure that delays do not occur. It implies that project management can use past experience of same nature to forecast vulnerable areas and act in advance instead of reacting to the forecasts of completion dates of the present project.

In ground realities, there are certain areas where delay occurs invariably after the zero date. Hence, project manager is to consider carefully the following areas to prevent possible delays. These are:

- Building up of project team.
- Finalization of Engineering designs, parameters, standards, extent of automation and spare philosophy.
- Finalisation of project execution strategy covering work packages division list for purchase, short-list of vendors and contractors, purchase and contract

procedures, overall schedules, budget, overall project layout and project coordination procedure.

- Finalisation of the task lists and operating level schedules.
- Bid document for turnkey packages.
- Import licence.
- Ordership cycle.
- Site infrastructural facilities.
- Receipt of vendor charges.
- Release of funds from financial institutions.
- Payment to vendors and contractors.
- Delivery of equipment and materials.
- Mobilisation of resources by contractors.
- Shipment of equipment and materials to site.
- Commissioning.

This list is likely to increase.

On going schedule control at the project level has to be done at three stages – project control, preventive schedule control and predictive schedule control.

Progress Control is to be exercised almost daily at the operating level where inputs or outputs are produced. It uses input output schedules as its basis.

Preventive Schedule Control is exercised at the project manager's level on daily basis. It uses the past experience on projects of similar nature and level two schedules as the basis.

Predictive Schedule Control is exercised both at the project manager's level and at corporate management level. Here, project completion forecasts are worked out through the use of feedback reports and network analyses as the base. The forecasts are discussed at project review meetings held each month at project manager's level and once in three months at corporate level. To ensure correct completion forecasts available at project revision meetings, outside monitoring agencies are appointed for management audit. A comprehensive project management audit covers scope audit, cost audit, systems and procedure audit and schedule audit. A schedule audit studies progress achieved vis-a-vis time of balance, float consumption trend, project completion outlook and identify the areas of concern and make recommendations. Such audit also highlights the delayed activities and comment on the reasons for delay. Wherever a project reviews its funds from the financial institutions, schedule control is achieved by linking fund disbursement to receipt of funds.

IV COST CONTROL

In the final analysis, it is the cost which reflects performance in all areas. It is obvious that a well managed project incurs least cost. In case the project cost is brought down without compromising on the parameters that make a project to perform, it is the case of excellent cost management. Hence, cost control is not merely a cost accounting to expenditures to budget. Its aim is to monitor all cost components and to ensure completion of the project at an optimal cost. Cost reduction budgeting without lowering the performance is cost control in real sense.

Ongoing cost control is the aim to control or reduce cost of work during any phase of the project to irreducible minimum. Each revised cost estimate is to be treated only as revised forecast of the total project cost. As all the forecast are for the things yet to happen, the extent to which the future events are manipulated will decide the final cost. Hence cost control refers to the manupulative efforts during the various phases of project for reducing costs not yet incurred.

Basically, the elements of costs are 'hardware', software' and "time induced". Hardware costs can be controlled through design and engineering. The software and time induced costs can be controlled through control systems and procedures. Software costs are forming very small part of the total costs. In case of time-induced costs, effective schedules and monitoring alone will help. Hardware cost control is to start before zero date of the project. It starts with the finalisation of the project design basis which is the starting point for conceptual design of the project. The different stages for ongoing cost control through design and engineering are:

- Finalisation of design basis.
- Finalisation of system design/ basic package.
- Issue of purchase/ tender specifications.
- Issue of purchase order / work contract.
- Review of vendor drawings.
- Issue of construction drawings.

These steps are broadly termed as "Value engineering effort".

Value engineering is not a cost control effort but when one looks at it as an ongoing effort for keeping unnecessary costs out it becomes a cost control effort as far as plant hardwares are concerned.

COST CONTROL METHODS

The cost control methods which can be used at different stages of the project for cost control are briefly explained.

A. AT ZERO DATE

On the basis of finalised basic package an itemised control estimate is prepared. Using the net-work plan, the control estimate is connected into cash-flow plan and annual or quarterly budgets. These control estimates and budgets provide onward control of commitment and expenditure.

B. DURING DETAILED ENGINEERING

The control estimate prepared before the zero date is soon overrun unless design and engineering procedures are constantly renviewed. Here, value engineering approach comes to help through overall plot plan, specifications of plant and machinery, utility system designs, building designs and standard specifications and drawings.

C. DURING PROCUREMENT AND SUB CONTRACTING

Procurement is the next area of cost reduction. This phase is more crucial because irreversible cost commitments are made during this phase. Cost reductions are possible only on commitments being made. Generally, competitive bidding is the most commonly used practice for proving a technically acceptable item at the lowest cost. However, competitive bidding is not going to help alone unless the following steps are taken:

- Vendor association in specifications.
- Detailed scope and specifications.
- General conditions of contract.
- Purchase procedure.
- Delivery in erectable sequence.
- Competitive bidding.

D. DURING CONSTRUCTION

Really, there is no much scope for cost reduction during construction phase. However there are certain items on which close cost control, must be exercised for keeping down the costs. These are:

- Extra items.
- Idle change.
- Inventory costs.
- Cash-flow planning.
- Cost of operating staff and administrative expenses.

Finally, as cash always shows a tendency to move up, cost reducing efforts have to be followed throughout the project life to keep cost under control. Cost control is not cost cutting recklessly. It is an attempt that should do the work of digging where gold is.

Hence, constant watch on behaviour costs is a must that calls for having comprehensive cost status report which is essentially a part of MIS of any organization.

CHAPTER BASED QUESTIONS

A. WRITE SHORT NOTES ON

1. Systems and procedures
2. Features of system
3. Design of system
4. Plan of systems and procedures
5. Project Direction
6. Review meetings
7. Project control
8. Performance control
9. Schedule control
10. Cost control

B. SHORT ANSWER QUESTIONS

1. What is a system ?
2. What is a procedure ?
3. What is a design of system ?
4. What is time management ?
5. What is man-management ?
6. What is cost management ?
7. What is risk management ?
8. What is project control ?
9. What is project direction ?
10. What is scope or progress control ?

C. ESSAY TYPE QUESTIONS

1. What do you mean by systems and procedures ? Explain system and procedure plan
2. What is project direction ? When there is need for direction ?
3. What is project control ? What are the components of it ?
4. What is progress or scope control ? How is it exercised ?
5. What is performance control ? How it is exercised ?
6. What is schedule control ? How it is exercised ?
7. What is cost control ? How it is exercised ?

* * * * *

Chapter 11

PROJECT MANAGEMENT FUNCTIONS PART-2

BACKDROP

In the foregoing chapter, we had the opportunity to discuss the managerial functions as regards project management namely, directing and controlling in the background of managerial systems and procedures. Now, we will concentrate on vital aspects of project management functions namely, project authority, team building, leadership, communication and project review meetings. The chapter ends with Chapter Based Questions.

I. PROJECT AUTHORITY

Authority is the legitimate right of superior to command and require his subordinates to perform certain activities. Authority is the right to give orders and the power to extract obedience. A manager's authority is his privilege to take decisions and the power to enforce those decision. It involves the right to use organisational resources. As a managerial aspect, authority is the power to command others, to act or not to act in a manner deemed by the possessor of authority to further enterprise or departmental purpose. To be very specific, authority is the sum of the powers and rights entrusted to make possible the performance of the work, delegated. Thus, authority is the right to decide or act and thereby guide actions of others.

THE FEATURES OF AUTHORITY

Authority as a managerial concept has its own features :

1. **IT IS THE RIGHT GRANTED :**
   Authority of a managers is his right as granted to him by his superior. That is a manager exercises his right by virtue of his formal position in a given orgnisation.

2. **IT IS THE POWER TO DECIDE AND COMMAND :**
   With the help of this right of authority, a manager takes decision and regulates the behaviour of his subordinates. This right or power enables him to decide and command the business scene.

3. **AN APPLIANCE TO GET COMPLIANCE :**
   This right puts a manager in a position by which he issues orders and ensures their compliance by the subordinates. The right to give orders is legitimate. That is, it is socially and ethically acceptable to all concerned unless subordinates accept the superiors command, authority can not be meaningful and operational.

4. **AUTHORITY IS RELATIVE :**
   The authority of a person is not absolute but relative. It is limited by several internal and external factors including the willingness of subordinate to accept the rights of the manager that is, a manager has his powers commensurate with his relative status or positions in a given organization.

5. **AUTHORITY HAS BOTH OBJECTIVE AND SUBJECTIVE FACETS :**

Authority in itself is an objective thing but its exercise is always subjective. The use of authority is determined by the personality factors of its possessor and the people over whom it is exercised. It means that a manager has powers or authority to use. But active use is left to the person. He may get the work done without using his powers by virtue of his leadership qualities. However, the objective behind the use of authority is to influence the behavior of the subordinates in the right direction, if at all exercised.

6. **AUTHORITY IS KEY TO MANAGE :**

Authority is the key to manage the job. The hierarchical structure of an organization is based upon the flow of authority. In fact, no manager can discharge his duties or functions and get one work done unless he has the necessary authority. That is, organized managerial action warrants authority. It is also supreme coordinating power or a binding force in an organization. Authority is the central mechanism through which the executive's decision-making activities take place.

DISTINCTION BETWEEN 'AUTHORITY' AND 'POWER'

Very often the terms 'authority' and 'power' are used interchangeably. However, these two terms are not one and the same. As the students of management we can not afford to commit such blunder. One can draw the clear distinction between the two on atleast nine counts. These points of difference are :

1. **MEANING :**

'Authority' is the set of rights inherent in a managerial position to give orders. It is the legitimate right to direct or influence the behavior of others. On the other hand, 'Power' is the ability to influence the behavior of others. 'Power' is personal while 'authority' is positional. That is, authority is institutionalised power.

2. **SOURCE :**

There are several sources of 'power' such as reward power, co-ercive power, referent power, information power, expertise power and so on. A person may be powerful by virtue of his position, knowledge, expertise and the like. On the other hand, 'authority' has one source-the position in the organizational hierarchy. Hence, 'power' is comprehensive than 'authority' is meaning and coverage.

3. **ASSOCIATION :**

'Authority' is associated with formal organizations, and therefore, it is always formal. However, 'power' can be both formal and informal. That is exercise of authority is formal while power is both formal and informal.

4. **NATURE :**

'Authority' is impersonal and objective but 'power' can be personal and subjective. That is, authority is not personal and subjective. Thus, a manager excersises authority that has been granted by his higher authorities and has to be used in an objective manner. Whereas 'power' is purely personal hence, it can be used in an subjective manner.

5. **SCOPE :**

'Power' is all pervasive. 'Authority' invested in a position whereas 'power' may be found in the lowest level also for instance, a trade union leader may have more power than even general manager. Again, a general manager has powers but the salary drawn is lesser to his status. In certain organisations, janitors draw higher salary than managers in an industrial or business setting.

6. **FLOW :**

'Authority' has a downwards flow from superior to subordinate. A subordinate can not exercise authority over his superior. Contrary to this, 'power' can flow from bottom to top. It is not the exclusive prerogative of superiors, even subordinates can posses it.

7. **DELEGATION :**

'Authority' can be delegated by higher authorities to the lower authorities or subordinates. However, some forms of 'power' can not be delegated at all. Thus, 'expertise' power can never be delegated.

8. **BALANCE :**

'Authority' is always related to responsibility. That is, authority and responsibility are co-extensive and balance each other. However, in case of 'power', there is no such balancing factor. Persons wielding power have no specific responsibilities to discharge.

9. **ACCEPTANCE :**

Acceptance of 'authority' is not left to the sweet will and discretion of individuals. In any organisation, subordinates have to either accept the authority of the superior or leave the organization. That is authority acceptance is mandatory. However, acceptance of 'power' is not mandatory. It is left to the individuals to accept it or reject it in full or part. In this sense, 'authority' is an artificial structuring of power while 'power' can create natural and spontaneous influence structures.

SOURCES OF AUTHORITY

The management thinkers have three theories to explain the sources of authority. The gist of these theories is given below.

1. **FORMAL AUTHORITY THEORY :**

As per this theory, all authority originates at the top in the formal structure of an organization and it flows downward to subordinates through the process of delegation. The ultimate authority in a company rests with the shareholders by virtue of their investment or ownership in the company. The share holders derive their authority due to the institution of private property. They delegate their authority to the Board of Directors which in turn delegates it to the CEO. Managers at each level of the organization derive their authority form managers at the higher level. Thus, formal authority that a manager has by virtue of his position in the organisation. Hence, it is the authority of position. Formal authority always comes form top to bottom and may therefore, be as well called "top-down authority". The authority conferred by law is also known as formal authority.

2. **ACCEPTANCE AUTHORITY THEORY :**

According to this theory, the degree of effective authority possesses by a manager is measured by the willingness of subordinates to accept the orders and command of the superior. The basic test of the existence of authority whether a managers subordinates will accept instructions. This order carries authority only if it is accepted by the recipient. Formal authority is nominal and becomes effective only when the subordinates accept the command of the executive. This works on: "One can take the horse to the water but not make it drink". As per this theory, authority flows upward from subordinates to superiors. That is, a manager gets authority if subordinates obey his command. Hence, acceptance of authority is called "bottom up authority". Acceptance theory interprets authority as leadership – the ability to persuade others to work well to accomplish group goals. The value of acceptance theory lies is its recognition of the individuals decision on whether to accept the formal authority.

3. **COMPETENCE AUTHORITY THEORY :**

As per this theory, authority is generated by personal qualities or technical competence of the manager. People accept the order of a person because he has specialised knowledge and skills. This opinion carries weight and people seek his advice irrespective of his position in the managerial hierarchy. We all know that staff specialists possess authority due to their expert knowledge. Thus, the personal authority is the authority of knowledge. That is why, it is well said: "Knowledge is power".

In a nut shell, the authority of a manager flows form different sources. That is, formal authority is conferred by the organisation, personal authority by subordinates' acceptance and the technical authority is implicit in specialised knowledge or skills. Though formal authority is the very foundation of the managerial job, he needs acceptance authority and competence authority to be more effective.

THE SCOPE OF AUTHORITY

It is worthwhile to note that the authority of a manager is not absolute or something abundant and unlimited. It is subject to certain limitations which can be :

1. **THE LEVEL OF THE ORGANIZATION :**
   The quantum of authority decreases successively lower levels in the management hierarchy. When a manager delegates authority, he places certain limits on the authority of his subordinates. People at higher levels enjoy greater authority than those at lower levels.

2. **LEGAL RESTRICTIONS :**
   The authority of a manager is to be exercised within the boundaries of a given Law or Act. Say Companies Act, MRTP Act, and so on. Thus, as a part of Companies Act, Memorandum of Association, Articles of Association, Company polices, Rules, Regulation, Resolutions and agreements clearly lay down the limits on authority.

3. **IMPLIED LIMITS :**
   The authority is to be exercised keeping in view the fundamental beliefs, codes, tradition, creeds and the like of the organisation. Social customs, religious beliefs do limit the use of authority.

4. **Biological Limits :**
   Biological and technological constraints limit the authority. Physical and mental capacity of a manager is limited. Climate, topography, market conditions, technology and the like also the effective determinants of scope of authority.

RESPONSIBILITY

The word 'responsibility' has different meanings to different people become some equate it to 'duties' and others 'obligation'. Some say responsibility, is the duties and activities assigned to a position or to an executive. Others say responsibility i`s the obligation of a subordinate to perform the duties or activities assigned to him. It means that these words have narrow and broad meaning. Hence, the word 'responsibility' is to be differentiated from 'duty' which is merely a task or functions to be performed. 'Responsibility' is the obligation to perform the assigned duties faithfully. Hence, responsibility is the obligation to perform certain, functions and achieve certain results.

MAIN FEATURES

The features of responsibility make its nature very clear and these are:

1. **OBLIGATION AS THE MAINSTAY :**
The essence of responsibility is the obligation to perform the assigned duty or task by the superior.

2. **OUTCOME OF SUPERIOR-SUBORDINATE RELATIONSHIP :**
Responsibility arises from superior-subordinate relationship when a superior assign some work to a subordinate, the latter becomes responsible for the performance of the task.

3. **IT MAY BE CONTINUAL OR SPECIFIC OBLIGATION :**
The responsibility of superior is of continuing nature while the responsibility of a consultant is specific and it comes to an end when the assignment is completed.

4. **IT CAN NOT BE DELEGATED :**
Responsibility is a personal attribute and it can not be delegated. No person can shift or transfer his responsibility by delegating his authority to others. Whether, an individual exercises the authority himself or delegates it to others, he remains responsible to his superior.

5. **IT IS CONCOMITANT OF AUTHORITY :**
That is, one is dependant on another. Hence, authority and responsibility should be equal. Inequality between authority and responsibility produces unwanted and undesirable results.

In a nutshell, authority is the right of a superior to issue commands to sub-ordinates while responsibility is the obligation of a sub-ordinates to obey those commands. Thus, authority flows down while responsibility is executed upwards.

PROJECT MANAGER'S AUTHORITY

A project manager's authority depends basically on his exact position in the organisation on one hand and his personality on the other. Hence, his scope of authority can be extended to two types of authority namely legal-'dejure' and real-'defacto'. One is able to have better understanding if he goes through the following figure that configures his exact role and authority in project organization.

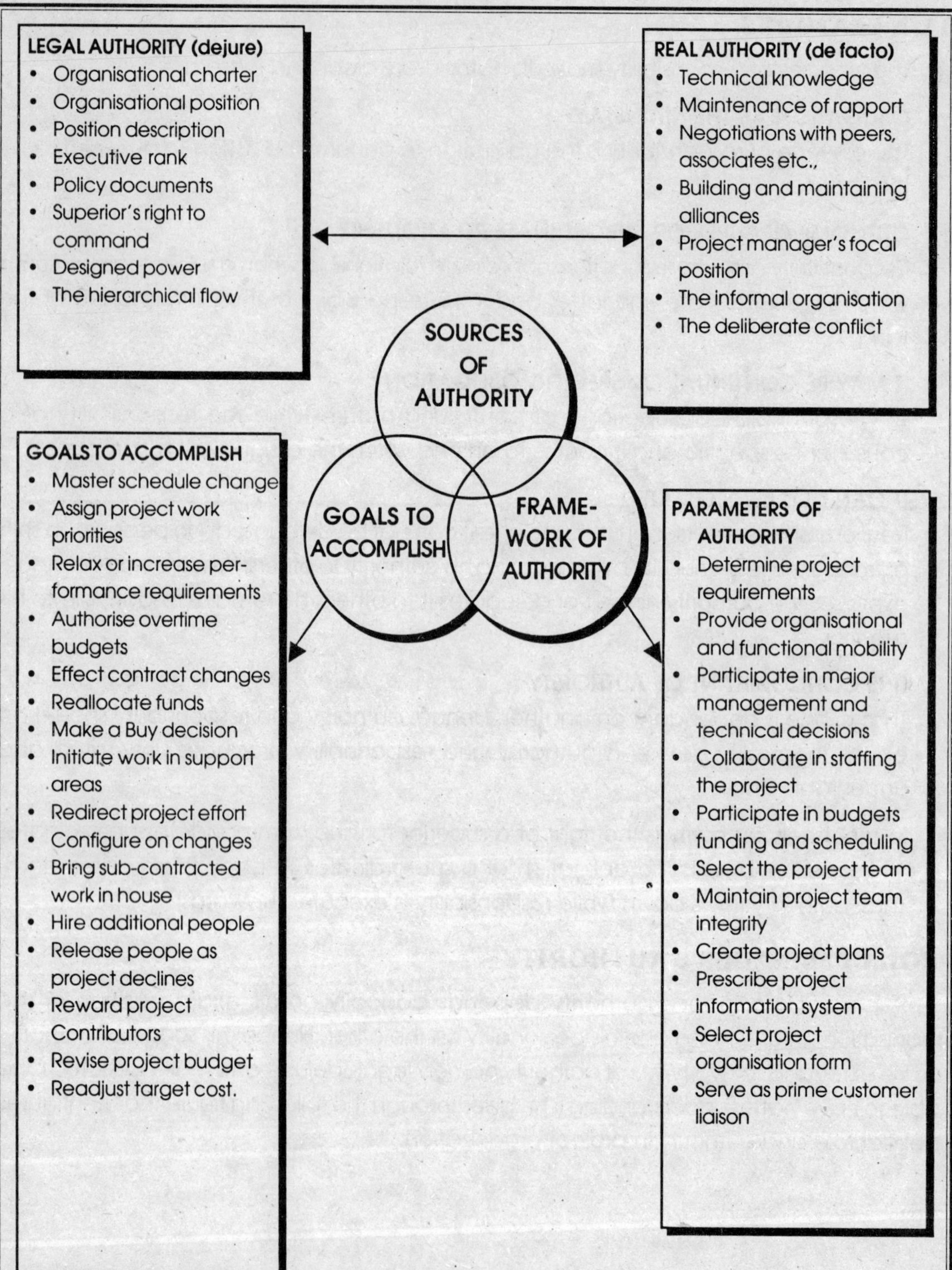

Fig. 11.01 Project Manager's Authority

A project manager has to make the vital and regular decisions to guide the actions of others. For taking sound and timely decisions, he needs authority that enables to make decisions and to delegate the authority to others. The scope of power and control exercised by the project manager is independent on his legal authority. However, project manager is expected to have broad authority over all the elements of the project. Though a good deal of his authority depends on his personal abilities, his position is strengthened by published documentations to establish his mode of operation and his legal authority. At the minimum level, the documentation should clearly define his role and prerogative as regards to :

- His focal position in the project activities.
- The need for a defined relationship between the project manager and the functional manager.
- The need for his influence to cut across functional and organisational lines to achieve unanimity of the project objectives
- Active participation in the overall managerial and technical decisions to compete the project
- Collaborating with personnel officer and functional supervisors while staffing the project.
- Selection of sub-contractors to support the project and the negotiations of contracts.
- Identifying the rights and resolving conflicts that jeopardise the attainment of project goals.
- Having a voice in maintaining integrity of the project team during the life of the project.
- Establishing project plans through the coordinated efforts of the project-team.
- Providing and maintaining a suitable information system for the project with sufficient data to control the project within the permitted cost, time and quality parameters.
- Providing leadership in the preparation of operational requirements, specifically, jurisdiction and the bid package.
- Liasioning with primary customers and contractors on project matters.
- Encouraging technological and managerial improvements throughout the life of the project.
- Establishes a project organisation for the duration of the project.

The above points speak of 'defacto' authority that a project manager should enjoy.

There are other authorities which are the results of delegation. These can be together called as 'dejure' or legal authority. These are :

- To organize, plan, direct and control the project utilising the advice and recommendations of the participating teams.
- To tailor the organisation of project office and the need and apply the management systems to the needs of the project within the limits specified by the program management directives and implementing command supplements.
- To make technical and business management decisions within the approved project to attain project objectives. Such decisions will be the directives on all the participatinsg groups.
- To establish the need, scope, cost and schedule for all project related efforts.
- To assess and document the impact of proposed changes with alter approved performance, schedule and cost objectives.
- To prepare and issue a comprehensive management plan in consonace within the top managements directives and implementing command supplements. The project plan is tailored to the needs of the project and will not require head-quarters approval unless such approval is specifically warranted.
- To assure adequate communication and coordination among all participating team members.
- To maintain a continuous assessment of his project's progress and preformance versus threats, schedules and costs, and to inform higher authorities of recommended changes as well as potential or actual breaches of project thresholds.

Thus, project manager needs authority in project management covering these areas :

- Project scope.
- Project goals.
- Project execution mode.
- Project organisation.
- Project purchase.
- Contracts, contractors and consultants.
- Project technical performance.
- Project schedules and budgets.
- Funds and other resources.
- Project personnel.
- Publics/Shareholders.
- Project environment.

- Management systems and procedures.
- Project performance review.

His authority – stems form his position in the organisation, his personality and his specialized knowledge. In other words, it is both 'dejure' and 'defacto' authority in right mix.

II. TEAM BUILDING

Today, most of the organisations face the formidable challenge of regaining or maintaining a competitive advantage with the intense global competition and the need for organizational renewal. Infact, when the managers are asked to identify the factors and trends driving the need for change in their organisation, they typically identify technological innovations, higher customer, expectations, new global entrants, increased or decreased government regulation and changing consumer, demand and demographs as being at the top of their lists. While the implication of these forces play out differently in each organisation all organisation must become adept at reading and responding swiftly and proactively to competitive forces. The ability to achieve, interpret, and act upon information with innovations in processes and products is a core competitive capability. To do this organisations need ingenuity-clever, imaginative out of-the-box responses that allow them to flex with their many competitive demands. It means that they must create favourable conditions for people to come together spontaneously to share knowledge and learn as they explore organisational challenges and identity novel ideas. Undoubtedly, team-work is the most efficient way for organisation to encourage and harness this creative potential.

WHAT IS 'TEAM WORK' AND 'TEAM'?

By teamwork we mean real team-work whereby the right people with right skills, knowledge and perspective join to collectively explore challenges, generate creative solutions and work diligently to build the necessary support and commitment for implementation. Not surprisingly teams have been identified as an integral part in developing and sustaining a high performance work culture. Teamwork leads to organizational health with decentralised decision-making and improvement as the basic principle of organisational design.

"Team" or "Project team" refers to all those individuals who have a significant contributions towards the successful achievement of the project through one or more factors such as technical or special expertise, sponsorship, political support or commitment expectations of and interest in its outcome. A team is a mechanism that enables the required quick responses and adaptation. It is aligned, cohesive and energetic group of people. A team is a unique type of group in two important ways. First, team has an objective a specific goal that the team is trying to reach. The goal is usually thought of as a performance objective that is, something the team trying to do rather than something the team is trying to be and performance objective is usually concrete or tangible. Teams are groups of people who design new products stage dramatic production, climb mountains, fight epidemics, raid crack houses, fight fires or pursue an inexhaustive list of present and future-objectives. Secondly, reaching the goal requires collaboration a coordinated effort. Advising the goal requires working together. Effective teams then, are made up of members who are not only technically competent but also good at collaborating with one another to reach their common objectives.

'TEAM' AND 'GROUP'

The distinction between the terms 'team' and 'group' is made to indicate difference in operating characteristics of each. A group is simply a collection of people. A 'team' is a unique group that has the following features.

1. **TEAM OUTPUT IS HIGHER THAN GROUP :**
   The output of the group is greater than the sum of outputs of the individuals. For instance, a team can engage in creative process say, idea generation-for more effective state than a collection of individuals.

2. **WIDE RANGE OF OPTIONS :**
   A greater range of options can be considered by exploring the differences in individual thought process. When people of like interests come together, there can be wider range of options as each is different from another in the same line.

3. **SUPERIOR DECISION-MAKING :**
   Decision-making by team is sure to be better. It is because a team is thought have members well versed in different sides of the same coin. That is, each member throws light on the problem to arrive at suitable decision. A problem is the gap between perception of an actual sutuation and that of the expected or required situation. The same issue is perceived by each in a different manner. Fianl shape will be the finest and very near to the reality.

4. **SHARED RISK :**
   Teams are more open to take risk as the risks is shared between the members rather than carried by one individual. A team member shares the risk.

5. **HIGHER OVERALL MOTIVATION :**
   There is overall high level of motivation as there is an inherent responsibility to others in the team and a strong desire not to let them down. After all, it is a prestige point. Team shows oneness in everything.

6. **TEAM PROVIDES BETTER SUPPORT :**
   There is better support for the individuals within the team who are more likely to be included in a greater range of activities than they would normally be exposed to, but without them having to work, alone.

'EFFECTIVE' VERSUS 'INEFFECTIVE' TEAMS

There are certain factors that make a team 'effective' or 'ineffective'. These points are:

1. **NATURE OF ATMOSPHERE :**
   Incase of 'effective' teams, the atmosphere tends to be informal and comfortable. That is people are really involved and interested. While in case of 'ineffective' teams the atmosphere is just formal, indifferent projecting lifelessness and – people are whispering and pulling the legs of one another. It is not an integrated atmosphere.

2. **UNDERSTANDING AND CONTRIBUTING :**
   In case of an 'effective' team, there is no scope for misunderstanding. Every one understands the team tasks. As a result, each one listens to another where every idea is given good hearing. As a result, every one is in bloomed mood whereby he takes active part in discussions by keeping him to the point whereas in case of 'ineffective' team no one known as to what is the group task. As a result, nobody listens to anybody very few people are to the point and most try to drift away from the group discussions.

3. **EXPRESSIONS OF OPINION :**
   In case of 'effective' team, the team members feel very frank and free to criticise and say honestly as to what they think of a particular issue. As against this, the members of 'ineffective' team are not frank and free as their way of argument has no logic at all. They more grumble on discussions and decisions once they are over and taken.

4. **VETO POWER :**
   In case of 'effective' teams, there can be disagreement. That is, the group is comfortable with disagreement. As a result, it works towards resolving it. That is, nobody is unhappy with decision made whether in favour or against. It is because, the team knows it has ought well for the best cause. On the contrary, incase of 'ineffective' teams, disagreements are not dealt with all the seriousness. That is, such issues are put to vote without much discussion. Only a handful of people are unhappy with the decisions so arrived.

5. **UNANIMITY :**
   Incase of 'effective' teams, everybody knows as to how others feel about what is being discussed at the forum. When action needs to be taken everyone is clear about what has to be done and team members help each other, while in case of 'inefficient' team hardly one or two people dominate the scene. Hence, what they say always goes up and stands. So for as action, nobody takes any interest in what has to be done and team members do not help each other in this context.

6. **LEADERSHIP :**

The leadership is really practised incase of 'effective' teams because different members of the team take over the role of a leader from time to time and situation to situation. As opposed to this, in case of 'ineffective' teams, one or two persons always take lead in discussion and decision-making and they are the permanent leaders for every issue and every occasion. That is, the participative leadership is not there because these leaders think that they are the only capable people.

7. **SELF CONSCIOUSNESS :**

In case of 'effective' team, the group is conscious of how well it is working and what is interfering with its progress. It takes care of on its own. As opposed to this, in case of 'ineffective' team, the group is not conscious of its working. It does not know about its achievements and failures. Only the third party will tell whether it is succeeding or failing-pin pointing the causes and remedies.

FACTORS THAT MAKE EFFECTIVE TEAM AND TEAM MEMBERS

After assessing the research findings, the researchers have given six factors that can make a team or team members effective or ineffective one. These factors are knowledge factors and team-work factors. The knowledge factors are experience and the problem solving ability. The team-work factors are openness, supporting action, orientation and personal style.

A. KNOWLEDGE FACTORS

When is comes to helping a team reach its goal, the first two distinguishing features that stand out among unusually effective team members are experience and the problem solving ability. The team-mates who are important to their team's success are knowledgeable about the business they are in, and they are effective problem solvers. These two factors combine to form the quality one calls "Working knowledge".

1. **EXPERIENCE :**

Experience is the first thing a team looks for in its members. Whether the team is about to embark on cardiac surgery, mountain climbers or building an airplane, once the goal is clear the question comes "Who has been here before ?" In other words, the team looks for practical knowledge that is relevant to its objective typically, the team looks hardest and longest in the direction of the leader. The leader is usually there precisely because of his or her practical knowledge, breadth of experience, or record of success. However, as work continues individuals rapidly discover that among the members of the team are those who know and those who do not, those who speak with voice of experience and those who simply speak. An experienced member knows his business. He has a clear vision. He has wealth of knowledge and experience. He has experience, sound judgment, good business sense. He has excellent grasp of that total technical capabilities and needs. He understands the jobs and knows putting together pieces of the big picture. He has great technical background.

2. **PROBLEM SOLVING ABILITY :**

As team-work progresses, another quality begins to emerge. Some members of the team are good at solving the problems that inevitably arise as obstacles to a team's success, irrespective of their level of experience. Problem solving ability can be manifested in various ways. Some team members are adapt in clarifying problems, bringing them into focus, getting them understood. Some are good at developing strategies for overcoming the problems, figuring out what's likely to work and what's not. Some know enough about the substance of the team's work to be able to make helpful constructive suggestions about overcoming a problem. Team members who help the team in resolving problems are seen as displaying strengths that keep the team focussed on the issues and moving towards the goal whatever their specific contribution maybe.

Productive problem solving is aggressive and proactive in problem resolutions. A problem solver is an active, constructive participant in team discussions of operations issues. He tries to keep people together focused. He provides through understanding of the key issues to the team and presents fact-based solutions very effectively. Contrary to this, ineffective approaches to problem solving typically involve carelessness, a lack of decisiveness or an inability to focus.

Both experience and problem solving ability are the core competancies. However, as important as these qualities are, they are not enough to make people effective team members.

B. TEAMWORK FACTORS

As much as team members value experience and problem solving ability, they recognize that social competencies are essential for effective teamwork. As noted earlier, there are four teamwork factors that determine whether or not an otherwise competent and knowledgeable group of individuals will be successful in working together to attain their common goal or goals-openness, supportiveness, an action orientation, and positive personal style.

1. **OPENNESS :**

Openness is the basic ingredient of team success. Openness is a pattern of behaviour. Those team members who are open are willing to deal with problem, surface issues that need to be discussed to help in creating an environment where people are free to say what is on their, minds, and promote an open exchange of ideas. These open team members tend to be effective communication, helping to create a climate in which communication flourishes and is used effectively to resolve whatever problems the team confronts to improve the team's performance.

The persons with openness are those who openly express their point of view. They are readily willing to bring up issues and offer possible resolution. They are ready to discuss the details of issue willingly. They do not shy about giving opinions and feedback. Conversely, those who are not open, make difficult to talk about the issues.

2. **SUPPORTIVENESS :**

Though supportiveness can take many forms, at the core it is a desire and willingness to help others succeed. This means encouraging some one whose confidence waning and wavering. It means placing charitable interpretation on people's difficulties when they are trying but struggling. It also means figuring on how to help some one to overcome an obstacle rather than taking advantage of momentary failure. Sometimes, it means defending someone who is being attacked. It always means putting the team's goal above any individual agenda being easy to work with ; and demostrate a willingness to help others in achieving.

A person is said to be supportive when he is dedicated to the team's success and wants what is best for the team. He works behind the scenes to aid the team. He is willing to pitch in whenever necessary. He has a positive outlook and a willingness to take more responsibility. He is very easy to work with and listens well to others ideas. By contrast, non-supportive member is seen focusing on 'me' than 'we' and very often achieving objectives at the expense of others and usually disinterested or insensitive to the concerns of other team members.

3. **ACTION ORIENTATION :**

Being action-oriented means having a tendency to act, to do something. It also means encouraging others to take action. It means being willing to prod to suggest courses of action to be willing to experiment, to try something different.

A person is said to be action-oriented when he rises to the challenge. He reacts positively to immediate needs. He has ideas to help the team bring in more business constantly. He is an energetic worker, fast learner; he organises his work well and has the courage to confront the issues. Conversely, passive orientation is to keep aloof, reacting negatively to immediate needs.

4. **PERSONAL STYLE :**

The personal style is the individual style of doing the things. There is fundamental difference among the people in form of whether they conceives a positive or negative attitude. Team members are positive styled people who are energetic, optimistic, engaging, confident and fun to work with.

Positive styled people are experienced motivators of people; they win with strong positive attitude and enjoy the work. They have positive energy, new ideas and good deal of creativity. They have in infectious enthusiasm about the work. They get along well with others. They are friendly and liked. They make everyone feel comfortable in whatever capacity they meet. Conversely, negative styled members are quite opposite of positive style of members.

EFFECTIVE TEAM WORK

Effective teamwork reflects the best results at least cost, intargeted time and expected quality performance. **Mr. C.E. Larson and F.M.J La Fasto** in their book TEAM-WORK- identify eight characteristics which can help to ensure the project success most of which are under the control of the project manager, is achieved. These are:

1. **A clear, elevated goal-** a sense of mission must be created through the development of an objective which is understand important, work while and personality or collectively challenging.
2. **Provide a result driven structure-** the structure and composition of the team should be commensurate with the task of being undertaken
3. **Competent team members-** need to balance personal with technical competence.
4. **Unified commitment-** create the environment of doing what has to be done to succeed.
5. **Foster a collaborative climate-** encourage reliance on others within the team.
6. Standards of excellence- through individual standards team pressure, knowledge of the consequences of failure.
7. **External support and recognition-** where good work is performed, recognize it. It is likely to be absent from the other stakeholders so will be the responsibility of the project manager to provide it.
8. **Institute principled leadership-** manager is the dynamic life going element in every business. Without this leadership, the resources remain resources and never become proceducts. In competitive economy, the quality and performance of managers determine the success of this business, ideas they determine its survival .

BUILDING SMART TEAMS

Professor Carol A Beatty and Brenda A Barker Scott both of Queen's University Ontario USA have given Nine Planner Elements in building the smart teams in their title "BUILDING SMART TEAMS". Following is the gist of nine planner elements.

1. **ARTICULATE YOUR PURPOSE :**
   Creation of the team's purpose for being is an important first step for newly forming teams. Powerful team building occurs as members jointly explore their challenge or the opportunity to develop a deep appreciation of their cause. Members together, can create a purpose that they all want to create a purpose and contribute to on that is fulfilling and meaningful for each member. A good team purpose has two key ingredients. First, it clarifies how the team's work will support the organisation as a

whole. This gives the team organisational relevance. Second, the purpose should tap into the team why it is important and relevant for each member. In addition, to organisational relevance, it creates personal relevance too.

2. **CREATE YOUR TEAM'S VISION AND STRATEGY :**

When a team understands why it was formed it can turn its attention to the important task of creating the ideal scenario – a vivid detailed account of what life will be like, in business terms, after the mission has been achieved. This is the step which the authors call it "beginning with the end in mind" Visioning has several steps all of which must be completed for the exercise to have value and credibility.

These steps are:

1. Begin with the end in mind.
2. Assess the vision for reality.
3. Organise priorities.
4. Supportive thinking for implementing change.

3. **DEVELOP CLEAR GOALS AND ACCOUNTABILITIES :**

Effective teams translate their purpose and priorities into clear goals aligning members around practical tasks and results that they can monitor and measure. Clear goals lead to higher performance and employee commitment when employees are involved in the goal setting process. Further, receiving feed-back on goal performance enhances productivity. Simply put, goal setting works because it clarifies what is expecting of the team, as well as how each member can contribute to goal achievement. How you are defining your team's goal or goals will depend on answers to the questions that follow:

- What are the specific objectives to be achieved ?
- What key activities are required ?
- What specific results or deliverables are expected of us ? By whom ?
- What are the expected dates for completion ?
- How, when and by whom will we be measured ?
- At what milestones should we report results and how should results be reported?

Accountability is another side. While the team as a whole is accountable for achieving its overall purpose and goals, each team must go through the important process of identifying who can be carry out each of the sub-goals and then shifting authority for goal completion to one member or members. These persons who are asked to achieve goals-rather sub-goals are better known as goal-leaders. Because members hold widely different assumptions about the notion of authority, it is suggested that teams explicitly define the expectation and parameters for that transfer of authority for goal completion. The goal leader, in turn, assigns tasks of other members of the team and elicit support of others essential to carrying out the goal. This technique is called as "accountability charting". This process warrants the leader and others whose roles interrelate formulate a list of actions, decisions and activities with respect to attaining the goal. These activities include collecting data, communicating with stakeholders, developing budget, allocating resources or running a pilot project.

4. **IDENTIFY YOUR AUTHORITY AND REPORTING STRUCTURE :**

Closely linked with the development of the teams purpose is the determination of the team's boundaries for responsibility, authority, and reporting requirements. Teams that do not have clear scope and boundaries may experience great confusion, frustration, and disappointment as they learn the hard way that they have overstepped their limits or not met their obligations. Unfortunately, this mismatch occurs often, as the concept of authority in organisation is laden with assumption. Some people crave it, while others fear it. Of course goal is to work towards more authority and accountability. It is generally behind that if teams are to be used at all, it is important that they begin with at least enough authority to determine their own goals, work-methods, and norms of conduct. As teams mature and gain both competence and confidence, the scope of their authority should be increased. Teams need to learn together by articulating goals, experimenting units options, taking action implementing solution, and reflecting on their success and failures.

Through this action learning process, teams become more able and willing to assume greater levels of responsibility over, time. Thus, collective responsibility for production processes, people management issues, and quality control all have a self-supporting effect on teams. By specifically defining the team's authority and then holding members accountable, members learn to work out the answers to their obligations. This strategy encourages learning and growth of team members.

5. **ESTABLISH THE TEAM MEMBERSHIP AND CONTRIBUTION :**

A critical issue for team success is team membership, having right mix of skills, experience and leadership to ensure that the team can deliver on its performance expectations. If the team's goals are complex, requiring team members to problem solve and reach consensus on major issues, teams of about SIX or SEVEN members are most effective. The research findings state that performance declines in smaller teams of TWO or THREE members, probably because teams do not have the necessary experience or expertise to draw from. In larger teams of TEN or MORE, group satisfaction declines. It seems that as the group size becomes too large, both interaction and communication tend to become difficult, resulting in dissatisfied members and unproductive interactions.

Generally, team membership should include individuals who :

- possess critical expertise knowledge or.information for the tasks at hand.
- have a slake in the final outcome.
- have responsibility for implementing whatever is decided.
- have relevant and diverse view points that will stimulate discussion and thinking.
- have the authority to decide on behalf of their constituents. Often, due to time and size constraints, the formal team can not include all relevant individuals. In such case, creativity is required to find the ways to bring necessary insights and perspectives to the team. The team can invite subject matter experts or key customers to providing briefings can form advisory boards composed of relevant stake-holder groups to impart feedback, can hold town hall meetings or can run a services of focus sessions.

6. DETERMINE NORMS AND PROTOCOLS FOR WORKING COLLECTIVELY :

When people get together in a group to make decisions, they need norms and protocols to structure their thinking and participation as they collect data, make some of the data and come to conclusions. What sets smart team apart from others which decision tools they use, last that they discuss and agree on norms and protocols for important aspects of working collectively. Norms are those consistent and enduring behaviour that group members have explicitly or implicitly agreed to. They support a set of shared beliefs, values, and expectations for team behaviours and determine "how we do things around ?" It is important to note and understand that if helpful norms are not explicitly defined unhelpful norms may implicitly emerge. Implicit or explicit some group's norms help by fostering interaction and effective decision-making, while some hinder performance by preventing dialogue or promoting premature decision-making.

Though there are many problem solving processes available, most are built on the following fundamentals: problem identification and description, problem analysis, option generation, solution selection, action planning and follow through. From time to time, most teams experience conflict that gets in the way of team progress. Very often, the conflict occurs due to a misunderstanding, or members may have different values, mindsets, or working styles. If these tensions are left unchecked members tend to act out their feelings in destructive behaviour such as discounting member input, emotional outburst, or formation of cliques. Teams that are skilled at conflict handling slave off this destruction conflicts by creating norms for welcoming diverse views, accepting controversial statements, and openly sharing feelings.

To be useful the norms and protocols should continue to evolve as members discovers what behaviours and processes are truly important for working together effectively. With each successive interactions the list of norms and protocols becomes smaller but will have more impact as team narrow down the behaviour and approaches that are truly helpful.

7. **DEFINE ROLES AND ROLE CLARITY :**
When team is formed, each member is faced with the questions about his or her role. The roles for team management are: The leader or facilitator, The scribe, The time keeper, Team coach or advisor and Team member.

TEAM LEADER OR FACILITATOR

As the ring leader guide, process expert and catalyst, the team leader has a critical role. Ever mindful of both the task and social complexities, the team leader is three parts process facilitator and one part project manager.

Leader as a Facilitator :

- Leads the team through a series of exercises and questions to co-create then team management practices.
- Plans and facilitates an agenda to ensure that members jointly share, analyse and evaluate data for synergistic decision making.
- Provides an overall road map for the groups approach to working together making sure to match the challenge at hand with the appropriate tools and technologies.
- Encourages balanced participation by creating a safe climate and protecting ideas.
- Helps members in working through differences of opinion constructively.
- Assists the team in addressing counter productive behaviours.
- Leads the team in developing and using group norms to guide behaviour.
- Ensures that team members understand their roles and responsibilities.
- Keeps team meetings focussed and productive.
- Ensures that relevant information is available for team's deliberations.
- Invites experts to meetings to supplement team's collective knowledge and experience.
- Checks for comprehension and understanding.
- Provides feed-back to team members.
- Asks effective questions.
- Develops team members and encourages shared team leadership.

Leader as Project Manager :

- Schedules, arranges and facilitates team meetings.
- Clarifies purpose and team goals.

- Summarizes and organizes ideas, checks for understanding and commitment, and assigns tasks.
- Ensures that team uses agree-upon problem solving methods.
- Ensure that action items are assigned and follows up to ensure completion.
- Keeps the teams coach and management appraised of team progress and issues.

Scribe :

The team leader is often too busy wearing his or her, 'task' and group process has to record group discussions and decisions. As such, a scribe or recorder should be appointed before each team meeting to take and distribute minutes to team members. It is recommended by the experts that scribe should capture only the relevant data, including the meetings purpose, relevant discussion themes points of agreement and disagreement, decision for action, and accountabilities.

Time-Keeper :

The role of time-keeper is to alert the team several minutes prior to the end of the time limit for each agenda item. His role is made to move the group to the next agenda item when the time limit is up. Rather, if an agenda item requires further time, the team will decide to either spend the required time of complete the agenda item or close the agenda item for completion at another time.

The Team Coach or Advisor :

Newly formed team can benefit greatly from the support of a team coach. The coach is not a member of the team but rather a resource assigned to the team to assist with solving political issues, opening communication channels with key stakeholder group and listing or refining ideas before they are shared widely. The role of coach is to:

- provide guidance, advise and development for the team primarily by coaching the team leader.
- when called up on by the team, act as team ambassador and communication link with senior management to remove barrios to team success.
- offer guidance on how to manage political issues, should they occur.

Team Members :

Effective team members are committed team members. That means they "show up" and participate enthusiastically throughout the team's life-cycle. While good team management practices help to build the necessary commitment, every member must personally agree to invest in the team by agreeing to:

- prepare prior to the meetings.
- attend team meetings on time for the full meeting.

- participate fully by providing key information, voicing opinion and listening actively.
- accept and complete work assignments set by the team.
- serve as facilitator, scribe, time keeper and process advisor as needed.
- accept ana support consensus decisions of the team.

8. DEVELOP RELATIONSHIPS AND COMMUNICATIONS :

A group is not an island unto itself. Most groups can not survive without the assistance and support of other individuals and groups within the orgnisation. The teams that view themselves as the part of larger organisation are acutely aware of the web of interrelationships, which are essential to achieve their goals. These interrealtionships provide the team with important information and feed-back that helps them to stay aligned with the overall priorities and goals of the organisation. In the early stage to team's development, members are to identify the key people and groups who have a stake in the challenge as well as how these key stake holders will be informed, involved and consulted. Involving key stake-holders early ensures that important perspectives, information and expertise are carefully considered so that smart workable solution are adopted and supported. Hence, stake-holder mapping is a useful toll for this important dialogue.

Stake-holders mapping involves brain storming the key relationships that need the manager for the team initiative to be a success. Stake-holders promote important information, perspectives and insight on most aspects of the planning process such as teams mission and scope. In addition, stakeholders involved in defining the teams mission goals scope membership, authority, and expected results will understand the full extent of the team's challenges and their role to helping the team to achieve its goals.

9. MAINTAIN TEAM ENERGY AND FOCUS :

It pays to take stock of things that have taken place. This is not a futile exercise but something that promotes the deepest learning. Most of the teams are too busy in doing their work to consider how well they are performing or whether they are abiding by their protocols for decision-making and social inclusion. It is extremely helpful for the team to stop and think about these issues, from time to time. That is, there should be team evaluation at definite time interval.

It is important that evaluating team effectiveness requires that members be willing to share how they are feeling about their personal experiences as the members of the team, candidly. Members must also be willing to accept feedback about how their own actions were interpreted by the group.

III. LEADERSHIP

WHAT IS LEADERSHIP ?

To 'lead' is to guide, direct, supervise, integrate and energise the efforts of others towards a common goal. It also means to excel to be in advance, to stand out. A leader is one who influences the behaviour of others in any organised activity. It is the ability to get people to do what you want them to do because, they want to do it. It stands for relationship between an individual and a group around some common interest and behaviour in a manner directed by him. It is the ability to induce subordinates to work towards the group ideals with confidence and keenness.

Professor George Terry says : "Leadership is the relationship in which one person, the leader, influences other to do the work. Willingly a related tasks to attain that which the leader desires." **Professor H. Koontz** and **O. Dounell** say : "Leadershop is the ability of a manager to induce subordinates to work with confidence and zeal".

In short, leadership is to do much with the art of changing the behavioural pattern of others in the pursuit of common goals. A leader is like a monitor of an orchestra as an integral part of it. Leader integrates, guides, supervises, and inspires the group members towards the predetermined goals.

FEATURES OF LEADERSHIP

Leadership is the product of many forces acting and interacting simultaneously. Existence of leadership speaks of certain features. These features also clear the nature of leadership. These are:

1. **EVERY LEADER HAS FOLLOWERS OR A GROUP :**

   Leadership can not be imagined in vacuum. It is for the simple reason that he is to be obeyed. There must be some people who are prepared to accept his leadership. Organisational leader has followers namely, subordinates, a team or a group just as 'Guru' nas 'chelas', a 'teacher' has 'deciples'. As leadersip is the process of influencing, it presupposes a group willing to carry out his wishes accept his advice and direction. A leader influences their behaviour, attitudes and beliefs.

2. **EXISTENCE OF WORKING RELATIONSHIP :**

   Leadership requires another important point of prevalence of working relations between himself and the group or the team. A leader is not a pusher. He is always to the fore front. He is not sacrificing his followers to test his plans validity. He pulls the followers to the height of accomplishments. He knows the individual features of key followers, knows what qualities will click their best efforts and services at the same time he leads. He has the ability to awaken emotional as well as rational powers of his followers. He inspires attains the work, shows how to do, assumes obligations and accepts blames.

3. **SETS IDEALS BY PERSONAL CONDUCT :**

   As leadership is always concerned with the task of influencing the behaviour of others, it can be done best by setting himself an ideal before his followers. His speciality, his behaviour should stimulate others for hard, smart and honest-work. It is not what a leader says-still what he writes-that influences the subordinates. He is what he is; and they judge what he is, by what he is, by what he does and how he behaves. A leader is admired for special qualities stemming from his knowledge, ability, expertise, skills and accuracy.

4. **EXISTENCE OF COMMUNITY OF INTEREST :**

   Leader has his own goals and objectives and his followers too. Both are to move in the same direction as the members of the team. If there is drag, there is no leadership. It is the activity of influencing the people to strive willingly for mutual goals. Leader reconciles the differences and brings about workable compromise between organizational and individual interests of employees to the general interest of the organisation. This is possible when subordinates develop a strong sense of belongingness. That is why, the leader shares everything credit, blame, ideas, opinions and even the experience.

5. **LEADERSHIP IS SITUATIONAL :**

   Leadership is always related to a particular situation, a point of time and a set of circumstances. It is particular than general. A leader can stick to a particular style of leading. Situations change with the change in time. Sometimes, autocratic style works; sometimes democratic and still sometimes the free-reign. To succeed at all the times and all the situations he cannot be stagnant and adamant. He is to be dynamic to read the situation and follow a maching technique to make much out of it.

PROJECT MANGER AS A LEADER

Just as the projects are unique in their gamut and approach, so also are the project managers or project leaders. That is, no two project managers can be compared as regards their styles, approach and performance. The ever changing project scenario is itself a valid proof that – all project mangers are successful or failures. It may so happen that two project managers may have technical knowledge, abilities, yet one is better than another. It is so because, the ability to lead is quality that is quite distinct from technical capabilities and it is something that stems from the varied endogenous and escogenous factors that make his personality. As noted, leadership means the abilities to influence and detect the group of people towards common goal or goals. It is the greatest knack exercising power through direction and control of the individuals and groups.

In that sense a project leader is one who :

- is responsible for the accomplishment of project goals which are limited but require transparent and dynamic activity. In relation to the project, the role is akin to that of a general manager.
- is unable to hide his traits. It is always apparent as to who is the in charge to bear the risks associated.
- has limited direct authority. This is something that varies according to the project leader's position, but is usually necessary to negotiate for resources and support from a wide network of people inside and outside the organisations.
- is expected to cut across normal organizational boundaries and traditions and customs to be unconventional in approach– dealing with resistance or opposition is highly demanding.
- is often working in new areas for the company – new technology, new markets, or new approaches to the old situations. The unknown and unpredictable are often feared by many in the main-stream organisation. Credibility may be low initially and needs to be developed over a period.

DIMENSIONS OF TEAM-LEADERSHIP

As a team leader, project manager is key player in a setting that is fraught with measing, challenge and the risk. Whether he is leading an exclusive management team in a Fortune 500 company or a team of frontline workers in a government agency or non-priofit organisation, his interest is focused on what he can do, personally and specifically, to be more effective at leading his team and helping his organisation succeed. His purpose as a leader is to add value to his team's effort. There are atleast six dimensions of team leadership that are to be given top priority by the leader in managing his teams. These are:

1. FOCUS ON THE GOAL :

The first responsibility of a team-leader is to keep his team focussed on its goal or goals. Here goal means– team mission, visions, strategy, primary objective or prime directive– whatever one calls. The first task of a team-leader is to clarify define the goal or goals. Goal clarity is critical for team members to have confidence in their direction and to be committed to making it happen. Clarity also derives the alignment of activities and trust in team-leader's ability to lead. As a team-leader his primary responsibility is to ensure that team reaches its goal. That is, he should not play politics in this regard. He is to help the team members to see their relevance to the goal. He has to keep the goal alive at any rate. The focus on the goal means:

- Clarity in goal setting.
- Articulation of goal.

- No compromise and no politics.
- Role and responsibility alignment.
- Reinforcement of goal in fresh and exciting ways.
- Giving reasons for adjustment in goal, if any.

2. **ENSURE A COLLABORATIVE CLIMATE :**

Once the team's goal is established, the most important contribution of a team-leader is to ensure a climate that enables team members to speak up and address the real issues preventing the goal from being achieved. Collaboration is the dual presence of openness and supportiveness; the abiliy to raise and resolve the real issues standing in the way of a team accomplishing its goal, and to do so in a way that brings out best thinking and attitude of every one involved. A collaborative climate is attained by talking about reinforcing it, and guaranteeing it. An able team-leader creates a collaborative climate by demonstrating and modeling it through the behaviours and process of making communication safe, demanding collaborative approach, rewarding collaborative behaviour, guiding the team's problem solving efforts, managing his ego and personal control needs.

3. **BUILD CONFIDENCE :**

Collaborative team-leaders bolster the self-assurance of team members. They demonstrate personal confidence in individual team members, transporting each person to higher self-expectation. They build trust by providing meaningful responsibilities accompanied by the freedom to think and act. They encourage team members to stretch. Collaborative team- leaders demonstrate a positive attitude that focusses on opportunities and accomplishments. They are fair and impartlal towards all team members, careful neither to reject nor to exclude. Building team confidence begins with achieving results.

The most authentic confirmation of confidence is being part of a solid, well-earned, winning experience. It is the most preferred measure of leader effectiveness and result based leadership is the end game of leadership for employee, the organisation, its customers and investors, The secret is, clarity derives confidence and confidence derives commitment. That is why, the team-leader is to make team members smart about key issues and facts, exhibit trust by assigning responsibility. He is fair and impartial. He accentuates positive. He is to acknowledge and appreciate team members for their contributions. In essence building confidence is to ensure team achievement of results, strengthening self-confidence of team members, trusting team members, fair and impartial, optimistic, focussing on opportunities and thanking the team members as a mark of acknowledgement.

4. DEMONSTRATE SUFFICIENT TECHNICAL KNOW-HOW :

Broadly, technical know-how means understanding the content, or body of knowledge, directly related to the achievement of a goal. This also means knowledge specific to a well-defined field. For instance, if the goal is to lead a team in construction the world's largest plane say Boeing 747, understanding the discipline of engineering is essential. If the goal is to lead a team in creating a substitute for human blood that can be used during emergencies, it is necessary to understand the relevant science of bio-chemistry. It also refer to understanding a product or service or market place. It could mean knowing a specific manufacturing process for a modelled product, or the distribution requirements for food or medical supplies. It could mean understanding an organisation's history, values, and culture. In short, technical know-how is a framework of understanding through which to identify and analyse key issues related to the team's objective. Usually, it is the knowledge comprised of study and direct experience.

Demonstrating sufficient technical know-how implies that the team-leader has understood the technical issues that come in the way of achievement; holds sufficient experience with the technical aspects of the team's goal; been open to technical advice from team members who are more knowledgeable than the team-leader; the capability of helping the team to analyse complex issues related to team goal; been accepted as a credible person and people outside the team.

5. SET PRIORITIES :

A leader's ability, or more correctly, inability to set priorities is the most vehemently advanced complaint by team members. Hence, the team-leader should have more focus, clear priorities, and be less ambiguous. Broadly, a priority is determined when one is confronted with choices and decide which of the two or more competing activities is most important. As a leadership trait, the ability to set priorities is the ability to reconcile competing demands for finite resources of time, money and energy. Effective team-leader understands the urgency of advancing toward the goal and translate that urgency into clear priorities. Able team-leader scrapes away the inessentials and concentrate on a handful of critical initiatives that will advance the team towards its goal. Equally important, he requires each member of the team to do the same in their respective area.

Setting priorities will mean: keeping the team focussed on a manageable set of priorities that will lead to the attainment of the set goal; both leader and team members agree on top priorities for attaining the goal; communicating and reinforcing focus on priorities. No dilution of team's efforts with too many priorities: changing the priorities with supporting reasons if need there be.

6. MANAGE PERFORMANCE :

Performance management is the final dimension of team-leadership that emerges from the insights of team-members. Performance management begins with making expectations clear. Further, expectations should focus on results that are mutually agreed on by the team-leader and team members. There are four ingredients of better performance management. These are :

1. Objectives.
2. Collaborate style.
3. Management skills.
4. Personal development.

A team-leader is working towards the dimension of management performance when he is: making performance expectations very clear; encouraging the team to agree on set of values that guides the team performance; ensures rewards and incentives are aligned with achievement of team's goal; assesses the collaborative skills of team members as well as the results they achieve; gives useful, developmental feedback to team members; confronts and resolves issues associated with inadequate performance by team members; recognizes and rewards superior performance.

IV. COMMUNICATIONS IN PROJECT MANAGEMENT

Perhaps the single most important thing in project management is communications. It is said that if good communications exist in a project, the team will be motivated, and the project will succeed in spite of problems that might kill another project. Even Dr. Peter Drucker said 60 per cent of the managerial problems are caused by faulty management communication– partly or wholly. Communication is the great linking pin that connects– direction, co-ordination and control. In fact, communication is the centre of all management functions which gives a life to the managerial process of planning, organising, directing, coordinating, motivating and control. The following diagram makes it amply clear.

That is why, it is essential that all project managers have a good understanding of communications. It is generally agreed among the project managers that communications skills are the most important skills that a project manager can have. These skills are considered to be more important than organization skills, team building skills, and leadership skills, and they are certainly considered more important for project managers than technical skills. As per one research studies conducted in the US, the following is the ranking by 600 project managers :

- Communication skills 84%
- Organisation skills 75%
- Team-building skills 72%

- Leadership skills 68%
- Technological skills 48%

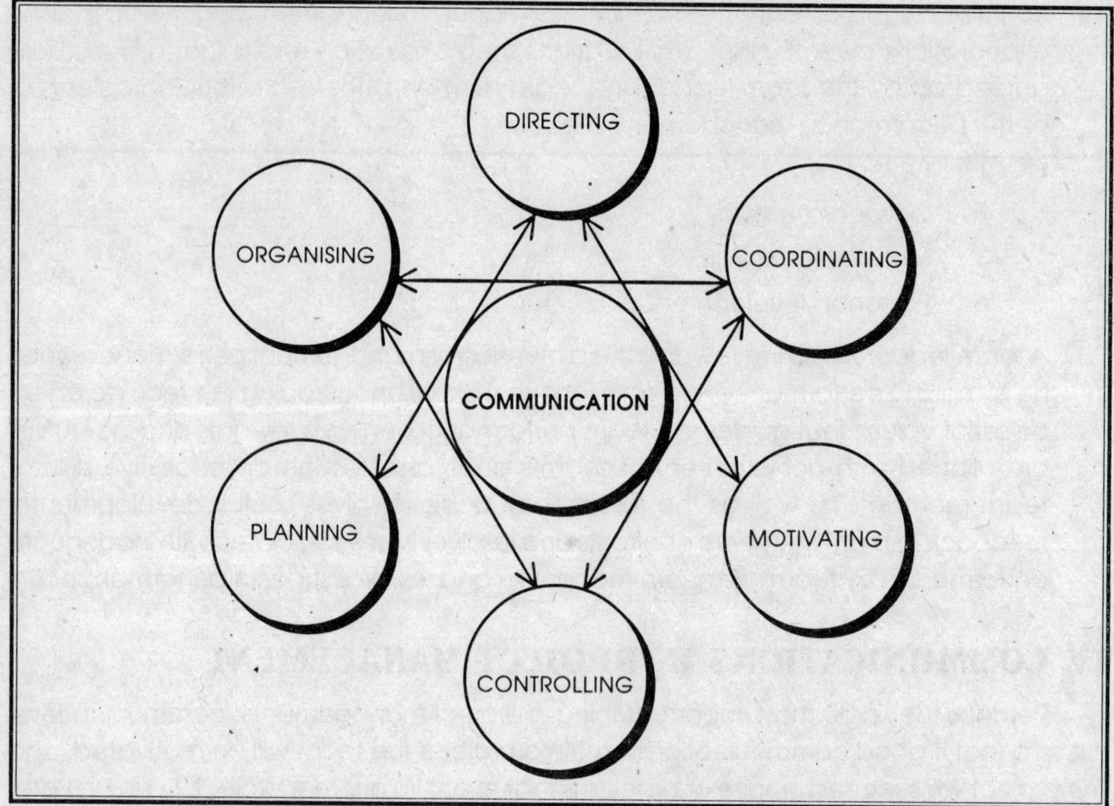

Fig. 11.02 Communication as key to other Management Functions

That is why, it is often said that if a project managers has good communications skills and no other skills at all, the project team will get the project completed successfully in spite of the project manager. Communication management in projects is the process required to ensure timely and appropriate generation, collection, dissemination , storage, and timely disposition of project information.

WHAT IS COMMUNICATION ?

The word 'Communication' is derived from the latin word 'Communis' which means 'in common' or "sharing in common". Two distinct meanings are possible in case of this word– 'Communication'. First, it stands for means of communication like telephone, telegraph, television, cable, radio, micro-wave and the like. The second the transmission of information in an organisation. It is the act of inducing others to interpret an idea in the manner intended by the speaker or a writer. It is the act of pouring the idea into the heads of others. It is the sum total of all those things one person does when he wants to create an understanding in the mind of another. It is the bridge of meaning. In the words of Prof Luis A. Allen,: "It is the bridge of meaning involving a systematic and continuous process of telling, listening and understanding". According to Charles E. Readfield: "Communication is the broad field of human interchange of facts and opinion and not the technologies of telephone, telegraph, radio and the like".

BASIC FEATURES OF COMMUNICATION

The nature of communication as a management function is very much clear from the following points.

1. **COMMUNICATION IS ADMINISTRATIVE :**

   Though communication is a common process In day-today life, it has specific stand in the world of business. It is administrative in nature. It is used to connect the function of management. Theoretically, it is possible to plan, organise, develop procedure, when it comes to implementation, communication becomes an essential tool. To be very precise, no function of management is going to be performed effectively without communication because management is not a one man show.

2. **IT IS INTERNAL TO THE ORGANIZATION :**

   Communication is purely internal to the organisation. It is intended to apply primarily to the persons who are the members of the organisation. Thus, a company discovering a new product reporting in news-paper is not communication in the strict sense of the term. On the other hand, a superior giving orders to his sub-ordinates is communication. By the same token, the progress reports moving from the sub-ordinates to the supervisors is communication.

3. **IT IS TWO WAY PROCESS :**

   At one time, it was the function of the boss to tell his sub-ordinates as to what to do. The sub-ordinates were to do and die but not to reason why ? Thus, communication was more an order giving. Lapse of time, warranted another aspect- namely, understanding. Thus, a manager speaks, informs and requests, he listens, answers and interprets. Communication to be the complete process, should be transmission supported by the mutual understanding. Thus, it is the two-way process of telling, listening and understanding on the part of parties involved in the exactly same manner.

BASIC ELEMENTS OF COMMUNICATION PROCESS

Communication, as an administrative process, has fine basic elements. These elements have been very aptly explained by Professor Lawrence A. Appley, a known figure in the management science. These elements are :

1. **CLARIFY THE DATA :**

The beginning of the communication is the idea. Unless the idea is clearly formulated in the mind of a transmitter, the message is likely to be misunderstood by the receiver or the respondent. One cannot make clear print from a blurred negative; so also the process of communication starts with careful and precise identification as the problem that requires an action.

2. **EMPLOYEE PARTICIPATION :**

This important step is to draw others into the problem crystallised. The purposes of such involvement are:

(1) to clarify and test his own thinking by sharing his ideas with others.

(2) to gather the ideas.

(3) to motivate those who are responsible for carrying out the decision by inviting others to participate. Productive participation demands- careful preparation, permissive climate, sensitive listening and willingness to credit others.

3. **TRANSMISSION :**

At this juncture, the communicator must plan very carefully, what to communicate ? Whom to communicate with ? And how best to communicate ? Utmost care is to be taken as to what he is going to say so that he says clearly and correctly. He should be aware of the fact as to whom he is talking- what barriers come in the way of effective communication. These barriers may be physical and psychological.

4. **MOTIVATION :**

A communication is not only to be understood but also to be accepted and acted upon. This warrants motivation. It should state, and inspire the receiver to do it. Employee morale and productivity are directly linked to the process of communication. Employee who knows what is expected of him, that is, work is tied to the objective of the company, learns changes before that occurring will work with enthusiasm and initiative.

5. **EVALUATION :**

Many a time, communication suffers from the failure to evaluate its effectiveness. It is necessary to investigate into the reasons why the manager succeeded in some meetings and not in others ? Why some talks of his produced wonderful results, while some merely indifference ? Why some only resistance ? The exact impact of communication can be traced from attitude surveys, productivity indicators, labour turnover and absenteeism and so on.

BARRIERS TO COMMUNICATION

There can be many barriers to communication. Messages can be blocked or distorted, and as a result, their meaning can be changed considerably. Each manager is aware of misunderstandings, frictions and the inconveniences that arise when the communication network breaks down. These breakdowns are costly in terms of treasure, time and talents. The most common types of barriers are:

1. **BARRIERS DUE TO ORGANISATIONAL STRUCTURE :**

   The structure of organisation has a significant influence on the ability of the members of the organisation to communicate effectively. Today's organisation structure is complex involving several layers of supervision, relations of staff to line, longer communication lines, creating an organizational distance of the workers at floor level to the top management. Such a vast distance by communication channels and lairs may breakdown at any point does filter in faulty transmission.

2. **BARRIERS CAUSED BY LANGUAGE :**

   Language is the method of using symbols namely, words to represent facts and feelings and it is the basis for communication. Though word serves some definite purpose, very often the same word carries different meanings for different people in different contexts. For instance, the word 'round' can be used as round as ball, walking round and round- a round dozen eggs- a round trip- a round beef- a round cylinder and so on. The point is that the sender has his own frame of reference and the receiver too. The word 'Profit' stands future growth for the management but exploitation to the employees.

3. **BARRIERS DUE TO RESISTANCE TO CHANGE :**

   It is the most natural tendency of human beings to resist change and to prefer status-quo. The listener will not receive message in its real sense if it is new as their receiving apparatus acts as a filter if does not match to the existing equilibrium in the mind. It is the set of predisposition that decides the acceptances of message and interpretation.

4. **DISTRUSTED SOURCES :**

   The source of a communication may be wrong about what he or she is communicating. It can be that source is really wrong, or it may be that one is just convinced that the source is wrong. When this condition exists in an extreme way, it makes no difference what is really said. The perception of the message will be similar to what is expected.

5. **DISTORTED PERCEPTION :**

   Many a times, the receiver is not in the proper frame of mind to receive the message. This may be due to many reasons, such as the environment, the mood of the receiver, or the subject matter being delivered. The status of the person sending the message may have an effect as well. When something is being said by a person working in the next cubical, the effectiveness of the communication will be different than if the person is the CEO of the company. So one can say that motivation and needs and even his or her experience affect a person's perception. The receiver's perception is also affected by the need to connect the new message to already received information that is stored in his or her memory. One tries to connect new information to the old in order to make it more meaningful.

HOW TO IMPROVE COMMUNICATIONS ?

Since effective communication is vital to successful management, the executive is to be familiar with the means of improving communications. These ways are :

1. **Enter the world of Receiver :**

   To communicate effectively, the sender must be sensitive to the world of receiver. He is to predict the impact of what he will pay on the feelings and attitudes of the receiver. The message should have more relevance to the employees. This warrants a common ground for the receiver and the sender. The sender is not to beat his own drum. Make messages linked with the employee feelings. Rather the communicator is to reach mutual understanding, the language used must be one of listener. That is, sender should be receiver friendly.

2. **LISTEN MORE :**

   The sender is to listen first the receiver instead of just pouring down his ideas to him or her. This enables the speaker to learn about the receiver's value and relationship to his work. Listening, in the sense, does not mean attention nor listening with the intent of finding faults. He is to listen to the meanings, the idea than the word. He is to know the hidden meaning and it is called as hearing with "third ear". It calls for improving listening. It means that one should not interrupt, put the speaker at ease, appearing interested, cutting out distractions and summing up at definite internal what is already said.

3. **ACTIONS SPEAK LOUDER THAN WORDS :**

   Every manager is to realise that he communicates by his actions as much as he communicates by words. The best way to communicate is to act according to the message. His verbal announcements are to be reinforced by actions. That is, he should mean as to what he says. A good communicator is an actor or a person who knows how to articulate and dramatise.

4. **BE REDUNDANT :**

   Certain amount of redundancy has often helped to overcome barriers of communications. This is especially so when each word in communication is important and directions are complicated. In, such cases, it is wiser to repeat them several times, probably best in different ways and means. However, too much is too bad. It should not defeat the every purpose of elaboration of deliberation. The degree of redundancy depends on the content of message and experience and back- ground of the receiver.

5. THE FEED-BACK :

The communication is to be assured that the receiver has received the message and understood it in its organisational and original sense. The simplest way to make certain this, he is to observe the receiver's non-verbal clues such as facial expressions like raising an eye-brows, or frowning. This is possible in case of face to face communication. The other ways are asking the questions, describing the situation frankly. Such verification helps a lot.

6. REDUCE THE MESSAGE TO ITS SIMPLEST TERMS :

When one communicates with someone, he is to keep the message as simple as possible. Many a times, the message is complicated with unnecessary details about the rationale and the justification of the project when the listener is already convinced and just wants to know what to do. The task of manager is to get the work done. This is possible when he puts his idea or ideas to the receiver of the message in the simplest words.

7. ORGANISE THE MESSAGE INTO A SERIES OF STAGES :

One of the reasons that verbal communication succeeds over written communication is the opportunity to keep things simple. The sender can send a simple part of the message and receive feed-back immediately. The sender can send another part of the message and receive feed-back on that too. In this way, the message is kept simple, and the receiver is brought to the complete understanding of the full message, one piece at a time.

V. PROJECT REVIEW-MEETINGS

Managers and project managers spend as much as 70 per cent of their time in meetings. Nearly, all managers complain that they spend more time in meetings than they should and that for the most part, meetings are a waste of time. If no one likes to attend meetings and everyone feels that they are a waste of valuable time, why then organisations call meetings ? The reason that meetings are held is based on the concept that two heads are better than one, three heads are better than two, and so on. Adding people to a meeting improves the chances that things can be accomplished in the meeting. The problem is that as number of people attending a meeting increases, the effectiveness of the meeting increases at a diminishing rate. The cost of additional people in a meeting continues to increase in a linear fashion, and very soon the benefit of additional people at a meeting is less than the cost of having them there.

WHY MEETINGS ?

Whenever the meetings are conducted properly, there are definite advantages that flow. They are :

- **SAVING IN TIME :**

  Meetings save good deal of time by bringing the number of people together to discuss and decide something than trying to deal with it in another way say- writing or dealing with them one at a time. It facilitates face to face discussion and exchange of information.

- **REFINED SOLUTIONS :**

  Meetings extend an opportunity for various views to be expressed, listened too and to be discussed and decided upon. Meetings ensure that everyone involved in a subject has an opportunity to make one's views known and to hear the views of others. This results in supporting or opposing proposals and assessment is the base for such support rejection.

- **POOLING OF RESOURCE PERSONS :**

  Meetings enable the pooling of knowledge, skills and resources of people who do not normally work together. This makes the outcomes the best possible as the problems are thrashed out at the hands of veterans.

- **ENHANCING SELF-CONFIDENCE AND CREATIVITY :**

  Meetings help to increase the self- confidence and creativity of individuals either in a leader role or as a member, particularly in a grouped team situation. Some individuals may not bring forward ideas when they are working alone; but in the atmosphere of meeting intervals, they are encouraged to express themselves or be creative particularly when they hear others speak out with less valuable contributions.

- **DEVELOPING TOGETHERNESS :**

  Meetings encourage good communication, co-ordination, improved relationships and co-working. Meetings can ensure the spreading of tasks among the number of people. This leads to building of working relationships among people from different parts of the company or different organisations. What is more important is that they are instrumental in establishing an uniformity or communality of attitude and action within the group, department or company or group of units.

TYPES OF MEETINGS

It is the objectives determined for the meeting will decide the exact nature of the meeting. Experts visualize six types of meetings namely, information giving, information seeking, consultative or general, problem-solving and decision-making, brain-storming, team-briefing. We are concerned here with the last type which is also called project review-meeting.

The project manager calls on regular basis, weekly or fortnightly on monthly review-meetings. These meetings are meant for project team. Hence, engineers, vendors, contractors are also allowed to participate in these meetings in addition to team members. It is obvious that for the reasons best known everyone cannot participate in the same meeting. Thus, reasons with contraction are normally held at the site, mostly every week. Similarly, all review-meetings, with vendors are held at vendors work site. These meetings have no fixed interval. Review-meeting with engineers can be a monthly or quarterly at the owner's office or at the site. However, reviews within an engineering company are generally held every month with all the interrelated disciplines attending at the same time.

Thus, team review or briefing meeting is one that combines information giving and information seeking and general discussion items. The team members are having the opportunities to raise questions or proposals relating to the team operations. They give feed back on what has been achieved over the last meetings targets. The reasons for achievement, non-achievement or under-achievement are thoroughly discussed. Each meeting sets targets for the coming period. It is a meeting of give and take on the progress of the project in question.

EFFECTIVE MANAGEMENT OF MEETINGS

Successful management of review-meetings can be divided into two sections namely, Before the meeting, During the meeting and After the meeting

Before the Meeting :

The project manager arranges to send a memo giving notice of the meeting. Notifying the people of a meeting by telephone is not the most reliable way to ensure that they will attend. Sending a written message increases the chances that they will attend. Most people are busy and are bombarded with meeting notices and telephone calls. On many occasions, these meetings are called at short-notice at the inconvenience of the attendees. This creates a feeling of imposition on the part of attenders and does not make for a good attitude towards the meeting. The participants are to feel that they are inseparable, contributing part of meeting. Hence, sufficient advance notice is to be given.

The written notice of meeting should contain time and place for the meeting, the subject to be discussed, the tentative agenda and the list of those who are invited. It is essential to fix up the agenda and frequency for these meetings at the beginning of the project so that everyone could do their homework for attending these meetings. That is, attendees should have time to prepare and should know who is attending the meeting. They should be specifically informed if they are going to be expected to make any presentation, or contribute something special to the meeting. Obviously, the agenda for different review meeting will be different. However, in general, a project review meeting has for discussion :

- Status of implementation of the decision taken in the previous meeting.
- Progress achieved during the review period vis-a-vis agreed targets.
- Problems and issues associated with the project.
- Decision regarding the problems and issues.
- Agreed action-program and progress target up to next review meeting.

During the Meeting :

Project manager opens the meeting by restating the objectives. It should be clear to all those attending the meting as to what the purpose and goal of the meeting is. He goes over the agenda and asks for additions. This is one of the most important aspects of making a meeting effective. One of the problems of meetings is that one of the participants is inspired to change the subject. Before anyone can stop it, the meeting heads off in a new direction and is no longer going in the direction of its stated goals. The problem with this is not that the discussion is not useful and that the new discussion is not beneficial, but that the purpose of the meeting side -tracked and that some of the people in the meeting are not necessary for the discussion now taking place. The wise use of an agenda avoids this problem. When a new and unrelated discussion begins, the leader of the meeting can use the agenda to bring things back on the right track. It is, therefore, important for the leader of the meeting to ask for additions or corrections of the agenda at the beginning of the meeting. Any additions and corrections made at this time will be likely to help in achieving the goal of the meeting. Later, when spontaneous discussion ensues, the agenda can be used to guide it back to the purpose of the meeting.

There should be record of the minutes of the meeting, all action items signed and any conclusions reached. The results of the meeting are to be recorded. In particular, the agreed upon action items must be recorded to ensure that they actually take place.

The use of recording devices and video cameras generally has a negative effect on the discussion that take place in the meetings. Transcribing tape recordings of meetings is generally time consuming and less effective than good note-taking.

After the Meeting :

The persons conducting these review-meeting are to distribute the minutes within twenty four hours. Each meeting should be followed up by the distribution of the minutes of the meeting. Like the meeting notes, the information and the results of the meeting must be distributed to the attendees and other interested parties. These minutes provide the necessary directions till the next review.

The review-meetings of the type that we have noted will force the people to be on the look out for signs of problems all the time. In spite of these meetings, problems crop up almost every day without notice and directions will have to be provided immediately as they can not be allowed to wait till the next review-meeting. Hence, there is need for sound communication system supporting project management where direction, co-ordination, control all can be taken care of.

CHAPTER BASED QUESTIONS

A. WRITE SHORT NOTES ON

1. Project authority
2. Sources of authority
3. Scope of authority
4. Project managers authority
5. Project-team
6. Team-building
7. Team-work
8. Team and group
9. Effective team-work
10. Steps in team-building
11. Leader as a team builder
12. Leadership
13. Project manager as a leader
14. Communication
15. Basic elements of communication
16. Barriers of communication
17. Review-meetings

B. SHORT ANSWER QUESTIONS

1. What is a project review-meeting ?
2. What is communication ?
3. What is leadership ?
4. What is project authority ?
5. What is the scope of authority ?
6. What is a project team ?
7. What is effective team work ?
8. What is an agenda ?
9. What is veto power ?
10. What are the team-work factors ?

C. ESSAY TYPE QUESTIONS

1. What is project authority ? What are the features of it ?
2. What is authority ? What are the sources of authority ?
3. Discuss the 'dejure' and 'de facto' authority of a project manager.

4. What is the difference between a 'group' and a 'team' ? How an 'effective' team differs from an 'ineffective' team ?
5. Discuss role of a project manager as a 'team-builder'.
6. What is leadership ? What are its features ? Discuss project manager as a leader.
7. What is communication ? What is its role in project management ?
8. What is communication ? What are barriers to communication ? How you will remove them ?
9. What is a project review meeting ? How you will manage them in an effective manner ?
10. Do you think the terms 'power' and 'authority' are same ? If not- how will you distinguish them ?

* * * * *

Chapter 12

PRICING ESTIMATING AND COST CONTROL

- COST ESTIMATING
- IMPORTANCE OF COST ESTIMATES
- TYPES OF ESTIMATES
- TECHNIQUES OF ESTIMATING
- SUITABILITY OF ESTIMATING TECHNIQUE AT DIFFERENT STAGES OF PROJECT
- PROJECT LIFE-CYCLE AND PROJECT COST
- ISSUES INVOLED IN LCC
- DISTINCTION BETWEEN 'TRADITIONAL' COSTING AND 'LIFE-CYCLE' COSTING
- AREAS WHERE LCC IS APPLIED WITH SPECIFIC BENEFITS
- COST FLOW
- PROJECT PRICING
- COST BUDGETING
- COST CONTROL
- REPORTING THE WORK COMPLETED
- CHAPTER BASED QUESTIONS

BACKDROP

Cost management is an essential part of project management because, it makes it possible to manage cost - baseline of the project. Without cost management projects will use more or less money than allocated, and it would be impossible to fund future projects. The project manager as in all things is the person responsible for the project cost management. Cost estimation is done over the life of the project. The work break down structure is the basis for cost-estimates. Since work breakdown structure identifies all the project work in a detailed workable way, it becomes the best place to determine the cost of the project. Equally important is pricing of projects because business is not a charity and risks need reward. In making project management a grand success, there is dire need for cost control in project management. This is achieved through the use of the earned value reporting system. Hence, this chapter plans to touch upon these to acquaint the readers as to what one should know in the cost and costing area of project management. The chapter ends with Chapter Based Questions.

COST ESTIMATING

As against ascertainment of actual cost, there is need of predetermination of costs. Cost estimation is the process of predetermining the cost of goods or services. Here, 'goods' we mean 'project' because 'Project' becomes the 'product'. The costs is determined in advance of production and precede the operations. Estimated costs are definitely the future costs and are based on the average of the past actual costs adjusted for the anticipated changes in future. A cost estimate is a prediction of the likely cost of the resources that will be required to complete all the work of the project.

Cost estimating is done throughout the project life cycle. In the beginning of the project proof of concept estimates must be done to allow the project to go on. An order of magnitude estimates in performed at this stage of the project order of magnitude estimates can have an accuracy of -25 per cent to +75 per cent. As the project progresses, more accurate estimate are required. Budget estimates are those that have an accuracy of –10 per cent to +25 per cent. Finally, at the time of creating the project cast base-line, the definitive estimate is 5 per cent to +10 per cent. Early in the project, there is much uncertainty about what work is actually to be done in the project. There is no point in expending the effort to make a more accurate estimate than the accuracy needed at the particular stage of the project is in.

IMPORTANCE OF COST ESTIMATES

The importance of cost estimates hence, estimating, can not be underestimated. The significance is self-evident from the following points.

1. MAKING PRICE QUOTATIONS AND BIDDING CONTRACTS

To enter into a contract for the execution of the project and to compare the price of the contract, a realistic cost estimate of the total project work as the basis for finalising the and to compare the price of the contract, a realistic cost estimates of the total project for which contracts is being finalised is essential. The estimated cost shall contract price and, hence, contract in question.

2. BASE FOR BUDGETING, MONITORING AND CONTROLLING

Budgets are the estimates for the future. Hence, cost estimates are the basis for budgeting business activities for a definite period of time. These estimated costs are 'standards' for the future and hence, there is a possibility of perfect monitoring of the project progress. Equally important is that of controlling the project costs. Thus, planning, monitoring and controlling are assured by cost estimates.

3. BOTTOM FOR PREPARING PROJECTED FINANCIAL STATEMENTS

Financial statements are needed for several reasons. Among them is the financial grant. Cost estimates help in preparing projected income statements and balance sheets for the future years. From these fund-flow and cash-flow statements can be prepared. Arrangement of funds for the project can be made only when the cost of the project is known in advance. To take advantage of different sources of funds and types of funds to the advantage, there is need for convincing the supplies the supporters of finance atleast cost and with least strings.

4. MEASURING THE PROFITABILITY

Cost estimation is almost unavoidable to assess the viability of the proposal. The commercial viability of a proposal can be determined in number of ways. It can be done by calculating payout period, rate of return on investment, present or net present value, internal rate of returns and so on. All these calculations are the of shoots of cost estimation from which cash flows statements are prepared and used in various calculations for ascertaining profitability.

5. GRANT OF APPROVAL TO GO AHEAD

Approval of higher or competent authority is a must. The higher authorities or competent authorities grant a green signal of go ahead only when they are convinced that the project proposed can be executed in the parameters of the cost, time and resources. It is the perfect cost estimates that have the power of winning the heads and hearts of higher authorities. It is necessary to know the cost of the proposal to decide the level of authority to whom the proposal shall be put up for approval. It is because, different levels of authorities have different powers to approve.

TYPES OF ESTIMATES

There are several types of estimates in common use. Depending on the accuracy required for the estimate and the cost effort that can be expended, there are several choices. These are:

1. TOP-DOWN ESTIMATES

Top-down estimates are used to estimate cost early in project when information about the project is very limited. 'Top-down' comes from the idea that the estimate is made at the top level of the project. That is, project itself is estimated with one single estimate. The merit of this type of estimate is that it requires much less effort and very little time to produce. The demerit is that the accuracy of the estimate is not as good as it would be with a more detailed estimating effort.

2. BOTTOM-UP ESTIMATES

Bottom-up estimates are used when the project baselines are required or definitive type of estimate is needed. These types of estimates are called 'bottom-up' because they begin estimating the details of the project and then summarise the details into summery levels. The WBS can be used for this 'roll-up'. The merit of this kind of estimate is that it produces accurate results. The level of accuracy of 'bottom-up' estimate depends on the level of detail that is being considered. Statistically, convergence takes place as more and more detail is added. The demerit of this is the cost of doing detailed estimating is higher and the time consumed is quite longer.

3. ANALOGOUS ESTIMATES

Analogous estimates are form of 'top-down' estimate. This process uses the actual cost of previously completed projects to predict the cost of the project that is being estimated. Thus, there is an analogy and the project between one project and another. In case of the project being used in analogy being estimated are very similar, the estimates control quite accurate. On the other hand, if projects are not very similar, the estimates may not be that accurate at all. For instance, a new software development project is to be done. The modules to be designed are very similar to the modules that were used on another project but current modules require more lines of code. The difficulty of the project is quite similar to the previous project. If the new project is 35 per cent larger than the previous project, the analogy might predict a project cost of 35 per cent greater that of the previous project.

4. PARAMETRIC ESTIMATES

Parametric estimates are similar to analogous estimates in that they are also 'top-down' estimates. Their inherent accuracy is not better nor worse than those of analogous estimates. The process of parametric estimating is attained by finding a parameter of the project being estimated that changes proportionately with project cost. A mathematical model is designed based on one or more parameters. When the values of the parameters are entered into the model, the cost of the project results.

In case there is close relationship between the parameters and the cost and the parameters are easy to quantifying, the accuracy can be improved. If there are, historical projects that are both more costly and less costly than the project being estimated and the parametric in relationship is true for both those historical projects the estimating accuracy and the reliability of the parameter for these project will be better. Multiple parameter estimates can be produced as well. In multiple parameters estimates, various weights are given to each parameter to allow for the calculation of cost by parameters simultaneously.

5. DEFINITIVE ESTIMATES

Definitive estimates are the 'bottom-up' variety. This type of estimate that is used to establish a project baseline or any other important estimate. In a project, the WBS can be used as the level of detail for the estimate. The accuracy of this estimate can be made to be quite high, but the cost of developing the estimate can be quite high and the time to produce it can be lengthier as well.

Definite estimates are based on the statistical central limit theorem that explains statistical convergence. If we have a group of details that can be summarized, the variance of the sum of the details will be less significant than the significance of the variance of themselves. All this means is that the more details one has in estimate, the more accurate the sum of details will be, because some of the estimates of the details will be over-estimated and some will be underestimated. The over-estimates and underestimates will cancel each other out. If one has enough details, the average overestimates and underestimates will approach a zero difference.

If one knows the mean or expected values and the standard deviations for a group of detailed estimates, one can calculate the expected value and the standard deviations of the sum. If one also is willing to accept that the probability of the estimate being correct follows a normal probability distribution, then one can predict the range of values and the probability of the actual cost.

TECHNIQUES OF ESTIMATING

There are several techniques of estimating, of which most widely used all over the world in case of project management are five. These are founded on historic cost and price data especially where:

- The data sample size is relatively large.
- The cost data relates to a specific base date.
- The data available are updated to values that are relevant to the base data by using an inflated index.
- The effects of market forces are duty accounted for. These techniques are:

1. GLOBAL ESTIMATING

This technique is also known as "order of magnitude", "rule of thumb" or "ball-park estimating". This technique relies solely on historic data and, therefore, must be used in conjunction with inflation and judgment of the trends in levels of prices (market influence) to allow for the envisaged timing for the project. The examples of the cost units applied are:

- Cost per mega watt capacity of power stations.
- Cost per meter or km of road or railways.
- Cost per square metre of building floor area or per cubic meter of building volume.
- Cost per ton of output for process plants.

The application of such type of "rolled up historical data" is beset withy the dangers under following situations:

1. Free play of inflationary trends.
2. Costs are undefined or ill-defined.
3. The measurement of the capacity is ill-defined or undefined.
4. The unit of measurement includes on infrastructure facilities.
5. The comparisons are made with dissimilar ones.
6. The standards of the quality are incompatible.
7. The cost base is different.

2. FACTORIAL ESTIMATING

Factorial estimating or estimates is generally applied in complex projects, where multiple projects are undertaken simultaneously which are similar in scope and size. As the name suggests the various factors of project costs are comprehensively covered such as pipe-work , electric instruments, structures and foundations and the like. The estimate for each peripheral is the product of its factor and estimate for the main plant items. Though this technique does not call for a detailed presentation, it necessitates a through scanning of the construction and inventory problems that go undetected many a times. The technique has a considerable advantage being predominantly based on current costs, thereby taking account of market conditions and placing little reliance on inflation. This technique is not advisable for site-works estimates such as civil construction, mechanical and electrical installations except in a series of projects where the site circumstances are nearly similar.

The success of this technique depends largely on:

- Experience on a similar projects would be a reliable factor in the long-run.
- The estimator has to make judgments on the values to include in his estimate depending on market conditions.
- A complete loyalty towards this technique may avoid deficiencies in some areas by mutual adjustments and timely compensation.
- Estimator's personal skills and dependence on proper judgment and application.

3. MAN-HOURS ESTIMATING

This is claimed to be the only original estimating technique. It is one of the most suitable techniques for estimating cost in labour-intensive projects such as fabrication, erection of piping, mechanical equipment, electrical installation-work, where a reliable records of production of different trades per man-hour are prevalent.

As per this technique, the estimated costs of the man-hours for a given task are determined according to the prevailing labour rules which are further added to the costs of materials and equipment. There is, however, an assumption, that the methods of construction will not vary form project to project in great detail and, hence, detailed program for such similar constructions is not essential. In fact, it is always advised and recommended for a detailed program in order to identify constraints specific to the project and avoid emergencies. The total cost is subjected to a change proportionately in case labour productivity varies. Therefore, this technique warrants an appropriate knowledge about the prevailing labour rates and advocates vehemently the estimator to ensure much care while managing the current-day projects.

4. UNIT RATES ESTIMATING

This technique is as old as the construction itself in the sphere of projects. It is based on the "Bill of Quantity" (BOQ) approach to pricing construction work. It is customary to have a detailed list of items to be purchased and used for which "bill of quantities" is prepared by the purchase manager, in case of each and every project. This BOQ contains the quantum of work to be constructed measured with an appropriate yardstick. The estimator selects historical rates or prices for each item in the bill, using information quantities or built up rates through his analysis. This estimating technique involves good deal of guesstimating than estimating as it relies on historical data. When the detailed bill of quantities is not available, quantities for the main items of work are priced using "rolled-up" rates that eventually account for the associated minor items.

This technique is suitable for building and construction projects where allocation of costs to specific operation can be very well defined at the same time to various similar operations and make it possible to manage risks. Its stability depends, however, on the executive experience and the skill and the accessibility of the estimator towards well knit bank comprising of 'rolled- up' prices. However, this technique is not free from limitations. The basic weak point is that the precision and the details of the limit rates can create unwanted misplaced level of confidence in the figures. It assumes that the previous work is similar to one that of present and having same time duration. It is because period costs have their own implications.

In spite of its weaknesses, this unit price estimating is most widely used because it can produce realistic estimates if the exercise is handeled by experienced estimators with good intuitive judgment having access to reliable data bank.

5. OPERATIONAL COST ESTIMATING

This is one of the universally applied technique. It is also known as "resource cost estimating". As per this technique, the total cost of the project is compiled by considering the constituent operations revealed by the resource schedules and demand estimates. The procedure of estimating costs is very simple as regards the materials, plant and machinery, labour and so on where current prices are applied. As the technique discloses the fundamental sources of costs, the sensitivity associated with the assumptions, methods and the reasons for variation in costs, it would be much of utility under heavy uncertainties. To determine the costs of most vulnerable project operations, sensitivity analysis may be carried out and appropriate allowances can be included.

This technique is most reliable in case of civil engineering works, and it is frequently used by major contractors and consulting project engineers. Though it is relatively time consuming and resource intensive comparatively, the project manager and engineers prefer this discounting the demerits. It is because it enables them to prepare preliminary estimates considering the common risks and uncertainties of the project.

SUITABILITY OF ESTIMATING TECHNIQUE AT DIFFERENT STAGES OF PROJECT

According to experts, there is definite co-relationship between five estimating techniques described above and the estimating stages. This relates the level of details available for estimating different costs attached to a project.

1. PRELIMINARY STAGE

As preliminary stage is a mere beginning for any estimate where one is unlikely to have design data avilable with crude indication of the project size or capacity, the estimate is likely to be in the form of provisional state of capital expenditure. Hence, the global estimating technique can be very well used which is a crude system that relies on the existence of data for similar projects assessed purely on a single feature such as size, capacity or output. For some projects consisting of process plants or with multiple projects simultaneously carried on, the factorial method can be applied where the key components can be easily identified and prices and all other works are calculated as factors of these components.

2. FEASIBILITY STAGE

Any estimate at this stage mainly focusses on the direct comparison of the alternative schemes under consideration. This estimate is more generally known as "appraisal estimate." All the estimates of alternatives that include them all costs that are charged against project to provide the best estimate of the anticipated total cost, in fact, and if it is to be used to update the original amount in the forward budget then it is escalated to cash estimate. Hence, the project price will be equal to estimated Cost + Risk + Overheads + Profit + Mark-up.

The basic cost estimate is the largest of all these valuations reflecting atleast say 90 per cent of the total price. The basic cost estimate is normally determined by using a unit rate or operational assessment of the materials, labour, plant to be used along with any sub-contracting cost details. Quotations are needed for details of materials and sub-contracting works. Typically, materials account for 30 to 60 per cent of the total value of the project whereas sub-contracting costs range between 20 to 40 per cent. Overheads for the project include allowances for site management and supervisions, accommodation for clerical staff and general employees, general items and sundry requirements.

3. DESIGN STAGE

At this stage the estimates are to be more dependable and must evolve from conceptual design until pre-tender definitive design is completed. Therefore, labour-hour method is most matching for labour-intensive operations like designing, maintenance or mechanical erection work that is estimated on the basis of total man-hour and costed in conjunction with the plant and material costs. Finally, these decisions of design focussing on the size, complexity, quality parameters will influence the capital costs deeply. The higher the amount of changes in the design, the higher will be the capital cost commitments for the sponsor and the contractor. This continues till the pre-tender design is completed and sanctioned for further proceedings. Hence, the design budget estimates should confirm the appraisal estimate and set the cost limit for the capital outlay of the project.

4. CONSTRUCTION STAGE

At this stage, the estimates are bound to be more refined. The estimator finds now it practically difficult to manage the budget according to the plan and any variation during the construction stage proves to be costly affair. Hence the estimates are the superfine and less subject to contingencies. In order to cope up with such intricacies, the tender money needs to be properly distributed over the bill of quantites (BOQ). The unit rate method is a matching technique based on the traditional BOQ approach where quantities of work are defined and measured in accordance with a standard method of measurement.

PROJECT LIFE-CYCLE AND PROJECT COST.

Of late, it has become important to consider the cost of project for the full useful life of the product or service that is created. This means that the cost of project does not end when final acceptance of the project has been completed. Guarantees, warranties and ongoing services that must be performed during the life of the project must be considered. With regard to project life-cycle, cost decisions are made with a clearer picture of the future commitments that the project requires. If life-cycle cost (LCC) is considered better decision will be made.

The concept of life-cycle costing is quite relevant to project management. LCC is the systematic analytical process of evaluating various alternative courses of action with the intent of choosing the best way to employ scarce resources. Put in the words, of Mr. Benjamin, S. Blanchard and Walter J. Fabrycky, LCC is an "accumulation of all costs associated with the system as applied to the defined life-cycle."

The function relevant to each phase of life-cycle costing are:

- Concept or need identification.
- Preliminary systems planning.
- Systems research.
- Systems design.
- Production and construction.
- Systems evaluation.
- Systems use and logistic support including project termination, material-disposal and reclamation or recycling.

The life-cycle, as tailored to the specific system being addressed, forms the very basis of LCC. Hence, the cost break down structure will be to be suitable to the life-cycle:

- Research and development costs.
- Production and construction costs.
- Operation and support costs.
- Retirement and disposal costs.

ISSUES INVOLED IN LCC

There are some important issues involved in LCC application. These are:

1. DEVELOPMENT OF COST PROFILE

This is the first basic task where project manager has to develop a cost profile immediately after:

- Identifying the activities.
- Determining the respective costs in each category.
- Establishing the cost factors.
- Projecting each cost element into the future for each cost category in accordance with the cost-breakdown structure.

2. ARRANGEMENT AND ASSIGNMENT OF APPROPRIATE INDICES

There is need for sound arrangement and assignment of appropriate indices to cope with inflation and other economic fluctuations that reflect in pricing of activities.

3. LEARNING CURVE EFFECT AND IMPACT

Learning curve shows quantitatively how, when activities are repeated, their cycle times reduce. There is need for acknowledging the "learning curve" effect and its impact on costs.

4. ESTABLiSHING COMMON POINT OF REFEREE

A common point of reference is expected to be established so that reckoning time value of money can be made easy and simple and all available alternatives can be compared on a standard level since revenues and costs are related to different activities at different points of time over the life-cycle.

DISTINCTION BETWEEN "TRADITIONAL COSTING" AND "LIFE CYCLE COSTING"

Traditional or conventional costing is generally referred to as either product costing or process costing. Its applicability is confined to the manufacturing industries, where production activities are repetitive in nature and rarely differ in size or scope. Hence, a fixed framework can be determined for such continuous process or product manufacturing activities and the cost can be determined without much fuss. As opposed to this **project costing** is unique which fails to fit into the outfit of process or manufacture. It is a known fact that each project is unique and unique in experience like the finger prints of human beings. To aevelop, therefore, a standard costing system in the project management, it is really challenging. Over the years, the veterans of the field tried their best to evolve a standard costing system to address to the peculiarities of the projects. Finally, there has been a headway made where contributions of **Mr. B.S.Blanchard and J.Fabrycky** are recognized who gave the world of project management a new system of costing the project management known as LIFE-CYCLE COSTING SYSTEM (LCC). The question is how this LCC differs from conventional, costing system (CCS). The major points of difference are:

1. ORIENTATION

As opposed to conventional costing system, the orientation or philosophy of LCC is towards the expected future cost and not historical costs. As the focus is on future trends of project performance, uncertainty is caught with and treated explicitly rather than being given a hideout.

2. TIME SPAN

LCC in a project costing system concerns the entire life span of a project from almost "womb to tomb". Hence, it consists of cost-conceptual, development, design, construction operation and maintenance and replacement costs. LCC approach helps to ensure that the total resource impact of a proposal is identified. The danger of forcibly operating costs are avoided by judicious enquiry into the intersection of cost at different cycles of the project.

3. APPROACH TO COSTING

LCC brings more dynamic approach to resource optimisation by challenging costs at different stages of creation, preservation and disposal using sound alternatives. The distinction between fixed and variable cost is not manifested rather the relevant objective function is applied for which the costs are incurred.

AREAS WHERE LCC IS APPLIED WITH SPECIFIC BENEFITS

There are certain areas where the LCC approach can be used with benefits. These are:

1. DEFENCE ACTIVITIES

The LCC that originated from the American Defence Department, was used extensively for cost analysis of variety of defence projects. For a proposed new weapon system, the cost of the proposal is lumped under three major cost classes namely:

- R. and D costs
- Investment costs
- Operating costs

R. and D costs comprise of resources required to develop new capability to the point where it can be introduced in the operational inventory at some desired level of reliability. Investment costs are one time required to introduce capability into the operational inventory. The operating costs are recurring costs needed each year to operate and maintain the capability while in service over number of years. The frame-work for military cost analysis falls under the following heads namely,

- Intra-system comparison (French and Swedish guns).
- Inter-system comparison (Air defence versus ground defence).
- Force mix comparison (the size of the force and the inter-system mix).
- The total force –structure comparison.

2. PRODUCT LIFE-CYCLE

As the students of marketing, one is aware that there are five distinct stages in the life cycle of a product. These are: Introduction - Growth - Maturity - Decline - Death. The nature of product development, production and distribution costs naturally vary at each stage and suitable costing methods and pricing policies are to be designed to adjust these stage wise marphology. In order to make it more meaningful, LCC is widely used for all costing purposes all through the product life-cycle stage.

3. CHOICE OF TECHNOLOGY

This is the age of fierce competition where market forces and technologies have upper hand in deciding the firms' competitive ability. LCC is of greatest relevance towards deciding on the choice of perfect technology among the alternatives. Each technology has its own plus and minus points. Thus, two technologies are employed to make Titanium dioxide - namely, sulphate and chloride routes. The sulphate route is more hazardous environmentally, but easy and cheaper. This technology creates large amount of residue in the form of dilute sulphate acid and generally heavy doses of pollution having its own problems. It is well known that chemical industries dealing with drugs dump wastes in drainage or rivers leading to water pollution. The living example is Hussain Sagar of Hyderabad, Yamuna around Taj Mahal belt, Ganga in Varnasi. The water pollution and allied environmental problems are overcome only at a high cost 25 per cent more than actual products by recycling. Here, LCC comes in selecting a technology that is not only economical but equally environment friendly.

4. PLANT CAPACITY

It is possible to decide on plant capacity to be put to use and get the merit of optimising the capacity both by controlling and culting down the major costs through LCC. Through LCC some decisions can be made on plant capacity in case of manufacturing unit exclusively. In order to popularise this LCC approach, Indian Government is granting licences in accordance with the criteria set. Thus, it has been instrumental in planning, pricing, expanding plant capacities to meet the individual requirements of the situation.

COST FLOW

Cost build-up for a project can be the total cost plus desired amount of margin or profit. In simple terms, following is the configuration of cost build-up:

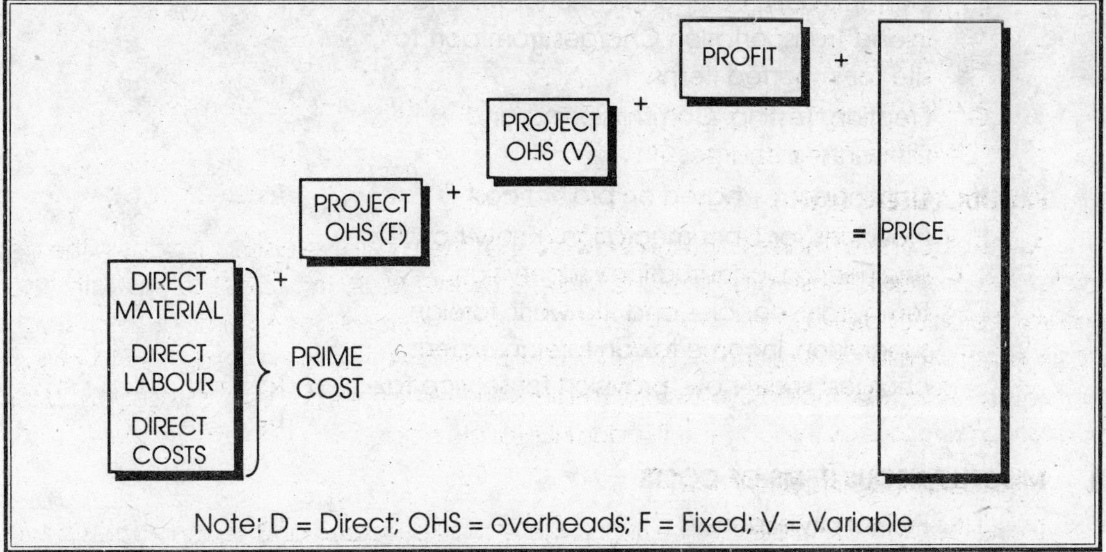

Fig.12.01 Elements of Costs and Profit

STATEMENTS OF COSTS AND PROFIT

Direct Material	Rs	
Direct Labour	Rs	
Direct Expenses	Rs	
PRIME COST		Rs ....
Overheads		
Variable	Rs	
Fixed	Rs	Rs ....
COST OF SALES		Rs ....
Desired profit		Rs ....
Sales/Price		Rs ....

The same cost build-up in case of project management language is presented in the following way:

I. ACTIVITY-WISE COST

A.	Equipment	Rs ....
B.	Civil Engineering, Structural, Refactories	Rs ....
C.	Spares/ Spare parts	Rs ....
D.	Excise duty, sales tax, works contract tax, Entry tax, Freight and Insurance on indigenous items	Rs ....
E.	Ocean Freight and Insurance	Rs ....
F.	Customs duty, Port handling charges and Inland Transportation Charges from port to site for imported items.	Rs ....
G.	Erection, Testing, Commissioning and Dismantling charges	Rs ....
H.	Contingency – based on project cost	Rs ....
I.	Provisions for Documentation, Know-how, engineering, construction , supervision, temporary, enables and site work, foreign supervision, income tax on foreign experts charges, know-how, provision for service tax	Rs ....
		Rs ....

II. MISCELLANEOUS ITEMS OF COSTS

J.	Preliminary expenses	Rs ....
K.	Land procurement	Rs ....
L.	Town ship	Rs ....

M. Interest during construction Rs ....

N. Margin Money Rs ....

Rs ....

Total Rs ....

ILLUSTRATION:

The following cost details are available for a replacement project undertaken by Gammon India Ltd for Modern Manufacturers Ltd.

Sl.No	Item		Cost:(Rs. in crores)
1.	Imported equipment		48.00
2.	Indigenous equipment		8.80
3.	Spares:		
		For imparted equipment	4.80
		For Indigenous equipment	0.44
4	Building Structure		12.80
5	Erection		6.40

Besides the above details, following information is made available:

1. Contingencies to be provided @ 3 per cent of the basic cost of project.
2. Engineers, supervisors construction plant equipment and enabling works to be provided @ 10 per cent of indigenous cost procurement.
3. Excuse duty to work @ 10 per cent of the indigenous cost of the procurement
4. Sales tax to work out @ 4 per cent
5. Entry tax to work out @ 1 per cent on the indigenous procurements
6. Inland freight and insurance @ 2 per cent of the indigenous cost of procurements
7. Ocean freight and insurance to be worker out @ 10 per cent on the FOB cost of the imports.
8. Customs duty to work out @ 20 per cent on CIF cost of imports.
9. Special duty to work out @ 2 per cent on the cost as per (8) above.
10. Countervailing duty to work out @ 10 per cent (the rate equivalent to the excise duty rate)
11. Interest during construction work to work out @ 15%p.a on the long-term loan assuming entire project cost to be finalised from the commercial borrowings and constructions period of two years. Expenditure in the first year shall be incurred for 40 per cent, in the second year 50 per cent and post commissioning payments – 10 per cent of the total cost excluding interest during construction.
12. Port handling and inland freight and insurance charges from port to the site of work @ 2 per cent of CIFcost of imports.

From the above details you are to workout the total capital cost estimates of the replacement project.

SOLUTION:

CAPITAL COST ESTIMATE OF REPLACEMENT PROJECT FOR MODERN MANUFACTURERS LIMITED

Sl.No	Details		Cost (Rs in crore)
1.	Equipment:		
	Imported Equipment	Rs. 48.00	
	Indigenous Equipment	Rs. 8.80	56.80
2.	Spares for 2 years normal operation:		
	Imported Equipment @ 10%	Rs. 4.80	
	Indigenous Equipment @ 5%	Rs. 0.44	5.24
3.	Building Structure		12.80
4.	Erection:		6.40
5.	Contingencies:		
	Basic Cost : Equipment	Rs. 56.40	
	Spares	Rs. 5.24	
	Building structure	Rs. 12.40	
	Erection	Rs. 6.40	
		Rs. 81.24	
	Calculated @ 3 per cent		2.44
6.	Excess Duty		
	Indigenous procurement cost	Rs. 8.80	
	Equipment	Rs. 0.44	
		Rs. 9.24	
	Calculated @ 10 per cent		0.92
7.	Sales Tax:		
	Indigenous procurement cost as above	Rs. 9.24	
	Add Excess duty	Rs. 0.92	
		Rs. 10.16	
	Calculated @ 4 per cent		0.40
8.	Entry Tax @ 1 per cent on the procurement cost and above (10.16 x 0.01)		0.10
9.	Inland freight and Insurance:		
	Indigenous procurement cost (S. NO. 6)	Rs. 9.24	
	Add Excise Duty	Rs. 0.92	

Add Sales Tax	Rs. 0.40	
Add Entry Tax	Rs. 0.10	
Rs.	10.66	
Calculated @ 2 per cent		0.20
10. Ocean freight and Insurance FOB		
Cost of Import:		
Equipment	Rs. 48.00	
Spares	Rs. 4.80	
	Rs. 52.80	
Calculated @ 10 per cent		5.28
11. Customs Duty including Special Duty:		
CIF Cost	Rs. 58.08	
Calculated @ 22 per cent		12.78
12. Countervailing duty @ 12.2 per cent on CIF Cost:		
(100 + 20 + 2) x 10 per cent		
= (58.08 x 12.2) per cent		7.08
13. Port handling charges:		
@ 2 per cent on CIF cost		
(2 per cent x 58.08)		1.16
14. Engineering, Supervision, Construction plant equipment and enabling works:		
Basic Cost of Project per (SN.5)	Rs. 81.24	
Add Contingencies	Rs. 2.44	
	Rs. 83.64	
Calculated @ 10 per cent		8.36
Sub total 1 to 14 points		119.6
15. Interest during Construction:		

Year	Phasings	Interest	
1.	48.00	48.00 x 0.15 x 0.5 =	3.60
2.	60.76	48.00 x 0.15 + 60.76 x 0.15 x 0.5 = 7.20 + 4.58	11.78
Post Commissioning PaymenT	11.20		
	119.96		15.38
Total Cost (119.96 + 15.38)			135.34

Foreign Exchange Component:	
Equipment Cost	48.00
Spares	4.80
Contingencies	1.58
Ocean Freight and Insurance	5.28
Sub total:	59.66
Landed Cost of Import:	
CIF cost of import as above	59.66
Add Customs Duty	12.78
Add Countervailing Duty	7.08
Add Port Charges	1.16
	80.68

PROJECT PRICING

Project pricing is the next step in project management, once the project cost is calculated. One should remember that business is not a charity and business involves shouldering of risks and uncertainties. In fact, profit is reward for the risks taken to venture a project.

Profit is the excess of cost incurred. That is, profit can be equated as:

1. Cost + Profit = Price
2. Price – Profit = Cost
3. Price – Cost = Profit

Let us prove these by figures:

1. Project Cost + Profit = Price

   Rs. 700 crores + Rs. 150 crores = Rs. 850 crores
2. Rs. 850 crores – Rs. 150 crores = Rs. 700 crores
3. Rs. 850 crores – Rs.700 crores = Rs. 150 crores

   If we express the profit as a percentage of price:

$$\frac{\text{Profit}}{\text{Price}} \times 100 = \frac{\text{Rs.}150\,\text{crore}}{\text{Rs.}850\,\text{crore}} \times 100 = 17.647\%$$

If we express the profit as a percentage of cost

$$\frac{\text{Profit}}{\text{cost}} \times 100 = \frac{\text{Rs.}150\text{ crore}}{\text{Rs.}700\text{ crore}} \times 100 = 21.428\%$$

Thus, we need the amount of profit though it is same, it is lower in terms of percentage on price while higher on cost. It means that when one wants to earn a profit of 20 per cent on the price he should earn 25 per cent on cost. By the same token, when a person when a person wants to earn 50 per cent of profit on price he should earn 100 per cent on cost.

In the above cases as 1, 2 and 3, which one is applied in a given case depends on whether price, cost or profit is fixed first. These differences can be explained as follows:

1. In case the price is fixed through legislation, or in case of a target costing, through market analysis.
2. In case the cost fixed first, generally through contract purchases which guarantees that goods will be supplied to you at a particular price. This fixed ones costs, whilst one's selling price and profits can be varied.
3. In cases where agreements make it clear as to the amount of profit which is otherwise known as cost plus pricing.

It is worth remembering that the statement of the cost estimation will not disclose the profit. It is left to the top management to decide. It is also because, the manpower that is working behind a given project should not be made known of surplus or profit. This may create labour troubles and degenaration of motivation and morale. The skilled, semi-skilled and technicians may not take keen interest in completing a given project because, they argue that they are not rewarded well for their hard and smart work.

COST BUDGETING

Cost budgeting is the process of allocating costs to the individual work items of the project. Project performance is determined based on budget allocated to the various parts of the project. The outcome of the cost budgeting process is the cost baseline of the project.

The cost baseline for the project is the expected actual cost of the project. The budget for a project should contain the estimated cost of doing all the work that is planned to be completed. In addition to the work that is required for completing the planned work of the project, cost must be budgeted for the work that will be done to avoid transfer, and mitigate risks, contigencies must be budgeted for the risks those are identified and may or may not come to pass. A reserve must be budgeted for risks those are not identified also. On most projects, the expected value for risk is budgeted. This is reasonable as it reflects the average risk exposure for the project.

These budgets for projects provide a guideline for future achievement. They are the base for performance evaluation. Budgetary-control as the last part of budgeting is like control step where actual costs are compared with budgeted, and variances are measured, reasons for the same are traced and necessary corrective action or actions are taken to put the project on the path of progress. This was what we referred earlier of conducting progress review reports.

COST CONTROL

We did touch upon cost control as a part of project control in chapter TEN. Therefore readers are advised to refer that chapter also.

Cost controlling is the process of controlling the project costs and taking correlative action when control indicates that corrective action is a must.

METHODS OF COST CONTROL

Though there are different methods of cost control, in respect of project costs, Earned Value Reporting is dominating the scene.

What is Earned Value Reporting ?

The earned value reporting (EVR) system is now most commonly used method of performance measurement and project control. This is a reporting system that works on tracking three measurements of the project namely BCWS, ACWP and BCWP. What these mean will see soon.

In any reporting system, the principle is to set some standards and then measure the actual performance to that standard and report on the observed differences. In the earned value reporting, a planned budget and schedule are used and then measured the actual progress in the budget and schedule. Frequently, the Gantt Chart is used to show progress and performance to schedule, but this does not state the case clearly. If a schedule activity is shown to be three days behind schedule, it is important to know if there is one person involved in this activity or if there are twenty. In reporting cost, actual is frequently compared to budget cost to date. This also does not show the full picture. If a project is behind schedule, the actual cost could be tracked nicely to the expected budgeted expenditures, and the project could still be in a great deal of trouble.

Using the earned value reporting system the progress of the project in terms of cost is measured in rupees. The progress of the project in terms of schedule is also measured in terms of rupees. This may sound confusing to people who are used to thinking of schedules in terms of days ahead or behind. In fact, it is more informational description of the condition of the project schedule. If project activity is reported as being five days behind schedule, and there is one person working on activity part time, it is very different than an activity that is behind four days that has twenty people working on it. Obviously, what is needed is reporting system that combines performance schedule and the budget. This is the purpose of the EVR system. This is the reason for the popularly of this reporting system in project management. That is, it includes performance to cost and performance of schedule in one report.

Earned value reports are cumulative reports. The values collected for the current reporting period are added to the values from the last reporting period, and the total is plotted.

Cumulative values will never go down unless a values is reversed. It is evident from Figure. 12.2 that cumulative cost curves have a feature 's' shape. This is because typically project teams start out spending money slowly and gradually increase their spending rate until a peak reached and then gradually decrease their rate of spending until the project is finally completed.

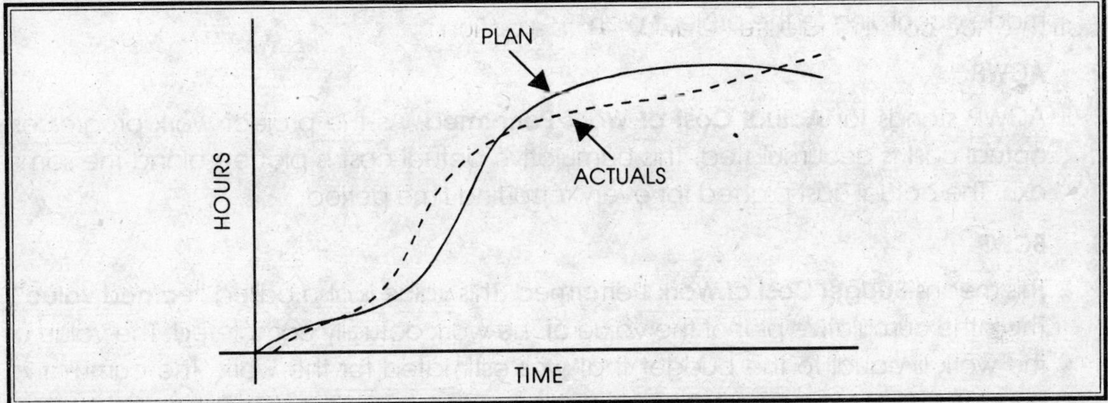

Fig. 12.02 Cumulative Work Hours

One difficulty in showing the cumulative cost curve for a large project is that the scale required to show the entire cost of the project may be so compact that relatively large variations are not visible. A 4000 crore project plotted on an 8.5 x 11.00 inch page has a crore rupees variation shown by one fifth of an inch. Hence, where large numbers are used, a plot of the variance can be used. The scale of this type of chart can be much less compact and still show the needed information. It is made simple by drawing a line as zero base and then plotting the difference between the actual and expected values as depicted in Fig. 12.03 below.

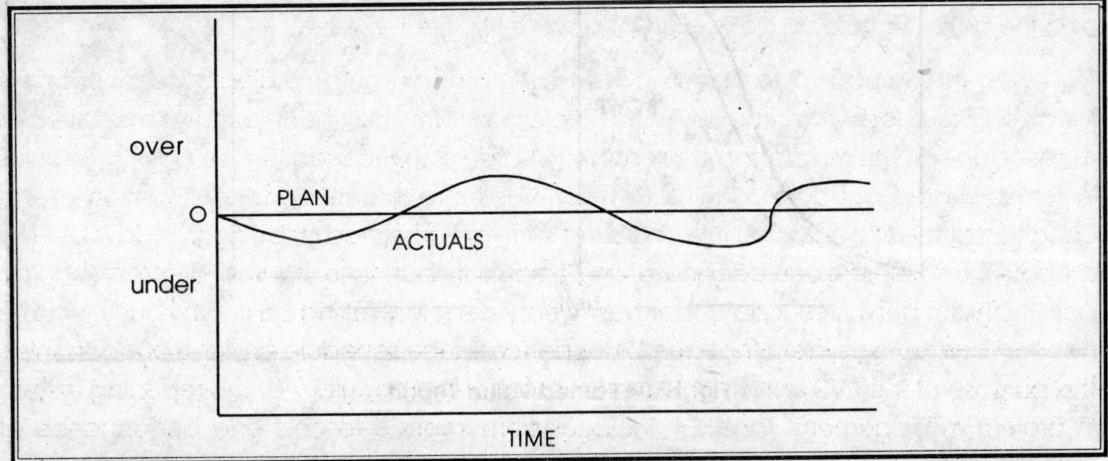

Fig. 12.03 Cumulative Variance Report

The parameters of earned value are three as earned value reporting system depends on the tracking of three measurement of the project. Those are:

1. **BCWS**

   BCWS means **Budgeted Cost Of Work Scheduled**. When one establishes three project baselines, one is definitely setting the cost & schedule baselines. Each of the activities in the project has its own estimated cost and schedule. The BCWS is the cumulative budget plotted on a time axis that shows when the expenditure is supported to be made according to the project plan.

2. **ACWP**

   ACWP stands for **Actual Cost of Work Performed**. As the project work progresses, actual cost is accumulated. This cumulative actual cost is plotted along the same axis. The actual cost plotted for every reporting time period.

3. **BCWP**

   This means **Budget Cost of Work** Performed. This value is also called **"earned value"**. This is the cumulative plot of the value of the work actually completed. The value of the work is equal to the budget that was estimated for the work. The cumulative budgeted cost of work performed is plotted on the same time axis. The earned values plotted for every time period based on the actual work that is accomplished.

In case project follows the project plan, each of these three parameters are exactly the same. Significant deviations between the values of the three parameters are real cause for concern. This is evident from Figure 12.4 given below.

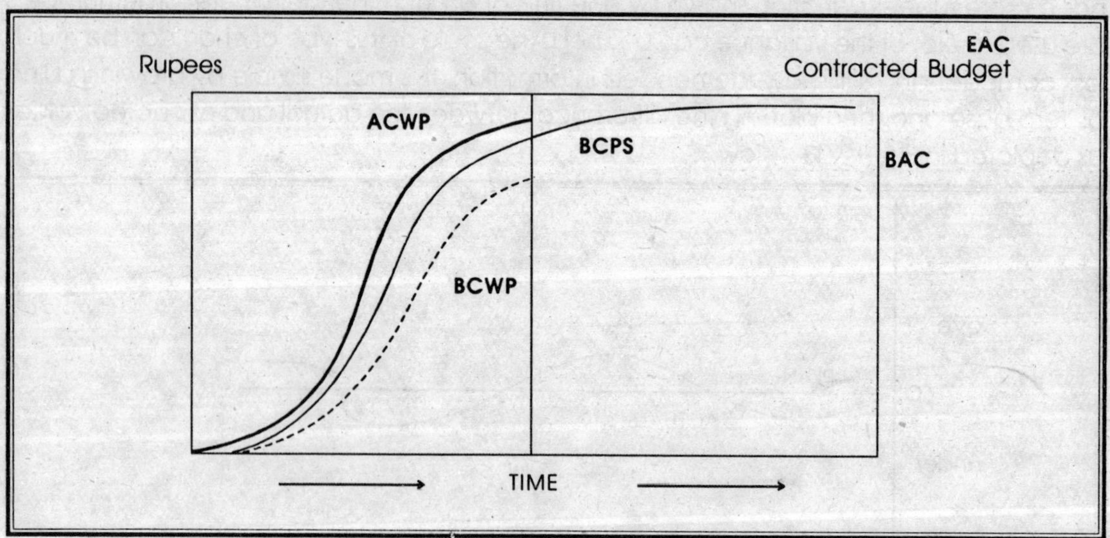

Fig. 12.04 Earned Value Report

Plotting the BCWS is rather straight forward. However, care should be taken that the time taken that the timing and the amounts that are plotted as BCWS are the same and that the timing is same as when they are reported as actual expenditures.

In the area of material cost, the timing of the budget and the reports of the actual expenditure are important. An expenditure may be recognized when the commitment is made to purchase the material. When the material is delivered, when the material is accepted, when it is invoiced or when it is paid for. All of these data may be quite different points in time. Care must be taken so that the timings of BCWS matches the timing of ACWP.

In the area of labour cost, difficulties frequently arise in the development of these estimates as well. Companies very often do not like to have their estimates know the salary cost of individual employees. People are generally grouped together by similar skills. Within the group there can be wide range of salaries. Since it is usually not possible to ascertain exactly who will be working on a project when the work is actually done, the average cost of a person is the group in used for estimating purposes. When the project is actually done, the average cost of a person in the group is still used.

REPORTING THE WORK COMPLETED

It is usual to find difficulty in reporting the work completed on a project. Good many people tend to report that the per cent that is completed on an activity is the same as the per cent of time that has elapsed. Thus, 50 per cent of time to do an activity in the project has passed but only 25 per cent of the work is actually done, misleading reports can come to light. There are several approaches to solve this problem. The "50 - 50" rule is one such approach. As per this approach, 50 per cent of the earned value is credited to earned value data collection, as earned value when the activity is begun. The remaining 50 per cent is not credited until all the work is completed.

The "50 – 50" rule encourages the project teams to begin working on activities in the project, since they get 50 per cent of the earned value for just starting an activity. As time goes by the actual cost of work performed accumulates and the project team is motivated to complete the work on activity so that additional 50 per cent of the earned value can be credited. This creates an incentive to start work and another incentive to finish the work that has been already started. This solves the problem of reporting per cent complete, and there should be few arguments about whether the work is actually begun or is complete on a project activity.

In fact, there are many variations of this "50 - 50" rule. Popular uses include "20 – 80" and "0 – 100" rule. These allow differing percentages of the carried value of the work to be claimed at the start and completion of the work.

CHAPTER BASED QUESTIONS

A. WRITE SHORT NOTES ON

1. Cost estimating
2. Importance of Cost estimating
3. Types of Cost estimating
4. Techniques of Cost estimating
5. Suitability of cost estimating techniques
6. LCC
7. Areas of LCC application
8. Cost Flow
9. Issues
10. Project pricing
11. Cost budgeting
12. Cost control
13. EVR
14. "50 – 50" Rule of Reporting.

B. SHORT ANSWER QUESTIONS

1. What is cost estimating ?
2. What are Bottom up estimates ?
3. What are analogous estimates ?
4. What are parametric estimates ?
5. What are the different estimating techniques ?
6. What is global estimating ?
7. What is LCC ?
8. What issues are involved in LCC ?
9. What is cost - flow ?
10. What is project-pricing ?

C. ESSAY TYPE QUESTIONS

1. What is cost estimating ? What is its importance ?
2. What is estimating ? What are the different types of cost estimates ?
3. What is cost estimating ? What are the different techniques of it ?
4. Explain the techniques of cost estimating and their suitability.
5. What is LCC ? What issues are associated with LCC ?
6. What is LCC ? Where is it applied with benefits ?
7. What is cost flow ? Present a chart that shows cost flows ?
8. What is project pricing ? How projects are priced ?
9. What is cost budgeting ? How does it help in cost control ?
10. What is cost control ? What is EVR system widely used in cost control ?

* * * * *

Chapter 13

SKILL DEVELOPMENT

- **CASE ONE – PROJECT LIFE-CYCLE CART**
- **ADDITIONAL ILLUSTRATIONS**
  1. **PROJECT LIFE-CYCLE OF ENGINEERING PROJECT**
  2. **PROJECT LIFE-CYCLE OF HOUSING PROJECT**
  3. **PROJECT LIFE-CYCLE OF ENGINEERING PROJECT**
  4. **PROJECT LIFE-CYCLE OF A COMPUTER INSTALLATION PROJECT**

BACKDROP

As the business managers of the days to come, you are to develop the managerial capabilities. One way is develop managerial skills. A skill is an ability or proficiency in performing a particular task. Skill is practical knowledge combined with ability, a craft, an accomplishment. A skill is acquired or learnt ability to translate knowledge into performance. It is the competency that permits super performance in the field in which the person has acquired the ability. Mere acquiring the knowledge has no meaning unless it is fruitfully utilized to solve problems that crop up in the way of achievement. The managerial skills are technical, analytical, decision-making, conceptual, inter-personal, human relations and political. By now, you have been acquainted with good amount of quality knowledge in project management. You are to apply this knowledge as the project manager in making. As a part of this, certain exercises are given. You are asked to design a chart with regard to project life cycle. To facilitate, some chart are given, in the following pages.

SKILL DEVELOPMENT CASE ONE – PROJECT LIFE CYCLE CHART

REQUIRED:

Prepare project life-cycle chart

SOLUTION:

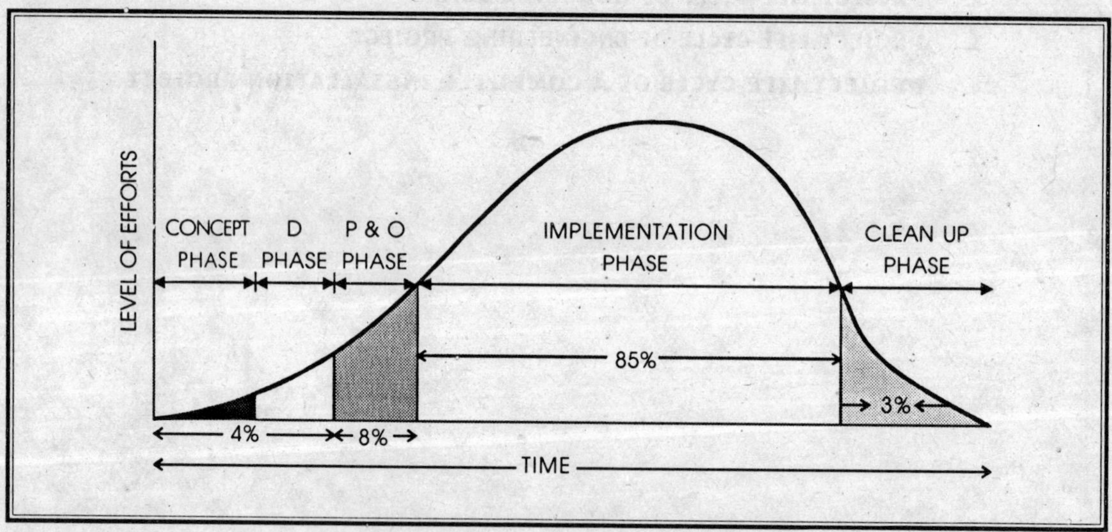

Project Life-Cycle Phases and the amount of efforts puf in

NOTE:

D = Development P & O = Planning and Organising.

Thus, it is evident that there are five phases of project life-cycle. Each phase needs efforts where share of concept phase is 2 per cent, development phase 2 per cent , implementation phase 85 per cent, and cleanup phase 3 per cent. These percentages are not permanent in all cases. This is only an illustration. Actual percentages differ from project to project in ground reality.

ADDITIONAL ILLUSTRATIONS

1. PROJECT LIFE-CYCLE OF ENGINEERING PROJECT

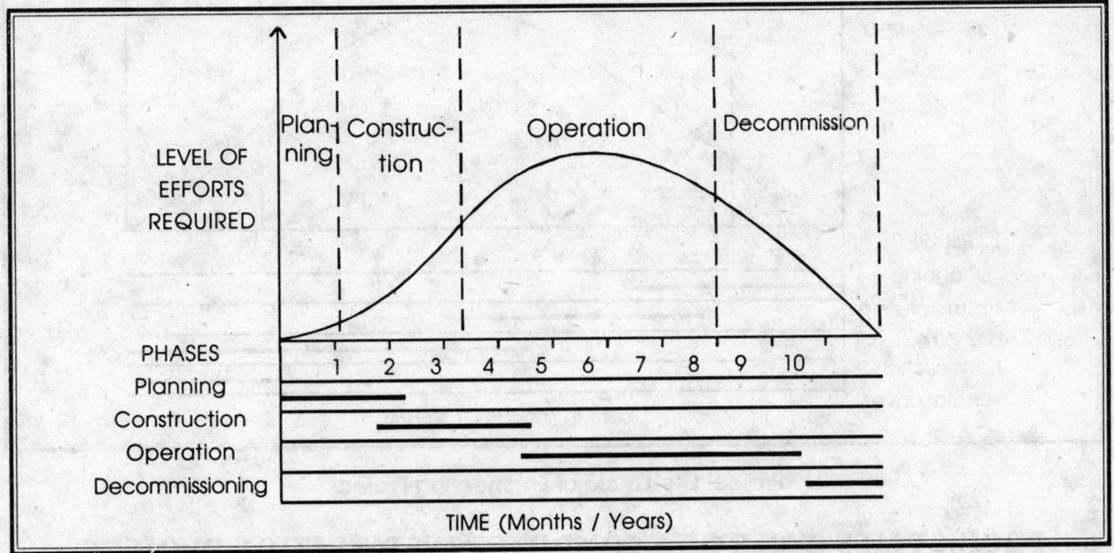

Project Life-Cycle of a Nuclear Power Station Project

2. PROJECT LIFE-CYCLE OF HOUSING PROJECT

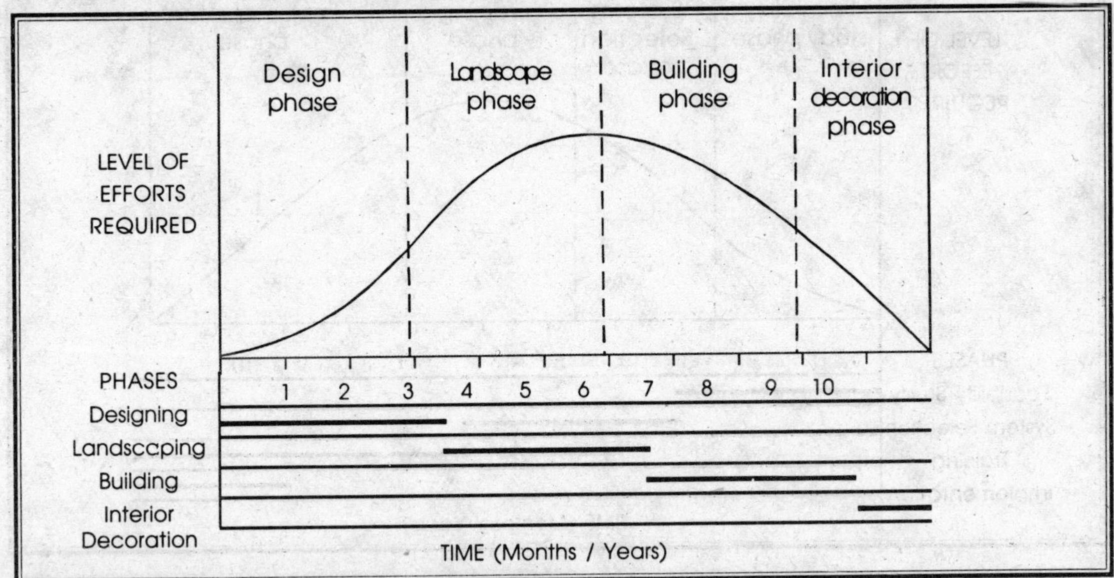

Project Life-Cycle of a Housing Project

3. PROJECT LIFE CYCLE OF ENGINEERING PROJECT

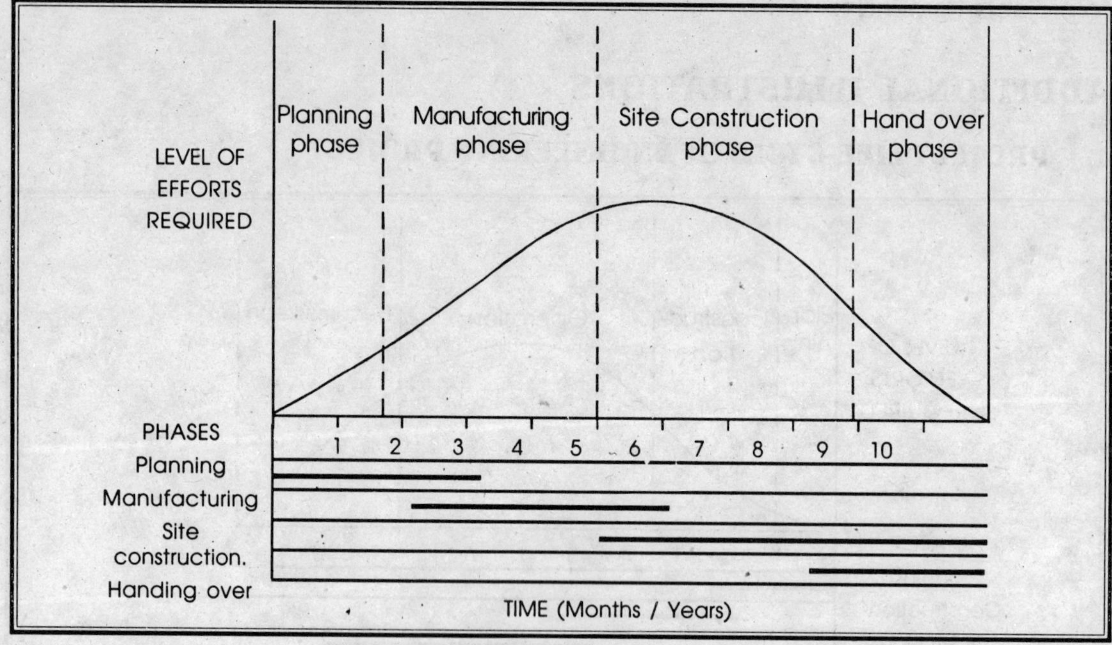

Project Life-Cycle of Engineering Project

4. PROJECT LIFE CYCLE OF A COMPUTER INSTALLATION PROJECT

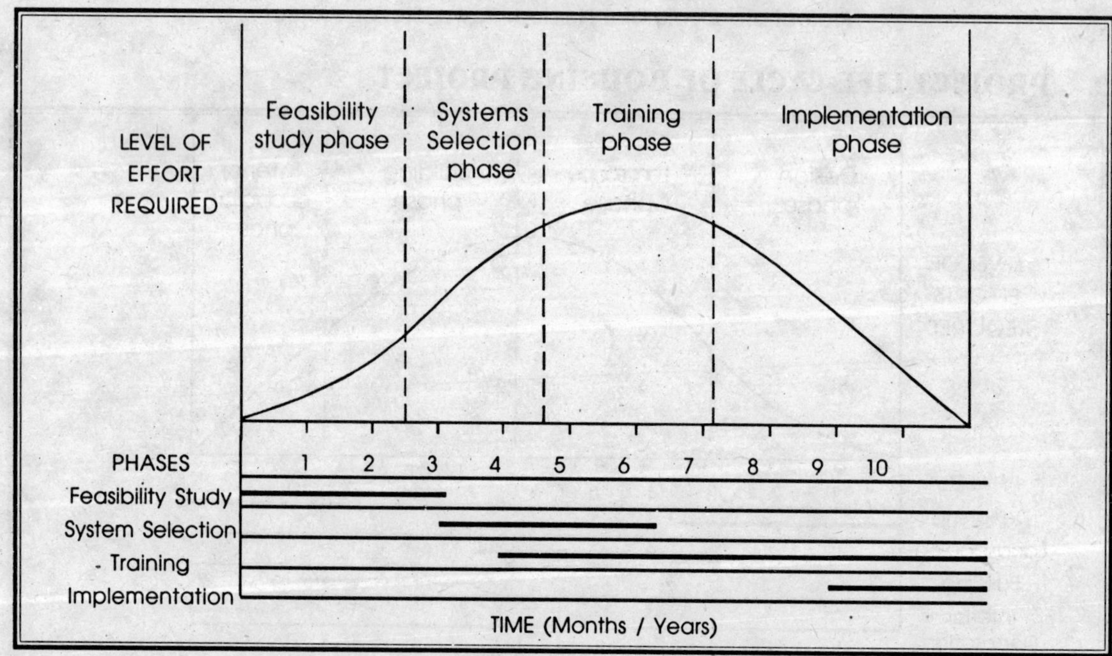

Project Life-Cycle of a Computer Installation Project.

* * * * * *